# Ableton Live 10 Power!
## The Comprehensive Guide

**Jon Margulies**

**Hobo Technologies**
hobo-tech.com

*Ableton Live 10 Power!*
*The Comprehensive Guide*

**By Jon Margulies**

Hobo Technologies
hobo-tech.com

Please send errors to: errata@hobo-tech.com

*Publisher:* Jon Margulies
*Editor:* Marta Justak
*Interior Design and Layout:* William Hartman
*Indexer:* Marilyn Augst
*Proofreader:* Charles Hutchinson

ISBN: 0692061355
ISBN 13: 978-0692061350

Printed and bound in the United States of America

# Acknowledgments

Getting a book like this done is a team effort, and I've had a great team to work with! Many thanks to everyone: Marta Justak for editing my writing and for her great expertise in the process of producing a book; Brian Jackson for keeping things on point with his technical editing; Michele Darling for helping me put together some of the content for this edition; Marilyn Augst for creating the index; and William Hartman for his great-looking layout.

Also, a big shout-out to Ben Casey, Dennis DeSantis, Dave Hillel, and Tony McCall at Ableton. Thanks for helping me out and generally being awesome.

# About the Author

Jon Margulies has been teaching and creating training materials for Ableton Live since 2005. His years of real-world experience in the studio and the classroom have given him a unique understanding of how musicians learn and use Live. Also active as a producer, engineer, and performer, he's appeared at festivals such as Coachella, SXSW, Winter Music Conference, and Burning Man. When he's not helping people become better producers, he makes music with his band Tiny Machines and works as a mixing and mastering engineer at his studio, Hobo Technologies.

# Contents

# Chapter 3
# Live Interface Basics                                                    37

# Chapter 4
# Making Music in Live                        75

# Chapter 5
# Clips                                                                123

# Chapter 6
# Tracks and Signal Routing                                185

# Chapter 7
# Using Effects and Instruments                             203

# Chapter 8
# Live's Instruments                                      231

## Chapter 9
## Live's Audio Effects       305

# Chapter 10
# Live's MIDI Effects                                    387

# Chapter 11
# Remote Control                                        403

# 1
# Live 10

**A**bleton Live has been regarded as revolutionary since its earliest days. Now at version 10, it's no longer just the upstart that transformed computers into playable musical instruments. Live has grown into a mature and deep program capable of many different workflows, used by musicians of every stripe. It's a program written for musicians by musicians, a fact that continues to be apparent in every release, as features are carefully selected and refined to support a creative, spontaneous workflow.

It all started with Robert Henke and Gerhard Behles (paired in the Berlin-based electronica group Monolake), who were looking for a better way to create their own music. Both were experienced sound designers and had spent time working for Native Instruments, one of the industry's chief authorities on software synthesizers. At the time, the industry lacked user-friendly software that was conducive to creating music in the intuitive, spontaneous manner they envisioned.

In 2000, they formed Ableton (along with Bernd Roggendorf and Jan Bohl) and released Live 1.0, an audio-only program oriented around live performance (hence the name!). What made Live so unique from day one was the Session View (see Figure 1.1), a customizable grid used to create and play musical elements on the fly, mixing and matching them at will.

**FIGURE 1.1** Here is a quick peek at Session View. The rows make up musical sections called *scenes*, and the columns function as virtual mixer channels.
*Source:* Ableton

Not strictly an improvisation and performance tool, Live also sports a traditional timeline similar to that found in other digital audio workstations like Pro Tools. Live's timeline (called the *Arrangement*) can be used to capture your improvisations for final polishing, or used to create music from scratch. How you use Ableton Live is up to you.

# What Sets Live Apart?

The digital audio world is full of incredible tools. Even the average computer is extremely powerful, and all the major software companies have studied their competitor's features and expanded their products in ways that make formerly incomprehensible innovations commonplace. There has never been a better time to get into the game; for a beginner, it's almost impossible to go wrong.

**FIGURE 1.2** If you are familiar with other digital audio workstations, Live's Arrangement View should look familiar.
*Source:* Ableton

That said, there are still many things that make Live a unique program (see Figure 1.2). Although this list is far from complete, these features show a few ways in which Live stands apart.

▶ Ableton is one of the original innovators in the area of real-time time stretching and pitch shifting. While all DAWs now have time and pitch manipulation features, Live's flexibility and ease of use remain unparalleled. With a few mouse clicks, you can adjust pitch and time for synchronization tasks or insane sound mangling.

▶ Live is exceptionally easy to use with MIDI controller hardware. Whether you're using a device designed for Live (such as Push or Launchpad), or a generic MIDI controller of some sort, it's simple to get your hands off the mouse and onto pads, knobs, and the like. Even if you don't have a controller, Live's flexible mapping feature allows you to control just about anything with a single keystroke on your computer keyboard.

▶ Live 10 introduces Capture, a feature that listens to MIDI input at all times so that you can grab performances without ever pressing Record. Jam on your keyboard or drum pads, and press Capture after playing something you like. A new clip appears in Live, ready to go.

▶ Live lets you build customized groupings of effects and virtual instruments called *Racks*. With powerful routing options, you can create layers, splits, and complex effects like never before. Drum Racks take this concept to another level, allowing you to build drum banks with combinations of audio samples, synthesized sounds, and effects.

▶ Max for Live allows Live to be infinitely extended. These extensions range from effects (such as convolution reverb) to step sequencers, parameter randomizers, and video tools. Max for Live devices are fully programmable, so if you've got the skills, you can modify any device to your particular taste or simply create your own from scratch.

# How to Use This Book

Great effort has been made to make this book readable from cover to cover, while maintaining its usefulness as a reference guide. That said, I have a few tips for maximizing your enjoyment of *Ableton Live 10 Power!*

If you're new to Live, and you're just plugging some headphones into a laptop to see what all the fuss is about, you can skip straight to Chapter 3, "Live Interface Basics."

Once you've had some fun with Live, take a few minutes to at least skim through Chapter 2, "Getting Live Up and Running," to get a sense of your configuration options. If you're more experienced with digital audio software or you're using (or planning to use) external audio and MIDI hardware, Chapter 2 is really useful. Because it's all setup information, it's one of the more dry chapters in the book, and at first you may not even know which setup options you want. But getting a sense of the possibilities will be very helpful as you dig into Live, slowly tweaking your setup to perfection.

The "File Management" section at the end of Chapter 3 is *very* important. Most new producers make a mess of their files at first, and that's totally fine. However, if you let it go for too long, you'll end up with chaos that will make you miserable. At best, it will be confusing and take hours of work to sort out. At worst, you'll end up losing work due to lost or accidentally deleted files.

Chapters 3–7 are the heart of this book, covering all of the essentials of using Live. For the average user, there's more detail here than you'll need right away, so don't worry: if you're getting music made, you're winning. If you notice yourself getting slowed down by certain things again and again, take the time to research them.

Chapters 8–10 are a reference guide to all of Live's effects and instruments. Most people learn how to program devices through experimentation, so feel free to just dip into these chapters as needed. At the top of Chapter 8, "Live's Instruments," there's a detailed explanation of Live's filters, which appear in many instruments and several effects as well. Since filters are such an important part of sound design, this is well worth going over even if you primarily learn through knob tweaking.

The remaining chapters are a mixed bag of specialized topics. If you're using a control surface such as Push or you want to supercharge your workflow with customized controllers and key commands, you may want to get to Chapter 11, "Remote Control," sooner than later. However, the basics of remote control are covered in Chapter 3, so many users can take their time getting to this.

# Live Power Downloads

To get you going as quickly as possible, this book comes with Live Sets that illustrate the topics in this book along with some other fun tools.

To download the files, visit hobo-tech.com/livepower and use the code GIMMEPOWER. After downloading and unzipping the files, make sure to read the included documentation for information on installing and using them.

# 2

# Getting Live Up and Running

**B**efore you dive in and start producing hits, it is important to take a moment to verify that your computer system is up to speed and that you've installed Live properly. This chapter will provide a few recommendations to help you through the installation process, along with some tips for fine-tuning your Ableton Live studio. I'll cover both Mac and PC setup and talk about several methods for optimizing your system. Also, remember that Ableton's technical support (www.ableton.com/en/help/contact-support/) is an excellent way to get to the bottom of anything not covered in this book, as is Ableton's online user forum (found at http://forum.ableton.com/), which is usually rich with tips, tricks, and advice.

## System Requirements

Listed in the pages that follow are Ableton's posted system requirements, followed by my recommendations. The minimum system requirements can be a very different matter from a *desirable* system configuration. This is true with most software applications, and Live is no exception. Ableton Live is a power-hungry program, and ideally your system should be put together with the most power you can afford. Don't worry, though: not only is power very affordable these days, but there are also strategies for making epic sounds with a less than epic computer. (See the "Latency Settings" section later in this chapter and "Freeze and Flatten" in Chapter 7, "Using Effects and Instruments," for more information.)

As of version 10, Live is a 64-bit only application. This means that any 32-bit plug-ins on your system will not work in Live (unless you use "bridge" software such as jBridge or 32 Lives).

## System Requirements for Macintosh

▶ Intel Core 2 Duo processor (i5 or faster recommended)

▶ 4GB RAM (8GB or more recommended)

▶ OS X 10.11.6 or later

## System Requirements for PC

▶ 64-bit Intel or AMD multicore processor (i5 or faster recommended)

▶ 4GB RAM (8GB Recommended)

▶ Windows 7, 8, or 10

# Installing, Running, and Updating Live 10

Live can be purchased as a download or in a boxed retail version. The download version is sold only through the Ableton shop (www.ableton.com/en /shop/). The only difference between the two is that the boxed version includes printed manuals, so if you don't care about those, go ahead and buy the download. The DVDs in the box do offer the convenience of not having to download the content packs, but the software itself is usually out-of-date by the time it gets to you, and you end up having to download the latest version anyway. The truth is that printed manuals are often a bit out-of-date as well, since features are regularly being improved and completed.

Live 10 comes in three versions: Intro, Standard, and Suite.

▶ **Intro:** A feature-limited version of Live with 16 tracks, 4 instruments, 21 audio effects, 8 MIDI effects, and 5+ GB of sounds.

▶ **Standard:** A full-featured version with unlimited tracks, 34 audio effects, 5 instruments, all 8 MIDI effects, and 10GB of sounds.

▶ **Suite:** Includes all instruments and effects, Max for Live, and 70GB of sounds.

▶ For a detailed comparison of the three flavors of Ableton Live, please refer to www.ableton.com/en/live/feature-comparison/.

# Live Installation Tips

Installing Live 10 on Mac OS X is a breeze. After downloading, open the disk image (.dmg file) and drag Live 10 to the Applications folder on your hard disk. For quicker access to Live, you may want to install a shortcut onto the OS X dock. To do this, simply open your Applications folder and drag the program icon to the dock. To remove the item from the dock, drag it to the Trash or to the desktop, and watch it go "poof" and disappear.

Installing Live onto a Windows machine is much like installing any other Windows-based application. After you open Setup and follow the instructions, Live's installer will ask you where you would like to place the Ableton folder and its files. It's recommended to use the installer's default setting, which will place Live in the Program Files folder.

The first time you launch Live, you'll be offered the opportunity to register Live or run it in Demo mode. Authorizing will open your Web browser and take you to ableton.com where you'll have to log in or create a user account. If you've bought the download version from ableton.com, your Live 10 serial number will already be entered in your account, and the authorization process should begin immediately.

Ableton enables you to install Live on two computers. If you replace one of your computers, it's possible that authorizing your new computer will fail because you've used up your "unlocks." Not to worry—just email customer support to explain the situation, and they'll take care of you.

# Updating Live

Like any good piece of modern software, Live is constantly under development, with bugs being fixed and functionality added and improved. Ableton releases updates quite regularly, so it's very easy to fall behind. This is not something you should lose any sleep over; not only is it very easy to update, but there's nothing wrong with taking an "if it ain't broke, don't fix it" attitude toward the software on your computer. However, before you tear your hair out trying to figure out why something isn't working on your system, it's a good idea to make sure that you're running the latest version.

The easiest way to stay up-to-date is to turn on Live's Get Software Updates feature (see Licenses/Management in the "Setting Preferences in Live" section of this chapter), which automatically downloads new versions as needed. This is done in the background and is usually quite fast since all that is downloaded are small patches to the program, rather than an entire new version.

For those of you who like to handle it manually, you'll find Check for Updates in the Help menu handy. This will take you to a web page to download the latest version. The advantage of this method is that the download page contains additional information and links, such as new features and available downloads. You can always find out what version you're running by opening the About Live screen (from the Live menu on a Mac, or the Help menu on a PC).

# Basic Computer Specifications

Since everyone uses Live differently, it's tricky to give a one-size-fits-all recommendation for computer specs. There are users who use almost nothing but Live's built-in devices, keep their track count low, and release great music using a four-year-old laptop. Others use power-hungry plug-ins extensively and make densely layered music with loads of tracks, challenging even a top-of-the-line system. Therefore, it's important to understand some of the details of how hardware affects performance and how you can get the best machine for your budget.

## Processor Speed

The biggest performance bottleneck for most digital audio computers is the processor speed. Live is a program that prioritizes elegance and ease of use, rather than extreme CPU efficiency. That said, there are many tasks that Live can handle even when running on a very humble computer. For example, playing back many tracks of audio takes very little CPU power, unless you're using a lot of effects. Sets that rely heavily on MIDI tracks and virtual instruments are often very demanding on the CPU, unless you're mostly using built-in devices like Simpler and Operator, which are very CPU efficient. Keep an eye on the CPU meter in the upper right-hand corner to get a practical feel for all this.

Obviously, a more powerful CPU will provide you with the most ease and flexibility. But this doesn't mean you have to break the bank buying the absolute newest and fastest. Buying a step down from the top can save you quite a bit of money, which you can put toward a quality soundcard and a good pair of speakers or headphones. Your music will be better for it.

## Hard Drives

Get the biggest hard disks you can afford. You *will* fill up every single drive you buy, and faster than you think. (And don't forget extra backup drives!) 7200 RPM drives are great for audio, providing fast performance for the price. SSD drives are even faster, but substantially more expensive. In a high-performance system, it's common to mix and match—for example, a smaller SSD for the drive containing the operating system and applications and larger capacity 7200 RPM drives for music projects and sample libraries.

5400 RPM is a common speed for small portable hard drives and PC laptop drives. These are fine for many live performance and production situations as well. A slower drive can become a problem when Sets grow large and complex with many audio tracks and samples playing back simultaneously. When this happens, you'll hear audio dropouts, and the "D" (Disk Overload) icon in the upper right-hand corner will begin to flash.

## RAM

As your Live Sets grow and become more complex, they use more RAM (memory). It's important not to run out of memory while running Live because when you do, it crashes. There's no built-in way to monitor memory usage (as there is with CPU power and disk usage), so you'll have to run Activity Monitor in OS X or Task Manager in Windows to see where your system memory is going.

If your system has a relatively small amount of RAM, it's important to quit other applications while running Live. Whether you're prone to running out of RAM depends on how you use your system. Some devices are more memory hungry than others; for example, if you're composing music for a sampled symphony orchestra, expect all those instruments to use a lot of memory. Max for Live and ReWire both demand more memory because they involve running additional software.

Live 10 is a 64-bit application, which means it can utilize an astronomically high amount of RAM (more than any computer actually has). While 8GB of RAM is fine for basic production work, 16GB or more is highly recommended if you can afford it. My studio computer has 64GB of RAM, which is way more than I need, but that's the point. If I'm working on a massive mix in Studio One, and I want to open a Live Set containing piles of virtual instruments at the same time, it's not a problem.

## Audio Interface Specs

Almost invariably, the audio capabilities that come standard with your PC or Mac are lacking. Without a specialized audio interface, sometimes called a *soundcard*, you'll find yourself hitting limitations in terms of routing flexibility, connectivity, and sound quality. Choosing an interface can be tricky since there are so many choices on the market. Here are a couple of items to consider when purchasing an interface.

Most soundcards have a minimum of two input channels, a right and left input, which can be used separately or together as a stereo pair. More inputs are a must if you're planning on recording multichannel sources, such as a live band. If you have multiple synthesizers and drum machines, multiple inputs can be very useful because you can leave them connected and record any piece of gear without having to re-patch connections. But for the many musicians who overdub one track at a time when recording, two inputs work just fine.

Multiple outputs are necessary for a DJ-style live setup, for which you'll need four outputs (two stereo pairs), which allows you to use one pair as your main output and the other for cueing (prelistening) to clips in your headphones. (See the "Performance Strategies" section in Chapter 12, "Playing Live… Live," for more information on setting this up.) In the studio, multiple outputs are used for external signal processing and mixing. For example, one might send each track in a Set to a channel on a mixing console, or use the External Audio Effect device to process tracks with hardware audio effects.

After you've decided whether you need two, four, six, eight, or more channels, you may also want to consider what types of connecters the interface uses. For example, if you're always connecting to DJ mixers, it may be more convenient to have RCA outputs on your interface, rather than ¼ inch or XLR. Ultimately, though, this shouldn't be a deal-breaker, since you can always connect with the proper cables or adapters.

# ASIO Drivers—A Must for Windows Users

ASIO (Audio Stream Input/Output) was first invented by German software-slinger Steinberg. It helps musicians running Windows record multitrack audio digitally with a minimal amount of time lag within their digital system. (ASIO is unnecessary on Mac OS X, thanks to Core Audio.) This time lag can be a real buzzkill, and it is called *latency*. Latency occurs because the sound you are recording is forced to travel through your operating system, your system bus, and host application to end up on your hard drive. Like bad plumbing, the signal may be coming down the pipe, but there are clogs and corners that must be navigated along the way. The gist is that your computer is performing calculations, and though they are blazingly fast, it takes a moment for the processor to finish, and the result is latency.

Many audio interfaces come with ASIO drivers, and those that don't can use the freeware driver "ASIO4ALL" available from www.asio4all.com.

# Choosing a MIDI Controller

Whether you're using Live to perform or produce, you're going to want some sort of MIDI controller as part of your setup. There is a lot you can do with only your computer keyboard and a mouse, but at some point, you'll want to play a melody, bang out a beat, or crank a knob to apply some effects.

The most important thing in picking a controller is to understand your needs, but this can be tricky if you are totally new to production. If that's the case, the best thing I can recommend is to get something affordable and push it to its limits—it's the one guaranteed method for discovering what your needs are!

Here are some factors to consider:

▶ **Grid:** Some controllers (such as the Novation Launchpad and Akai APC 40 mkII) feature a grid of buttons for launching clips in the Session View. When connected, a colored rectangle appears in the Session View to indicate which area of the clip grid is available to the controller. On the controller, each grid button that corresponds to a clip will light up, while buttons corresponding to empty clip slots remain dark. These are fun in the studio, and a must-have for many live performers. Ableton's Push is designed around a button grid, which can launch clips, and do much more as well.

▶ **Keys:** Even if you don't play the piano, you'll probably want to have at least two octaves of piano keys to play with. Some keyboards come with extra controls (faders, knobs, etc.), and may be all you need. Simple keyboard controllers may need to be supplemented with another controller for knobs and buttons. There's nothing wrong with the latter approach. In fact, it can be quite convenient to have several smaller controllers. After all, you might not need one of them for gigs, and you'll save space in your gig bag over a larger, fully featured controller.

▶ **Drum Pads:** Some people can't live without them. If you like to bang out your beats, drum pads can make it much more fun. That said, I know folks who have no problem playing great beats on a piano keyboard or simply drawing in every note with the mouse. Drum pads vary in feel and sensitivity, so make sure to get ones you like.

▶ **Knobs:** Some knobs have a nice smooth feel and have a limited range, just like a knob on an old synth. Others turn endlessly and click as you turn them. (These are usually referred to as *encoders.*) The former are much better for musical tasks (such as filter sweeps). A bad feeling or awkwardly placed knob is no fun to use, so try before you buy.

▶ **Faders (and Crossfader):** For many of us, volume controls just make more sense on faders rather than knobs. For precision studio work, a nice big fader with a long *throw* (range of motion) is handy, but not essential. Motorized faders are great in the studio, but probably not necessary on stage. In the world of MIDI, a crossfader is just a sideways fader. Whether or not you need one depends entirely on your style. Live's crossfader can be controlled by any MIDI input, so you can get the functionality of a crossfader from a variety of nontraditional controls.

▶ **Buttons:** Some light up, and some don't. Some have a nice chunky feel, while others are downright wispy. For use in the studio, turning the metronome on and off, or controlling Live's transport, these issues probably aren't very important. But during a gig, having nice buttons that light up when you click them can make all the difference.

▶ **Joysticks and Touchpads:** These are often referred to as X-Y controllers since they can be moved along two axes. From a MIDI standpoint, a joystick or touchpad is seen as two separate controllers: one for the horizontal axis and one for the vertical. As you move one of these controllers, two different control messages are simultaneously transmitted.

## Control Surfaces

Another factor to consider when picking a control surface is whether or not it is a supported *control surface* for Live. In Live's MIDI preferences (see "Link/MIDI" later in this chapter), there is a menu that will show you a list of controllers that can be plugged into Live and use remote controlling immediately without any mapping.

Because there are so many different styles of controllers, this technology varies widely from device to device. To see how it's implemented for various controllers, open up Help View from the Help menu and refer to the Control Surface Reference, which documents the behavior of all supported controllers.

It's also possible for third parties to allow any MIDI controller to behave as a control surface in Live, but this involves the installation of a script file on your computer. The details of this process will be included in the manufacturer's directions for any controller promising custom control surface support.

# Setting Preferences in Live

This section covers a wide range of settings from simple (such as clip colors) to esoteric (like clip update rate). Most users won't have to read it from beginning to end and can just refer to it as needed. However, skimming it over is recommended because it will acquaint you with various configuration options that will come in handy later.

If you're using an external audio interface, you'll need to visit the Audio preferences tab to get it set up. MIDI devices are set up on the Link/MIDI tab, although you may not have to set up your MIDI devices manually because Live automatically configures many MIDI devices for basic use when they are connected to your computer.

To open the Preferences window on a PC, select Options → Preferences; on a Mac, select Live → Preferences. When you first open the preferences, you will see a small pop-up window with a number of tabs marked on the side: Look/Feel, Audio, Link/MIDI, File/Folder, Record/Warp/Launch, and Licenses/Maintenance. We'll have a look at each of these in turn.

# Look/Feel

On the Look/Feel tab (see Figure 2.1), you'll find a number of settings having to do with Live's appearance and the way it presents information to you. Let's look at all the settings.

The Language setting chooses the language to use for Live's menus and messages. The internal help menus, interface text, and informational messages can be set to read in French, Spanish, German, and English.

The "Don't Show Again" Warnings setting deals with the various warnings that come up when you first perform certain actions in Live. Typically, these warnings will only be seen the first time you perform a particular action, and then you won't see them again. If you want to bring back all these messages and restore Live to the state it was in when you first installed it, click Restore here.

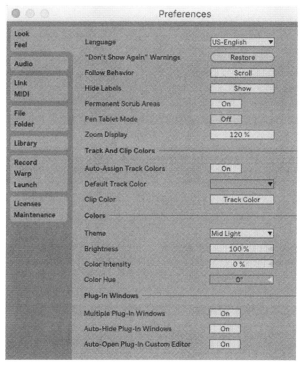

**FIGURE 2.1**

The Look/Feel tab in Live's Preferences. Use the tabs on the left to show the other preference views.

*Source:* Ableton

The third option, Follow Behavior, determines the graphical style used when following the song position in the Arrangement and Clip Views. When set to Scroll, the playback cursor will stay in place while the window moves smoothly under it. When set to Page, the window will stay stationary while the cursor moves. When the playback cursor reaches the right edge of the screen, the window jumps ahead so the cursor appears again on the left. The Scroll option is much harder on your CPU, so if you are experiencing dropouts or a sluggish response, set this option to Page.

The next option here, Hide Labels, gives you a little more screen real estate once you've memorized all of Live's components and don't need the labels anymore. When set to Show, the Live interface will look normal. When set to Hide, all of the little labels on the interface (such as Track Delay and Audio To) will disappear.

Permanent Scrub Areas turns on or off the scrub area at the top of the Arrangement View and Clip View (right below the ruler), and the lower half of the waveform display in the Clip View. With this preference turned on, your mouse will turn into a speaker icon automatically in these locations and can be used to jump to any location. With it turned off, you'll have to hold down the Shift key to see the Scrub tool.

Pen Tablet Mode can make Live easier to use when using a graphics tablet instead of a mouse or when controlling Live with a touch screen. Some of these devices have the disturbing behavior of returning the mouse pointer to the center of the screen when the pen or finger is removed from the device. Turning Pen Tablet Mode on changes this behavior so the pointer stays where you leave it.

Zoom Display is used to scale the entire Live interface larger or smaller. During gigs, I set my display to 120% so it's easier to see what I'm doing.

## Track and Clip Colors

With Auto-Assign Track Colors turned on, Live will randomly choose a color for each new track you create. If Auto-Assign Colors is off, the Default Track Color determines which color Live will assign to all new clips. Of course, color will not affect the sound and is purely aesthetic.

The Clip Color switch can be set to either "Track Color," which colors new clips to match the track they are created in, or "Random," which assigns a random color every time a clip is created.

## Colors

The Theme setting sets Live's overall color scheme. To find the scheme you like best, simply click the drop-down menu and use the up and down arrows on your keyboard to scroll though the options. The three controls below are used to customize the theme you select. Brightness adjusts the overall lightness of the theme. Color Intensity and Color Hue work in conjunction with each other. With Color Intensity set to a non-zero value, you can adjust Color Hue to pick a specific color tint.

## Plug-In Windows

The three options in the next section of the Look/Feel preference tab determine how Live will display a plug-in's custom display window.

When Multiple Plug-In Windows is activated, you can open more than one plug-in window at a time. When this is off, open plug-in windows will be closed anytime a new one is opened. Keeping this option off can help minimize screen clutter. With this preference turned off, you can still open multiple plug-in windows manually by holding down the Ctrl (Cmd) key when opening a new plug-in window.

The second option, Auto-Hide Plug-In Windows, will make plug-in windows appear only for those plug-ins loaded on a selected track. For example, if you have a MIDI track loaded with Maschine and another track with Serum, Maschine will be hidden when the Serum track is selected and vice versa. This can also help minimize screen clutter and thus is especially useful for laptop users.

The third option here is the Auto-Open Plug-In Custom Editor box. When active, the plug-in window will be opened immediately after the plug-in is loaded onto a track. This makes perfect sense, since you'll usually need to make some modification to the plug-in after you load it.

# Audio

The next tab in Live's preferences, the Audio tab (see Figure 2.2a), is used to select an audio interface and makes adjustments to its performance.

## Audio Device

The first section of the Audio tab is labeled Audio Device. The first setting you can choose here is the Driver Type you want to use for your audio interface. On the PC, options will include MME/DirectX and ASIO, and in Mac OS X, you will see just one choice, Core Audio. After you select the driver type you want to use, you will have a selection of audio devices to choose from in the subsequent drop-down menus. As noted previously, you will always get better performance with ASIO drivers, so you should always choose ASIO on a PC if this option is available.

Next after Driver Type is the Audio Device setting, where you actually choose the specific soundcard you want to use. In Windows, you will see only a single menu here; in Mac OS X, you will see separate settings for Audio Input

**FIGURE 2.2A**

Live's Audio Preferences tab. If you're using a PC, this window looks a little different, but the basic functionality is the same.

*Source:* Ableton

Device and Audio Output Device. Theoretically, you could choose different devices for input and output; in practice, however, you will probably get the best performance by using a single audio interface at a time, so you'll probably want to choose the same device for both input and output. (If you are not recording, you don't need to choose an input device at all.)

Please note that Live will always seek out the audio interface last saved in the preferences each time the program launches. If Live cannot find it—if, for instance, you have unplugged it or swapped it out—Live will still launch, but with no audio enabled. In this instance, the CPU meter will be red and display the word OFF. You won't be able to play any sound in Live until you go to Audio Preferences and select a new audio device.

The Channel Configuration settings include two buttons: Input Config and Output Config. Clicking one of these opens a window for activating and naming inputs and outputs on your audio interface (see Figure 2.2b). Only those inputs and outputs that you activate here will appear in Live. If you don't need to use all of the inputs and outputs, you may want to leave them inactive here, as doing so will save you a little computing power. Naming is useful in complex setups with a lot of I/O, particularly when hardware devices are permanently connected to certain inputs and outputs.

FIGURE 2.2B The Input Configuration window. If you give inputs names, they will show up in Live's input and output choosers, as seen on the left.
*Source:* Ableton

## Sample Rate

The In/Out Sample Rate setting in the Audio Preferences tab will determine the recording quality of both Live's output and recorded input. The most common sample rate is 44,100Hz (44.1kHz), which is the sample rate for CDs and most consumer digital audio. The sample rate for digital video is 48,000Hz. Some producers work at higher sample rates, in the interest of sound quality, and *downsample* the audio in the mastering process. There is much debate on this topic, the details of which go beyond the scope of this book. Bear in mind that higher sample rates mean larger file sizes and greater CPU demand.

There is also another setting here labeled Default SR & Pitch Conversion. When set to High Quality, Live will set the Hi Q switch to its On position for all newly created clips. This causes Live to use a cleaner algorithm when converting sample rates and transposing clips. Unless you're really strapped for CPU power, leave this in the Hi Quality position. You can always turn it off for individual clips, which you may want to experiment with when using transposition for sound design purposes.

## Latency Settings

The next section of the Audio tab adjusts a number of settings relating to the buffer size and latency of your soundcard. You may need to experiment with these settings a bit to get the best possible performance on your particular computer system. Before we get to the experimentation, though, let's make sure you understand the problem.

First, recognize that there is both output latency and input latency. There is a minimum amount of latency that must occur as the signal passes through your A/D converters into your computer, just as there is also a certain amount of time that it takes for your computer to send audio to your soundcard and through the D/A converters. While this is a very short period of time, things are complicated somewhat by the fact that you need your audio to play back without interruption, while at the same time your CPU is being interrupted constantly, handling myriad other tasks while your audio is playing back. This is where buffers come into play.

If something causes your CPU usage to spike momentarily, and you don't have a big enough buffer, audio mayhem will ensue! Audio playback will glitch or drop out completely while your computer handles some other task. So, how big should you set your Buffer Size? It depends.

A very small buffer gives you low latency and makes your system very responsive, but it demands a lot of your CPU. A large buffer is easier on the CPU and ensures smooth performance, but increases latency. Therefore, you may have to experiment with your system to get the settings right, and you may have to change them, depending on what you're doing.

For example, on stage you want to make sure that you've got a big enough buffer to avoid audio dropouts or artifacts without generating so much latency that you can't perform comfortably. In the studio, you might keep the buffer low during the early parts of the production process, increasing as your song becomes more complex and more CPU power is needed.

It's possible you may not be able to adjust the buffer size of your audio interface from the Buffer Size menu. In Windows, you will probably need to open the interface's proprietary control panel, which can be launched with the Hardware Setup button. The need to set the buffer outside of Live can arise on OS X as well, although it is far less common.

Next, see the Input Latency and Output Latency values. Output latency is the amount of lag time between when you trigger a sound or action and when you hear it. If you're cranking a knob and can hear Live lagging behind you, that's output latency at work. Input latency arises because audio is buffered on the way into the computer, so Live receives this audio a little later than it should. Fortunately, Live can compensate automatically for this when recording.

## ROUND IT OFF

While some audio drivers will allow you to adjust the buffer in increments of one sample, Ableton recommends that you set your buffer to one of the binary "round numbers" that we see so often on our computers: 64, 128, 256, 512, 1024, and so on.

Audio interfaces are designed to report their latencies to Live so that it can offset its operations properly. However, in practice, the reported amount is sometimes not completely accurate, and you'll find that your audio recordings are slightly out-of-sync. To correct this, you must enter the unreported latency manually into the Driver Error Compensation box. Follow the step-by-step instructions in the Driver Error Compensation lesson from the Help View to determine and correct unreported latency.

# Test

The Test section of the Audio Preferences generates a test-tone sine wave so that you can test your system. You can also adjust the volume and frequency of the test tone using the other parameters in this section. Here are the steps for testing your system:

1. Turn on the test tone.
2. Set the CPU Usage Simulator to its maximum value (80%).
3. Decrease the buffer size until you start to hear crackling or dropouts in the test tone.
4. Increase the buffer size until those artifacts go away.

This test will yield a buffer size that will guarantee smooth audio performance in almost all situations. This will be a good value to use for live performance where stability is paramount. For situations where you need lower latency, you can test with a lower simulated CPU usage, or as long as you are working in the studio, just lower the buffer size as low as you want and increase it if you have problems.

# Link/MIDI

This brings us to the third Preferences tab, the Link/MIDI tab, shown in Figure 2.3. This is where you configure MIDI devices, such as keyboard controllers, drum pads, and synthesizers. You'll also use this tab to configure Link, a technology developed by Ableton for synchronizing multiple computers and mobile devices such as iPads and Android phones.

## Link

As you'll see in Figure 2.3, there are only two preferences for Link. That's because Link is designed to be almost completely automatic. If you want to use Link, Show Link Toggle must be set to "Show." A switch marked Link will appear in the upper left-hand corner of Live, which you can use to enable or disable Link. When it's enabled, Live will synchronize other Link

**FIGURE 2.3**

The Link/MIDI tab found in Live's Preferences box.

*Source:* Ableton

applications on the network. When Start Stop Sync is enabled, you can start and stop playback of other Link applications simultaneously. For more information, see the Link section in Chapter 13, "Live 10 Power!"

## Control Surfaces

Below Link, you'll find options for setting up natively supported control surfaces in Live. If you are using a controller that Live supports, you can use one of the drop-down choosers in the first column (labeled *Control Surface*) to select it from a list. Once selected, Live will have all the necessary information to support the device. In many cases, the Input and Output ports will be selected automatically, but if you need to select them manually, they are usually the ports with names similar to the control surface.

Depending on which controller you are using, Live may need to do a "preset dump" to the device after you have selected it, in order to initialize it with the correct control values. In this case, the Dump button at right will become active (not grayed out), and you will need to click it once to do the dump.

## MIDI Port Settings

This area shows a list of the MIDI Input and Output devices available on your computer. There are columns for the names of each MIDI port found by Live, plus columns named Track, Sync, and Remote. In order for a MIDI device to communicate with Live, it has to be enabled as a Track Input or Output, as a Sync source, or as a MIDI Remote Control.

Enabling Track for a MIDI Input device means that you can use it as an input to a MIDI track. This would be enabled for something like a keyboard that you use for playing notes on a virtual instrument. Enabling Track for a MIDI Output allows Live to send MIDI data from a MIDI track to an external piece of hardware, such as a synthesizer.

The Sync option enables the port as a MIDI Sync source or destination. This will have to be turned on for at least one port for any of the Sync functions to work. When you are using Sync input, the EXT switch will appear in the Control Bar and can be used to force Live to slave to an external tempo source.

The last column, Remote, is especially nifty. By enabling a remote input, you can map any of Live's on-screen controls to a physical controller. Remote output is used for sending MIDI feedback to MIDI controllers with motorized MIDI knobs and faders, or those with light-up encoders, and so forth. If you have a control surface with these types of controls, moving an on-screen control with the mouse will cause the MIDI controller to reflect that change.

Each MIDI port in this display has a triangular "unfold" button on the left. Click this to reveal these advanced synchronization options, as follows:

▶ **Midi Clock Sync Delay:** Set this value to correct for synchronization timing errors. If the synchronized device is late, use a negative value. If it's early (usually caused by latency compensation errors), a positive value is what's called for.

▶ **Sync Type/MTC Settings:** When Live is receiving sync, it can synchronize to the tempo only (MIDI Beat Clock) or to MIDI Time Code (MTC), which synchronizes the song position in addition to tempo. When MTC is selected, two additional controls are enabled. Select the frame rate being sent by the master device in the MTC Frame Rate menu, or select All to have Live automatically detect the frame rate. If MTC Start Offset is specified, this location in the MTC source will correspond to the start of the Arrangement in Live.

▶ **MIDI Clock Type:** When Live is sending sync, it can operate in Pattern mode, which sends tempo and start/start information only. (This is all that's needed for simple hardware like a drum machine.) Song mode sends the song position to the external device as well.

## Takeover Mode

The Takeover Mode menu (located above MIDI Ports) helps with handling control surfaces and MIDI remote devices that do not receive MIDI feedback. With these devices, moving a control with the mouse causes the physical controller to become mismatched with its associated on-screen control. When set to None, the controls on-screen will jump to whatever value the MIDI controller is sending immediately. This is very simple, but can result in sudden volume changes and other unnerving parameter jumps. Pick-up mode requires that you move the MIDI control to the value of the on-screen control, while Value Scaling moves the on-screen control in the direction that the MIDI control is moved, until the upper or lower limit is reached, at which point normal MIDI control resumes.

# File/Folder

The File/Folder tab is used to specify various external file locations, manage plug-ins, and handle Live's cache for decoded MP3 files (see Figure 2.4).

The first setting here, Save Current Set as Default, is used to save the current Live Set as the template Set that will be loaded each time Live is launched. This can be helpful for preconfiguring commonly used settings, such as MIDI assignments, input and output routings, and common effect patchwork (such as EQs on every channel). Note that you can save only one template in this Preferences tab. For additional templates, you can create additional Sets and store them in the Templates folder of your User Library. (More on this in Chapter 13.)

**FIGURE 2.4**

The File/Folder tab.

*Source:* Ableton

The Create Analysis Files option lets you determine whether Live will save audio analysis data for quick loading in the future. The first time an audio file is used in Live, the program will create a waveform display and perform additional analysis on the file. When this option is enabled, Live will store this information in a file on your computer's hard disk. The file has the same name and location as the sample it is associated with and uses .asd as its extension. The next time the audio file is used in a Live Set, you won't have to wait for the graphical display to be rendered again because the file analysis has been saved.

The Sample Editor setting is for defining the location of your favorite wave editor, such as Wavelab, DSP-Quattro, or the excellent freeware program, Audacity. The editor will launch when you press the Edit button in an audio clip.

Temporary Folder determines where Live will store any temporary files it creates. This is the folder into which Live places all new recordings made before a Set is saved for the first time. In most cases, you won't need to change this from its default setting.

## Decoding Cache

Before Live can play compressed audio files, such as MP3s, it must decompress them into standard WAV files. These decompressed files are created automatically and stored in the Decoding Cache. The parameters in this section determine how Live will handle the creation and cleanup of the decoded files.

While high-quality compressed audio files sound good enough for many applications, bear in mind that you won't save any disk space when using them in Live. In fact, you end up using *more* disk space because you're storing both a compressed *and* an uncompressed version of the file. If you have to work with a lot of compressed files and you're relying on a small laptop hard drive, you'd be better off converting them to WAV files before you add them to Live. (There are many cheap/free utilities for doing this.)

The first option, Minimum Free Space, is the amount of free space that you always want available on the hard drive. If you set this to 500MB, Live will stop increasing the size of the cache once there is only 500MB available, which can be extremely important if you only have one hard drive on your entire computer system (frequently the case for laptop users). This setting will ensure that a minimum amount of space is available on the drive for swapping files and other housekeeping tasks. Alternately, Maximum Cache Size can be used if you would rather set a hard limit for the Decoding Cache. For example, you might want to make sure that the cache never gets bigger than 10GB, regardless of how much drive space you have left.

You'll notice that if you add an MP3 to your Set and Live decodes it, Live will not have to decode the file again if you drag the same MP3 into a Set at a later time. This feature works this way because the decoded file is still in the cache. If the decoded file gets deleted, you'll have to wait again for the previously decoded MP3 to be decoded again. The larger your cache is, the less this will happen.

## Plug-In Sources

To use plug-ins in Live, you'll need to have at least one of these options turned on. In OS X, just enable Use Audio Units to enable Audio Units, and Use VST System Folders to enable VST plug-ins. PCs can't use Audio Units, and don't have a VST system folder, so you'll have to specify the folder on your hard drive that contains your VSTs, typically Program Files/Steinberg /VstPlugins.

On a Mac, you can also specify a custom location for VSTs that can be used instead of, or in conjunction with, the System folder. For complex setups, or when testing new plug-ins, it can be handy to have a separate folder for certain VSTs that can be enabled or disabled with a single click.

### MAC USERS TAKE NOTE

OS X has a built-in location for storing all of your plug-ins (Library /Audio/Plug-ins). I find that it's handy to drag this folder to the Favorites area in a Finder window for easy access.

Within the Plug-ins folder, VSTs live in a folder called "VST," while Audio Units are in the nonintuitively named "Components" folder.

# Library

The first option in the Library tab is Collect Samples on Export (see Figure 2.5). This affects Live's behavior when saving presets for Simpler or Sampler and when clips or tracks are dragged into the Browser in order to export them as Sets or Live Clips. If it's set to Yes, Live will always copy any necessary samples into the new location, along with the new Sets or Live Clips you are creating. If it's set to Never, the new Sets or Clips will refer to the original locations of the samples they use. I recommend setting this preference to Ask, which invokes a dialog asking you if you want to export files. This gives you additional control and allows you to learn by doing.

By default, the Packs View of the Browser will display all Live Packs registered to your account whether or not you've installed them, and any available updates for those Packs. If you'd prefer that these downloads and updates be hidden, turn Show Downloadable Packs off.

**FIGURE 2.5**
The Library tab.
*Source:* Ableton

## Content Locations

The first option here is the location of your User Library. This can be any location on your hard drive. The User Library is where any custom presets you save will be stored, so it's highly recommended that you place it in a location that gets backed up regularly.

Installation Folder for Packs enables you to select where Ableton will install any new Live Packs that you install. Live Packs can contain many different types of content including presets, samples, clips, and Sets. They can be downloaded from ableton.com and from some third-party vendors such as Loopmasters. Once you've installed a Live Pack, its content will be accessible from the Browser, as explained in Chapter 3, "Live Interface Basics."

# The Record/Warp/Launch Tab

As you might guess, this tab contains settings dealing with Live's recording, launching, and clip launch functions (see Figure 2.6).

## Record

Anytime you record new audio, whether through resampling or from an input on your soundcard, it will use the Record parameters you set here. First, you can record in WAV or AIFF format. Sonically, these file types are identical. Historically, WAVs are associated with the PC and AIFF with the Mac, but nowadays the difference is largely irrelevant and both types can be used on both platforms.

More important is the Bit Depth, which should usually be set to 24. At 24-bit, you can capture highly detailed recordings at lower levels. If you have to record at 16-bit for some reason, you need to be more conscious about getting a higher level into the computer while being cautious not to overload the

**FIGURE 2.6**

The Record/Warp/Launch tab.

*Source:* Ableton

inputs ("go into the red"). At the time of this writing, true 32-bit recording is exceedingly rare because 32-bit A/D converters are virtually nonexistent. If you're someone who needs to record at 32-bit, you know who you are.

The next option in this section is Count In. When set to None, Live will begin to record immediately when the transport is engaged. If you select a value here, such as 1 Bar, Live will provide one bar of count-in time (the metronome will sound, but Live will not be running) before it begins to record. This feature is useful if you're recording yourself and you need some time to get to your instrument after you've engaged recording.

The Exclusive buttons are used to determine whether or not more than one track's Solo or Arm switch can be engaged simultaneously. For example, when Solo Exclusive is on, only one track may be soloed at a time. If you click the Solo button of another track, the previous track's solo status will turn off. The same is true for Arm Exclusive. Only one track can be armed to record when this button is active. You can override the Exclusive setting for either Solo or Arm by holding down Ctrl (Cmd) while clicking these switches in the Mixer.

The Clip Update Rate is the frequency with which Live recalculates changes made to a clip during playback. For instance, if you transpose a clip in Live while the Clip Update Rate is set to 1/32 note, you will hear nearly instant changes to the pitch of the loop in the clip. Conversely, choosing a Clip Update Rate of 1/4 note or the even slower rate of Bar (meaning one update per measure) will result in changes occurring more slowly.

Record Session Automation specifies how the Session View behaves when the Automation Arm switch is turned on and Session Record is enabled. When set to Armed Tracks, automation in the session view will only be recorded into tracks that are armed for recording. If this option is set to All Tracks, all your knob movements and other automation will be recorded, regardless of whether the tracks are armed or not.

Finally, use the Start Playback with Record setting to determine Live's behavior when the Record button is pressed. When turned off, Record can be enabled and then playback started with the spacebar, by clicking a clip slot's record button or by launching a scene. Turn it on if you want playback to begin immediately when Record is pressed.

## Warp/Fades

This section includes various settings relating to Live's Warp engine, which controls the time flow of clips, keeping everything in sync.

The Loop/Warp Short Samples menu determines the default state of a new audio clip, be it a loop or a one-shot sound. The Auto setting will cause Live to try to determine the nature of an imported sample on the fly and set its loop and warp settings accordingly. Live typically does well at automatically determining settings for short samples, and when it makes mistakes, they are easy to correct.

The next option relates to Live's Auto-Warp feature. When the Auto-Warp Long Samples option is on, Live will attempt to determine the tempo of the imported audio file and will place Warp Markers into the audio clip automatically. This will only happen on long samples—files that Live assumes to be complete songs. Auto-Warp works better with some kinds of material than others (for example, dance music with clear tempo and transients), so what you do with Live will determine whether or not you want this setting enabled. With long samples, Live sometimes makes mistakes that are difficult to correct, so turning this feature off can be desirable. You can still use Auto Warp, but you'll invoke it manually, as explained in Chapters 5, "Clips," and 12, "Playing Live…Live."

Default Warp Mode specifies which of Live's warping algorithms will be applied to new clips. Five of Live's six Warp modes are available to set as the default. (Complex Pro is not an option due to its high CPU usage.) All of these modes produce different results when modifying the tempo or the pitch of a clip. The Warp modes are explained in detail in Chapter 5. Until you've mastered these, it's just fine to leave this setting on its default setting of Beats.

Finally, the Create Fades on Clip Edges preference can be turned on or off. In its On position, the Fade switch will be turned on for all new Session View clips (which creates a fixed 4ms fade at the start and end) and will create an editable fade whenever an Arrangement View clip is created or split. Fades are typically desirable because they prevent the ugly digital popping that can occur when editing or looping audio. For more about fades, see Chapter 4, "Making Music in Live."

# Launch

When you are triggering a clip to play, Live's behavior varies depending on the clip's *Launch mode*. The full rundown on these modes can be found in Chapter 4. For now, I recommend leaving Default Launch Mode for new clips on Trigger, and return to this preference once you're familiar with the four Launch modes.

The next setting, Default Launch Quantization, determines the default point at which new clips will be launched in relation to the time grid. Unless you've got an advanced understanding of this subject, you should leave this set to Global, which means the clip's quantization will follow the global quantization value in the Control Bar. Launch quantization is discussed in detail in Chapters 3 and 4.

When Select On Launch is turned on, launching a clip will also select it. This means its waveform and properties will be displayed in the Clip View, and editing commands like Duplicate will affect the launched clip. If you discover a situation in which you need to launch clips while performing operations on other clips, turn this preference off. Select Next Scene on Launch is a setting designed primarily for live performance. Anytime a scene is launched by keyboard or remote control, Live will advance the scene selector to the one below it. If you've already laid out the sections of your song in a top-to-bottom arrangement in the Session View, you can progress through the song with just one button.

Start Recording on Scene Launch determines if clips will begin recording when launched by a scene. Having this option off will allow you to launch Scenes without recording, even if some tracks are armed. Having this option turned on can be useful for recording several clips simultaneously or starting recording in one track and playback in another at the same time.

# Licenses/Maintenance

The top of this screen will display your current Live authorization and how many add-ons are registered to your account. Typically, authorization is done the first time you run Live, but if you need to do it after the fact, you can use the Authorize at ableton.com or Authorize Offline buttons on this screen (see Figure 2.7). Offline authorization is only necessary for computers that are never connected to the Internet. If you select this option, follow the directions that appear on-screen. Live will give you a code to enter into your ableton.com account. You can then download a file that can be copied to the offline computer to authorize Live.

Turn on Get Software Updates to make Live keep itself up-to-date automatically. Updates are downloaded while Live is running and take effect the next time the software is launched.

Send Usage Data is a feature that shares configuration and usage information anonymously with Ableton. This data is used to fix bugs and develop improvements based on common usage habits.

**FIGURE 2.7**
The Licenses/
Maintenance tab.
*Source:* Ableton

# 3

# Live Interface Basics

One of Ableton's defining achievements is Live's simple, elegant interface. Only two views are needed to accomplish everything in Live: Session View and Arrangement View. Session View is geared for use in live performance, for loop experimentation, and as a quick multitrack sketchpad, while Arrangement View facilitates detailed editing and song arranging.

In this chapter, we'll be covering the basics of getting around Live. I'll also mention a few things that you may not use until you're deeper into the program, but nevertheless need to be discussed at the outset.

## Before We Begin...

To get started, it's important to know that a Live file is called a *Set*. When you first open Live, you're presented with an empty Set containing four tracks (two audio and two MIDI). To the Set you'll add prefabricated elements, such as samples or Live Clips, and create new parts by recording audio or programming MIDI parts with virtual instruments. Don't worry if you don't know what all of this means. That's what the book is about!

To switch between Session and Arrangement Views, press Tab. You can also use the horizontal and vertical line icons in the upper right of your screen. But seriously—use Tab. Try it now.

Be aware that there are often a few different ways of doing something in Live. For example, you can also switch between Session and Arrangement by selecting Toggle Arrangement/Session View from the View menu. Notice that most menu commands have keyboard shortcuts next to them. Keep an eye on these and learn them as you go. When keyboard shortcuts are referred to in this book, the format PC (Mac) is used.

## Showing and Hiding

As you work with this book, you may notice that the figures don't always match what you see on your screen. This is because Live allows various interface elements to be shown or hidden. At the far right of Live's screen, you'll see a set of show/hide switches. Try clicking on them, and you'll see various sets of controls appear and disappear. The ones pictured in Figure 3.1 are for various aspects of the mixer, but that's not important yet. Just be aware that these turn up in various parts of the program. Whenever you see them, click them on and off to see what happens.

**FIGURE 3.1**
Switches like these appear in various places in Live to show or hide interface elements.
*Source:* Ableton

In the corners of the screen (except for the upper right), you'll see show/hide buttons containing a triangle (see Figure 3.2). These are used to show or hide the Browser, Info View, and Detail View, all discussed later in this chapter. Similar triangular "unfold" switches appear elsewhere throughout the interface to reveal additional controls and features. Make sure to try these out as you come across them.

**FIGURE 3.2**
Some views are shown or hidden using these triangular fold/unfold buttons.
*Source:* Ableton

Finally, you'll find all of Live's optional views can be shown or hidden from the View menu. Open this menu and learn the keyboard shortcuts that are displayed next to the various commands. You'll be glad you did.

# Working with Knobs, Sliders, and Boxes

Live has several different controls for adjusting values, which all have a lot in common, even though they look different (see Figure 3.3). Sliders are adjusted by dragging vertically, just as you'd expect. What might not be obvious is that knobs and numeric boxes are dragged in the same vertical fashion. These controls can also be adjusted by single-clicking and then using the up- and down-arrow keys. Finally, numeric boxes can be adjusted by simply typing in a value, which is often faster than dragging the mouse.

Any control can be returned to its default value by double-clicking on it, or by selecting it and then pressing Delete. Additionally, some knobs have a triangle, which can be clicked to reset to default (see the Transpose knob in Figure 3.3 for an example).

**FIGURE 3.3** All three of these control types can be adjusted by dragging vertically.
*Source:* Ableton

# Common Editing Commands

Under the Edit menu, you'll see Live's editing commands. Some of these are specialized commands we'll be discussing later, while others are common commands you'll want to learn right away because they are used throughout the program. For example, Duplicate can be used to make a copy of just about anything you can select with the mouse: clips, tracks, scenes, and devices. Rename works the same way. It's good to get in the habit of naming things (especially tracks and clips) before your Sets get too big and confusing. When using Rename, press Enter to confirm the name, Esc to cancel, or Tab to confirm the name and jump to the next object. As you'd expect, Live supports Cut, Copy, and Paste for moving and duplicating clips, tracks, and devices as well.

There are many editing commands that can be applied to multiple objects simultaneously. For example, it's possible to duplicate several clips in one step or to adjust the volume of several tracks simultaneously. To select multiple objects, hold down Ctrl (Cmd) while clicking on them. Alternately, Shift-click can be used to select a range. In other words, to select tracks 1 through 8, click on the title bar of track 1 and then Shift-click on the title bar of track 8.

## Context Menus

Context menus contain a list of commands relevant to a particular object. They are a very useful part of Live's interface and are something you should plan on becoming very familiar with. For example, the context menu for a track contains commands to create additional tracks, as well as commands to delete or duplicate the selected track.

Context menus are typically invoked by right-clicking with the mouse. If you're on a Mac, you may need to configure your OS X Keyboard and Mouse preferences to enable the right mouse button, or you can Control-click with the left mouse button instead. If you're using a MacBook, you can also configure the trackpad to register a right-click when you click with two fingers.

## The Info View

The Info View is a retractable display in the lower-left corner of Live that provides information about whatever control your mouse is hovering over (see Figure 3.4). The information displayed here is brief but very handy, and even if it doesn't answer every question, it will at least tell you the name of the thing you're looking at, which is a great help if you want to look it up in this book or (gasp!) in the Live manual.

I strongly recommend you keep the Info View open while learning Live. The "?" key can be used to quickly hide it to protect your reputation when a friend looks over your shoulder.

**FIGURE 3.4**
The Info View can be hidden or expanded to give you quick bits of pertinent Live wisdom.
*Source:* Ableton

# The Help View

This view can be opened by selecting Help View from the View menu (see Figure 3.5). This view differs from the manual in that it provides step-by step tutorials organized by task, such as recording or programming beats. Exploring these topics is highly recommended for new users or experienced users moving into a new area of the program.

**FIGURE 3.5**
The Help View offers useful lessons and reference guides.
*Source:* Ableton

# Session View

Live's Session View (sometimes referred to as the *Session* for short) is far more than just a tool for live performance. It's the launch point for many compositions, where ideas are sketched out and quickly captured without worrying about how and where they'll be used in the final production. The next phase of the process is handled in the Arrangement View, but there's no need to worry about that right now. Just focus on having fun in the Session View.

---

**SPACE OUT**

The spacebar starts and stops audio in Live, as it does in most audio software.

---

# Clip Slot Grid

The Session View's defining characteristic is the grid that covers most of the screen. Live's clip slot grid is a palette upon which to create, organize, and experiment with the sonic colors that will eventually become your masterpiece. Just as a painter will mix colors before starting to paint, today's music producers will often gather and create appealing sounds in the clip slot grid before giving form to a song.

Each cell in the grid shown in the Session View—Ableton calls them *clip slots*—can contain a clip (see Figure 3.6). A clip is a piece of audio or MIDI that can be launched via the mouse, computer keyboard, or MIDI controller. Drag clips or samples from the Browser, the OS X Finder, or Windows

**FIGURE 3.6**
The clip slot grid with a few clips loaded in some slots. Each clip has its own launch button.
*Source:* Ableton

Explorer and drop them into clip slots. Then launch them by clicking their triangular "play" buttons. (For more information about loading clips into slots, read "The Browser" later in this chapter.)

Every empty slot contains a square stop button. (The bottom of the clip slot grid also contains a permanent row of stop buttons that will remain visible even if you've filled every slot in the grid above.) Clicking the square in one of these slots will cause any clip playing on the track above it to stop. Also, there is another box labeled Stop Clips in the Master track at the right. This button, as its name implies, will stop all clips—both audio and MIDI—when triggered.

There's another way to stop a clip—by launching a different clip in the same column. In other words, Live only allows one clip at a time to play back in any given track. This means that any time you have two clips you want to play simultaneously, they must be in separate tracks. That's why Figure 3.6 is organized as shown, with the drum parts in one track, the bass parts in another, and so on.

## Tracks and Scenes

The columns of the grid are referred to as *tracks,* while the rows are called *scenes.* The type of track determines what type of clips it contains: audio tracks can only contain audio clips, while MIDI tracks are strictly for MIDI clips. There are also types of tracks that can't contain clips at all, but we'll get to those in Chapter 6, "Tracks and Signal Routing." We'll also be getting further into the workings of scenes later, but for now just know that scenes are a handy way to organize musical ideas. For example, when you've got drum, bass, and keyboard parts that work well together, drag around the clips in the grid so the ones you like are all in the same scene.

## The Scene Launcher

At the far right of the screen, you'll see a special track called *Master.* Each slot in this track has a Scene Launch button, which is used to launch every clip in the scene simultaneously (see Figure 3.7). When you launch a scene in this way, it's as if you clicked in every single clip slot—even the empty ones containing stop buttons. Therefore, launching a scene also stops playback in any

**FIGURE 3.7**
Click the triangle to launch all the clips in the scene (row).
*Source:* Ableton

tracks that don't have a clip in that particular scene. Spend a little time playing with this, and you'll get a sense of how powerful this feature is for quickly arranging musical ideas.

# The Mixer

Live's mixer (see Figure 3.8a) is made up of several sections, which can be shown or hidden independently using the View menu or the buttons shown in Figure 3.1. One of these sections is called *Mixer*, and contains basic mixing controls such as volume. When I refer to the Mixer (with a capital "M"), I'm referring to this component, while other references to the mixer are considering the conceptual whole. Live has several different types of tracks (covered in detail in Chapters 4 and 6), some of which have unique mixer features, but most of them share the controls shown in Figure 3.8b.

Like many features of the Session View, the mixer is also available in the Arrangement View. However, the Session View is more intuitive to use for many tasks and offers a few additional features. I'll use the term *Session Mixer* when it's necessary to differentiate the two.

Let's take a look at each section now.

## Mixer

▶ **Volume:** Drag to adjust the volume of a track, or type in a decibel value into the numeric display if you're in the expanded view.

▶ **Pan:** Drag to move the signal left or right in the stereo field. Right-click and select Split Stereo Pan Mode to switch to a control that allows you to adjust the left and right channels of a stereo signal separately.

In/Out

Sends

Mixer

Track Delay

Crossfader Assign

Crossfader

**FIGURE 3.8A** Here's the Mixer with every section shown. Each of these sections is explained on pages 44 and 46.
*Source:* Ableton

Peak Level

Numeric Volume Display

Split Stereo Pan Control

Standard Pan Control

Track Activator (mute switch)

Solo/Cue Switch

Record Arm

**FIGURE 3.8B** Two fully expanded Mixer channels. Live 10 introduces an optional split stereo panning mode, shown on the left.
*Source:* Ableton

▶ **Track Activator:** In most mixers, this is referred to as the "mute" switch. When turned off, the track is silenced.

▶ **Solo:** Activating Solo mutes all other tracks. If you want to Solo more than one track at a time, Ctrl (Cmd)-click the Solo switch, or change the Exclusive preference on the Record/Warp/Launch tab of the Preferences dialog. This button can be switched to act as a Cue switch, as explained in Chapter 6.

▶ **Arm**: Allows new clips to be recorded. If you want to Arm more than one track at a time, use Ctrl (Cmd)-click or change the Exclusive preference on the Record/Warp/Launch tab of the Preferences dialog. The Arm button can also be used to enable Session Automation recording, which is discussed in Chapter 4, "Making Music in Live."

If you click and drag the top edge of the Session Mixer upward, you can resize it better to see levels when mixing (see Figure 3.8b). When resized, the Peak Level display appears, indicating the maximum level reached during playback. Click on Peak Level to reset it.

## Sends

Sends are used to route audio into Return tracks, which are covered in Chapter 6. For example, if you turn up Send A on a drum track, the audio from that drum track will now come out of Return A as well. This feature is typically used for effects processing, in particular to add time-based effects, such as reverb and delay.

## In/Out

The In/Out section is used for recording and for various advanced routing techniques. The "From" menus specify the source that the track will receive from (Input), while the "To" menus determine where the signal from the track goes (Output). Both sections contain two menus: the top two menus are called Input Type and Input Channel; the bottom two are Output Type and Output Channel.

In audio tracks, Input Type determines the source that the track will record or monitor, while Input Channel is used to specify a specific input from the selected source. For example, if you want to record a guitar that's plugged into Input 2 of your audio interface, you'd select Ext. Input from the top menu and 2 from the second.

For MIDI tracks, the Input Type is used to select which MIDI device you'll use to record a performance. By default, this is set to All Ins (All Inputs), which typically works just fine unless you have a very complex setup with a lot of MIDI gear. You can then use Input Channel to limit input to a specific MIDI channel, or leave it on the default, which receives all channels.

Output Type and Output Channel are used to route audio to outputs on your audio interface or MIDI to external hardware. You may notice that the Output Channel menu is disabled by default. This is because the default Output Type is Master, which has no channel settings. There's a lot more information about signal routing in Chapter 6, but these basics should be plenty to get you started.

The Monitor switches determine what signal passes through the track: the input source or the currently playing clip. With MIDI tracks, you can also monitor both at once (using Auto mode, explained next). Let's look at the three options:

▶ **In:** The input source is passed through. Audio or MIDI coming from clip playback is ignored.

▶ **Auto:** For audio tracks, the input source is passed through to the mixer if the track is armed for recording, and there is no clip playing back in the track. For MIDI tracks, the MIDI input is passed through when the track is armed for recording, regardless of whether or not a clip is playing back.

▶ **Off:** The input source is ignored. Only audio or MIDI coming from clip playback will be passed through the track.

If you're an experienced engineer, these modes should be quite familiar. If not, don't worry. Just leave your tracks set to the default (Off for audio tracks, Auto for MIDI tracks). If you plug in a microphone or an instrument, you may need to switch to Auto or In to hear the signal, but in most cases the best way to monitor audio input is to use the monitoring features of your audio interface. I'll be explaining different routing configurations as necessary throughout the book, and you can refer back here if you don't remember what the different modes mean.

## Crossfader

Live also features a DJ-style crossfader. For many years, analog crossfaders have been used by DJs to enable the mixing of two tracks together, with one simple gesture. Scratch DJs have taken crossfader technique to incredible levels, transforming the mixer into a musical instrument.

Live's crossfader consists of two components: the crossfader itself (located at the bottom of the master track) and the Crossfader Assign switches at the bottom of every other track. To use it, you will have to assign tracks to either the A (left) or B (right) side of the crossfader. As you move the crossfader to the right, you increase the volume of all channels set to B, while decreasing the volume of all channels set to A. The reverse holds true when you move it to the left. Unassigned tracks are disregarded by the crossfader and play back regardless of its position.

Opening the crossfader's context menu reveals the transition modes, which determine the volume curve used when transitioning between A and B. Constant, Dipped, and Intermediate are curves that slowly change the volume across the entire range of the crossfader. With all three of these modes, there's a gain reduction to both sides in the center position (Dipped reduces gain the most, Constant the least) to compensate for the volume overload you can get from mixing together two powerful sources (like dance tracks). Fast Cut, Slow Cut, and Slow Fade have both sources at maximum amplitude before the center position is reached. Slow Fade provides the largest amount of transition between the two, with Fast Cut providing almost none. The last mode, Transition, keeps the gain constant across most of the range, with both signals rising rapidly to a peak at the center.

## Track Delay

Track Delay isn't a mixer control in the traditional sense, but it provides a very valuable service in the world of digital audio. It allows the output of a channel to be delayed or advanced by small amounts of time (measured in milliseconds or samples) to compensate for sluggish hardware, plug-ins that generate excessive latency, or as a creative tool. (Theoretically, Live can automatically compensate for all plug-in latency, but this depends on the plug-in accurately reporting its latency to Live, which not all plug-ins do.)

Positive values make the track play back later, while negative values make it play earlier. For example, you might be sending MIDI to an external synthesizer and hear that it's responding late and messing up the groove. Set track delay to –50ms to bring it into sync. Or maybe you've got a hi-hat clip that you think would sound better if it lagged a little behind the beat. Set its Track Delay to 10ms to add a little vibe.

Note that in order to hear the effects of Track Delay, Delay Compensation must be activated under the Options menu. To make the Track Delay setting visible at the bottom of each track, select the Track Delay option under the View menu.

# Arrangement View

Beginners may think of it as merely Live's "other" window, but Arrangement View (sometimes called the *Arrangement* for short) is incredibly important. It's the place where final decisions about composing and arranging are made, and where songs are completed. If Session View is the spontaneous right-brain-tickling screen, Arrangement View is the analytic left-brain-stimulating, "finishing touches" side of Live.

You may notice that Live's Arrangement View closely resembles other multitrack applications (see Figure 3.9). These programs, such as Cubase, Logic, and Pro Tools, are based on horizontal, left-to-right audio arrangers (also called *timelines*). If you like this method of working, you will be right at home making music in the Arrangement.

For those who didn't read the figure caption, here it is again: Each track in Session View corresponds precisely to its track counterpart in Arrangement View. If you have eight tracks in Session View, you will have eight tracks in Arrangement View. You can add a track in either view, and it will appear in the other.

Clips can be added to this view by dragging and dropping (just like you would in Session View), or by using a method called *Arrangement Record,* which allows an arrangement to be created interactively by launching clips and tweaking controls, such as track volumes and effect parameters. While this is a fairly deep topic, the basics are quite simple.

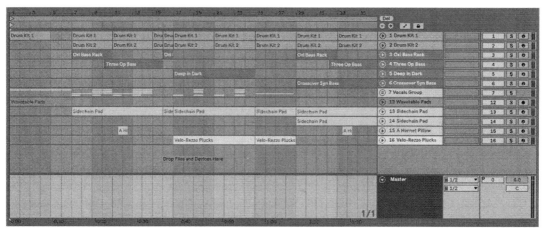

**FIGURE 3.9** Live's Arrangement View is where songs are finished. Each horizontal row represents a track that corresponds to a vertical channel in the Session Mixer.
*Source:* Ableton

Try this out:

1. Click on Arrangement Record, the solid circular "record" button at the top of the screen (next to Play and Stop).

2. Launch some clips in the Session View and adjust some track volumes.

3. Press the spacebar to stop and press Tab to switch to the Arrangement View.

4. You'll see every clip you launched laid out left to right in the time-line, and the movement of every volume you adjusted represented as a red line called *automation*.

When you start playback while looking at your new arrangement, Live may not do exactly what you expect. Instead of playing back the arrangement you just recorded, Live ignores it and resumes playing the same clips that were playing back when you stopped recording. Confused? Excellent. Everyone is at this point!

To hear the arrangement, you'll have to click on Back to Arrangement, as seen in Figure 3.10. Once you do, you'll immediately start to hear the Arrangement View clips play back, and you'll also notice that they pop into full color instead of being dimmed out as they were before. So what's going on here? Read on and I'll explain.

**FIGURE 3.10**
The button in the top-right corner of this figure is called Back to Arrangement. This all-important control allows you to hear the contents of the Arrangement View.
*Source:* Ableton

# Relation to the Session View

Although the Arrangement and Session Views may seem very different, they are closely related. The main difference is the way in which they handle clips. Arrangement View deals with them in a linear fashion: clips play in the order they show up in the timeline, from left to right. Session View is a nonlinear beast: clips are launched interactively to play in any order you want. Both views allow you to place multiple clips in a track, but in any given track, *only one clip can play back at a time.*

In the Session View, this is seen in a behavior described earlier—launching a clip stops playback of any currently playing clip in the same track. In the Arrangement View, this behavior can be demonstrated by dragging a clip and dropping it on top of an existing clip. The clip you dropped *replaces* what was there before. They can't "overlap" and both play simultaneously.

The same rule applies to clips in the Session and Arrangement Views. As mentioned previously, the two views are just different ways of looking at the same set of tracks. Therefore, any given track can either have a clip playing back from the Session View or the Arrangement View, never both simultaneously. In order to hear clips play back from the Arrangement View, you need to *explicitly give control to Arrangement View;* otherwise, the clips in the Session View will win out.

This takes some getting used to, and like all good rules, there are a couple of exceptions. But not to worry! Read on and practice using the program. It will all make sense eventually, I promise.

While playing back an arrangement, you're free to return to the Session View to launch clips. When you do this, two things will happen in the Arrangement to show you that clips from the Session have taken over: the clips in the Arrangement will be dimmed (grayed out), and a triangular "play" button will appear at the far right of the track (see Figure 3.11).

FIGURE 3.11
The top track has been overridden by a clip in the Session.
Source: Ableton

To hear what's going on in the Arrangement again, you have two choices. Click Back to Arrangement (as described previously) to restore the Arrangement for *all tracks,* or click the triangular button at the right edge of the track display to restore an *individual track.*

This relationship between the two views means that you can arrange a song in the Arrangement View, but return to the Session View at any point for further experimentation. For example, maybe you're not crazy about a percussion track in a song you're working on. Just head back to the Session View to launch a few percussion loops while listening to your arrangement. If you find something you like, click Arrangement Record to replace the part. When you're done, use the methods described previously to return control to the Arrangement.

## The Arrangement Mixer

The Arrangement View's mixer controls, as seen in Figure 3.12, are located on the right side of the screen. Also notice that there's a triangular "unfold" switch, which is used to enlarge the track so that all of the mixer controls are visible and a detailed view of the clips in that track can be seen as well.

Every mixer control seen in the Session is also available in the Arrangement. The only difference is visual: the controls have been turned on their sides and are represented by values instead of graphical controls. Also, unlike Session View, the sends are displayed as part of the Mixer section.

FIGURE 3.12
All the mixer controls can be accessed from Arrangement View.
Source: Ableton

# Clip View and Device View

The bottom of your screen is shared between two views: the Clip View, which allows detailed manipulation of audio and MIDI, and the Device View, which is for working with devices such as effects and instruments.

To access the Clip View, double-click on a clip. In the Session, you can double-click anywhere but on the launch button, while in the Arrangement, you can click anywhere except for the waveform/MIDI display that's visible when the track is unfolded.

The Device View is accessed by double-clicking on the top area of a track where its name is shown (called the *title bar*). You can easily switch between these views using the Shift+Tab keyboard shortcut. Both views can be hidden or shown by using Show/Hide Detail View from the View menu.

The best way to understand how these two views work together is to think of the Device View as happening "after" the Clip View. For example, let's say you have a bass loop playing back in a track. The Clip View is where you would change the loop itself, modifying its key, timing, and loop points. The sound then flows into the Device View and is processed by any effects you've added. In the case of MIDI clips, there's no audio flowing out of the clip; instead, it's MIDI data, which is like a set of instructions (for example, what notes to play when). These notes flow into whatever instrument is hosted in the Device View, which, in turn, produces sound and sends it into the Mixer.

## The Clip View

When the Clip View is open, it shows the details of whatever clip is currently selected in the Session or Arrangement (see Figure 3.13). In the lower-left corner, there are switches used to show and hide the different sections: Launch, Sample (for audio clips), Notes (for MIDI clips), and Envelopes. When you're in the Arrangement, the Launch box isn't shown, since its settings are only relevant in the Session.

The parameters in the Clip View are a big subject that we'll be covering over the next three chapters. At first, all that's important to know is that this is where you refine, tweak, and mangle individual clips. Launch an audio clip and then explore this view and experiment a little bit.

**FIGURE 3.13** Here's the Clip View for an audio clip.
*Source:* Ableton

Crank the Transpose knob, and you'll hear the pitch change immediately. Next to Transpose, there's a volume slider, which can be used to adjust the volume for this clip only (unlike the volume control in the Mixer, which will change the volume for any clip playing back in that track). Press the button marked Rev. to make the audio play backward.

# The Device View

The Device View is home to devices: Audio Effects, MIDI Effects, Instruments, and Plug-Ins (see Figure 3.14). Until you add some devices, the Device View will be empty, except for a caption that tells you what sorts of devices the track will accept. Audio tracks can only accept Audio Effects, while MIDI tracks can use any type of device. Signal flows from left to right in the Device View, passing from one device to the next.

**FIGURE 3.14** Here's the Device View with a couple of effect devices loaded in.
*Source:* Ableton

To see the Device View in action, click on the Audio Effects View in the Browser and drag an effect device into a track. All clips played in this track will now be processed by this effect. We'll be discussing effects and instruments in greater detail in Chapters 7, 8, and 9, but for now all that's important is to have fun and experiment.

# The Browser

Before you start having fun with Session and Arrangement views, it's important to familiarize yourself with Live's content portal, the Browser. The Browser window (see Figure 3.15) provides the means to access all of the elements you will add to a Live Set, such as samples, Live's built-in devices (Instruments, MIDI Effects, and Audio Effects), and third-party plug-ins. The Browser is available in both the Session and Arrangement Views, and it can be hidden to save space when you're not using it.

**FIGURE 3.15**

The Browser is for accessing instruments, effects, and samples. It's where you'll save and organize your presets, and manage any additional Live Packs you download.

*Source:* Ableton

Some of the content you'll access from the Browser is installed with Live, and some it you'll create yourself and save into the User Library. There are also many additional Live Packs to download from ableton.com. Obviously, there are quite a few different things in the Browser, and you'll need to know more about the details of each one before understanding the how and why of using them in a Set. Everything you need to know will be explained in the coming chapters.

# In Use

Items from the Browser are added into Sets by dragging and dropping them into tracks. You can also double-click (or press Enter), but I strongly recommend using drag-and-drop until you're quite familiar with getting around the program. Double-click doesn't always do what you'd expect, and it can be a bit confusing.

Basic navigation of the Browser should be familiar to anyone with a working knowledge of Windows Explorer or the Finder on a Mac. Any item containing additional content (such as a folder) has a triangle to its left, which can be clicked to expand the item and display the contents within. The left- and right-arrow keys can be used for expanding and collapsing as well.

The Browser can also perform functions similar to the Explorer or Finder. You can rename and delete files, and in some areas drag and drop files and folders to reorganize them. Right-click in the right-hand pane of the Browser to reveal options for creating folders and other common tasks.

# Collections, Categories, and Places

The left area of the Browser is divided into three sections: Collections, Categories, and Places. Below these headings, you'll see icons that I'll sometimes refer to as *views*. These views display content by type (Categories), location on disk (Places), or user preference (Collections). Even though Collections appears at the top, I'll cover it last because it makes more sense once you understand the others.

# Categories

The Categories area displays factory content, content from any additional Live Packs you install, and items you save into your User Library. If you're new to working with devices and presets, don't worry because these are explained in Chapter 7, "Using Effects and Instruments," along with some additional examples of real-world Browser use.

▶ **Sounds:** This view shows Live's factory Instrument and Instrument Rack presets organized by type of sound. This is a great place to begin if you just want to make some music and don't care too much about what's going on under the hood.

▶ **Drums:** Here you'll find Drum Rack presets, both those from Ableton and any that you create yourself. This view also contains a folder called "Drum Hits," which contains both drum samples (with .wav and .aif extensions) and individual drum presets (with .adg extensions) for adding to your Drum Racks.

▶ **Instruments, Audio Effects, MIDI Effects:** These views display Live's built-in devices, which are described in detail in Chapters 8, 9, and 10. Devices can be expanded to show their presets. Any device presets you save will appear here in addition to the User Library. For example, if you create an Auto Filter preset, it will appear under Auto Filter in the Audio Effects view.

▶ **Max for Live:** In this view, you'll see that Max for Live devices are categorized by Instrument, Audio Effect, and MIDI Effect, just like Live's built-in devices. Many of these devices will operate in ways very similar to the built-in ones, while others go far beyond and extend Live in all sorts of wild and wonderful ways.

▶ **Plug-ins:** This is where you access your third-party software effects and plug-ins. You can use a wide variety of third-party plug-ins with Live, in either VST (PC/Mac) or AU (Mac only) formats. Plug-ins can be either instruments or effects, but aren't automatically separated into categories. To tell them apart, you'll notice that instrument plug-ins have a small piano keyboard in their icon, while effects do not.

▶ **Clips:** Live Clips are musical parts saved in a special format that allows them to also contain devices and automation (which can't be saved with standard audio or MIDI files). Bear in mind that while Live Clips can be audio or MIDI, there's no way to tell them apart in the browser, so you'll just have to jump in and try them out.

▶ **Samples:** Here you'll see every audio file in the Live Library and the User Library. This is typically a pretty gigantic list of files, so it's mostly used in conjunction with the search function described next.

## Places

Places is customizable, but by default it only contains the following views:

▶ **Packs:** Live Packs contain content for Live such as presets and samples. This view allows you to view all of the packs you've installed and browse their contents. As you load up your computer with Packs, you'll find this is an incredibly handy way to explore. Scroll down to the bottom of this view, and you'll see any Live Packs that need updating and ones you haven't downloaded yet. Click the down arrow icon to begin downloading.

▶ **User Library:** This area separates your personal content from that installed by Live or add-on Live Packs. Whenever you save your own device presets, Live stores them in the User Library. For presets that have associated sample files (such as Simpler presets), the sample files are copied here as well. This area also contains the Defaults folder where default settings for devices and tracks are saved when the "Save as Default" command is used.

▶ **Current Project:** This view displays everything contained within the project folder of the currently open Set. Typically, this is samples and Sets, but other files of your choosing can be stored here as well. (For more information on Project Folders, please see "Saving" later in this chapter.)

You can also add any folder from your hard drive to Places by using the Add Folder option at the bottom. For example, you might want to add sample libraries or DJ music folders. Folders added here will be scanned and added to Live's database, so they can be searched quickly. Be aware that this can take awhile if the folders are large. Occasionally, Live won't display all of the content in a newly added folder until the next time it's launched.

## OPEN AND CLOSE

Expanding an item in the Browser causes any currently expanded item to collapse. Use Ctrl (Cmd)-click to expand an item without collapsing the others. To collapse all items in a view at once, double-click the view name in the left pane of the Browser.

## Collections

A collection is a color-coded view that displays anything you want. Want one place to view your favorite instrument presets, from both built-in devices and Audio Unit presets? Need quick access to a few go-to drum samples, Drum Racks, and Drum Buss presets? Collections are the answer.

Live starts you out with an empty collection called *Favorites*. For a first experiment, navigate to the Audio Effects view of the Browser and right-click on the Auto Filter effect. Select Favorites from the context menu. That's it! Auto Filter now appears in the Favorites view. Repeat this process with other content types, and you'll see that this is a really flexible feature. Expand devices to add presets to the Favorites collection, or navigate the Places section to add a Live Pack or a folder full of samples.

Now, try removing an item from the collection by right-clicking one of the items you added and selecting Favorites once again. Each color in the menu is an on/off switch that adds or removes the item from the collection. When it's been added, there's a black rectangle highlighting the color. It's a little hard to see because it's small, but once you notice it, it's hard to miss.

To create a new collection, right-click on an item and select one of the other colors from the context menu. You'll see the color appear under Collections immediately. Since you probably don't want a collection named "Yellow" or "Blue," this would be a good time to rename it. Right-click the collection and select Rename to get this done.

As you continue to create and customize collections, you'll notice that an item can be added to multiple collections. You may not find this to be necessary, but it's an important part of the collections feature. Adding an item to a collection isn't like putting it in a folder—it's more like adding a "tag." At the top of the context menu, there is a "Clear All Colors" command for removing an item from all collections with one click.

# Searching for Files

Even with all the views offered by the Browser, you'll still find the Search function to be quite handy. To get started, just type something into the search box at the top of the Browser. As soon as you begin to type, you'll see a new view called *All Results* appear in the Browser (see Figure 3.16). As you'd expect, this view displays every file containing the search term, regardless of its type.

The real power of the Browser is revealed by clicking on the other views, which will display a filtered list of content matching your search term. For the search shown in Figure 3.16, the Instruments View will show only instruments that have presets with "pad" in the name. The same holds true for Places. By combining search terms with filtering by type (Categories) or location (Places), you should be able to find anything you need without much suffering.

**FIGURE 3.16**

Searching the word "pad" and selecting All Results on the left shows you every file from every place that has "pad" in its name. Use the Ctrl (Cmd)+F keyboard shortcut to jump to the search box at any time.

*Source:* Ableton

# Preview

The Preview tab is located at the bottom of the Browser. Previewing can be toggled off and on by clicking the headphones icon shown in Figure 3.17. When turned on, the icon turns blue, and you'll be able to hear the sounds you're browsing right away. Audio files and Live Clips will play back automatically when selected, and an image of the waveform will appear to the right of the headphones.

**FIGURE 3.17** Preview lets you hear what you're getting into before you add an instrument or clip to your Set.
*Source:* Ableton

## QUICK PREVIEW

The right-arrow key can be used to preview individual files when the Preview switch is disengaged.

Every instrument preset installed with Live has a preview snippet built in. When you are previewing a Drum Rack or Impulse preset, the preview will be a simple beat made with the sounds from that preset. For presets from Live's other instruments, you'll hear a two-second sample of the instrument playing middle C. Presets from older versions of Live, or those created by third parties, may not have preview snippets. When you come across these, you'll have to add them to your set and try them out in order to hear them.

If you use preview during playback, Live will play back the preview at the current tempo if possible. For drum presets and longer sample files, the preview won't begin when you click—Live will wait until the beginning of the next bar. If you want to override synchronization, click the Raw button (see Figure 3.17), and the preview will play back at its original tempo. Very short samples, such as drum hits and instrument previews, aren't synchronized, so they play back immediately, and the Raw button is hidden.

Drum presets and longer samples will loop indefinitely when previewed. To stop the looping, press Esc.

While these features are generally predictable when previewing Live's factory content, you may notice a few quirks. For example, you may find that Live tries to synchronize longer drum hits like cymbals and that some samples can't be automatically synchronized. In these cases, you can use the Raw switch or just stop playback before previewing.

### CUEING THE MIX

You can adjust the volume of previewed sounds by adjusting Preview/Cue Volume in the Master track. In Session View, this control appears as a knob with headphones next to it. The Arrangement View displays this control as a number box to the right of the Master track's nearly identical-looking volume control. Preview/Cue Volume also adjusts the level of the metronome.

# The Control Bar

Running across the top of the screen is the Control Bar, which handles all common transport functions (start/stop, playback position, loop, tempo), along with important system information and helpful tools, such as tap tempo and a metronome. In this section, we'll take a look at every function.

## Tempo and Time

The left side of the Control Bar deals with all things timing related (see Figure 3.18). Some of these controls are used every day, while others are more esoteric. I'll discuss the most common controls first.

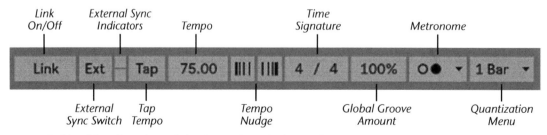

**FIGURE 3.18**  This subsection of the Control Bar is devoted to time. You probably won't see the External Sync controls or Global Groove Amount on your screen—they are hidden by default.
*Source:* Ableton

## Tempo

The Control Bar offers two ways of setting Live's tempo: adjusting it manually using the Tempo control or tapping it in. When using the Tempo control, drag vertically to the left of the decimal point to adjust the tempo in whole numbers, to the right to make fractional adjustments, or just type in a value. To tap in the tempo, rhythmically click on the Tap Tempo control four times, and Live will jump to its best approximation of the tempo you clicked. If you continue to tap, Live will continue to adjust the tempo, getting more and more precise.

If you tap in a tempo while playback is stopped, Live will begin playing after four taps. This makes it possible to "count in" a live performance. In a real-world situation, the mouse isn't ideal for doing this, so you'd be better off making a Remote mapping to the tap control. (See "MIDI and Computer Keyboard Remote Control" later in this chapter to get started.)

To the right of the Tempo control, you'll find Tempo Nudge Down, followed by Tempo Nudge Up. These controls are used to change Live's master tempo momentarily in order to bring it into sync with another source, much the way a DJ beat matches two tracks by physically dragging the record back or speeding it up slightly before letting go of it. Tapping these controls will yield very slight tempo changes (less than 1 BPM), while holding them down can be used to slow the tempo to a third of its original value or speed it up by as much as two-thirds. Releasing either control immediately returns Live to its original tempo.

## Time Signature and Metronome

The Time Signature control can handle numerators ranging from 1 to 99, and denominator choices of 1, 2, 4, 8, and 16—but if you're making pop or dance music, you'll rarely move this from 4/4. Changing the time signature won't change how your music sounds. What it will do is change how Live numbers the Beat Time Ruler, where the accent is placed when the metronome is running, and how it interprets settings like "1 Bar" in the Quantization Menu (explained later in this section). If you work in a different time signature but don't specify it here, Live's interface will be confusing and its behavior will be awkward.

When the Metronome button is engaged, you will hear a rhythmic click that can serve as a guide for new recordings and editing tasks. The volume of the click can be adjusted by using the Preview/Cue volume knob in Live's Master track.

On the right side of the metronome, there's a small arrow for opening the Metronome Settings menu. The settings are as follows:

▶ **Count-In:** Determines how many bars of click you'll hear before playback begins when recording. For example, if you set a Count-In value of 1 Bar and press Record, the metronome will click for a single bar before recording begins.

▶ **Sound:** Sets the sound of the metronome.

▶ **Rhythm:** Sets the beat division of the metronome. The default (quarter notes) works for most situations. However, for very slow or very fast tempos, it may be helpful to select a lesser or greater division.

▶ **Enable Only When Recording:** When the metronome is enabled, it will play during recording and be silenced during standard playback.

## Quantization

Finally, we come to the Quantization menu, which is used to set Live's *global quantization* for clip launching (and a handful of other timing-related features). You may be familiar with the concept of quantization if you've worked with sequencers or drum machines before. In music, quantization means eliminating or reducing imprecision by forcing rhythms to conform to a predefined set of values. For example, you might play a drum part on a set of pads and then quantize it to correct any hits that were played early or late.

The quantization dealt with in this menu is for *launch quantization,* which is a little different than the common example shown previously. You may have noticed while experimenting in the Session View that clips don't start playback immediately when you click on them. Instead, they wait until the beginning of the next bar and play back in sync with the other clips that are currently playing. In other words, the launching of the clip is being quantized to 1 Bar, the default value in the Quantization menu.

Exploring this menu, you'll see that you can quantize to a whole range of values, including None, which allows clips to play back immediately. I strongly recommend that you experiment with different values to get a feel for this feature and that you return quantization to 1 Bar when you're done. It will make life much easier as you're learning the program. Also, bear in mind that there's lots more information on launch quantization in the "Clips" section of Chapter 4.

## Link n' Sync

While you could have an entire musical career without ever having to synchronize Live to another computer or external hardware device, you may one day find yourself wanting to integrate a drum machine into your setup, or have a jam session with some other laptop-wielding musicians. For these situations, you'll need to keep everything in sync using Ableton's futuristic Link technology, or old-fashioned MIDI sync, which has been around since the 1980s.

When you enable the Link switch, Live will automatically synchronize its tempo with other Link-enabled programs running on the same local network. It's a remarkably simple process that you'll probably be able to get working with a few minutes of experimentation. There's a detailed explanation of Link in Chapter 13, "Live 10 Power!"

The External Sync controls will only appear if you've set up an external sync source or destination in the Link/MIDI Preferences tab (see Chapter 2, "Getting Live Up and Running"). The External Sync switch engages or disengages MIDI synchronization to an outside source, while the External Sync Indicators blink to indicate if sync is being received (top indicator) or transmitted (bottom indicator) by Live.

Monitoring lights announce that the MIDI sync signal is being sent or received.

### SO FINE

To make fine adjustments to the Tempo or other controls such as volume, hold down the Shift key while dragging.

# Transport, Recording, and Automation

This area of the Control Bar is for controlling playback and recording in Live (see Figure 3.19). It contains some important automation features as well. Recording and automation are complex topics that are dealt with in Chapter 4, so I'll just be giving basic definitions of these controls here.

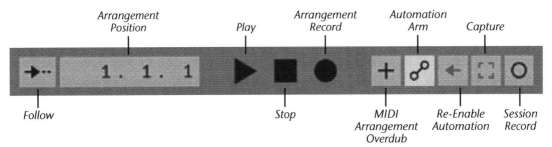

**FIGURE 3.19** This section of the Control Bar handles playback, recording, and automation. *Source:* Ableton

> ▶ **Follow:** When turned on, Live's display will follow the song position (in the Arrangement) or the clip position (in the Clip View) to keep the currently playing part visible. It works in conjunction with the Follow Behavior preference in the Look/Feel tab of Preferences.

> ▶ **Arrangement Position:** This box provides a continuous readout—in measures, beats, and subdivisions—of where you are in the song, whether you're listening or recording. You can manually enter a start time value into this box or drag up and down with the mouse to change the setting.

> ▶ **Play & Stop:** These buttons start and stop playback. You can also toggle between play and stop using the spacebar.

> ▶ **Arrangement Record:** This button is used to initiate recording clips and automation into the Arrangement.

> ▶ **MIDI Arrangement Overdub:** When you are recording MIDI into the Arrangement, this button can be enabled to allow notes to be added to existing MIDI clips. When disabled, MIDI clips are overwritten during recording.

▶ **Automation Arm:** This control enables the recording of automation. Manual adjustments, such as changes to track volume and device parameters, can be recorded into clips in the Session View or tracks in the Arrangement View. Automation is a somewhat complex topic and will be covered in detail in Chapter 4.

▶ **Re-Enable Automation:** Just as it's possible to override Arrangement clips by launching clips from the session, it's also possible to override automation by manually changing an automated parameter. Whenever automation has been overridden, this button will light up. Clicking on it will restore automation for all clips and tracks.

▶ **Capture:** This button makes it possible to create a new clip from a MIDI performance without recording. Whenever you play a MIDI controller into an armed MIDI track (or a track with its Monitor status set to In), Live is listening. If you like something you played, hit Capture and it's added to your Set.

▶ **Session Record (Session View only):** This is a multifunction button that works in close conjunction with the Push controller, but is used without Push as well. It is used to record new clips, as well as to overdub MIDI and automation. These topics are covered in the "Recording" section of Chapter 4.

# Punch In/Out and Arrangement Loop

This section of Live's Control Bar is used in conjunction with the Arrangement View. In the center is the Loop Switch, which you can enable to repeat a range of the arrangement indefinitely. Looping the arrangement is really handy for working on new musical parts and for all sorts of editing tasks as well.

The range that gets looped is controlled by a brace that appears over the looped bars (as seen toward the bottom of Figure 3.20). Drag the edges of the brace to change the size of the loop, or drag it from the center to reposition it. The loop range is also displayed numerically as seen in Figure 3.20. The left box displays a number indicating the loop's starting point, while the one to the right shows the length. In other words, Figure 3.20 shows that the loop

**FIGURE 3.20**
In this image, the Loop Switch is enabled, and the brace below sets the loop from bar 49 to bar 53.
*Source:* Ableton

starts at the beginning of bar 49 and is 4 bars long. Adjust these values directly instead of dragging the brace if you prefer.

The brace is also used to specify the Punch In and Punch Out points. These can be used to automatically enable recording temporarily, so you don't have to worry about recording over sections you want to keep. The switch to the left of the Loop switch enables Punch In, while the one to the right enables Punch Out. Punching is covered in the "Recording" section of Chapter 4.

# Mode Switches and Diagnostic Tools

Figure 3.21 shows the final section of the Control Bar, which contains some important mode switches and displays useful diagnostic information.

**FIGURE 3.21**
The final section of the Control Bar contains a variety of useful odds and ends.
*Source:* Ableton

## Draw Mode

The first item in this area of the Control Bar turns Draw Mode on and off. This is colloquially referred to as the *pencil tool* (but you won't find that term anywhere in the Live manual). Used for drawing automation and MIDI, this mode is toggled on and off with a quick press of the B key, or temporarily invoked by clicking and holding B.

## Computer MIDI Keyboard

The piano keyboard icon turns MIDI input from the alphanumeric computer keyboard on and off. This is a feature that allows you to use your computer's keyboard as a MIDI input device, which can be handy when working on a laptop on the go. The M key can also be used to turn Computer MIDI Keyboard on and off. When enabled, the top two rows of the computer keyboard are used to trigger MIDI notes, while the Z and X keys are used to transpose the keyboard down or up in octaves.

## Key Map and MIDI Map Mode

The Key and MIDI buttons enable Live's mapping modes, which are the gateway to completely customized control of Live with MIDI controllers or your computer keyboard. This feature is called *remote control* and is discussed in the next section.

## CPU Load and Disk Overload

The CPU Load Meter and Hard Disk Overload Indicator let you know how well your computer is keeping up with Live's demands. If the CPU percentage approaches 100 percent, you'll experience performance degradation or audio dropouts. The Hard Disk Overload Indicator will flash red if your computer is not able to get data from the hard drive quickly enough. This will also result in dropouts and usually occurs because your hard drive is too slow for the number of audio clips you are trying to play back simultaneously.

## MIDI Track and Remote Indicators

Figure 3.21 shows two sets of indicators, both of which are useful for troubleshooting. The MIDI Track indicators at the far right light up when a conventional MIDI signal is sent or received. The indicators between the Key and MIDI switches flash to show the presence of a remote control signal. Keep an eye on these as you experiment with remote control in the next section. The top indicators show input, the bottom ones output.

# MIDI and Computer Keyboard Remote Control

Just about everything in Live, from launching clips to tweaking device parameters, can be *remotely controlled* from a MIDI controller or the computer keyboard. What follows is a brief introduction to a topic that is covered in detail in Chapter 11, "Remote Control."

To assign a key on your computer keyboard, first click the Key Map Mode switch (refer to Figure 3.21), or press Ctrl (Cmd)+K. An orange overlay will appear over any control that can be mapped. Click on the control you want to map and press a key on your keyboard to map it. Then press the Key Map Mode switch again to restore Live to normal operation, and you're done! Turn off Computer MIDI Keyboard when experimenting with key mapping—when it's enabled, much of the computer keyboard will not function for remote control.

Before you can use a MIDI controller for remote control, you must visit the Link/MIDI tab of the Preferences screen and set Remote to On, as explained in Chapter 2. After you've done that, click the MIDI Map Mode switch in the Control Bar (shown in Figure 3.21) or press Ctrl (Cmd)+M. The blue overlay that appears indicates the controls that can have a MIDI message assigned to them. Click on the control you want to map and move the MIDI control you want to map it to.

## WITH THE PUSH OF A KNOB

Live will allow you to assign MIDI knobs and sliders to on-screen buttons. In this case, the button in Live will turn on when your MIDI control passes its midpoint (64 on a scale of 0 to 127). It will switch off when you move the control back under 64.

You can also assign a MIDI button or computer key to an on-screen slider or knob. In this case, pressing the button or key will make the slider or knob toggle between its lowest and highest settings.

Key and MIDI mappings are saved with the Set, so every song can have a different control scheme. If you find yourself always making common assignments, you can assign them and save them as part of your default set (see "File/Folder" in Chapter 2).

# Overview

Just below the Control Bar is the Overview, shown in Figure 3.22. (If you don't see it, select Overview from the View menu.) Resembling a very small timeline, it's used for navigation and reference purposes to show you where you are in the Arrangement.

In the Arrangement, the Overview contains a black rectangle to indicate the portion of the Arrangement that is currently visible. Dragging the edges of this box causes the display to zoom in or out, making more or less of the timeline visible.

You can also use the Overview for navigating. Place the mouse pointer over the portion of the Overview bar you want to move to, and a magnifying-glass icon will appear; click once, and you will be moved to the corresponding location in the arrangement. To zoom in or out, click and drag vertically in the Overview. Clicking and moving the mouse left or right will scroll the visible area of the timeline.

In the Session View, the mouse transforms into a launcher when placed over the Overview. Clicking will cause Live to jump to that point in the Arrangement.

**FIGURE 3.22** Live's Overview is a view from above.
*Source:* Ableton

# File Management

Learning how to do effective file management seems incredibly boring at first, but yields great benefits later when you are enjoying the creative process of making music, rather than tearing your hair out searching for lost samples and digging through multiple versions of songs, trying to figure out the right one. Here's my advice: adopt good practices at the outset, rather than make a mess and have to clean it up later.

## Sets and Projects

The first time you save a Set, Live will automatically create a project folder called *<Set name> + Project* to hold all the files associated with the Set. Before you get too deep into using Live, choose a location on your hard drive to save all of your Live projects. Whenever you start a new song, save it into this folder. For example, let's say you create a folder called *Live Projects.* Every new song you start gets saved into this folder, so eventually you will have a folder full of projects, as seen in Figure 3.23.

What you want to make sure you *don't* do is save all of your new Sets into an *already existing* project folder, as seen in Figure 3.24. This becomes a nightmare when any sort of project sharing or advanced file management is necessary later.

This is not to say that you never want to save multiple sets into the same project folder. In fact, this is often a desirable thing to do when saving *multiple versions of the same song* using the Save As command, as seen in Figure 3.25.

Saving multiple versions is an essential part of any experienced producer's process. How often you save a new copy is up to you. The important thing is to leave a *breadcrumb trail*—a record of what changed when. Having done this, you can recover previous settings in case they are accidentally lost, or you can simply decide you don't like the direction you've gone and go back and try again. In combination with Live's automatic backup feature (discussed later in this section), this technique will keep your creative process organized and save you from losing important ideas.

**FIGURE 3.23** A neatly organized projects folder. Each new song has its own project. Inside the project folder is the Set (.als) file.
*Source:* Ableton

**FIGURE 3.24** A project folder with several unrelated Set files inside it. This will eventually drive you crazy.
*Source:* Ableton

**FIGURE 3.25** A project folder with several versions of the same song in it. These might be Sets with different purposes (such as radio edits or alternate mixes) or simply a way of ensuring that you can get back to an old version in case you change something and want to go back.
*Source:* Ableton

# Saving

Live offers four ways to save, all available in the File menu: Save Live Set, Save Live Set As, Save a Copy, and Collect All and Save. Save, Ctrl (Cmd)+S, saves the Set in its present state, with its current filename. Every time you save, Live backs up your Set before overwriting it with the new version. The backup is given a timestamp and added to the Backups folder. Live will save 10 backups; when you go over 10, the oldest backup is deleted.

Save Live Set As is the command for saving the Set under a *different* name. This is useful for saving multiple versions of the same song, as described earlier in this section. To do this, select File > Save Live Set As, select the location where you would like to place the file, and type the song's newest name. Save a Copy is similar to Save As in that it allows you to save the file under a new name. However, instead of opening the newly named file, the Save a Copy command will keep the version you are currently working on open.

The most comprehensive save method is Collect All and Save. Live allows you to add files to a Set from anywhere on your hard drive(s). This is very convenient, as you may have sample libraries used across many different projects. However, over time, hard drives can get reorganized or become unavailable, and you're faced with the inconvenience of opening a Set and discovering there are samples missing. Collect All and Save eliminates this problem by copying all files used by the Set into the Project folder. This command is also important when transporting a project from one computer to another. Collect All and Save before copying the Project folder and you know everything you need will be there when you need it.

### NO PLUG-INS

Even though Collect All and Save works wonders for keeping all your files together, keep in mind that any external plug-ins (VST and AU) used in a Set cannot be saved within the project. This means that if you transport your song to a different computer, all of the plug-ins used on your song must be present on that computer as well. Unless you know you'll have all the necessary plug-ins on the system you are moving to, it's a good idea to Freeze plug-in dependent tracks before moving your session (see Chapter 7).

# 4

# Making
# Music in Live

In this chapter, we'll be covering the core concepts and basic workflow of Live. This is a big chapter with a lot of information, but if you spend the time to take it all in, you'll find the rest of the book much easier to manage. Bear in mind that this chapter assumes you're familiar with terms and concepts introduced in Chapter 3, "Live Interface Basics."

I'll be introducing many important commands in this chapter. While Live has a very manageable set of commands compared to other programs, there are still quite a few to learn. With a few exceptions, I'll be directing you to Live's main menu bar and various context menus when new commands are introduced. The menus display keyboard shortcuts next to the commands, and I strongly recommend taking a moment to learn them as you go.

While the fundamental concepts behind Live are equally important to all users, the actual music-making process differs quite a bit from person to person. Like most things, discovering your method is a matter of practice and experimentation. We'll be looking at some standard approaches here, so it's well worth your time to familiarize yourself with them; however, in most cases there's no one "right" way to do things, so don't be afraid to find your own way.

**UNDONE**

There's a good reason that most programs have the Undo command as the first option in the Edit menu. The only way to learn a program is to get in there and experiment, knowing you can back out of any mistakes you make. It may sound funny to say, but Ableton Live has one of the best Undo features in the business. Unlike some other programs, almost everything you do can be undone. (Exceptions include the Solo and Arm switches, some file operations in the Browser, and certain parameter changes in complex plug-in devices.) Be aware that the Undo queue is emptied when you quit Live.

The basic procedure goes like this:

▶ **Create individual musical parts:** Record bass parts, guitar riffs, keyboard lines, drum grooves, and MIDI instruments, or import samples and MIDI sequences. These are called *clips.*

▶ **Create song sections:** Arrange clips that go together horizontally in the Session View to make *scenes.* Each scene represents a section of your song, such as intro, verse, and chorus.

▶ **Record an Arrangement:** Launch clips and scenes in the Session while using Arrangement Record to capture your song into the Arrangement View.

▶ **Finalize the song:** Edit the Arrangement, add effects to the mix, layer additional parts, finalize the automation, and export a mixdown of the song.

# Clips and Tracks

Clips are the musical building blocks of Live. They come in two varieties: audio and MIDI. Audio clips produce sound from audio files on disk, while MIDI clips contain MIDI data for playing either virtual or hardware instruments.

Clips in the Session View are played or *launched* by clicking the triangular Clip Launch button at the left side of the clip. Clips in the Arrangement View are played as the playback cursor (the thin vertical line that moves from left to right when Live is running) passes over them.

In the clip slot grid, audio and MIDI clips look exactly the same, and there's no way to tell them apart. However, in the Clip View the difference is apparent immediately, as seen in Figures 4.1a and 4.1b. It's also easy to tell audio and MIDI apart in the Arrangement, as seen in Figure 4.2.

**FIGURE 4.1A**  Audio clips display a waveform.
*Source:* Ableton

**FIGURE 4.1B**  MIDI clips display sequences of MIDI notes.
*Source:* Ableton

**FIGURE 4.2**

Clips in the Arrangement View can be resized to change how long they will play. Note that it's easy to tell the MIDI track (notes are displayed) from the audio tracks (waveform is displayed).

*Source:* Ableton

As briefly explained in Chapter 3, clips are contained within tracks. Before going further into the details of working with clips, let's take a closer look at tracks.

# Creating Tracks

Tracks are created using the commands in the Create menu (Insert Audio Track, Insert MIDI Track, and Insert Return Track). These commands can also be accessed in the context menu that appears when you right-click in the title bar of any existing track. To remove a track, click on its title bar and press Delete.

Tracks can also be created by dragging items from the Browser into the Drop Area, the empty part of the Session and Arrangement Views labeled *Drop Files and Devices Here.* For example, you could drop an audio file here to automatically create an audio track or drop an instrument to create a MIDI track. If you drop a Live Clip, which can be either audio or MIDI, Live will automatically create the right type of track. You can also drag clips and devices from existing tracks into the Drop Area to create new tracks.

# Audio Tracks and MIDI Tracks

Audio tracks can contain audio clips and audio effects. All that an audio track requires to produce sound is an audio clip—effects are completely optional (and completely fun). MIDI tracks can contain MIDI clips, instruments, and MIDI effects. A MIDI track is a little more complicated than an audio track, in that a MIDI clip alone isn't enough to produce sound—an instrument is required as well.

Figure 4.3 shows an empty MIDI track, which looks a bit different than the tracks next to it. A MIDI track without a virtual instrument inserted does not output audio; thus, there are no Volume, Pan, or Send knobs in the mixer. You still have the Track Activator, Solo/Cue, and Arm buttons, which function the same way as their audio track counterparts.

**FIGURE 4.3**

An audio track, an empty MIDI track, and a MIDI track with an instrument device loaded. Notice that the Arm switch of the MIDI tracks displays a note icon, which makes it possible to tell them apart from audio tracks, even when an instrument is loaded.

*Source:* Ableton

When an instrument is loaded onto the track, the full set of mixer controls will appear. Drag an instrument from the Sounds, Drums, or Instruments view of the Browser into an empty MIDI track if you want to see this transformation in action. A MIDI track with an instrument inserted is essentially a hybrid MIDI/audio track. It passes MIDI input from MIDI clips (or a MIDI controller) into an instrument, which produces audio in response. The audio is then optionally processed with effects and passed into the mixer.

A MIDI track without an instrument can be used to control external hardware, such as synthesizers. Notice MIDI the lower menu in the empty MIDI track shown in Figure 4.3 is labeled MIDI To. To sequence external hardware, select the port and channel the hardware is connected to, and you're all set. (You can also use the External Instrument device for this purpose, as explained in Chapter 8, "Live's Instruments.")

# Importing Audio and MIDI

A great way to get to know Live is by using premade content such as audio loops and Live Clips. This makes it easy to explore Live's features without having to focus on playing or singing at the same time. You'll find some loops to get you started in the content that comes with this book. There are more available in Live's library, downloadable from ableton.com, and available for purchase from companies like Loopmasters.

Don't underestimate the power of what can be done with prerecorded loops. As you become expert at manipulating clip properties, editing clips in the Arrangement, using effects, and other features such as Slice to New MIDI Track, you'll discover that loops are just raw material from which a large variety of useful and original sounds can be created.

The most common method of importing content into Live is by dragging an audio file, standard MIDI file, or Live Clip from the Browser into a track. Files can also be dragged into Live from Windows Explorer, the OS X Finder, and some other programs such as iTunes. You can also use the Import Audio File or Import MIDI File command from the Create menu to import files into the currently selected track.

Audio tracks can only contain audio clips, and MIDI tracks can only contain MIDI clips. However, if you drop a file onto the wrong kind of track, Live will help you out if possible. For example, if you drop an audio file onto a completely empty MIDI track, Live will convert it into an audio track. But if you drop an audio file onto a MIDI track that already contains clips or devices, Live will display the Convert Audio to MIDI dialog (which is covered in Chapter 5, "Clips").

You can also grab multiple files (Shift-click to select a range of files or Ctrl (Cmd)-click to select multiple nonadjacent files) and add them all at once. By default, the clips will all be placed on the same track. To have Live drop the files into separate tracks, press and hold Ctrl (Cmd) before dropping the files.

Live can work with just about any audio you've got—any audio file (in WAV, AIFF, SDII, MP3, Ogg Vorbis, Ogg FLAC, or FLAC format) on your computer is fair game in Live. (If you're planning on using compressed audio files like MP3 or FLAC, make sure to read up on the Decoding Cache in Chapter 2, "Getting Live Up and Running.")

Standard MIDI files have a file extension of .mid. They are included with some third-party content libraries and can be exported from other programs, such as Reason and Logic Pro, for use in Live.

You can also explore the Clips view of the Browser to find clips to use in Live. These are files saved in the Live Clip format. Live Clips can be audio or MIDI and can contain devices as well. For example, a MIDI Live Clip can contain not just a MIDI sequence, but an instrument as well. So it's like a preset that contains a sound *and* a musical part.

One caveat to know when working with Live Clips is that their devices only get loaded if the track you drag it into *does not already contain any devices*. In other words, if the track has even one device in it, you'll only get the audio or MIDI. If this sounds like a lot right now, don't worry. Live Clips will make much more sense once you've got a handle on the various elements they contain.

## Understanding Audio Clips

Audio clips *refer* to audio files. They do not *contain* them. An audio clip contains the information necessary for Live to play an audio file from disk. However, audio clips have all sorts of special properties, such as the ability to flexibly adjust the pitch and tempo of the audio. Not only that, but you can also create many different clips from the same audio file without needing multiple copies of the audio on your hard disk. A single audio file can be referenced from as many clips as you want, each having its own parameters: loop points, transposition, Warp markers, automation, and so on.

This ability to duplicate, chop, and mangle clips all day without affecting the underlying audio file is sometimes referred to as *nondestructive editing*, and it is one of the things that makes Live (and every other modern DAW) so powerful. However, this fact also warrants a few words of caution.

Should a referenced audio file become altered by another application, such as a wave editor, each clip that used that file will now play with the same alteration. If you delete the file that is referenced by a clip, the clip and any other clips that used that file won't play anymore! This is why it can be very important to use Collect All and Save (see Chapter 3) to copy audio files into your project folder, in order to help protect them from being modified by other projects or programs.

Unlike audio clips, all of the data in MIDI clips is saved in the Set—even if that MIDI clip was created by importing a MIDI file or Live Clip.

# Organization

Before getting into recording and automation, let's adopt some good organizational habits.

Like most modern music programs, Live gives you the power to create a lot of content very quickly. The downside of being able to move quickly is the potential for confusion and stress as musical ideas pile up. Don't skimp on organization. Trust me, your music will be better for it.

The first step is to use the Rename command frequently, as explained in Chapter 3. You don't have to worry about naming every single clip, but naming tracks is essential. Any name will do, but "Synth 1" is infinitely superior to "29 MIDI." You can always rename it later if a more descriptive name comes to you.

The next step is to use color. You can right-click on clips, track title bars, and scenes to bring up a color chooser and apply colors in any way that makes sense to you. For example, you might want to make all your drum tracks and clips shades of red and your basses blue.

It's also important to move clips, tracks, and scenes to meaningful locations. It may sound obvious, but don't underestimate how much easier it is to work on a Set where all of the drum tracks are next to each other, as opposed to scattered around. This logic applies to clips and scenes in the Session View as well. Tracks and scenes can be moved by clicking and dragging the titles, while clips can be moved by dragging the main body of the clip.

### DRAG TO COPY

If you hold down Option (Alt) while dragging an object, you'll create a copy instead of just moving it. This works for copying clips, devices, and even tracks. For example, you might create multiple copies of a clip and set different loop points, or make a copy of an entire track and apply radically different effects to create a layered sound.

# Recording

Unless you're strictly using Live to DJ or work with pre-existing material, you'll need to create some clips of your own. The basic process for recording new audio and MIDI clips is very similar, so we'll be taking a general look at recording first. Obviously, there are some big differences between audio and MIDI, and these will be discussed next.

Regardless of whether you're recording into the Session or Arrangement Views, the first two steps of recording are the same: select a valid input source and arm the track for recording (see Figure 4.4). Input/Output and Arm are both introduced in the Mixer section of Chapter 3.

If you're making an audio recording, make sure that the inputs you want to record from are enabled in the Input Configuration screen. If you're making a MIDI recording, make sure that your MIDI controller's input has Track set to On in the MIDI/Sync tab of Live's Preferences. (Review the Audio and Link/MIDI tabs in the "Setting Preferences in Live" section of Chapter 2 for more information.)

Arming a track is simple: just click the Arm switch so that it lights up. Be aware that if no input is selected, or the selected input has become invalid (for example, your audio interface has been disconnected), the Arm switch may not appear or will be disabled. You're free to arm multiple tracks and record many clips simultaneously if you want.

**FIGURE 4.4**

An audio and a MIDI track, both ready for recording.
*Source:* Ableton

## MULTIRECORDING

Can't seem to arm more than one track at a time? Hold down the Ctrl(Cmd) key and then click the Arm buttons. To allow multiple tracks to be armed without doing this, change the Exclusive setting under Record/Warp/Launch in Preferences (see Chapter 2).

# Recording in Session View

Once a track is armed for recording, all of the square Stop buttons in the track's clip slots will turn to circular Record buttons (see Figure 4.5). Click one of them to start recording a new clip and then bang on your MIDI controller, yodel into your microphone, or slap the bass. You stop recording by clicking the Clip Stop button or by clicking on the Clip Launch button of the clip you're recording. This second method is really handy because the new clip will immediately start looping, and the music keeps flowing!

## NO LOOP?

If you click a Clip Launch button to stop a recording and the clip doesn't start looping, this means the Default Launch mode has been changed in Live's Record/Warp/Launch Preferences. Set it to Trigger, and you'll be all set. There's a full discussion of Launch modes in Chapter 5.

Recording loops in the Session View is made easy by the fact that Live uses launch quantization to start and stop recordings. Assuming that the Quantization menu in the Control Bar is set to its default value of 1 Bar, all recordings will start and stop at the beginning of a bar, and you'll always end up with loop lengths that make sense.

**FIGURE 4.5**
The track on the right is armed, so the empty clip slots now contain circular Clip Record buttons. Notice that there is a Stop button below the clip slots in both tracks.
*Source:* Ableton

Doing multiple takes is as easy as clicking additional Clip Record buttons in the track. Every time a new recording starts, the previous one ends. You can then go back and listen to each take individually to find the best one. Or you can use the Arrangement View to combine the best parts of each take into one perfect "supertake."

Of course, the nicest thing about this workflow in the Session View is that it allows you to quickly build layers and sections of a song without ever stopping Live. You can then audition all of your new clips and organize scenes to start arranging the sections of your song.

## ON THE LEVEL

Before you start an audio recording, check your input signal level to make sure that it's not too high or too low. The track's meters will show the volume of any incoming signal as soon as the track is armed. Play as loud as you plan to play during the recording while watching Live's meters. If the signal is too loud (the meters reach the top and turn red), it could distort, or clip, the recording. If the level is too low, your sound may become grainy when turning it up to match the rest of your song.

If you're recording at 24- or 32-bit, you can record at lower levels and still have excellent audio quality, so this is generally recommended. If for some reason you need to record at 16-bit, it's more important to get the highest level possible without clipping.

# Session Record Button

The Session Record button (see Figure 4.6) is a multifunction button, which is relevant to the prior section because it can be used to record new clips. It's also relevant to the upcoming sections because it is used to overdub automation and MIDI in the Session View.

**FIGURE 4.6**

Session Record can be used to record new clips. It also enables MIDI and automation overdubbing.

*Source:* Ableton

When you click on Session Record, it will start recording in the empty clip slots of the highlighted scene for any armed track in which a clip is not currently playing. Clicking it a second time will stop recording and begin playback of any newly recorded clips. Just like the Clip Record buttons, Session Record is quantized to make it easy to record properly timed loops.

Session Record's role in MIDI overdubbing recording automation will be discussed later in the section entitled "MIDI Overdub." Because this button does several different things, it provides a very streamlined workflow, but it also creates the potential for confusion. Make sure to take some time experimenting with this button as you learn about its different functions to avoid surprises later.

## Arrangement Record Button

The Arrangement Record button also handles several functions (see Figure 4.7). It's used to record new clips in the Arrangement View, as well as to overdub automation and MIDI. Arrangement Record is also used to initiate recording clips from Session into Arrangement. This might sound like a lot, and it is!

**FIGURE 4.7**
Arrangement Record is used to record new clips into the Arrangement. Like Session Record, it also has several other functions that are discussed later in this chapter.
*Source:* Ableton

Depending on your workflow, you'll probably use some of these functions more than others. So as you get familiar with the Live workflow, all of this will make sense eventually. For starters, though, you'll want to take some extra time to familiarize yourself with each of these functions as they are explained in the upcoming sections.

## Recording in Arrangement View

If you've made recordings in just about any other DAW, from Pro Tools to GarageBand, this way of working will be familiar. To record clips into the Arrangement View, just arm a track and click Arrangement Record. To stop recording, you can click Arrangement Record again, disarm the track, or simply press the spacebar.

In addition to allowing the type of recording described here, Arrangement Record also causes clips to be recorded from the Session into the Arrangement, which can take some getting used to. If you want to avoid this behavior, make sure that there aren't any clips playing in the Session before you record new clips in the Arrangement. This can be done by clicking Back to Arrangement or Stop Clips.

### READY, SET, GO!

The Count In feature can be accessed easily from the Control Bar by opening the Metronome's drop-down menu. Select the number of bars of count-in you want, and you're ready to go. The next time you start recording, Live will count you in with the metronome so you can get a clean start.

## Punching In and Out

In the good old days of recording to tape, it was common to replace only a section of a recording using a technique called *punching*. If you had a good vocal track with a weak phrase, the engineer would wait until that moment, press Record while the singer replaced it, and then disable recording before erasing the next phrase. In digital audio, we do the same thing, but it's much less nerve-wracking since digital recording is nondestructive.

Punching in Live is easy. While playing back, click Arrangement Record to start recording and click it once again to stop. No special steps are necessary. However, you can also make Live begin recording automatically at a specified point and stop at another. This is really handy if you're both the engineer and performer.

In Chapter 3, there's a brief introduction to setting these points, known as *Punch In* and *Punch Out*. They can be set visually by dragging the bracket that sits above the track display, or set numerically in the Control Bar. Once the points are set, punching is enabled with the switches located to either side of the Loop button, as seen in Figure 4.8.

When you click Record, Live will start running but will wait for the Punch-In time before it actually starts recording. It will continue recording until it reaches the Punch-Out point. You may, of course, use either Punch In or Punch Out by itself if you choose.

**FIGURE 4.8**
Configured as shown, Live will automatically begin recording at bar 21 and then stop recording four bars later. The two bent line icons are the Punch-In and Punch-Out switches.
*Source:* Ableton

# Capture

Capture is new to Live 10. This feature makes it possible to create a clip from a MIDI performance without recording. To use Capture, first arm a MIDI track or set its Monitor switch to In. Play a musical phrase and then press the Capture button (see Figure 4.9). A new clip containing the most recently played phrase will appear and begin playing back. Capture can be used whether or not Live is playing. If Live is stopped when Capture is pressed, its tempo will be set to the tempo of the musical phrase you just played.

**FIGURE 4.9**
Capture will grab your last MIDI performance so that you never miss a musical idea.

Not only is this feature a great fail-safe to prevent you from missing out on great musical ideas, but it also encourages a free-flowing creative mindset. Sometimes, pressing Record can create a sense of pressure that's not present when you're just messing around. Capture makes it possible to keep things casual, just grabbing the phrases you like.

Capture can also be used to overdub notes into an existing MIDI clip. Just jam along with the clip while it's playing back. When you press Capture, your new performance will be added into the clip.

As you might imagine, quite a bit has to happen behind the scenes to make Capture work. For example, Live has to guess the tempo of your performance and decide what constitutes a "phrase." Phrases are determined by pauses. It's worth taking a moment to understand how Live interprets pauses.

When you stop playing, your performance is stored indefinitely. As soon as you play another note, however, one of two things will happen. In the case of a pause of 20 seconds or more, playing a note will cause the previous performance to be discarded. If you pause for only a few seconds, Live will retain the previous performance but exclude it from the looped region of the clip created with Capture. If you want to use the performance before the pause, all you have to do is adjust the clip's loop boundaries.

Generally speaking, Live's tempo analysis is quite good. However, if you already know the tempo you want, you'll find that playing along to the metronome or a drum beat produces the most accurate results.

You may find that Capture works seamlessly. However, because there's a lot happening automatically, you may not always get exactly the results you expect. Sometimes, you'll have to do a little editing on clips created with Capture to get them just right.

# MIDI Overdub

MIDI Overdub allows you to record additional note or controller data into a MIDI clip without erasing what's already there. This is a handy feature when it comes to programming drumbeats, since you can build them one piece at a time. For example, you could make a two-bar loop with just a kick drum and then play the additional parts (snares, hi-hats) layer by layer as the clip continues to loop.

MIDI Overdub has all sorts of uses. If a piano part is really tricky, you can record the left-hand and right-hand parts separately. Or you can build a drum part one drum at a time and generate variations while you're at it. For example, start with a simple drum pattern (perhaps just a kick drum and hi-hat for the intro of your song); then use Duplicate to copy the clip and launch the copy. Now you can use MIDI Overdub to add snare hits. This will leave you with two MIDI clips: one with just kick and hats, and the other with a snare added. You can then duplicate the MIDI clip again and layer on an additional part, such as a shaker or congas. Using this technique, you can build a collection of drum variations quickly.

To overdub MIDI into an existing MIDI clip, you must first arm the track for recording. Once you've done that, the procedure for MIDI overdubbing differs in Session and Arrangement.

# Overdubbing in Session View

In the Session View, launch the clip you want to overdub on and arm the track. You'll be able to play your controller and hear what you're playing along with the clip. At this point, your playing isn't being recorded, so this is a handy way to practice before doing the overdubbing.

MIDI overdubbing is initiated by clicking on the Session Record button (see Figure 4.10). After doing this, you'll see the clip's Launch button turn from green to red. Now any notes you play (or knobs you turn) on your controller will be recorded into the clip.

Enable Session Record ——

This clip records and plays —— back simultaneously.

Arm Track ——

**FIGURE 4.10**

MIDI overdub recording allows you to record into an existing MIDI clip without erasing what's already there.

*Source:* Ableton

# Overdubbing in Arrangement View

In the Arrangement View, MIDI overdubbing is enabled with the MIDI Arrangement Overdub switch, shown in Figure 4.11. (It's on by default.) After it's enabled, just arm a MIDI track, press Arrangement Record, and you're in Overdub mode.

**FIGURE 4.11**
MIDI Arrangement Overdub enables overdubbing into Arrangement clips.
*Source:* Ableton

It's important to understand that recording in the Arrangement works differently and requires more caution than it does in the Session View. This is because you can destructively record *over* MIDI clips in Arrangement—something that is not possible in Session. In other words, if you arm a MIDI track and click Arrangement Record while MIDI Arrangement Overdub is *disabled*, you'll start recording a new MIDI clip that contains only your new performance.

Fortunately, Live has an Undo command!

# Recording Automation

Nearly everything in Live can be automated. Want a synth part to slowly fade in over 32 bars? No problem, just automate the volume. Want an effect to kick in on every other snare drum hit? Automate the effect's Device Activator. Automation has been an important part of sound mixing for a few decades now. In contemporary electronic music, it's more important than ever because it's an essential tool for building evolving arrangements out of loop-based elements.

To record automation in Session or Arrangement, enable Automation Arm, shown in Figure 4.12. The basic process for recording automation is incredibly simple. Just move the controls you want to automate while recording. These could be mixer controls such as volume and pan, or effect and instrument device parameters, whether built-in, VST, or AU.

**FIGURE 4.12**
Automation Arm is the key to recording automation.
*Source:* Ableton

## Session Automation

Session automation can be recorded while you record new clips, or it can be overdubbed afterward. In order to record automation, the Automation Arm switch must be enabled. It is turned on by default, so you may have already started recording automation without doing anything special.

The process of recording automation couldn't be easier. While recording a new clip, modify the device or mixer controls of your choosing. For example, while recording a new MIDI clip, tweak the filter cutoff of the virtual instrument you're using. The change to the filter is recorded into the clip alongside any notes you've played. Once you're done recording the automation, it can be viewed and edited in the Clip View as seen in Figure 4.13.

Automation overdubbing is enabled with the Session Record button. Again, the basic process is simple. Make sure that Automation Arm is enabled, click on Session Record, and make some parameter changes. When you're done, click Session Record again to stop recording automation.

There's one very important preference you have to consider when overdubbing Session automation. It's in the Record/Warp/Launch tab of Live's Preferences and is labeled *Record Session Automation in.* When set to Armed Tracks, you'll only be able to overdub automation into tracks that are armed. The appeal of this setting is that it prevents you from unintentionally recording automation by forcing you to arm tracks.

**FIGURE 4.13** Session automation is viewed in the Clip View. This is covered in detail in "Automation Editing" later in this chapter.
*Source:* Ableton

The other setting, All Tracks, allows you to record automation into any clip, regardless of the track's Arm status. This setting is extremely flexible, and it comes with a different advantage: you can record automation without arming any tracks, so you have maximum improvisational freedom.

If you find that you're generally focusing on one track at a time, recording clips and automation in a single pass, you're probably best served by using the Armed Tracks preference. If you prefer to jump around, creating clips in many tracks, and then recording automation for several at a time, you'll find All Tracks is easier to use. Like many workflow choices, it's a trade-off. The only way to find what's best for you is to experiment boldly and use Undo to clean up any messes you make.

## Arrangement Automation

Just like in the Session View, the Automation Arm button must be enabled for automation to be recorded. While you are recording new clips, any parameter changes you make will be recorded and displayed, as seen in Figure 4.14. To show or hide automation in the Arrangement, press A or select Automation Mode from the View menu.

**FIGURE 4.14**
Arrangement automation shows up in the timeline as seen here.
*Source:* Ableton

Overdubbing automation into the Arrangement is also quite simple. Just enable Automation Arm, click Automation Record, and start twisting knobs and pushing buttons. However, there's one important caveat here. Unlike Session View, which can be set to record automation into only armed tracks, Arrangement automation is always recorded into all tracks. Not only that, but you must also take extra care to make sure that you haven't unintentionally left tracks armed. For example, if you want to record some simple volume automation into an audio track you just recorded, you need to disarm the track beforehand. Otherwise, you'll end up simultaneously recording the automation *and* recording over the track! Probably not the desired result.

## ALWAYS AUTOMATED

When you are recording clips from Session View into Arrangement View, automation will be recorded no matter what. If there's Session automation contained in the clips, it will always be recorded into the Arrangement. Additionally, manual tweaks made in any track in which you've launched a clip will be recorded, even if Automation Arm is disabled. See "Recording from Session into Arrangement" later in this chapter for more information on this process.

## Disabling and Re-Enabling Automation

When a parameter is being automated, a red "LED" (see Figure 4.15) appears next to it so that you know it's being controlled by automation. If you change an automated parameter manually, the automation will stop immediately, and the LED will turn gray to indicate that it's been disabled. The automation lines shown in Figures 4.13 and 4.14 will turn gray as well.

**FIGURE 4.15**
The small circle next to the Freq knob indicates that it's being automated.
*Source:* Ableton

Another thing happens when you manually change an automated control. The Re-Enable Automation switch turns orange, as seen in Figure 4.16. Clicking on this causes automation to resume for all automated parameters in all tracks and clips immediately.

**FIGURE 4.16**
Click Re-Enable Automation to bring all your disabled automation back at once.
*Source:* Ableton

Re-enabling automation is an area where there's a difference between Session and Arrangement. Session automation is automatically re-enabled whenever you launch a clip containing automation. In other words, Session automation can only be disabled if you manually change the automated parameter while the clip is playing back. The next time you launch the clip, its automation will be active.

**DELETE AUTOMATION**

If you decide that you want to get rid of all automation for a given control, there is an easy shortcut. Just right-click on the control (knob, slider, and so on) and select Delete Automation from the context menu. Be aware that this is a very powerful command, since it deletes all the automation for that control from the timeline and from all Session clips.

# Using Scenes

In the studio, the Session View is conceived of primarily as a powerful sketchpad for creating parts and experimenting with ideas. And indeed, it shines in this capacity. However, unless you take some time to organize your ideas, it can quickly turn into an unwieldy mess. You think you'll remember which parts went well together and what order you were launching the clips in, but next week when you come back to it, you'll remember nothing. Trust me, this is based on a true story.

The ultimate solution to this problem is to create an arrangement in the Arrangement View. This is the place where you make final decisions about the flow of your song. That said, there's often an intermediate step where you want to organize your ideas and create sections before beginning the process of creating a final arrangement. This is where scenes really come in handy. On stage, scenes are a powerful tool, as well. Not only do they allow multiple clips to be launched simultaneously, but they can also be used to adjust tempos and time signatures automatically.

Scenes are horizontal rows of clips in the Session View. Drag clips that go together into the same scene and use the Scene Launch buttons (in the Master track) to launch them all simultaneously. As shown in Figure 4.17, this method can be used to build an arrangement that is both clear and very flexible. Scenes can be launched in any order and allowed to play for as long as you like.

The song shown in Figure 4.17 is organized from top to bottom with the topmost scene being the intro and the song progressing downward. Each row can house whole musical sections, new song directions, or merely a slight modification in the piece currently playing.

**FIGURE 4.17** Scenes can be used as song sections, such as the verse, chorus, or bridge.
*Source:* Ableton

If you run out of scenes, or just want to add a new one at a specific location, select Insert Scene from the Edit menu. The new scene will be inserted below the currently highlighted scene. You can also create a new scene containing clips you like in one step. When you come across a combination of clips that sound good together, select Create → Capture and Insert Scene to create a new scene that is populated with the currently playing clips.

To change the location of scenes as you create them, just click on the scene's title (or number) and drag it to the new location. To rename a scene, use Edit → Rename. Press Enter (Return) to accept the new name or Escape to leave it as it was. Or you can press Tab to rename the next scene down.

## TWO SCENES ARE BETTER THAN ONE

When you are working on a song arrangement, it can be really useful to make a copy of an entire scene and use it to create some variations. Click to the right of a Scene Launcher to select a scene and then use Duplicate to copy the scene directly below the scene you are working in. Now delete or modify clips in the new scene to create variations.

There are a number of different ways to launch and move between scenes. In addition to pressing the Scene Launch button, you can trigger a scene by pressing the Enter (Return) key, as long as the scene number/name is high-lighted. Changing the highlighted scenes can be done with the arrow keys, so it's easy to navigate and trigger each scene from the computer keyboard without doing any special mapping.

Live also features a couple of Preferences specifically for working with scenes (see Chapter 2). When Select Next Scene on Launch is set to On, Live will automatically move down one scene every time a scene is launched with the

Enter key. The Start Recording on Scene Launch preference can be turned on to allow recording to be initiated by launching Scenes. By default, a track's Arm status is ignored when launching clips, so empty clip slots in armed tracks will simply cause the currently playing clip in that track to stop.

## Programming Scene Tempos and Time Signatures

From time to time, you may want to make instantaneous jumps to different tempos while in the Session View. By naming a scene using a special convention, you can cause Live to change tempos when the scene is triggered. To switch the tempo to 85 BPM, just include "85BPM" in the name of the scene and launch it. The scene can be empty; you don't need to trigger any clips when you launch this scene if you merely want to change tempos. You can remove all the Clip Stop buttons (select them and press Ctrl (Cmd)+E) so that none of your clips are stopped.

One instance where programming scene tempos is particularly helpful is when you're organizing a large batch of clips into a Set so that a single Live Set contains multiple songs. One group of scenes may belong to one song at a given tempo, while another group of scenes represents a different song and tempo, and so on.

Scenes can also be named to create changes in the time signature. Time signatures are represented as fractions with the numerator (number of beats per bar) being any value from 1 to 99 and the denominator (type of beats) being 1, 2, 4, 8, or 16. Scene names can contain both time signature and tempo changes as long as the two values are separated by at least one character (see Figure 4.18).

**FIGURE 4.18**

Live is smart enough to recognize tempos and time signatures in scene names. Launching these scenes will cause the indicated changes to take effect immediately.

*Source:* Ableton

## Removing Clip Stop Buttons

In Figure 4.19, you'll see that only some of the empty clip slots have square Clip Stop buttons. Removing the Clip Stop button from a clip slot will allow a playing clip on the track to continue playing when the scene is launched. To remove a Clip Stop button, right-click in a clip slot and select Remove Stop Button. Don't worry, you can get the Stop button back by right-clicking again and selecting Add Stop Button.

This feature is particularly handy when working with longer clips. For example, let's say you have a long clip containing ambient sound effects in scene 1. You want them to keep playing in scene 2. If you copy the clip into scene 2, the sound effects clip will start over again from the beginning when the scene is launched. By removing the Stop button from scene 2, you can allow the ambient effects to continue playing instead of restarting.

**FIGURE 4.19**
Notice the missing Stop button in scene two of the FX track. Launching the second scene in this example will allow the Ambient FX clip to keep playing while launching drum and bass parts.
*Source:* Ableton

# Arrangement View

Where the Arrangement View fits into your workflow depends a lot on what you do. If you're primarily interested in producing music, it's absolutely essential. The Arrangement is where you really put the song together—beginning, middle, and end.

In fact, for many producers the Arrangement comes into play quite early in the production process. The Session View is great (maybe one of the greatest things ever) for the initial part of the production process, but even if you're clever at organizing ideas with Scenes, you'll find that laying your ideas from left to right forces you to make decisions and get clear on where a song is going. The beauty of Live is that moving to the Arrangement View doesn't mean you have to be done with the Session View. You can continue returning to it to compose new ideas and experiment with old ones.

If you're only using Live as a performance platform, the Arrangement will likely be of secondary importance to you. However, there are many exceptions to this. There are some performers who organize performances using the Arrangement View and take advantage of Live's unique locators, which can be launched like clips. There are also certain types of editing that are impossible in the Session, so you may end up using the Arrangement to prepare clips for performance.

There are a few methods for getting clips into the Arrangement. You can add files from the Browser and record new clips, just like you would in the Session. Or you can use the fun and interactive process of recording clips from the Session View.

# Recording from Session into Arrangement

When Live 1.0 first hit the scene, there were two features that immediately made it stand out. The improvisational Session View really made eyes pop. But no less significant was the ability to perform with Session clips and capture every move—every launched clip, mixer adjustment, and device tweak—into the traditional timeline of the Arrangement View. To this day, it remains a uniquely fun and musical way to compose with a computer. Let's take a look at the process.

Start off by clicking Stop in the Control Bar twice. The second click sets the Arrangement playback position to 1.1.1. Next, click Arrangement Record and perform your song by launching clips, moving sliders, and turning knobs. Remember that Arrangement Record is also used to record brand new clips into the Arrangement, so make sure that no tracks are armed.

When you click Arrangement Record, recording will begin immediately. Depending on how you work, this may or may not be a problem. Here are a few methods to get a clean start.

▶ Use the Metronome's drop-down menu to select a count-off. This will give you a moment to get ready after pressing Arrangement Record.

▶ Launch all of the clips for the intro of your song and then click Stop twice. When recording begins, these clips will start playing back, and you can take it from there.

- ▶ Shift-click Arrangement Record to arm recording without start-ing playback. As soon as you launch a clip, recording will begin.

- ▶ Right-click on Record and uncheck Start Playback with Record. Now you can click Record without starting playback. Launch a clip or click Play to begin recording.

When you're finished, press the spacebar to stop or click Arrangement Record to disable recording while playback continues. If you want to re-record a sec-tion or add new clips, just press Arrangement Record again. Newly launched clips will be recorded; clicking Clip Stop buttons will cause Arrangement clips to be erased. Everything else will be left alone.

When you are recording clips from Session to Arrangement, automation is *always* recorded, regardless of the Automation Arm status. Also note that if you launch Session clips containing automation, that automation will be recorded as well. After recording, this automation will no longer be shown in the Clip View (as Session automation is), but will instead be shown in the track display of the Arrangement View. For more information on viewing and editing automation, see the "Automation Editing" section later in this chapter.

When you're finished recording, take a look at the Arrangement View. The tracks will now be filled with clips, as seen in Figure 4.20. However, you'll also notice that every clip is grayed out, and starting playback does not cause the arrangement you just created to play back. What's going on here? The answer lies with Back to Arrangement.

**FIGURE 4.20** After recording, every clip launched in the Session appears in the Arrangement. The clips are grayed out, however, and the Back to Arrangement button appears above the upper-right corner of the timeline. This indicates that the Session clips are still in control.
*Source:* Ableton

## SESSION TO ARRANGE (AND BACK AGAIN)

As you work on your masterpieces, you'll sometimes want to manually drop a Session clip into the Arrange View. To do this, click a clip and hold down the mouse button as you press and then release the Tab key. Now you can drag that clip to wherever you want it in your arrangement and drop it in. The same technique also works for dropping clips from the Arrangement into the Session.

# Back to Arrangement

Since the Session and Arrangement Views share the same set of tracks, there has to be a way to determine which view will be in control. Remember, any track can only play back one clip at a time. This means it's an either/or situation. A track plays back either Arrangement clips or Session clips, but never both.

Ableton's scheme for handling this problem is to allow Session clips to automatically override Arrangement clips whenever they are launched. Arrangement clips are re-enabled manually via the Back to Arrangement buttons. When a Session clip is launched, any Arrangement clips in that track are grayed out to indicate that they are currently disabled. This explains the grayed-out Arrangement mentioned above. Until you explicitly give control to the Arrangement, the Session stays in control.

There are two global Back to Arrangement buttons, both of which function identically. One is located in the Session View, next to the Stop Clips button in the Master track (see Figure 4.21). The other one appears conditionally in the Arrangement View, as seen in Figure 4.20. By default, the Session's Back to Arrangement button is gray, and the one in the Arrangement is completely invisible! As soon as anything is done to override the Arrangement, they both light up. Clicking on either one causes the Arrangement to take control immediately.

**FIGURE 4.21**
The Session View has a Back to Arrangement button in the Master track.
*Source:* Ableton

You can also give control to Arrangement tracks on a per-track basis. Whenever a Session clip is launched, a triangular button appears at the far right of the corresponding Arrangement track. In Figure 4.20, you'll see these buttons displayed at the right edge of every track. Click on a button to re-enable Arrangement clips for that track only.

Bear in mind that you don't have to have anything in the Arrangement to "override" it. For example, when you first launch Live and are looking at a completely empty set, the Back to Arrangement buttons are gray. As soon as you launch a single Session clip, they turn orange. Clicking Back to Arrangement will stop playback of any Session clips you've launched because Live will give control to the tracks in the Arrangement View, which are currently empty.

# Navigation and Selection

Before digging into the details of navigating and editing in the Arrangement, let's get some terms straight. The Arrangement View has several different areas and a few interface elements that might not jump out at you at first. Figure 4.22 shows them all.

The Beat Time Ruler displays bar numbers, and if you zoom in enough, it will show beats and sixteenths as well. When you float your mouse pointer over the Beat Time Ruler, it turns into a magnifying glass, which can be used to zoom (by dragging vertically) and scroll (by dragging horizontally). To zoom from the keyboard, use the + and – keys. Pressing Z zooms in on the current arrangement selection and Shift+Z zooms back out.

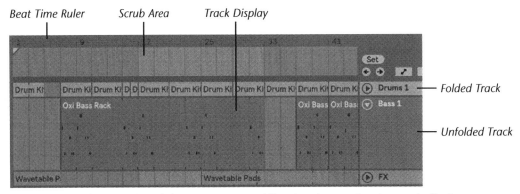

**Figure 4.22** The majority of the Arrangement View is taken up by the track display.
*Source:* Ableton

## SCROLL WHEEL

The scroll wheel on your mouse can be used to zoom and to pan the display left or right. Hold down Ctrl(Cmd) while scrolling to zoom, hold Shift to pan, or hold Alt(Option) to change the height of the currently selected track.

Next is the Scrub Area, where the mouse turns into a speaker. Click to make the Arrangement play back from where you clicked. If Live is running when you click in the Scrub Area, playback will jump according to the global quantize setting. If you want Live to respond immediately, or you want to be able to drag the speaker for traditional scrubbing behavior, set Quantize to None in the Control Bar.

The final method for controlling the transport involves mousing over the Scrub Area of the Arrangement. When your mouse turns into a speaker icon, you can click, and Live will immediately begin playing from this location. You can even do this while the transport is running to jump to a different position in the arrangement.

There are two ways to view tracks in the Arrangement View: folded and unfolded (refer to Figure 4.22). Unfolded tracks can be resized by dragging the bottom edge of the track's title bar or Mixer section. To fold all tracks, press S or hold down Alt (Option) while clicking a track's fold switch.

While keeping tracks folded is convenient for getting an overview of your arrangement, unfolded tracks are easier to edit. When a track is unfolded, a miniature waveform or MIDI display is revealed for the clips. I'll be referring to this area as the *display* and the colored bar above it as the *title bar* of the clip. (These aren't official Ableton terms, but we've got to call them something.) When a track is folded, only the clip's title bar is visible.

## Insert Marker and Arrangement Selection

To navigate and edit in the Arrangement View, you'll need to know how to place the *insert marker* and create an *arrangement selection*. The insert marker is shown as a blinking vertical line. The arrangement selection is shown as a highlighted range of time in one or more tracks.

To place the insert marker, click anywhere in the track display, except in the title bar of a clip (see Figure 4.23). Once the insert marker is placed, it can be moved using the left and right arrow keys. In folded tracks, you can place the insert marker by clicking in an empty part of the track; if you click on a clip in a folded track, you'll create an arrangement selection as explained below.

To create an arrangement selection, click on the title bar of a clip or click and drag in the track display. If you click in the title bar of a clip, you create an arrangement selection the length of the clip, as seen in Figure 4.24a. If you click and drag, you can make an arrangement selection as long as you want. Drag over empty areas of the track display, within clips or any combination thereof. Figure 4.24b shows an arrangement selection within a clip. To extend an existing selection, Shift-click at the location you would like to extend it to. To create an arrangement selection from the keyboard, place the insert marker and then hold down Shift while pressing the left or right arrow. Once an arrangement selection is created, it can be moved using the arrow keys.

## FOLDED TRACK TRICK

To place the insert marker within a clip in a folded track, hold down Shift+Alt (Option) while clicking. This keyboard combination also works when dragging to make an arrangement selection.

**FIGURE 4.23**

The insert marker shows up as a blinking cursor in the track display and a downward-pointing arrow above.

*Source:* Ableton

**FIGURE 4.24A**

The arrangement selection is indicated by the pair of angled triangles above the track display. Clicking on a clip in a folded track, or in the upper half of a clip in an unfolded track, selects the entire clip.

*Source:* Ableton

**FIGURE 4.24B**

This arrangement selection was created by dragging over a range of time in an unfolded track.

*Source:* Ableton

## Setting Playback Position

When you stop and start Live, it doesn't resume playback from where you stopped. Instead, playback begins from either the insert marker or the arrangement selection. (If you want to resume playback from where you last stopped, use Shift-spacebar.) If you want to temporarily play back from a different location, click in the Scrub Area to change the playback position without relocating the insert marker. To play back from the very beginning of the Arrangement (1.1.1), click Stop while Live is already stopped.

## Looping

You can loop a section of your arrangement by enabling Loop in the Control Bar (see Figure 4.25). To the left of the Loop button is a numerical display indicating the bar and beat that the loop begins, while on the right you will see another numerical display showing the length of the loop. These values can also be edited by moving the brace that sits above the track display and dragging its edges to resize.

**FIGURE 4.25**

Turn on Loop to repeat a section of the Arrangement.
*Source:* Ableton

Often, you'll find that you want to set the loop points to match the exact length of a clip, or a series of clips, in your arrangement. To do so, select the clip(s) and use Edit → Loop Selection, which automatically sets the loop points to the position and length of the selection and enables Loop in one step. The keyboard shortcut for Loop Selection, Ctrl (Cmd)+L, can also be used to turn the loop switch on and off.

You'll also notice there's a Select Loop command in the Edit menu. This enables you to create an arrangement selection across all tracks from the loop points. The more editing you do in the Arrangement, the more this will come in handy. For example, you might use Select Loop and then use Duplicate to copy the part of the song you're currently looping.

## SELECT LOOP

Click on the loop brace that sits above the track display to create an arrangement selection from the loop position. Or use the Select Loop command from the Edit menu.

# Grid Spacing

Whether you are creating an arrangement selection, moving clips, or tweaking automation, all editing in the Arrangement is constrained by the current grid setting. For example, anytime a clip is resized or moved, it will snap to the closest grid line. You can change the grid to suit your workflow, or even turn it off completely for free-form editing.

Live has two grid modes: Adaptive and Fixed. Adaptive mode (the default) automatically changes the grid spacing as you zoom in and out. In Fixed mode, you manually set the grid spacing, and it stays put until you change it again. The current grid spacing is displayed in the lower right-hand corner of the Arrangement at all times. To change the grid spacing, right-click on it (or anywhere in the track display) to open the context menu.

## BREAK OUT OF THE GRID

To temporarily disable the grid, hold down Ctrl (Cmd) while dragging clips, MIDI notes, or automation.

In this menu, you can customize the Adaptive behavior to make the grid tend toward wider or narrower spacing (Wide, Medium, Narrow, etc.) or select a Fixed value instead. For many users, the default Adaptive mode (Narrow) works just fine. Power users, however, don't want to be stuck having to change the zoom level just to change the grid spacing.

Fortunately, Live has a few keyboard shortcuts for adjusting the grid. I urge anyone learning Live to learn them because they will speed up your workflow and make your life much easier! Mastery over the grid is one of the keys to being a speedy and effective editor.

▶ **Ctrl (Cmd)+1:** Decreases the grid spacing. If the grid was set to 1/16 before, it will be 1/32 after using this key command.

▶ **Ctrl (Cmd)+2:** Increases the grid spacing. A grid value of 1/16 will change to 1/8 after using this command.

▶ **Ctrl (Cmd)+3:** This key command toggles Triplet mode on and off. A previous setting of 1/8 will turn to 1/8T (1/8-note triplet) after pressing these keys. Use this key command again to switch Triplet mode off.

▶ **Ctrl (Cmd)+4:** This turns the entire grid on and off. When the grid is off, the grid value display will turn gray. You will be able to place MIDI data anywhere you like while the grid is off. To re-enable the grid, use this key command again.

It is worth noting that these shortcuts will function differently depending on what you're doing in Live. For example, if you're working in the clip slot grid in Session View, they will adjust the global Quantization value shown in the Control Bar. If you're editing MIDI in the Clip View, they will change the grid spacing in the MIDI editor.

# Locators and Time Signature Changes

Locators are used to mark sections of a song, such as the start of a verse, chorus, or bridge. However, Ableton did not stop there—it has given you the ability to launch the locators like you would clips, thus allowing you to perform custom arrangements right in the Arrangement View.

## Creating Locators

To place a locator, right-click in the Scrub area and select Add Locator from the context menu. Or you can set locators interactively using the Set button in the upper-right corner. This method will place a locator at the position of the playback cursor while Live is running or at the insert marker (or start point of the arrangement selection) when Live is stopped (see Figure 4.26).

Locators created with the Set button will be assigned a number. To give the locator a more useful name, right-click on the locator and choose Rename. You can change the position of locators after you've made them by clicking the locator and dragging it to a new location in the timeline. If you want to

**FIGURE 4.26** Click Set to create a locator at the current play position. Use the arrow buttons below to jump from one locator to the next.
*Source:* Ableton

remove the locator, click to select it and then press Delete. You'll also notice that when the insert marker lines up with a locator, the Set button changes to read Del and can be used to delete the current locator.

### QUANTIZED LOCATORS

If you use the Set button to place locators while Live is running, the locators are placed according to the current global Quantization value. If Quantization is set to its default value of 1 Bar, locators will always get placed at the beginning of a bar.

## Jumping to Locators

The best part about locators is your ability to jump between them seamlessly while the arrangement is playing. All you have to do is click on a locator (it will begin to flash green) and playback will jump to that location, subject to global quantization. You can also use the two arrow buttons below the Set button to jump to the previous or next locator.

What makes Live's locators unusually cool, though, is that you can assign MIDI messages and computer keys to these locators, just like any other control in Live. This means that the arrangement is now nearly as flexible as the Session View in that you can repeat sections of the song at will or jump to other areas as you see fit. Even the most complex of arrangements is now opened up for your experimentation, thanks to these locators.

## Time Signature Changes

Time signature changes can be created by right-clicking in the Scrub area, choosing Insert Time Signature Change from the context menu, and typing in the time signature you want (see Figure 4.27). Editing and deleting a time signature change are done from the context menu as well. Just right-click on

**FIGURE 4.27**
Time signature changes
in the Arrange View.
*Source:* Ableton

the time signature change and select Edit to alter the time signature or Delete
to remove it.

## LOOP RECORD

The Arrangement Loop can be quite handy for recording. For example,
perhaps your song is done except for lead vocals. Create a loop around
any part the singer is having trouble with and start recording. Go make
a cup of tea while the singer sings it over and over and pick the best take
(or edit together a few takes) when he's done.

# Arrangement Editing

By editing the contents of the arrangement, you can fix mistakes, change the
structure of your song, and creatively modify clips in ways that go beyond
what's possible in the Session. Unless otherwise specified, the examples that
follow will assume you're editing unfolded tracks. Working with folded
tracks is great when you need to fit as much as possible on the screen, but
when you are learning Live's editing features, unfolded tracks offer more
options and make it easier to see what's going on.

The standard Cut, Copy, Paste, Duplicate, and Delete can all be used in the
Arrangement View to copy clips or automation. Paste will place the contents
of the clipboard at the insert marker, while Duplicate will place a copy immediately to the right of the selection. It's important to note that Duplicate operates on a range of time, not just the clips or automation. For example, you can
select a full bar of time in a track, even though it only contains one short clip
on the first beat, and use Duplicate to place a copy of the clip one bar later
(see Figure 4.28).

When your mouse hovers over the upper half of a clip, it turns into a hand.
Drag clips with the hand to move them, or click to select and use the arrow
keys to move. To move multiple clips, first drag across them to create an
arrangement selection and then drag with the hand to reposition them.

**FIGURE 4.28**
Selecting the clip and the rest of the empty bar allows you to duplicate both the clip and the empty space. This way the clip lands at the beginning of the next bar.
*Source:* Ableton

At the left and right boundaries of a clip, your mouse turns into a bracket ( ] ), and you can click and drag the clip's edge to change its length. If an audio clip's Loop switch (in the Clip View) is enabled, you'll be able to resize the clip beyond its original length and cause it to loop as long as you want. Otherwise, you can only drag until the start or end of the audio file it references. MIDI clips can be extended indefinitely in either direction, which will just add empty space to the clip.

If you hold down Shift while dragging a clip edge, the audio will be stretched (if you're extending the clip boundary) or time compressed (if you're making the clip shorter). Before Live 10, this sort of time adjustment was done exclusively using Warp markers, which are explained in Chapter 5. For some tasks, particularly those that require very detailed time adjustment, Warp markers are still the way to go. However, this method makes it very easy to quickly fit any piece of audio into any space on the timeline.

If you hold Shift+Alt (Option) while hovering over a clip, you'll see a hand icon with a pointing index finger. Drag the pointing finger horizontally to move the contents of a clip while leaving the clip boundaries in place.

## Cut Time, Paste Time, Duplicate Time, Delete Time

In the Edit menu, you'll also see a set of basic editing commands with the word "Time" appended. These commands work on all tracks simultaneously, based on the arrangement selection. While the standard editing commands operate only on clips and automation, these commands allow you to edit *time itself.* (Welcome to the future.)

Let's say you want to move the bridge of a song. It's currently after the second verse, and you decide you want it after the third verse. In the track display, select the range of time where the bridge is currently located. It doesn't matter what track you make the selection in, or even if there are any clips in that track. As long as you create an arrangement selection from the start of the bridge to the end, you're all set.

Cut Time will remove every clip in the bridge and slide over everything that happens after it to fill the gap. Now, place the insertion marker after the third verse, where you want the bridge to begin and use Paste Time to insert the clips you just cut. Live pushes the rest of the arrangement over to the right to make room for the clips you're pasting. Note that you must click in the *top-most track* when placing the insert marker. Live pastes the tracks from the top down, so if you click in any other track, the clips will get pasted into the wrong tracks.

This example should give you a pretty good idea of how Duplicate Time and Delete Time work as well. Duplicate Time places a copy at the end of the selection, shoving everything in the way over to the right. Delete Time simply removes an entire chunk of the song.

The keyboard shortcuts for these commands are easy to remember. Just add Shift to the key command for the standard version. For example, Cut Time is Shift+Ctrl(Cmd)+X. (The exception is Delete Time, which is Shift+Ctrl (Cmd)+Delete). Take a moment to test out these commands and familiarize yourself with how they work. They are one of the most powerful features of the Arrangement View.

## Insert Silence

Insert Silence is found under the Create menu. It's similar to the Time commands in that it allows you to insert empty space in the arrangement, moving clips and automation to the right to make room. Before using Insert Silence, you must create either an arrangement selection or place the insert marker at the location you want to add silence to. Depending on which you do first, the command will behave differently.

If you use Insert Silence after making an arrangement selection, it will place a range of empty space equal to the length of the selection. If you place the insert marker instead, Live will display the dialog shown in Figure 4.29 asking how much space you want to insert.

**FIGURE 4.29**

Type in the amount of space you want to insert.

*Source:* Ableton

## Splitting and Consolidating Clips

You can break a clip into smaller clips using the Split function. Find the point at which you want to split the clip, click to place the insertion marker, and use Edit → Split. The clip will be split into two clips (see Figure 4.30). These new clips will be completely independent of one another, meaning they can have their own unique clip settings (such as transposition, warping, loop points, and so on).

You can also join several clips into one clip for easier use. Select the clips that you want to join and select Consolidate from the Edit menu. Live will quickly render a new clip containing all the parts you had selected. When Live consolidates a clip, it creates a new audio file in your project folder, in Samples / Processed / Consolidate.

### WHO'S GOT TIME TO SPLIT?

If you're moving a segment of a clip, there's no need to use the Split command first. Just highlight the segment you want to move and drag. Or, to make a copy, Alt(Option)-drag.

**FIGURE 4.30**

Just click and split to break clips into smaller ones for independent editing.

*Source:* Ableton

Bear in mind that Consolidate operates on a range of time, not just clips, so you can make new clips by combining empty space with existing clips. For example, you could use Consolidate to create a one-bar clip out of a mostly empty bar with a short audio clip in the middle (see Figure 4.31). This new clip could be copied to the first beat of any bar and retain the placement of the sample.

**FIGURE 4.31**
Consolidating this short sample into a bar-long clip makes it easy to copy to other locations while retaining the timing of the sample.
*Source:* Ableton

# Automation Editing

Automation editing is important for a few reasons. First, no matter how well you perform automation while recording, there will be times when you want to change it later. Often, it's easer to make changes by editing instead of re-recording. There are also cases where it's easier to draw in automation manually rather than record it.

Automation is displayed as a line graph representing changes to a parameter over time. In the case of level controls, such as Volume or Send, level increases as the line moves upward. For Pan automation, the center of the track represents the center position. Lower values move the pan left, while higher values move the pan right.

## Viewing Automation

Before you get into editing automation, though, there are a few things you need to know about viewing it. Session automation is displayed by clicking on the Envelopes box of the Clip View (see Figure 4.32a). Arrangement Automation is shown in the track display when Automation Mode is active, as seen in Figure 4.32b.

*Check here to display automation.* —
*Device Chooser* —
*Control Chooser* —

**FIGURE 4.32A** Session automation.
*Source:* Ableton

— *Automation Mode On/Off*
— *Device Chooser*
— *Control Chooser*

**FIGURE 4.32B** Arrangement automation. You can click the Automation Mode switch to show or hide automation, as shown here, or press A on your keyboard.
*Source:* Ableton

As seen in Figures 4.32a and 4.32b, both Session and Arrangement have a pair of menus known as the *Device Chooser* and the *Control Chooser*. The Device Chooser displays the devices contained within the track as well as the Mixer. The Control Chooser selects a specific parameter from the device selected in the first menu. For example, to see the track's volume automation, you'd select Mixer in the first menu and Track Volume in the second menu. If an Auto Filter effect is loaded onto the track, you can view its Cutoff automation by choosing Auto Filter and then Cutoff Freq.

Live makes it easy to find automated parameters by placing a red LED next to devices and parameters containing automation. At the bottom of both menus, you'll also find the Show Automated Parameters Only command, which collapses the two menus into one and shows only automated parameters. You can select Show All Parameters from this menu to return to the default view.

If you select a parameter that has not been automated, a light, dotted line is displayed. Click on this line and use the editing techniques explained in "Automation Editing" to create automation manually.

### SKIP THE CHOOSERS

Here's a trick that lets you view automation without navigating the automation choosers at all. First, select the view that contains the automation you want to see (Session or Arrangement). Then click on the control you want to view automation for.

For example, to view Arrangement Automation for the feedback of a Ping Pong Delay, switch to Arrangement and then click on the Feedback knob. The track will display the automation immediately. (Automation Mode must be active for this to work!)

## Automation Lanes

In Arrangement View, it's possible to view more than one lane of automation at a time. The easiest way to view all of a track's automation is to right-click in the area below the Control Chooser and select Add Lane for Each Automated Envelope from the context menu (see Figure 4.33a). Note also that from this same context menu, you can delete all envelopes with Clear All Envelopes if you want to start over with a clean slate.

**FIGURE 4.33A** The Add Lane for Each Automated Envelope command will automatically create a new lane for each automated parameter.
*Source:* Ableton

If you want to view only certain envelopes, you can click the plus sign seen in Figure 4.33b. This will add a new lane for whatever envelope you are currently viewing on the track. To add additional lanes, select a different envelope from the Device and Control Choosers and click the plus sign. Conversely, each automation lane has a minus sign that can be used to remove the lane.

**FIGURE 4.33B**

Click the plus sign to add a new lane for the currently displayed parameter. Click the minus sign to remove a lane.

*Source:* Ableton

## Editing Automation

There are two techniques for editing automation, one of which involves the standard mouse pointer and another that uses Live's pencil tool, known as *Draw Mode*. (Toggle Draw Mode on and off with the B key.) In Draw Mode, you'll draw with the pencil, creating flat "steps" that are each the same width as the current grid setting (see Figure 4.34a). This will allow you to create tempo-synced automation effects, such as volume gates or timed effect sends. The pencil will overwrite any ramps that may have been made in the breakpoint mode in favor of its flat-step style.

**FIGURE 4.34A**

In Draw Mode, it's easy to create tempo-synced steps in your automation.

*Source:* Ableton

When Draw Mode is off, automation is displayed as lines with little circles known as *breakpoints* (see Figure 4.34b). The lines and circles together are referred to as a *breakpoint envelope*. Click on the lines to create breakpoints and click on breakpoints to delete them. Double-click to create a breakpoint wherever the mouse is positioned, even if it's not on a line.

Drag the breakpoints to reshape the breakpoint envelope or move the lines directly. To move a line, position the mouse pointer adjacent to the line until it turns blue and then click and drag. To curve the line instead of moving it, hold down Alt (Option) while dragging.

It's also possible to adjust a range of automation. First, create an arrangement selection over the automation you want to adjust and then click and drag a breakpoint or line. The Cut, Copy, Paste, and Duplicate commands can all be used on a range of automation as well. To delete a range of automation use Ctrl (Cmd)+Delete.

To make fine adjustments, hold down the Shift key while dragging. Shift has the added bonus of confining horizontal or vertical movement. In other words, if you drag vertically while holding down shift, you'll be prevented from moving the automation horizontally and vice versa.

**FIGURE 4.35**
Automation curves in action.
Double-click while holding Alt
(Option) to restore the curve
to a straight line.
*Source:* Ableton

## Lock Envelopes

To the right of the Scrub Area is a switch with a lock icon, shown in Figure 4.36. This is Lock Envelopes, which is used to lock automation to the time-line. By default, moving, copying, or deleting clips will move, copy, or delete automation as well. If you want to edit clips without editing automation, turn on Lock Envelopes. This will cause automation to remain at its current location, regardless of the movement of the clips.

**FIGURE 4.36**
The Lock Envelopes switch.

# Fades

While fades can be used for what is commonly thought of as a fade (a song slowly decreasing in volume or smoothly transitioning into another song), they are particularly useful for solving common problems in digital audio editing.

First, with digital audio there is always the "zero-crossing" problem. If a digital audio file is ever suddenly cut off anywhere other than the zero point (the exact center of the waveform display), there can be an unpleasant popping sound. In the real world, it's simply not possible to make every single edit at a zero crossing (and ever get anything else done, that is). The simplest solution is to place an extremely short fade at every edit point. Fortunately, Live does this by default! Longer fades come in handy for a wide variety of editing tasks. You might want to shorten a note in a live bass performance or trim an excessively long "ssss" in a vocal performance. In both of these cases, a fade can make an otherwise unnatural edit go unnoticed.

When "comping" together takes (such as multiple passes of a vocal track), it's sometimes necessary to make extremely precise edits—placing an edit in the middle of a word, for example. In these cases, crossfades are essential. By simultaneously fading out one piece of audio while fading in the other, these minute transitions can be made far more smooth and convincing.

To edit fades, you'll need to hide automation, so press A on your keyboard if automation is currently showing. When you hover the mouse pointer over an audio clip, fade "handles" appear in the four corners of the clip, as seen in Figure 4.37.

Drag the top and/or bottom handles to adjust the length of the fade (or click the handle and adjust with the arrow keys). Adjusting the bottom handle moves the boundary of the clip, but it's different than just changing the clip length as we did earlier in this chapter. When you move the bottom handle,

**FIGURE 4.37**

Clip 1 shows the fade handles used to adjust fades. Clips 2 and 3 have been crossfaded using the Create Crossfades command.

*Source:* Ableton

it doesn't affect the position of the top handle; moving the clip boundary moves both handles. Once you've created a fade, an additional handle appears in the center of the fade line. This handle controls the fade's slope, changing it to more of a "scoop" or a "bump" shape.

To create a crossfade, drag to create an arrangement selection over the two clips you want to crossfade and then select Create Crossfade from the Create menu. To adjust the range of the crossfade, drag the two handles that appear at the top of the crossfaded region. The center handle is used to change the crossfade from a linear to an exponential shape.

Bear in mind that in order to create crossfades, *the clips have to have audio beyond the clip boundaries.* If the clips you're trying to crossfade are fully extended, there's nothing to crossfade, and nothing will happen when you use the Create Crossfade command.

### NO FADES ON ME

To remove a fade, click on a fade handle and press Delete. To delete all fades or crossfades from one or more clips, highlight the clips and press Ctrl (Cmd)+Delete, or select Reset Fades from the context menu.

If you want to turn off Live's default behavior of creating fades, you can right-click on a fade handle and turn off the *Create Fades on Clip Edges* preference.

# Exporting Audio

After you have finished your song, it is time to get it out of Live and into the world. To do this, you need to render your arrangement to a stereo audio file. There are other reasons to export audio from Live as well. For example, you may want to export all of the individual tracks for mixing in another DAW.

To export, select Export Audio/Video from the File menu.

The first choices to make are the Rendered Track and the length of the exported file (see Figure 4.38). For a final mix, Rendered Track is set to Master (the default). The Master is the track that combines all of the other tracks into a single stereo signal. When mixing down, you want to write to disk (render) the output from the Master track.

**FIGURE 4.38** The top of the Export Audio/Video dialog. Notice that the Render Start and Render Length fields have been automatically filled with the range of time selected in the Arrangement. *Source:* Ableton

Unless you're doing some fancy routing, the exported file will match what you hear coming out of your speakers. If you need to make an alternate mix, mute or solo tracks as necessary. For example, if you want to make an instrumental version of a vocal song, just mute the vocals and export.

In the Rendered Track menu, you'll find options to render any individual track, all currently selected tracks, or all individual tracks. All Individual Tracks is the option you'll select to export tracks for mixing in another program. This option exports all tracks, Group Tracks, Return tracks, and the Master track to separate files (see Chapter 6, "Tracks and Signal Routing," for more on tracks). This can add up to quite a few files, so good track naming habits are essential. I find it useful to adopt some naming conventions as well. For example, I always capitalize the names of Group Tracks to make it easy to tell them apart in the exported files.

Render Start specifies what bar the export begins at and Render Length specifies the total length in bars. By default, these are set to the position and length of the arrangement selection. Before exporting, I usually select the entire range of my song so I don't have to worry about setting these manually.

While a typical mixdown is always done from the Arrangement, it's also possible to export a mix of clips playing in the Session View. This would typically be done for a more specialized purpose, such as combining several clips into a new audio loop.

To render from Session View, the basic steps are as follows:

1. Launch all of the clips you want to be rendered. Once you've got them all playing, click Stop.

2. Select File → Export Audio/Video to call up the Export Audio/Video dialog and type in the length of the file to be rendered.

3. Click Export or press Enter and select the drive/folder where you want to save your new loop.

Before you click Export and select the location where you want your exported file to be saved, there are a few other options to consider. The rest of the options in Export Audio/Video are as follows:

▶ **Render as Loop:** It is primarily used to export loops with reverbs and delays. Live calculates the decay tail of the effect that would occur *after* the exported file ends and renders it at the *beginning*. This avoids the problem of the decay cutting off abruptly when looping the exported file.

▶ **Convert to Mono:** The exported file is mono instead of stereo.

▶ **Normalize:** It analyzes the exported file to find the highest peak; then increases the volume of the file by the amount necessary to make this peak 0dB. This makes the file as loud as possible without clipping. Leave it off for most applications.

▶ **Create Analysis File:** When this setting is activated, Live will also create an ASD file in addition to the rendered audio file. This is helpful when exporting files that will be reimported into Live, since the ASD file contains waveform display data and information, such as tempo.

▶ **Sample Rate:** If you're exporting audio that will be sent out for mixing or mastering, you should select the highest sample rate used in your set, typically the same as the In/Out Sample Rate in the Audio tab of Preferences. If you're exporting audio that's going straight to consumer formats like MP3 or CD, use the standard rate of 44100.

▶ **Encode PCM:** Set this to On to export full-resolution audio files (as opposed to MP3).

▶ **File Type:** The supported PCM are WAV, AIFF, and FLAC. WAV and AIFF files are identical in sound and size, and only differ in terms of the metadata that is stored within the file. If you want a smaller file, choose FLAC, which is a compressed lossless format, meaning that the file size is smaller but no quality is lost. If you want to make an MP3, see the section on MP3 below.

▶ **Bit Depth:** When you are exporting for digital distribution or CD, bit depth should be set to 16. When you are exporting for mixing or mastering, higher bit depths are typical. Live's internal bit depth is 32; therefore, any audio that is processed within Live is technically 32-bit. Most pro audio programs can handle 32-bit files these days, so this is typically safe to select. If file size or compatibility is a concern, 24-bit works great. If in doubt, ask your mixing or mastering engineer.

▶ **Dither:** Dithering adds low-level noise to digital audio to hide the distortion that occurs when reducing bit depth. It is commonly accepted that when outputting at 16-bit, some dithering should be used. (Try POW-r 2 as a default for most pop and electronic music.) If you're outputting at 24-bit, Triangular is the safest dither method to use, although some say not to use any at all. Search the Internet for endless pages of incomprehensible discussion on the topic.

▶ **Encode MP3:** Selecting this option will create a 320kbit/sec MP3 compressed audio file. Note that you can also have Encode PCM enabled and the export will give you two audio files, one PCM and one MP3.

▶ **Upload Audio to SoundCloud:** SoundCloud is an Internet service for sharing your music. If you have an account with the company, this option streamlines the process of uploading your song.

▶ **Create Video:** If you have a video in the Arrangement view and want to export a video, switch Create Video to On. There's more information about working with video in Chapter 13, "Live 10 Power!"

▶ **Video Encoder:** Select the encoder to use for rendering. The selection will depend on the video encoders installed on your system.

▶ **Encoder Settings:** Click Edit to access advanced settings for video encoding. For most purposes, you can easily find out the best settings for your video's destination (YouTube, etc.) with a quick Internet search.

# 5
# Clips

Clips are the musical building blocks of Live. As such, you'll eventually want to gain a deep knowledge of their inner workings, and this chapter is designed to help you do just that. From simple tweaks, like clip name and color, to the far-out manipulations possible with Warp Markers and grooves, there's an awful lot going on in the Clip View that you need to know about.

## Common Properties of Clips

While MIDI and audio are very different animals, there are a number of behaviors and settings that are common to both types of clips, all of which will be discussed here. The Clip View is divided into several different areas: the *editor* on the right, which displays audio waveforms, Warp Markers, MIDI notes, and envelopes; and several parameter boxes to the left: the clip box, which is always shown, and the Launch, Sample (audio clips), Notes (MIDI clips), and Envelopes boxes, all of which can be shown or hidden using the switches in the lower-left corner. See Figure 5.1.

*Show/Hide*                                                    *Editor*
*Switches*

**FIGURE 5.1** The Clip View contains multiple sections that can be shown and hidden using the icons at the lower-left corner of the window. A MIDI clip is shown. For Audio clips, the Notes box is replaced by the Sample box. The Launch box only appears in the Session View.
*Source:* Ableton

Be aware that the editor can display either the audio/MIDI data of a clip or its envelopes. Click in the title bar of the Envelopes box to show envelopes; click on the Sample/Notes box to view audio or MIDI. If you're not focusing on envelopes, it's a good idea to hide the Envelopes box. This will save space and help avoid any confusion.

# The Clip Box

The clip box is always visible in the Clip View (see Figure 5.2). Here you'll be able to adjust some basic properties of the clip and enable a groove if you choose.

**FIGURE 5.2**
The clip box is always visible. It contains some basic and some advanced controls, explained next.
*Source:* Ableton

## Clip Activator

The circular "power switch" in the upper-left corner can be used to disable the clip. This is handy if you want to leave a clip in place, but signify that it is not being used. It is particularly useful when working in Arrangement View, because it will allow you to mute a clip but leave it in place in case it is needed later. Clips can also be deactivated by selecting them and pressing zero on your computer keyboard, or by selecting Deactivate Clip from the context menu.

## Clip Name and Color

The first two settings in the clip box (see Figure 5.2) are purely cosmetic—they have no impact on the behavior or sound of the clip. The first field is the Clip Name, which can be as many characters as you want. Clips can also be named using the Rename command, and colors can be selected by right-clicking on a clip and using the color chooser.

If you create a clip by dragging a file from the Browser, the clip will be named the same as the file. When you record a new clip, it will be given the name of the track in which it is created. To help keep multiple takes (recordings) in order, Live adds a number to the beginning of the clip (and file) name as each new one is created. If you use long clip names, you'll only see the first nine characters in Session View when using the default track width. This can be remedied by dragging the right edge of a track's title bar to widen the track.

Clip color may seem like a bit of aesthetic fluff at first, but color coding your clips can be a huge benefit in performance or when working on complex productions. For example, you could make all your bass parts shades of blue in your songs or use colors to indicate different genres in your DJ set.

## Time Signature

The clip's Time Signature (labeled *Signature*) determines the numbering of the grid markers in the editor. What it does *not* do is change the time signature, tempo, or any other audible aspect of the clip. This parameter is strictly to make the editors visually coherent when working in different meters.

## Clip Groove

The Groove section is one of the more complex (and mind-blowing) features found in the Clip View. Using Live's Groove features, you can modify the timing and dynamics of your clips in unlimited ways. Groove is a deep topic that requires a good knowledge of clips, so it's explained in a separate section later in this chapter.

## Nudge Backward/Nudge Forward

These two buttons at the bottom of the clip box are useful for live performance or Session View loop experimentation. Clicking a Nudge button changes the playback position of a clip while it's playing back

The playback position is adjusted by the global Quantization setting displayed in the Control Bar. For example, if Quantization is set to 1 Bar, clicking the Nudge Forward button will make playback jump forward one bar with every click. If you want to offset by a smaller amount, select a smaller Quantize value. With global Quantization set to None, the Nudge buttons will offset the clip by minute increments, allowing you to make your clip sit just the tiniest bit ahead of or behind the beat.

### THE THIRD CONTROL

While it looks like the Nudge controls are limited to only two buttons, there is a third control that can be accessed only through MIDI assignment. When you enter the MIDI Map mode (Ctrl [Cmd]+M), you'll see a tiny box appear between the arrow buttons. Click this box and twist a knob on your MIDI controller. Now you can twist the knob to perform the nudge. You should use an endless encoder knob for this.

# The Launch Box

In Live, we use the term *launch* to indicate the playing back of a Session clip. Launching is a customizable behavior that offers a variety of creative options. These options are set in the Launch Box, which is only available to clips in Session View. You can show or hide the Launch Box using the L icon in the lower left-hand corner of the Clip View.

## Launch Mode

The Launch mode (see Figure 5.3) determines what happens when a clip's Launch button is pressed, or the clip is launched via MIDI or the computer keyboard. Be aware that the behavior of the Launch modes is linked to the Quantization setting (explained next). To experiment with the different modes, I recommend that you set Quantization to a relatively low value (such as 1/16), as it will make the differences in the modes much easier to understand.

▶ **Trigger:** The most common Launch mode for use in most performance situations is Live's Trigger mode. Each time you fire a clip, it will launch. Once a clip is launched and playing, you will be able to stop its playback only by pressing one of the Clip Stop buttons located in the same track. This mode ignores the up-tick (release) of the mouse button, computer keyboard key, or MIDI note. Each clip can be fired as rapidly as the quantization will allow, and each time the clip is fired, it will restart the clip from the beginning, even if it was already playing.

▶ **Gate:** When triggering a clip in Gate mode, you will hear the sound only for as long as your mouse or keyboard key is depressed. This is an excellent setting for dropping in snippets of sound without playing the entire clip. In short, holding down your left mouse button (or MIDI/computer-keyboard key) will play the clip continuously until you let up.

**FIGURE 5.3**

Launch modes are a powerful and simple way to get creative with clips.

*Source:* Ableton

▶ **Toggle:** With Toggle mode engaged, the Clip Launch button basically turns into an on/off switch for the clip. If you launch a clip
that is playing, it will stop. Launch the stopped clip, and it will
begin playing. This also works at the scene level if you trigger a
scene with clips set in Toggle mode. Each time you trigger the
scene, clips that are playing will stop, and stopped clips will
start. Bear in mind that stopping of the clip will respect the current quantization, just the way launching does.

▶ **Repeat:** Repeat mode is a way of retriggering a clip by holding
down the mouse or assigned key/MIDI note. Anytime the mouse
or key is held, the clip will continuously restart itself at the rate
specified by the clip's Quantize setting. If the setting is 1/4, holding down the mouse/key will cause only the first beat of the clip
to play over and over again. When the mouse or key is released,
the clip will play through its entirety like normal. This mode can
create fun stutter effects, but should be used sparingly—probably
not a good choice for default behavior.

## Legato Mode Switch

Below the mode menu is the Legato switch. When enabled, the clip will begin
playback from the relative position of the currently playing clip in the same
track. For example, let's say you have two eight-bar clips set to Legato mode.
The first clip is launched and allowed to play for two bars before the second
one is launched. Instead of playing from the beginning, it starts at bar 3 since
that's where the previous clip would have been had it been allowed to keep
playing.

This feature allows you to switch between several different clips, dipping in
and out of various sections of each clip. With low launch quantization values,
this feature makes it possible to generate a large number of variations from a
relatively small number of clips.

## Clip Quantization

You may be familiar with quantization as a technique to correct the timing
of MIDI performances. However, the Quantization menu in the Launch Box
deals with something called *launch quantization,* which is quite a different

animal. It still deals with correcting timing, but only in terms of launching and stopping clips (as the name suggests!). Proper Clip Quantization settings ensure that clips will start on time and in sync with each other, even if they are triggered a little early by us sloppy humans.

When you launch a clip, Live waits to play it back until the next quantization interval is reached. For example, with a quantization setting of 1 Bar, the clip will wait until the downbeat of the next bar to begin playing. In the interval between when a clip is launched and when it actually begins playing back, the Clip Launch button blinks. With quantization set to None, a clip will start playing the instant it is launched.

Quantization is selected from the drop-down menu shown in Figure 5.4. By default, clips are set to Global, which causes the clip to follow the Quantize setting in the Control Bar. In Live's Preferences, it's possible to change the default quantization to a value other than Global, but for most applications you probably don't want to do this. It's handy to have most clips follow global quantization and override that behavior only when necessary.

**FIGURE 5.4**
The Quantize settings for a clip.
*Source:* Ableton

## Velocity

Just below the Quantization box is the Velocity Amount. This value works only for clips launched via MIDI. It uses the incoming velocity level of the MIDI note to set the playback volume of the clip. At 0%, the velocity has no effect on clip playback volume—it plays at its original level. At 100%, the clip's velocity sensitivity will be extreme—probably too sensitive for most situations. This works for both audio and MIDI clips.

## Follow Actions

Live's Follow Actions allow an amazing level of automation within the Session View. Using Follow Actions, you can set rules by which one clip can launch another. Any particular clip can launch clips above and below it, replay itself, or even stop itself—all based on odds and a time period that you can program. You can think of Follow Actions as a virtual "finger" that launches for you. You'll find a list of potential applications for Follow Actions listed in Chapter 13, "Live 10 Power!"

Follow Actions work on *groups* of clips, which are clips arranged above and below one another in the same track (see Figure 5.5). An empty clip slot inserted between two clips divides them into separate groups. Follow Actions cannot be used to trigger clips in different groups or tracks.

The time and conditions for a Follow Action are set in the three sections at the bottom of the clip's Launch window. The first section, the Follow Action Time, determines how much time elapses between when the clip is launched and the Follow Action occurs. Figure 5.6 specifies that the action Play Next will be performed after one bar elapses.

The options in the Follow Action menus are as follows:

▶ **No Action:** No action is performed. This is the default action for all new clips. With No Action selected in both menus, no Follow Action will occur.

▶ **Stop:** Stops playback.

**FIGURE 5.5** The track on the left has two groups of clips, while the track on the right has one group.
*Source:* Ableton

**FIGURE 5.6** These parameters determine the Follow Action behavior of the clip. If Chances A and B are both set to a non-zero value, Follow A or B is randomly chosen, based on their ratio.
*Source:* Ableton

▶ **Play Again:** Relaunches the currently playing clip.

▶ **Previous/Next:** Triggers the clip above or below the current one. If the clip at the top of a group triggers the Play Previous action, it will "wrap around" and trigger the bottom clip of the group and vice versa.

▶ **Play First/Last:** Triggers the top or bottom clip in a group. If the top clip in a group triggers the Play First action, it will relaunch itself.

▶ **Any:** Launches a randomly chosen clip from the group. Live might retrigger the same clip with this option.

▶ **Other:** Launches a *different* randomly chosen clip from the group. The same clip will never be launched.

What makes Follow Actions particularly interesting is the ability to create two possible actions for each clip. Live will choose between Follow Action A and Follow Action B at random, but this randomness can be constrained using a mathematical ratio.

Chance A and Chance B are used to set the odds that each action will occur. By default, the odds are 1:0, meaning that the Follow Action on the left will always be performed. Odds of 0:1 will cause the right Follow Action to always be performed. Odds of 1:1 will give you a 50-50 chance of either action being performed. You can put in any values you like, such as 2:3 or 1:200.

Bear in mind that whenever No Action is encountered, no further Follow Actions will occur, even if the clip is looped. This is because Follow Actions are only evaluated after a clip is *launched.* If you want to create a chance that a clip will either continue to loop or launch another clip, use Play Again instead. This way, the clip will continue to evaluate its Follow Actions.

### PLAYING THE ODDS

Note that odds are calculated afresh every time a Follow Action is performed. If you have a clip with Follow Action odds of 1:1 and Live chooses the left Action the first time, it does not mean that Live will choose the right Action the next time. Just as it is possible to roll the same number on a die time after time, it is quite possible for Live to choose the left Follow Action several times in a row, even with 1:1 odds.

# Sample/Notes

The next box in the clip view differs for audio and MIDI clips. Audio clips display a box called *Sample*, while MIDI clips have a box called *Notes*. The left sides of these boxes differ in the Sample and Notes boxes, but the right sides contain identical parameters for adjusting the clip's playback range and loop length.

## Start and End

The Start and End values allow you to adjust where a clip begins and ends playback, regardless of how many bars of audio or MIDI are contained within the clip. For example, you might have a 16-bar drum loop, but only want to play bars 13–14. Or you might have a 2-bar MIDI clip, but want to add 2 empty bars to the beginning. These adjustments are made using the Start and End controls.

Start determines where the clip begins playback. The Start position is shown both as a numeric value and as a right-pointing flag in the editor to the right. End determines where the clip stops playback when the Loop switch is disabled. This is an important point, so I'll also say it a different way: when Loop is enabled, End has no effect. This parameter is displayed as a left-pointing flag in the editor and as a numeric value directly below Start. Both of these values can be edited by dragging the flags or by editing the numeric values directly, as shown in Figure 5.7.

**FIGURE 5.7** You can define a smaller section of a clip to use by setting the Clip Start and End Markers.
*Source:* Ableton

## EXTRA SPACE

Want to add space to the beginning or end of an audio clip? Adjust the Start or End number boxes to give yourself some extra bars. Unlike MIDI clips, audio clips can't be extended beyond the contents by dragging the Start and End markers. But using the number boxes, you're free to enter any values you want—even negative numbers.

If you mostly work in the Arrangement View, you may almost never think about the Start and End values. That's because dragging a clip's boundaries in the track display is really just another way of adjusting its Start and End. The next time you edit a clip in the Arrangement, keep an eye on the Clip View, and you'll see this in action.

## CLIP TRANSPORT

You can start playing a clip from any point you choose without having to move the Start Marker. To do this, simply hover the cursor just above the editor, which turns into a speaker icon. When you click, the clip will begin playing from the closest location allowed by the clip's Launch Quantization.

## Loop Settings

Loop settings are important to both Session and Arrangement clips. In the Session View, a clip that is set to loop will play indefinitely. Otherwise, it will stop playing as soon as the Clip End is reached. In the Arrangement View, the looped portion of a clip can be extended indefinitely by dragging the clip boundaries.

The loop settings consist of three controls: Loop, Position, and Length. The first of these, Loop, is a large switch that enables or disables the loop. The second two controls determine where the loop begins and how long it is. These parameters, Position and Length, are displayed as numeric values and as a brace running along the top of the editor (see Figure 5.8).

**FIGURE 5.8** It's easy to loop any portion of the audio or MIDI within a clip.
*Source:* Ableton

Dragging the right edge of the brace changes the Length while dragging the left edge will change both Length and Position simultaneously. Drag the brace from its center to change the Loop Position while leaving its Length the same. A single click on the Loop brace will select it and allow you to adjust it with the arrow keys. The left and right keys will move it by the grid size, and the up and down keys will move it by the current Loop Length.

Live also lets you define the loop points as the clip is playing by pressing the buttons marked "Set" next to Loop Position and Loop Length. These buttons are both quantized to the value in the global Quantize menu, so it's easy to create perfect loops interactively.

Bear in mind that Start and Loop Position can be adjusted independently. This means that you can have clips that don't begin to loop right away, as seen in Figure 5.9.

This is useful in a variety of situations. For example, imagine that you have a drum loop that starts with a crash cymbal. Instead of looping the entire clip, resulting in the crash cymbal sounding every time the loop repeats, you

**FIGURE 5.9**

A clip can be set to loop at a different point than it initially plays back from. Notice the Start marker at bar 1 and the loop brace running from bar 2 to 3.
*Source:* Ableton

can specify a loop area after the crash cymbal. This way you'll hear the crash the first time you trigger the clip, but you won't hear it again until you relaunch the clip.

It's also possible to place the clip's Start within the loop, at a point other than the loop's Start (see Figure 5.10). By offsetting loops from each other, a great deal of rhythmic variation is possible. To get a feel for this, try launching a drum loop and a bass loop on two different tracks. While the loops are playing back, move the Start position of the bass loop and listen to how the groove changes.

**FIGURE 5.10**
Try offsetting the clip's Start to create loop variations.
*Source:* Ableton

### ORANGE DIGITS

When adjusting loops, you may occasionally find numbers in the loop settings or Start/End display that are orange. This means that the number displayed is not exact. For example, if a loop length is listed as 1.0.0 with the last 0 in orange, the loop is a small fraction off. A loop this long will at first sound correct, but will drift over time.

This can be fixed easily by typing in the correct number and pressing Enter.

# Editing Multiple Clip Parameters

Many of the clip parameters explained here can be edited for multiple clips simultaneously. When you select multiple clips, only the controls that can be changed for all selected clips will be shown (see Figure 5.11). Controls that are set to different values will display an asterisk (*) instead of a value.

Some of the options, such as Clip Name and Clip Color, will be set identically for all clips. For example, if you change the Clip Name to Hot Drums, all of the selected clips will take on the same name. This same behavior is true for nearly all of the available fields when editing multiple clips.

**FIGURE 5.11**
Edit multiple clips
simultaneously and save
yourself some time.
*Source:* Ableton

The Transpose, Detune, Velocity, and Volume settings of audio clips can be adjusted by a relative amount. For example, if the Transpose setting of one clip is –2 and another is +3, turning up the Transpose knob 2 ticks while selecting both clips will result in the first clip being set to 0 while the second clip is set to +5. To reset a control of all selected clips to the default value, select the control and press Delete.

It's also possible to view and edit the notes of multiple MIDI clips simultaneously. This is covered in the following section on MIDI clips.

# MIDI Clips

If you're using Live to compose music, you'll probably be using MIDI clips extensively. Whether you're performing with a controller or drawing in parts from scratch, you'll need to know your way around the MIDI clip. In this section, we'll take a closer look at their properties and at MIDI editing in particular.

## Editing MIDI Clips

MIDI is incredibly flexible. Recorded notes can be effortlessly transposed to different pitches, extended or shortened, and moved to a different location in time. When you edit MIDI clips in Live, you not only have the ability to change the notes that were recorded, but also to create new ones by hand. For example, some producers prefer to draw drum parts instead of playing them. Editing also allows you to create precise automation, such as perfect volume fades and quantized filter modulations.

If you ever want to create a MIDI clip entirely through editing, there's no need to record at all. There are several different ways to create empty MIDI clips:

▶ Double-click in an empty clip slot of a MIDI track.

▶ Double-click in an empty area of a MIDI track in the Arrangement.

▶ Select an empty clip slot in a MIDI track and use the Create MIDI Clip(s) command from the Create menu.

▶ Select an empty range of time in one or more MIDI tracks in the Arrangement and use the Create MIDI Clip(s) command from the Create menu.

# Adjusting the Grid

All editing in a MIDI clip is governed by the current grid spacing, which you'll see displayed in the lower right-hand corner of the editor (see Figure 5.12). Anytime a note is created or moved, it will snap to the grid. When you are moving notes, the grid acts like a magnet. If you drag slowly and deliberately, you can slide notes in between the grid lines. You can change the grid spacing to make precise rhythmic adjustments, or even turn the grid off completely for free-form editing.

The grid can be adjusted by right-clicking anywhere in the Note Editor and selecting from the context menu. Just like the Track display in the Arrangement View, the MIDI editor has two grid modes: Adaptive and Fixed. Adaptive mode changes the grid value according to the zoom level, while Fixed grid keeps the resolution at whatever value you select, regardless of zoom.

**FIGURE 5.12**
Look in the lower-right corner, and you'll see the current grid setting is 1/16. Notes will snap to 1/16-note timing when dragged, and any notes drawn will default to a duration of 1/16.
*Source:* Ableton

## QUANTIZE KEYS

You can manually change the grid resolution with these keystrokes:

**Ctrl (Cmd)+1:** Makes the grid smaller.

**Ctrl (Cmd)+2:** Makes the grid larger.

**Ctrl (Cmd)+3:** Toggles triplet mode on and off.

**Ctrl (Cmd)+4:** Toggles the grid on and off. Alternately, you can temporarily disable the grid by holding down Ctrl (Cmd) while editing.

Before using these key commands, click in the MIDI editor to select it. Otherwise, you might end up adjusting the global Quantization value or the grid in the Track Display.

# Editing Notes and Velocities

After you've got your desired grid timing selected, you're ready to start manipulating MIDI notes. Live displays MIDI notes in a style known as a *piano roll*. This term comes from the old player pianos that were programmed using rolls of paper. These rolls had small slots cut into them, each representing a specific note on the piano keyboard or one of the other instruments mounted inside. A note that played for a long time was triggered by a long slot in the paper. As the paper rolled by mechanical sensors, it triggered servos to play notes on the piano.

## Viewing MIDI Data

The Piano Roll View in Live features a lane for each note on the MIDI scale. When looking at Figure 5.13, you'll see an image of a piano keyboard at the left side of the window. From each of these keys is a lane extending to the right where notes can be placed. Notes placed in these lanes trigger their corresponding key in the scale. Turn on Preview to hear notes as you draw or move them.

You can zoom in and out of the vertical piano keyboard, thus allowing you to see more or fewer of the 128 possible notes in the MIDI scale. Zoom in by moving your mouse over the piano keyboard at the left of the window. When the mouse changes to a magnifying glass, you can drag horizontally to zoom and vertically to scroll. To enlarge the editor, move your mouse above the

**Figure 5.13** The MIDI editor can be resized, and the piano roll zoomed and scrolled, so you can always see what you need to see.
*Source:* Ableton

editor until it becomes a splitter and then drag upward. If you want, you can make the editor take up the entire screen and use Shift-Tab when you need to see the clip grid or track display.

Just like the Arrangement View, horizontal zooming is done by clicking and dragging in the time ruler that runs along the top of the editor, or using the plus and minus keys on your keyboard. Use Z and Shift+Z to zoom in or out on a selected range of notes.

### INTO THE FOLD

Live's MIDI display has a unique feature that hides any lanes that don't contain notes. When the Fold button (located just above the Piano Roll display) is activated, the display will be condensed, and you'll see only the lanes that contain notes.

## Basic Editing

There are two methods for editing MIDI data: with the standard mouse pointer or with Live's pencil tool, known as *Draw Mode*. To enable Draw Mode, click the pencil in the Control Bar or simply press the B key on your keyboard (see Figure 5.14). A short press toggles Draw Mode on and off, while holding B will temporarily enable Draw Mode and restore the standard mouse

**FIGURE 5.14**
Enable Draw Mode to draw and erase notes with a single click.
*Source:* Ableton

pointer when you release it. This technique works in reverse as well, temporarily enabling the standard mouse pointer while in Draw Mode.

When Draw Mode is on, you can add notes in the editor by single-clicking. The notes you create will automatically be set to the length of the current grid setting. If you continue to hold the mouse button after you create the note, you can drag up and down to set its velocity. If you click and drag horizontally, the pencil will create a series of notes in that lane, which is great for hi-hat patterns. (You can also drag up and down to set the velocities of the whole group.) Clicking an existing note with the pencil will erase it.

While Draw Mode is very convenient for many editing tasks, there are a few things you can only do with the standard mouse pointer. For example, you can click and drag notes to relocate them, or draw a marquee around a group of notes to select them, and then move or edit them as a group. Once notes are selected, they can also be moved using the arrow keys. To create a MIDI note with the standard mouse pointer, double-click in the editor. Double-clicking an existing note will erase it.

Regardless of which mode you're in, the mouse will change into a bracket-shaped (] or [) trimmer tool when moved to the edge of a note. This tool is used to change the length of notes. When you are dragging with this tool, the note length will change smoothly at first, only snapping to the next grid line when dragged very close to it. Once it snaps to the next grid line, it will continue to snap, only allowing you to make edits sized to the grid. Not to worry, just hold down Ctrl (Cmd) while dragging to disable the grid.

Note lengths can be adjusted from the keyboard by holding down Shift and using the left- and right-arrow keys. Add Ctrl (Cmd) to disable the grid while resizing.

## QUICK SELECT

There's a quick shortcut for selecting every instance of a particular pitch or drum in a MIDI clip. Just click in the piano keyboard (or next to the drum name if you're using Drum Rack or Impulse) to select all of the notes in that lane.

The area directly above the note editor will display a highlight called the *selection area* whenever a selection is made. A selection can be made by clicking on a note, Shift-clicking to select a range of notes, or clicking and dragging to draw a selection marquee. Note that it's even possible to create a selection area without selecting any notes, simply by dragging in an empty area of the editor.

The length of the selection area is particularly important when using commands that operate on a range of time. For example, when Duplicate is used on MIDI notes, the copy will be placed at the end of the selection area. Therefore, the notes shown in Figure 5.15 will be placed at the beginning of the next beat. The note editor also supports the Cut Time, Paste Time, Duplicate Time, Delete Time, and Insert Silence commands described in the "Arrangement Editing" section of Chapter 4, "Making Music in Live." These commands will replicate or remove ranges of time according to the current selection area.

**FIGURE 5.15**
The selection area shown is a quarter note long, even though the notes are all on the first 1/16th. The Duplicate command could now be used to place a copy of these notes at the start of the next beat.
*Source:* Ableton

Clicking in an empty area of the editor inserts a blinking cursor, which is useful if you're using the standard Cut, Copy, and Paste commands. Once you've cut or copied a selection, click to place the cursor before pasting to determine where the notes will be placed.

Bear in mind that whenever you've selected a group of notes, they can all be edited simultaneously. Not only can you move them, but you can also resize them, or you can scale their velocities all at once.

## Editing Velocity

Directly below the note editor is the velocity editor. Typically, changes in velocity will result in a change in the volume of the note. However, this behavior is actually controlled by the instrument receiving the MIDI, and you'll find that some sounds are velocity sensitive while others are not. Some presets will map velocity to other values such as filter cutoff. To learn more about mapping note velocity, read up on Live's instruments in Chapter 8, "Live's Instruments."

The velocity editor can be folded or unfolded, and resized by dragging the lower boundary of the note editor (see Figure 5.16). When Draw Mode is turned off, the velocity of each note is represented by a vertical line with a small circle at the top. To adjust the velocity, just drag the circle up or down. With Draw Mode on, the circle disappears, and you can draw velocities directly into the velocity editor.

**FIGURE 5.16**

The velocity lane can be enlarged by dragging at the top, or hidden by clicking the fold switch in the lower-left corner.

*Source:* Ableton

When there are multiple notes on a single beat, the velocities are stacked on top of one another, making it difficult to change the velocity of a particular note (as shown in Figure 5.16). To work around this, select the note in editor first, and you'll then be able to edit its velocity. Using Draw Mode in this situation will set all the notes to the same velocity.

Fortunately, there's also an easy shortcut for editing velocity that works whether or not Draw Mode is turned on. Just hold down Ctrl (Cmd) while holding the mouse pointer over a note, and it will change into a splitter. Drag the splitter up or down to change the velocity. Since Live adjusts the color of notes to show their velocity, you may not have to use the velocity editor at all and can just fold it to save space on your screen.

## RISE AND FALL

To create a ramp of rising or falling velocities, first select a range of notes. Then, with Draw Mode turned off, hold down Ctrl (Cmd) and draw a ramp in the velocity lane.

To set a range of notes to the same velocity, select them and drag up or down until all notes are at the maximum or minimum. When you move back toward the center, they will all remain at the same velocity.

# Stretch Markers

With one exception, creating a selection area causes a set of handles called *MIDI Stretch Markers* to appear above the editor. (No markers appear when you select a single note or only simultaneously occurring notes.) These can be used to flexibly adjust the duration and timing of the selection. If the Envelopes view is showing, these markers can also be used to adjust automation or modulation (see Figure 5.17).

**FIGURE 5.17**

The outer two handles are the MIDI Stretch Markers that appear when you create a selection area. The handle in the middle is a Pseudo Stretch Marker.

*Source:* Ableton

Dragging the markers works similarly to moving notes, in that they move smoothly at first and then snap to the grid once the first grid line is reached. The way they adjust notes, however, is unusual and can take some getting used to. The marker that is moved will adjust the notes, while the other marker acts as an anchor.

The way the notes are adjusted depends on which direction you drag. If you drag a marker to increase the size of the selected area (you drag it *away* from the other marker), the notes are elongated and their timing is slowed down. Dragging a marker toward the other one compresses the timing and duration of the notes. If you continue to drag the marker, you can actually drag it *past* the other one and reverse the order of the notes. (This last trick only works if the selection is created by selecting notes in the editor. If you create the selection by dragging in empty note lanes, it won't work). If you want to stretch or compress a subset of the notes in between the markers, hover the mouse in between the two markers, and you'll see a third Pseudo Stretch Marker appear. Click and drag to adjust it.

## Multi Clip Editing

Live 10 makes it possible to view and edit multiple MIDI clips simultaneously. To get started, all you have to do is select more than one MIDI clip. Figures 5.18a and 5.18b show you what you'll see in the Clip View.

Even though you can view more than one clip in the editor, you're only allowed to edit one at a time. To control which clip is currently available for editing, Ableton has introduced the *multiclip loop bar.* You'll see this running across the top of both Figures 5.18a and 5.18b. Only the currently active loop bar and notes are shown in color; the rest are grayed out. As you hover your mouse over the inactive loop bars, they'll turn to color and the name of the clip will be displayed below. Click on the loop bar of the clip you want to edit.

In Figure 5.18a, you'll see multiple iterations of a one-bar loop called *Bass 1*. Any edit made to this loop will appear in all of the copies. This is no different than Live's typical behavior—the only difference is that when you are editing multiple clips, Live will show you the loop repeating in the Clip View. In the Session View, you'll see the loop repeated as many times as necessary to match the longest selected clip. For example, if you select an eight-bar loop and a one-bar loop, the one-bar loop will be shown eight times.

**FIGURE 5.18A** This figure shows two clips from the same track in Arrangement View. *Source:* Ableton

**FIGURE 5.18B**
When Session clips or Arrangement clips from different tracks are selected, you'll see a stack of multiclip loop bars along the top of the editor.
*Source:* Ableton

# MIDI Editing Tools

In the Notes box, there are several buttons used for MIDI editing, as well as a handy Transpose function (see Figure 5.19).

**FIGURE 5.19**
The MIDI editing tools in the Notes box. When the Loop switch is turned off, the Duplicate Loop button becomes the Duplicate Region button.
*Source:* Ableton

## Transpose

This nifty box shows you the range of the selected notes in the clip, or all notes if none are selected. For example, if you program a melody that runs from middle C to the G above, Transpose will display C3-G3. Drag up or down in this box to transpose the notes up or down, or type in a numeric value. For example, typing in –7 will move the notes down seven semitones (a perfect fifth). Alternately, you could move the notes this same amount by typing the new bottom pitch (in this case F2) or the new top pitch preceded by a minus sign (–C3).

## Play at Double Tempo/Half Tempo

These buttons can be used to exactly halve or double the playback speed and the duration of selected notes. If no notes are selected, all of the notes are adjusted, as is the clip's loop length. The first thing you might notice about them is that their markings seem counterintuitive. The reason that Play at Half Tempo is marked *2 is that playing something at half tempo means it takes *twice as long to play*.

## Reverse and Invert

Want to hear what your MIDI sequence sounds like backward or upside down? These buttons have got you covered. The results that these buttons produce are often in the strange and twisted category, but sometimes that's just what you need. Like the double/half buttons, these operate on selected notes or the entire clip if none are selected.

## Force Legato

*Legato* is an Italian word that's used to signify that notes should be played or sung such that they are smoothly connected to one another. This button provides an easy way to move the end of every selected note so that it reaches the start of the next one. If no notes are selected, the entire clip is modified.

## Duplicate Loop/Duplicate Region

When the Loop switch is enabled, this button duplicates the looped portion of the clip. When Loop is disabled, this button reads "Duplicate Region" and will duplicate everything between the Start and End points.

This button addresses one of the most common needs in MIDI programming, duplicating an entire pattern. A very common workflow is to program a one-bar loop and then double it and add variations to create a two-bar loop. This process can be repeated indefinitely, having the two-bar loop become four bars and so on.

# Quantizing Your Performance

*Quantizing* is the process of aligning events to a timing grid. When quantizing a MIDI clip, you're making sure that the notes are aligned (fully or partially) to the grid. Quantizing can be done either while you record or after the fact. Figures 5.20a and 5.20b show the effect of using quantization on a live performance.

If you want to quantize while recording, you'll have to visit the Record Quantization submenu (under the Edit menu). After you select a quantization value here, any recording you make will be perfectly aligned to the rhythmic subdivisions you have selected. If you're new to working with quantization, 1/16 works well for many situations.

**FIGURE 5.20A**  Here are some unquantized MIDI notes.
*Source:* Ableton

**FIGURE 5.20B**  The same part after quantizing. Notice how each note's left edge is aligned with one of the grid lines.
*Source:* Ableton

Of course, music does not always demand strict rhythmic quantization. Many musicians prefer to keep the natural feel of a performance, only using partial quantization or none at all. You can turn off Live's automatic quantizing by choosing No Quantization from the Record Quantization menu. For many situations, this is the best choice, since it's easy to quantize later if you choose.

## THE UNDO TWO-STEP

If you recorded a performance with Record Quantization turned on and you wish you hadn't, it's not a problem. Just use the Undo command and the quantization is removed. A second Undo will remove the recording entirely.

To quantize an existing clip, first select the notes you want to quantize. If no notes are selected, Live assumes you want to quantize the whole thing. Select Quantize Settings from the Edit menu (see Figure 5.21). If Quantize Settings is grayed out, click in the MIDI editor and try again.

**FIGURE 5.21**
The Quantize dialog box lets you tailor Live's quantization to your needs.
*Source:* Ableton

The first value at the top sets the quantize grid. Generally, this should be set to the smallest subdivision that occurs in the part. In other words, if you've played a part containing 1/8 notes and 1/16 notes, you'd select 1/16. If you select 1/8, the Quantize function will move the 1/16 notes to the closest 1/8 note and mess up the part. The Current Grid option will quantize to the size of the grid shown in the MIDI editor.

Below the Quantize selection is the Adjust Note selection, with two buttons labeled *Start* and *End*. By default, only Start is enabled. This means that Live will change only the start location of a note when it quantizes—the length of the note will remain the same. If you enable End as well, Live will make sure that the note ends on a grid subdivision, too. This is handy for rapid-fire synth bass sequences, because each note will be on beat *and* the same length. If you wanted, you could deselect Start, making Live fix only the end of each note.

The last parameter in the dialog box is the Amount value. By default, this is set to 100%, which forces every note to the nearest grid division. If you set this value to 50%, Live will move the notes only halfway to the grid. The result is a tighter performance, but one that is not completely rigid.

---

**PARTIAL QUANTIZING**

When you're programming drums, combining quantized and unquantized parts can work really well. Just select different drums before quantizing and experiment. For example, try quantizing the kick and snare parts in a drumbeat to 100% and leave the hi-hats unquantized. If the hi-hat feels too loose, try quantizing it to 50%.

---

After you've set up your quantize settings, you can immediately apply them to any MIDI clip without opening the Quantize window by using the Ctrl (Cmd)+U keyboard shortcut. When combined with the Current Grid setting in the Quantize dialog, this shortcut can be a real time-saver.

# Step Recording

Live offers yet another way of creating MIDI clips: step recording. Step recording allows you to place notes into a MIDI clip from your controller keyboard without having to perform them in real time. This technique can only be used to add notes to an existing MIDI clip, so you'll be using it to overdub notes either into a clip you've recorded or an empty clip you've created manually.

To do step recording, arm the MIDI track for recording and turn on the Preview switch in the MIDI editor. Now, while holding down notes or chords on your controller, press the right-arrow key to determine the length of the notes. Each press of the right arrow will make the note one grid segment longer. The right- and left-arrow keys are also used to navigate through the clip, so pressing the right arrow without holding down notes allows you to enter rests or skip ahead to another part of the clip entirely.

When in the MIDI map (see Chapter 11, "Remote Control"), you'll notice two arrows appear below the Fold switch in the MIDI editor. These can be remote-mapped to allow you to step back and forth through your MIDI clips from your controller, without using the arrow keys on your computer's keyboard.

# Program Change

Program Change messages are used to recall presets on the destination MIDI device. By setting the Program and Bank values in the Notes box (see Figure 5.22), each clip can recall a different preset from the same instrument when it is launched. Hardware instruments are typically configured so they automatically respond to program changes. Software instruments vary. Some will work automatically, while others may require special configuration in order to recall presets. Live's built-in instruments don't respond to program changes, so this is a technique for third-party plug-ins and hardware devices only.

**FIGURE 5.22**

Use the Program Change settings to automatically recall presets when a clip is launched.

*Source:* Ableton

A Program Change is a MIDI message with a value between 0 and 127 and refers to a memory location in your MIDI device's sound bank. The way a manufacturer maps the program message to the memory slots is entirely up to them, but generally a Program Change of 0 will cause the first sound on the instrument to be loaded. So, using the Program Change message, you can recall up to 128 presets.

But what if your device has more than 128 sounds? That's where the Bank Change message comes into play. A bank holds 128 programs. So you can recall any sound in your MIDI device by first specifying the containing bank followed by the program number. Some devices require that banks be specified with two numbers, the Bank and Sub-bank. Thus, the presence of the Sub setting below Bank in Figure 5.22.

# Importing and Exporting MIDI Files

Live stores all MIDI data and parameters for MIDI clips within the Live Set. You can see the individual MIDI clips and tracks within the Browser. While audio clips must play a specific audio file stored on a hard disk, the MIDI clips don't require any sort of external support file that you need to keep track of. When you import a MIDI file, Live copies the data from the MIDI file into the Live Set. Live will never use the original MIDI file again, so should that file be changed or lost, the Live Set will still play perfectly.

Live imports MIDI parts from Standard MIDI Files (SMFs), which come in two flavors: Type 0 and Type 1. Unless your MIDI file has only one part in it, Type 0 won't do you any good in Live—all the parts are squished into one track. Type 1, on the other hand, has the MIDI parts split into separate tracks for each instrument. If you view a multipart MIDI file in the Browser, you can open it like a folder and display each part. To import, just drag in the parts you want or use the Import MIDI File command from the Create menu.

If you've got a song in another software, or perhaps something stuck in an older hardware sequencer, and you want to transfer it to Live, SMFs will usually take care of the job. The format has been around for a long time, so you can be assured of compatibility; however, SMFs don't necessarily retain *everything* from a computer project. For example, application-specific features such as automation won't appear in an SMF export.

If you need to take the MIDI part from a clip and send it to another Live Set or a different program, you can export the MIDI data as an SMF. Select the clip and choose Export MIDI clip from Live's File menu. You'll be prompted to give a name and destination for the exported data. Choose a location and name and click Save.

# Audio Clips

You may be surprised to discover just how creative you can get with audio in Live. Obviously, if you're going to be recording live instruments and vocals, audio clips will be a big part of your life. But even if MIDI is the backbone of your compositional process, you'll still find that manipulating audio can produce a broad array of weird and wonderful results. Live's warping features can be used to synchronize any sample to the tempo of your track. And, of course, if you're going to be DJing with Live, you'll need to have a solid understanding of working with audio.

Before digging into the details of warping, let's take a look at the basics of the Sample box (see Figure 5.23).

**FIGURE 5.23**
The Sample box contains controls concerning audio speed, pitch, volume, and warping. In the Arrangement, you'll notice that the Fade switch does not appear, and there's an extra switch marked Slave.
*Source:* Ableton

## Basic Sample Controls

At the top of the Sample box, you'll see the name of the audio file referenced by the clip. Click on it to show the file in the Browser. There are three simple controls below to get familiar with right away: Transpose, Detune, and Gain.

### Transpose and Detune

The Transpose and Detune controls (see Figure 5.23) change the playback tuning of the clip without changing its playback speed. Transpose shifts pitch in semitones, while Detune adjusts it in small steps known as *cents* (one-hundredth of a semitone).

While transposing generally produces artifacts in the audio, small shifts in pitch can often be made with acceptable sound quality, as long as you use the appropriate Warp mode for the audio you're transposing. The Complex Pro mode can produce some very high-quality results when transposing, at the cost of high CPU usage. There's more about Warp modes in the "Warping" section.

**GOING WAY OUT**

Although Transpose is useful to make a loop match the key of your song, you'll discover that wild new sounds can be found by tweaking the tuning up or down by multiple octaves and experimenting with different Warp modes. Once a sample is altered this much, new textures and sounds can emerge. Take time to experiment!

## Clip Gain

The Clip Gain slider, which is unlabeled and located just to the right of the Transpose knob, is used to adjust the individual volume of a clip. This is a very convenient way to balance audio levels without using automation. Just bear in mind that you're changing the volume of the audio *before* it flows through effect devices. This is particularly important when using gain-sensitive effects (such as compression and distortion), which produce different results depending on the volume of the incoming audio.

# Warping

*Warping* is the term for Live's time-stretching and compressing technology. The technique of warping an audio file to match the tempo, groove, and pitch of a song involves many parameters, but the most important of these is the Warp button at the top of Figure 5.24. With Warp off, the clip plays the audio at its original tempo. However, once Warp is engaged, you can change the playback speed and pitch of the audio independently, as well as make adjustments to its timing and groove.

**FIGURE 5.24**

The warping controls of the Sample box. When a different Warp mode is selected, different controls will appear below the mode menu.

*Source:* Ableton

In order for Live to work its warping magic, it needs some information about the audio it's working with. To match a file to the current master tempo, Live needs to know the original tempo of the audio so that it can determine how much to speed it up or slow it down. For music with a completely steady tempo, this is a simple matter. However, in cases where the music wasn't played to a click track or programmed with a sequencer, it's a bit more complicated, since the actual tempo changes from bar to bar. It might only fluctuate by a fraction of a BPM, but it still matters.

When working with short, properly cut loops, Live can typically determine the necessary information for warping automatically. However, there are many cases where you'll need to specify where important timing events occur using Warp Markers (see Figure 5.25). You might do this to move an individual note with bad timing, or even to dramatically change the timing and sonically mangle a chunk of audio. If you're trying to sync up a song with a constantly fluctuating tempo, this can require quite a few Warp Markers, but don't worry. Live's *Auto-Warp* feature can usually be coaxed into doing most of the work for you.

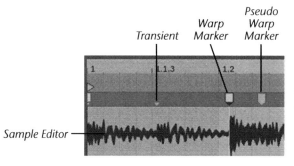

**FIGURE 5.25**

Double-click to create Warp Markers—the key to total timing control (or intentional timing madness!)

*Source:* Ableton

# Warp Markers

Warp Markers are like "pins" that fix audio events to a specific moment in time. An audio clip always has a minimum of one Warp Marker, which by default is placed at the very beginning. In the simplest situations, this is all that's needed. In more complex scenarios, numerous Warp Markers can be used to radically reshape audio, changing the timing and duration of numerous individual segments. If you have an audio file that has sloppy timing, you can use a few Warp Markers to move individual hits to just where you want them.

Setting up Warp Markers can be done manually or by using Live's Auto-Warp technology. When working with short audio files, such as prerecorded loops, Live automatically detects the tempo with a high degree of accuracy. If you're a DJ, you'll probably be using Auto-Warp extensively to prep your music library to play back in sync. For rhythmically imprecise material or material that you want to change dramatically, you'll be creating and moving Warp Markers manually.

When a piece of audio requires manual adjustment to get it to sync up (or to get it mangled to perfection), these are the tools you'll be working with. First, let's get our terms straight:

▶ **Warp Marker:** Locks a segment of audio to a location on the timeline. They appear as yellow markers directly above the waveform display. Warp Markers can be created by double-clicking just above the sample editor.

▶ **Transient:** Transients appear as small gray triangles above the sample editor. They indicate accents, such as the beginning of a note or a drum hit. Transients are automatically placed by Live, and can also be manually inserted or deleted from the editor's context menu or by Alt (Option)+click.

▶ **Pseudo Warp Marker:** When the mouse is moved over a Transient, a gray Pseudo Warp Marker appears. When dragged, these markers will become permanent Warp Markers if there are any Warp Markers to the right. Otherwise, they can be dragged to adjust the timing of the clip, and will return to being normal Transients when released.

To correct the timing of the audio shown in Figure 5.26a, hover the mouse above the snare hit right after beat 1.2. After the transient turns into a Pseudo Warp Marker, drag it to the left so that it lands on beat 1.2. Notice that this moves not just the snare hit, but also the audio before and after it. The only place the audio doesn't move is beat 1, where Live has placed a Warp Marker (see Figure 5.26b). The rest of the audio stretches like a rubber band, while the Warp Marker at beat 1 acts like a pin, holding it in place.

**FIGURE 5.26A** Transient markers temporarily become Pseudo Warp Markers when you hold the mouse over them.
*Source:* Ableton

**FIGURE 5.26B**
When the snare hit is moved to beat 1.2, the hits to either side are also moved. All of the transients now line up with the grid.
*Source:* Ableton

Now, let's say you want to create a rhythmic variation by moving the kick drum at 1.1.3 (see Figure 5.27a). If you use a Pseudo Warp Marker again, you'll just end up moving the audio off the grid, undoing the work you did in the first step. Double-clicking to create a Warp Marker at beat 1.2 will solve this problem (see Figure 5.27b).

This process can be repeated indefinitely to put every hit just where you want it. There's also a shortcut that makes it easy to move any snippet without worrying about throwing off the timing of the surrounding audio. Hold down Ctrl (Cmd) before double-clicking to create a new Warp Marker, and Live will also create Warp Markers at the preceding and following transients.

**FIGURE 5.27A** If you want to move the kick drum hit at 1.1.3 without moving everything else, you need Warp Markers.
*Source:* Ableton

**FIGURE 5.27B**
The Warp Marker at 1.2 locks down the audio from that point on, making it possible to move the kick drum, as shown here.
*Source:* Ableton

While it's important to know how to manipulate markers manually, Live has a couple of different methods for automatically fixing timing and creating markers: Auto-Warp and Quantize. In the upcoming sections, you'll learn to work with these and save yourself a lot of time.

### WARP 'EM ALL

If you're looking to do some serious mangling with Warp Markers, drag in the editor to select a range (or use Ctrl [Cmd]+A to select the whole clip) and use Insert Warp Marker from the Create menu. A Warp Marker will be created for each transient in the range.

## Auto Warp

When working with longer audio files, Live uses a technology called *Auto-Warp* to analyze the file and insert Warp Markers where needed. This process, however, is not perfect, and you may still have to adjust the Warp Markers manually. There are two ways to use auto warping: first, let Live do it automatically, and second, manually invoke it using the Warp commands from the context menus.

By default, Live will analyze and add Warp Markers whenever you add a long audio file to your set. In the Record/Warp/Launch tab of the Preferences screen, you can disable this behavior by setting "Auto-Warp Long Files" to Off. Depending on the material you're warping, you may find it quicker to turn this setting off and manually invoke Auto-Warp instead (see Figure 5.28). When you do it this way, you can give Live hints about the contents of the file and how to place the Warp Markers.

**FIGURE 5.28**

Right-click in or above the sample editor to select a Warp command.
*Source:* Ableton

## TEMPO TIP

Before using Auto-Warp, it's a good idea to set the tempo of your Set to the approximate tempo of the audio you're importing. For example, if you're preparing a techno DJ set, try setting the tempo to 127 BPM. (If you're not sure what tempo to use, tap the tempo in while playing the audio back unwarped.) This prevents Live from detecting a tempo that is half or double the desired result. Live uses the current tempo as a hint, so if you import the techno tracks I just mentioned while Live's tempo is set to 70 BPM, they'll end up warped as being 63.5 BPM. They'll be in sync with the clock, but will play back at double their original speed when Live is set to 127 BPM! (This may cause you to lose your residency at the club.) To fix this problem if it occurs, use the Half or Double BPM buttons explained earlier.

The Warp commands are accessed by right-clicking in or above the sample editor display and selecting one of the following options.

▶ **Warp from Here:** This tells Live to analyze the clip starting at the selected location and continuing to the right. It will attempt to detect tempo based on the audio, tracking fluctuations and placing Warp Markers as needed. Everything to the left of the selected marker will remain intact.

▶ **Warp from Here (Start at X BPM):** This option uses the current project tempo as a starting point and attempts to detect any tempo variations that occur later. If you've already determined the approximate tempo of the audio file using Tap Tempo, this option will often yield good results when the standard Warp command fails.

▶ **Warp from Here (Straight):** This mode attempts to set the tempo of the clip using one Warp Marker only. This should be used only when warping music that you know to have a completely steady tempo. This command is very handy because it prevents Auto-Warp from becoming confused by syncopations which otherwise might cause it to incorrectly detect a tempo fluctuation and place incorrect Warp Markers.

▶ **Warp X BPM from Here:** This simply sets the current Warp Marker to the current tempo of the Set. If there are any Warp Markers to the right, they will be erased in the process.

▶ **Warp as X-Bar Loop:** If you already know that the file you're working with has an even number of bars, you can select this option to automatically turn the clip into an even loop. The number shown here will depend on the current project tempo. If Live determines that it will have to do the least amount of warping to turn the clip into a one-bar loop, as opposed to a two-bar loop, the program will display "1" in place of "X" in the menu item above. If you increase the project tempo by almost double, Live will see that it is now easier to make the clip a two-bar loop and will suggest that by showing "2" in place of "1" in the menu option.

Note that there are also a number of other options in this context menu to help you work with your sample files, including the important "Set 1.1.1 Here" command. This command will renumber the grid to start from beat 1 at the selected location.

## Quantize

One of the cool features that comes with Live is the ability to quantize audio clips, much the way you can with MIDI (covered earlier in this chapter). To get started, select Quantize Settings from the Edit menu. If Quantize Settings is grayed out, click in the sample editor and try again.

The Quantize To setting specifies the location on the grid to which transients should be moved. In other words, if this value is set to 1/16, Live will find each transient most closely adjacent to the 1/16 note divisions of the grid and automatically move them there. Setting Amount to a value less than 100% will yield partial quantization. In the prior example, 70% quantization would cause each accent to be moved 70% of the way to the nearest 1/16th, rather than all of the way.

Once you're done with the Quantize Settings set, just click OK. You can also use the Quantize command from the Edit menu to apply quantization to a clip using the existing Quantize settings. By default, quantization is applied to the entire clip. To quantize a portion, select a range of time in the sample editor before quantizing.

## Setting Warp Markers for Multiple Clips

If you have two or more clips based on audio files of exactly the same length, Live will allow you to set Warp Markers across multiple clips simultaneously. This is especially convenient when you are working with a multitrack recording of a performance and you want to give all the tracks exactly the same warp timing.

To do this, select multiple clips before making warp adjustments. The sample editor will show the waveform for the clip selected last. The underlying audio files of the clips must be *exactly* the same length. If they aren't, the sample editor will display a message indicating that clips of different lengths are selected.

Let's say you want to sync a live band recording to Live's tempo. First, turn off Auto Warp Long Samples in the Record/Warp/Launch tab of Live's preferences. If you don't do this, you'll probably have to turn off the Warp switch in each clip because this technique won't work if the clips start out with different Warp Markers. Import the files into separate tracks in Arrangement View.

Select each clip, saving the rhythmically clearest track for last—that's the one that will appear in the sample editor. You need something that will give you some good visual cues for setting the Warp Markers. A kick drum track is probably your best bet, but obviously it depends on the material you're

**FIGURE 5.29**
When multiple clips are selected, the sample editor displays the waveform for the one selected last. Also notice the striped pattern in the title bar of the Sample box.

working with. Create and move Warp Markers as necessary. When you're done, you'll see they have been applied to all of the tracks.

### WARPING WORK-AROUND

You can still warp multiple clips, even if the underlying audio files aren't of the same length. You just have to generate new audio files first. Line up the files in the Arrangement View and trim them until they are the same length. If you need to make a clip longer, hold down Shift and highlight both the clip and the necessary amount of empty space in the timeline. Then use the Consolidate command to write new audio files of the specified length.

# Warp Settings

The Sample box (refer to Figure 5.23) contains a variety of settings and tools for warped clips. The BPM controls assist you with getting audio synced up, while the Warp controls are used for optimizing sound quality and doing sound design.

## Segment BPM

Segment BPM calculates the tempo of the audio in a clip, based on the position of its Warp Markers. This value is then used by Live to set the playback speed. Let's start off with a simple example. If Live's tempo is set to 70 BPM and Segment BPM is 70, then Live will not change the playback speed of the audio. If the tempo is changed to 140 BPM, however, Live would know from the Segment BPM value that it needs to play the audio at double its original speed to match the master tempo.

When a clip has more than one Warp Marker, Segment BPM refers to the segment of audio in between two Warp Markers. Click on a Warp Marker to display the Segment BPM of the audio in between the selected Warp Marker and the one preceding it.

For an audio clip with a completely steady tempo, no additional Warp Markers are necessary, and the Segment BPM will reflect the original tempo of the entire clip. In this case, type the original tempo of the audio into this box and Live will match it to the master tempo. You might need to adjust the clip's Start position so that it's aligned with the grid.

## Half/Double BPM

The two buttons below the Segment BPM window will either double or halve the tempo of the clip. Pressing the *2 button will multiply every Segment BPM by two. The result is that the clip will play at half speed. This may be counterintuitive, but remember that you're not telling Live to "play this clip at twice the speed," but rather you're telling it "the actual tempo of this audio is twice as fast." Pressing :2 will have the opposite effect. This is helpful when Live incorrectly guesses the length and tempo of a new audio clip. For example, if Live identifies a 170 BPM drum 'n bass loop as 85 BPM, a click of the "*2" button will fix this immediately.

## Warp Modes

Choosing the correct Warp modes is essential for clean, musical warping. The Warp mode determines how Live approaches stretching and pitch-shifting an audio clip. There are six different Warp modes: Beats, Tones, Texture, Re-Pitch, Complex, and Complex Pro. Each mode features special controls that appear when the mode is selected. Also, don't forget that you can simply turn off the Warp switch to play the sample at its default speed and pitch.

### Beats

Beats mode is a great mode for rhythmic loops, percussive samples, and even entire songs. You will usually want to use Beats mode with percussion, drums, and sounds characteristically containing minimal sustain. This includes samples that you might not think of as beats, such as a funk rhythm guitar part or perhaps a minimal techno track. When Beats mode is used with sounds that are too textured or lack rhythmic definition, you may hear artifacts.

## DEFINITION OF TRANSIENT

The Transient setting is a critical element of Live's beat-warping functionality. But what is a transient to begin with? A transient is the short, sharp attack portion of a sound. A transient occurs at the instant a stick hits a drum or a string is plucked. The soft attack of bowed strings may have no transient. In warping terminology, *transient* is often used to mean a chunk of audio (such as an entire snare hit) with a transient at the beginning.

Beats mode looks at your audio as a series of segments, the size of which is determined by the Preserve menu. The default value in the Preserve menu—Transients—uses the location of the clip's transients to time-compress or stretch the audio. Conceptually, the way this works is quite simple. When Live detects transients in a drum loop, it is identifying each hit in relationship to its position in the bar: this kick drum occurs on beat 1, this snare drum occurs at beat 2, and so on. Live then knows where to put each drum hit, regardless of the tempo, just like it does with a MIDI file.

For most rhythmic material, preserving transients will produce the best results. The other options in the Preserve menu provide compatibility with earlier versions of Live and allow you to tell the Warp engine to look at the audio as a series of evenly spaced segments (such as 1/8 or 1/16). If you have a one-bar loop with the Transient value set to 1/16, Live's default behavior will be to treat the file as if it were 16 equally sized segments. Live then plays these chunks back as if they were sixteenth notes at the current tempo.

Next, let's further examine what happens to your audio when you speed it up or slow it down. If the beat being warped needs to be sped up to match the tempo of Live, the segments will be moved closer together. As this happens, Live will time-compress the end of each segment, making the duration of each drum hit slightly shorter, so the decay doesn't get cut off due to the faster tempo. If the beat is getting slowed down, Live has to either stretch out the playback of each segment or leave a space between segments, since the original decay of the hit won't be long enough to fill the space at the slower tempo.

To stretch out the decay, Beats mode loops the last portion of the segment—the fading sound of the transient. If you're thinking that this might end up sounding a little strange, you're right. It is, however, the best solution, given that Live is doing all of this time stretching in real time. That said, it is generally easier to speed beats up without noticeable artifacts than it is to slow them down.

Live gives you full control over how this looping is done via the Transient Loop Mode menu (see Figure 5.30).

**FIGURE 5.30**
Transient Loop Mode and Transient Envelope have a big impact on the results when changing the tempo or pitch of a clip. *Source:* Ableton

▶ **No Loop** (single arrow): Live plays each segment to its end without doing anything to fill the space until the next segment plays. This yields extremely clean results (because there's no looping), but it may leave audible spaces in between each note or drum hit. Let your ears decide whether or not this is acceptable or desirable.

▶ **Loop Forward** (double forward arrows): Loops the decay of each segment forward. This mode tends to produce glitchier results and works more like an effect.

▶ **Loop Back-and-Forth** (bidirectional arrows): Live loops the decay of the segment forward and backward in order to fill empty space at slowed-down tempos. Generally speaking, this mode will yield the most artifact-free stretching. This is the default setting.

The numeric box next to Transient Loop Mode is the Transient Envelope. This value determines if a fade should be applied to each audio segment. In No Loop mode, reducing this value can be used to create dramatic gating effects, even when you're playing the audio at its original tempo. Playing with this value is highly recommended! When Transient Loop Mode is set to either of the looped modes, lowering the envelope tends to produce less dramatic results, but can still be very useful for smoothing out time-stretching artifacts.

## Tones

Tones mode is based on a technique called *granular resynthesis.* As a file is played back, it is broken into grains. The idea is that when you loop a grain, you get a continuous tone that represents that sound "frozen in time." By splitting the audio into grains and spreading the grains apart, Live slows down the tempo of the audio playback; however, since each grain is still played at its original pitch, there will be empty space between each grain. Looping each grain fills space to time-stretch the file.

Of course, looping each grain isn't necessary when speeding up playback of a file. As the grains are brought closer together, they will overlap one another. Each grain will therefore cut off the one before it, resulting in a continuous sound, but with one playing faster than before. For this reason, you'll probably find that you have better success speeding up loops or transposing them down (both methods use the same process) than slowing them down or pitching them up, which requires looping the grains.

With careful setting of the Grain Size value, you can achieve nearly transparent warping. Tones such as bass guitars, synthesizers, vocals, keyboards, or other long-sustaining instruments will usually sound much less processed when playing in Live's Tones mode. You can adjust Live's Grain Size to help reduce undesirable audio artifacts.

## Texture

Texture mode is built for atmospheric sounds with no definite pitch, but it can also work well on other complex sounds, such as orchestral samples and keyboard pads. Like Tones mode, Texture mode is based on granular resynthesis. In an effort to cloud the repetitive artifacts from looping grains, a Flux value is added that, when increased, allows Live to randomly change the grain sizes used in the process. This also adds a sense of stereo imaging to mono files.

## Re-Pitch

Re-Pitch mode is more like vinyl DJing—Live will alter the pitch of the sample, depending upon the playback speed. This mode produces no artifacts and thus usually sounds the best, especially if the sample is played close to its original tempo. Re-Pitch merely alters the file playback speed, which results in pitch changes.

## Complex and Complex Pro

Designed for use on entire songs, the Complex modes are the ones to go for when none of the other modes produce sufficient quality. Complex Pro also comes in particularly handy when transposing vocals, since it allows you to change the pitch (within reason) without making the singer sound like a chipmunk or a troll.

The magic of these modes comes at the cost of higher CPU usage, with Complex Pro being the more power hungry of the two. Unless you're strapped for computer power, or you like the artifacts produced by Complex mode, you should generally use Complex Pro for its higher sound quality. Just be aware that the Pro version can strain Live enough to produce glitches in the audio output without the CPU meter reporting abnormally high usage. If your computer is having a tough time keeping up with the added load of the Complex mode, you can Freeze the track (see Chapter 7, "Using Effects and Instruments") or resample the clip (see Chapter 6, "Tracks and Signal Routing").

# Tempo Master/Slave

If you are in the Arrangement View, you will see another control just above Seg. BPM: the Tempo Master/Slave switch (see Figure 5.31a). This control allows you to designate any clip as the tempo master by toggling its Master/Slave switch to Master. The current tempo master clip will always play as if Warp were *off,* but will cause the master tempo to follow the timing of the clip's Warp Markers instead of the other way around (see Figure 5.31b). This means that all warped clips will follow the timing fluctuations of the Master clip.

Let's say that you have a piano recording that you want to add some additional programmed parts and loops to. It's a well-played part with a mostly steady tempo, but since it wasn't recorded to a click track, there is some

**FIGURE 5.31A** Master/Slave only appears in Arrangement View. Click the switch to toggle between Slave and Master.

**FIGURE 5.31B** When an Arrangement clip is set to Master, pseudo tempo automation appears in the Master track based on the location of the clip's Warp Markers.

natural variation to the time. One way you could use warping in this context is to straighten out the timing of the piano track by adding Warp Markers so the piano lines up perfectly with the sequencer tempo. However, if the piano has a nice feel, this could make the whole recording feel rigid and dull.

Instead, you could add a Warp Marker to the downbeat of each bar in the piano part and set the clip to Master. Now, Live's tempo will breathe with the pianist's rhythm, and all of your MIDI clips and warped loops will breathe along with it!

If you toggle the Master/Slave switch back to Slave or delete the clip, the tempo automation will stop, and the former tempo will resume. If you want to keep the tempo information from the clip, right-click on the Control Bar's Tempo field and choose the Unslave Tempo Automation command. All clips will then be set to Slave, and the tempo information will become standard automation in the Master track.

Bear in mind that if you set more than one clip to be the Tempo Master, the bottommost one will be in control, and the others will be ignored. When Live's *EXT* switch (visible only when an external tempo source is enabled) is enabled, the Master/Slave switch has no effect and will appear to be disabled in all clips.

# Advanced Clip Settings

The two rows of buttons that run across the Sample box handle a variety of advanced settings for audio clips. It's good to be familiar with them, but depending on how you use Live, you may not find yourself using them very much.

## Edit

Clicking the Edit button will open the audio file in the sample editor you have selected in File/Folder preferences. Audio editors are useful for performing a variety of operations on your audio files, particularly when you want to edit *destructively.* Now, this may not sound very appealing at first, but there are times that you want to make a change that permanently affects the audio file itself. Modifying the Sample properties in Live only changes that audio file's playback characteristics. That's why it's called *nondestructive editing.*

While you are editing your sample file, the Clip View's waveform display will say Sample Offline. When you finish editing, just save your changes and return to Live. Bear in mind that every clip in every Set based on this audio file will be affected as well!

## Save

By default, adding an audio file to Live causes an analysis (.asd) file to be created in the same folder as the audio file. This file contains basic information about the file, including the data needed to draw the waveform display in the Clip View. When you click Save, *all* of the current clip settings (warping, loop settings, and so on) are written into the analysis file. The next time you add the audio file to a Set, these clip settings will be recalled automatically.

## Reverse

Live's Reverse feature (the Rev. button) is not instantaneous—don't expect it to be. It is, however, a whole lot of fun when used properly. Click the Reverse button, and Live will create a new audio file—a reversed version of the original. This new audio file will be named the same as the original, but it will have the letter "R" added to the end.

Okay, so it's not truly a Reverse button, as in "play the sample backward." Instead, the Reverse button means "play a backward version of the sample." This means you'll have to wait for the "R" file to be made the first time you reverse, but from that point on, Live will just choose the original or reversed file to play, allowing you to switch directions almost instantaneously. Because of the nature of the Reverse feature, you may want to avoid using this button during live performances. Instead, I recommend you make two clips: one normal and one reversed.

## Hi-Q

This button simply switches the audio clip between high-quality and low-quality interpolation (used for transposition). If this button is on, the clip will play using better pitch shifting and resampling algorithms, but it will also place a slightly heavier strain on your CPU. I recommend leaving this option on for all clips (setting Default SR & Pitch Conversion to "High Quality" in Preferences → Audio will make this the default) and turning it off only if you have a slower computer, and you need to save every bit of CPU power.

## Fade

To help an audio file loop seamlessly (no clicks or pops when the file loops around), Live can perform a quick (4ms) volume fade at the end of the clip. I recommend leaving this option on as the default, unless the downbeat transient seems too quiet. It is possible that the fade can soften the initial attack of the downbeat (for instance, shaving the attack of a one-shot sample), so you may need to turn this off from time to time. Because the Arrangement View contains a more sophisticated set of tools for creating fades, this option is not available there.

## RAM

Live streams audio files from disk as they play. With each additional audio clip that plays, the computer will have to stream another file from disk. Your hard disk can stream only a finite amount of data per second, and when Live requires more than the disk can provide, you get audio dropouts. When you hear audio problems, check to see if the Hard Disk Overload Indicator (the letter "D") in the right-hand corner of the Control Bar is lighting up.

To alleviate this, you can load audio clips into your computer's RAM, which is accessed much faster than the hard disk, by pressing the RAM button. Remember to be conscious of the size of the files you're loading into RAM. Even if you're using only 10 seconds of an 8-minute file, Live will still load the whole file into memory. The problem with this feature is that your operating system may decide to swap contents from RAM to hard disk. Live has no control over when this happens, so you may not always see the performance benefit you expect from using the RAM switch. If rapid access to audio files is a major concern for you, purchasing a solid-state drive (SSD) is probably a better option.

# Clip Modulation

To the right of the Sample box (for audio clips) or the Notes box (for MIDI clips), you'll find the Envelopes box. (If it's hidden, click the "E" icon in the lower left-hand corner to reveal it.) Click in the title bar of the Envelopes box to make the editor display envelopes. To return to the standard display, click in the title bar of either the Sample box or the Notes box.

Within the editor, there are two different types of envelopes that can be edited: automation and modulation. Automation envelopes were covered in Chapters 3 and 4. Modulation envelopes are very similar in that they can be used to automatically change device or mixer parameters, but they are very different in a few other respects.

First, modulation is *relative* as opposed to automation, which is *absolute.* In Figure 5.32a, you'll see an automation envelope for the mixer volume. The first breakpoint is highlighted, and a box appears above showing that the breakpoint is set to a value of –6dB.

In Figure 5.32b, you'll see a modulation envelope for the same parameter. It's roughly the same size and shape, but notice that the value displayed for the first breakpoint is 70%. What's going on here?

**FIGURE 5.32A** Automation is used to set absolute values.
*Source:* Ableton

**FIGURE 5.32B** Modulation makes relative changes to a control's state. Modulation envelopes are displayed with a shaded area below to differentiate them from automation.
*Source:* Ableton

When you automate a control, you're specifying absolute values, such as "set the volume to −6dB." When you modulate a control, you're specifying a relative change to the control's current value, such as "set the volume to 70%." For most device and mixer controls, the current position is considered to be 100%, and you can modulate it all the way down to its lowest possible value, which is considered 0%. (That means you can't modulate a control that's turned all the way down: 100% of zero is zero!).

Therefore, unlike automated controls, you can freely make manual adjustments to modulated controls. Manually changing an automated control causes the automation to be disabled, while manually changing a modulated control simply causes the range of the modulation to change.

Another feature of modulation envelopes is that they can be used to tweak some properties of audio clips, such as the transposition and clip gain. You can even modulate the clip's playback position (Sample Offset) as a way to create variations and glitches.

To get started, first select the clip you want to add modulation to. Then right-click on the control you want to modulate and select "Show Modulation" from the context menu (see Figure 5.33a). You'll then be able to draw the modulation you want in the editor (see Figure 5.33b). Clip modulation can't be recorded like automation—you have to create it manually.

With a few exceptions, anything that can be automated can be modulated as well. The editing techniques for modulation are identical to automation. You'll be using breakpoints and Draw Mode as explained in Chapter 4. Once you've created modulation, it will be accessible from the Control Chooser. In

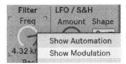

**FIGURE 5.33A** Show Modulation reveals the modulation editor in the Clip View. In this example, we're adjusting the Frequency parameter of Auto Filter.
*Source:* Ableton

**FIGURE 5.33B** Use the editor to create modulation. Once the modulation is programmed, you can get back to it easily from the Control Chooser.
*Source:* Ableton

Figure 5.33b, notice the item called *Frequency Modulation*, which reveals the modulation envelope for the Frequency control. Above it, there's another called *Frequency*, which reveals the automation envelope.

When modulation is affecting a parameter, it doesn't directly change the knob, slider, or number box the way automation would. Instead, it makes a subtler indication. Knobs will highlight the area of the knob's range that is being modulated, while sliders will display a small dot indicating the current modulated value.

### WARP AND STRETCH

Clip envelopes can also be moved and resized using Warp Markers and Stretch Markers, both of which appear as handles directly above the envelope editor.

A final, and very important, difference between automation and modulation is the relationship to the Arrangement View. When Session clips containing automation envelopes are recorded into the Arrangement, the automation is recorded into the timeline and no longer appears in the Clip View. Modulation, on the other hand, remains in the clip. This is because modulation and automation can actually be used simultaneously. For example, you could have automation slowly sweeping a filter's cutoff frequency from low to high, while the clip's modulation moves the frequency above and below the automated value in a rhythmic pattern.

### WARP AND STRETCH

Here's another way to get to Clip Modulation: use the Device Chooser and Control Chooser to show automation for a control; then right-click in the editor and select Show Modulation from the context menu.

## Modulating Audio Clip Properties

As mentioned previously, it's possible to modulate properties of audio clips. These deserve special mention since they're fundamentally different than the device and mixer adjustments discussed in Chapter 4. Revealing the modulation for clip properties is easy. Just select Clip in the Device Chooser, and they'll appear in the menu below.

## Volume

The Volume Modulation envelope changes the clip's gain. It provides an easy way to quickly cut chunks out of a loop or make small dynamic changes. Because it doesn't interfere with any automation or manual volume changes you may make to the track, it's very simple to use at any point in the production process. (see Figure 5.34).

**FIGURE 5.34** This modulation silences every other 1/8th note chunk.
*Source:* Ableton

## Transposition

The Transposition Modulation envelope will modulate the location of the Transpose knob, allowing you to program pitch changes, slides, or entire harmonic progressions for the clip. Because changing the pitch of a clip often produces interesting artifacts, this can be used as a sound design tool as well. Transposition begins as a line running across the center of the editor. Every line above zero is one semitone up, while every line below zero is a semitone down, as seen in Figure 5.35.

**FIGURE 5.35** Transposition can be modulated up or down by 48 semitones. Don't forget to try it on drum loops.
*Source:* Ableton

Be aware that to make smooth pitch slides, you'll have to be using a Warp mode other than Beats, which only allows one transposition change per transient. Also notice that you can scroll the range of the editor vertically by dragging the scale at the left, or you can enlarge the editor (by dragging upward at the top) to reveal the full range of +/−48 semitones.

## Sample Offset

Sample Offset allows you to manipulate the clip's playback position as it plays back. The horizontal grid lines represent sixteenth notes. The area above the centerline moves the playback position forward, while the area below moves it backward (see Figure 5.36). Sample Offset only works when a clip's Warp mode is set to Beats.

**FIGURE 5.36**

This Sample Offset modulation causes the first drum hit to repeat four times. The first step down causes playback to jump back one sixteenth, the second step causes a jump of two sixteenths, and so on.

*Source:* Ableton

Bear in mind that the value in the Preserve menu will determine the size of the chunks that get offset. If Preserve is set to Transients or 1/4, you'll get some unusual results if you make a lot of sixteenth note offsets. However, unusual results are generally what you're going for with this envelope, so take your time and experiment. If you're looking to do some meticulous micro-editing of your beats, you'll be happier doing it in the Arrangement View.

## Grain Size and Flux Modulation

These two specialized modulations work in conjunction with the Tones and Texture Warp modes. These parameters affect how the Warp engine handles pitch and timing changes, so don't expect these modulations to produce much result unless you're also doing some dramatic changes to pitch and/or tempo. Grain Size can be modulated when the clip is set to Tones or Texture; Flux modulation only works with Texture mode.

# MIDI Controller Envelopes

In addition to all of the types of automation and modulation discussed so far, MIDI clips also have the ability to send standard MIDI control messages, such as Pitch Bend, Modulation, Volume, and Foot Pedal (sustain). Control messages can be recorded from a MIDI controller during any recording, regardless of whether or not Automation Arm is enabled. That's because technically they are not automation at all—these messages are recorded as MIDI data, just like the notes are. For this reason, MIDI control messages also can't be viewed or edited in the track display of the Arrangement. They appear only within the clip.

To reveal controller envelopes, select "MIDI Ctrl" in the Device Chooser. The Control Chooser will then display a long list of MIDI control messages (see Figure 5.37).

**FIGURE 5.37**
MIDI controller envelopes can be edited just like standard automation.
*Source:* Ableton

When you look through the list of available MIDI controllers, you'll see some of them have already been named, such as Volume, Breath, Pan, and Expression. This is because part of the MIDI standard defines certain controller numbers for certain musical tasks. Controller 10 is generally Pan. Controller 7 is usually Volume, and so on. Whether these controllers actually have any effect will be determined by the MIDI device on the receiving end. Just about any virtual or hardware instrument will respond to pitch bend and modulation, but beyond that you'll need to look at your MIDI device's manual, specifically the MIDI implementation chart (usually at the end of the manual), to see a list of the MIDI controllers and messages for the instrument.

# Unlinked Clip Envelopes

Until this point, we've been talking about editing loops of a given length. After all, a loop is, by definition, a repeating sample or phrase. That is just what loops do—they loop. And by default, each envelope in a clip is the same length as the clip itself, allowing you to create repetitive automation or modulation patterns that recur every time the clip repeats itself. However, by *unlinking* an envelope, you can create modulations or automations with lengths and loop points independent of the clip, which gives you a mind-boggling array of options.

Sometimes, you may want to extend a given loop beyond its original borders. For instance, you have a repetitive two-bar drum loop, and you really wish that you had an eight-bar loop to make it sound more lifelike and less repetitive. One way to accomplish this is by *unlinking* the clip's envelopes. By changing the length of an envelope so that it is different from the length of the clip, you can introduce just this kind of variation to your loops.

To unlink an envelope, click the Link/Unlink switch so it reads "Unlinked" (see Figure 5.38). When you do this, you'll notice that the audio or MIDI note display disappears from the editor, because the envelope is now an independent entity with its own length and looping properties. These points are adjusted using a loop brace and familiar looking Start, End, Position, and Length controls in the Envelopes box—but in this case, you're affecting the envelope only. Feel free to make an unlinked envelope of eight bars over a

**FIGURE 5.38** The Start/End and Loop properties of the envelope are enabled when Unlinked is activated. The clip shown is an eight-bar loop but the envelope is a two-beat loop.
*Source:* Ableton

two-bar loop, or one that starts on beat one, goes for four bars, and then starts looping.

Bear in mind that each envelope, be it modulation or automation, can be linked or unlinked as you choose. This means you can have envelopes of many different lengths all happening simultaneously. You can also create envelopes of odd lengths that will change their position in relationship to the loop points of the clip over many bars. Imagine taking a two-bar MIDI clip and modulating a synth's filter with an envelope 7 bars long, while modulating the parameters of a delay and a distortion using envelopes 3 and 5 bars long. To the average listener, the pattern would be nearly impossible to discern, and the modulations would sound random.

# Audio to MIDI

Live provides several ways to start with an audio clip and create a MIDI clip from it. Slice to New MIDI Track provides an easy way to chop up a sample and trigger it via MIDI, while the various Convert modes actually analyze the musical information in the audio and generate a MIDI clip based on it.

## Convert to New MIDI Track

This feature comes in three flavors. There's a method optimized for melody, one for harmony (chords), and another specifically for drums. What these functions do is analyze the audio clip to detect pitches and transients and generate a MIDI sequence from them. This sequence can then be used to trigger the sound of your choice. So, for example, you could record yourself singing a melody and then convert it to a MIDI track and have the melody played by a synthesizer.

You shouldn't expect this feature to extract parts from fully mixed songs. It's much better suited to converting individual parts. Depending on the material, you may not get a high degree of precision in the conversions. The conversion process is very sensitive to a wide variety of factors, and it's better to expect a conversion to give you a starting point, rather than a finished product.

On the other hand, as a tool for generating raw material that you'll make new parts out of, you may have a lot of fun with this feature. Take a melody and convert it using the drum's algorithm or the harmony algorithm, for example. Obviously, not everything you get from intentionally misusing the technology will be great, but occasionally it will get the creative juices flowing.

The basics of using these commands are very simple. Right-click on an audio clip and choose Convert Harmony to New MIDI Track, Convert Melody to New MIDI Track, or Convert Drums to New MIDI Track, depending on the audio you're converting. All of the methods create a new track with a default instrument loaded and a new MIDI clip generated from the analysis. After the conversion, you can swap out the instrument to customize the sound. You can also drag an audio clip to an existing MIDI track, and a dialog will appear giving you the three conversion choices.

- ▶ **Convert Drums to New MIDI Track** analyzes audio, assuming it contains drums, and produces a new MIDI clip that will play a similar pattern on a Drum Rack. Generally, this technique does a very good job of identifying clear kick, snare, and hi-hat parts. However, it will falter, depending on how unusual and complex the drum sounds are. Not to worry, though, with a bit of editing this conversion method produces very usable results on a wide variety of material.

- ▶ **Convert Melody to New MIDI Track** will typically generate usable results if the source has strong transients and the signal is steady in pitch. Complex, modulating synthesizer tones and weak vocal performances (or emotional ones with a lot of note sliding and other vocal artifacts) will produce less accurate results.

- ▶ **Convert Harmony to New MIDI Track** is the fussiest of all of the methods. Even with a solo keyboard or guitar part, it will often generate chords containing strange extra notes or leave notes out entirely. Your mileage will vary greatly, depending on the material you feed it, so keep it simple and be prepared to edit the results.

# Slice to New MIDI Track

Slice to New MIDI Track is a whole different animal than the conversion methods discussed earlier. This method breaks the original audio into slices and then creates a new track containing a MIDI clip to trigger the slices in order.

To invoke this command, right-click on a clip and select Slice to New MIDI Track from the context menu. Next, you'll be presented with a dialog offering a couple of options (see Figure 5.39). The first menu allows you to choose how many slices your audio should be divided into. A good value to start with here would be whatever value you would use for the Transients setting in Beats mode. If the beat is based on 1/8th note divisions, try slicing at this value. There's also an option to slice at Warp Markers. This means that anywhere you've created a Warp Marker, a slice will be created. In other words, you can control how many slices are generated by adding Warp Markers before doing the slicing.

**FIGURE 5.39**
The Slice to New MIDI Track dialog. Make sure to experiment with the different slicing presets!
*Source:* Ableton

The Slicing Preset menu gives you a few presets that will affect the MIDI track that gets created. To fully understand these options, you'll need to know a bit about Drum Racks and Sampler so you may want to explore Chapter 8. The first option, Built-In, creates a MIDI track containing a Drum Rack. Each slice of the loop will be mapped to a pad in the Drum Rack, and a MIDI file will be generated to play the slices back. The Drum Rack comes equipped with some preprogrammed Macros for tweaking the envelope and the loop properties of each slice. Try turning Loop Length up and Loop Compress down for some buzzing glitchy madness.

Many of the other options in the menu place the slices into Zones within a Sampler instead. These presets use a wide variety of Sampler's modulation options to generate sonic variation. Make sure to try out your keyboard's modulation wheel while using these presets, as many of them are programmed to respond to it. Ableton updates these presets when new versions of Live are released, so don't be surprised if the contents of this menu change from time to time.

After you've clicked OK and waited for a few seconds, you'll have a brand new MIDI track all loaded and ready to go. Just launch the new MIDI clip, and you'll hear your loop playing back just as if it were the original audio clip. This is where things get interesting. Try rearranging, deleting, or adding MIDI notes, or try creating a brand new clip and using individual slices to program a beat! Also, make sure to check out the macros that have been programmed for you in the new Drum Rack.

For most rhythmic material, selecting Transient in the top menu will yield good results. Occasionally, you might find that Live is chopping the audio into too many slices. For example, sometimes Live will place a transient in the middle of a drum hit, causing it to be chopped into two separate drum pads in the resulting MIDI track. If this happens, examine the transients and right-click on any that you think are unnecessary and use the Delete Transient(s) command. For completely customized beat slicing, use Warp Marker as the slicing division after placing a Warp Marker at each segment you would like to have sliced.

# Groove

Before we get too far into discussing Live's groove features, let's talk a little bit about the concept of groove in general. Simply put, musical parts that have a certain amount of rhythmic variation or imprecision, as well as changes in dynamics, often have a more compelling feel than parts that are perfectly quantized and even in volume. This is not to say that absolute precision always sounds bad, but sometimes, it's useful to contrast extremely tight tracks against looser ones. There are also cases where a robot-like beat is just the thing. It all depends on the musical context.

Using music technology to adjust the timing of a beat automatically is not new. Many classic drum machines, like Roland's TR-909, have a shuffle control. The shuffle control delays certain beats of a sequence to create a shuffle or "swing" feel. A swing is a very simple type of groove. To create a 1/8th note swing, all you have to do is slightly delay every other 1/8th note in a beat (starting with the second). The more you delay the alternate 1/8th notes, the more intense the swing will be.

While a swing control on a drum machine isn't news, Live's Groove Engine does a few things that are downright futuristic. Not only can Live apply a traditional shuffle to both MIDI *and* audio clips, but it can also quantize audio to correct timing or *remove* swing, as well as apply a whole variety of other grooves, such as those associated with samba and rumba. Far from simply being able to delay certain beats to add swing to a loop, the Groove Engine can shift individual beats in either direction and add some randomization to the timing as well. Grooves can also contain velocity changes, which can be used to modify dynamics as well. This could be a simple matter of making the downbeat of a bar slightly louder than the other beats, or it could be a complex flow, rising and falling throughout the bar.

To apply a groove to a clip, press Hot-Swap Groove, as seen in Figure 5.40. This will cause the Browser to display the groove files in Live's Library. Now you can browse until you find the groove you're interested in. If you're new to working with grooves and shuffles, open up the Swing folder and select one of the groove files contained within to get started. If you're an experienced percussionist, or perhaps a user of Apple's Logic Pro or Akai's MPC-series drum sequencers, you'll be happy to find all sorts of familiar grooves contained within the other folders.

After you've selected a groove by double-clicking it, you should hear it take effect immediately, and it will appear in the Groove Pool. The Groove Pool displays one row for each groove that is used in the current Set.

Groove Pool

Show/Hide
Groove Pool

Hot-Swap
Groove
Clip Groove
Commit Groove

**FIGURE 5.40**
Using the Hot-Swap Groove
button enables you to browse
through Live's Groove Library.
After you select a groove, you
can customize it in the Groove
Pool. Click the wavy lines
above the Clip View to open up
the Groove Pool. You can also
drag grooves directly from the
Browser into the Groove Pool.
*Source:* Ableton

For each groove, the following parameters are available:

▶ **Base:** In order to shift the timing of certain beats in a clip, Live
needs a point of reference. For example, if Base is set to 1/16, it
will examine every 1/16 note chunk of a clip and evaluate how
much (if at all) the accents within it need to be moved to match
the timing of the groove.

▶ **Quantize:** This setting determines how much real-time quantization is applied to the clip, based on the setting of the Base parameter. In other words, if Base is set to 1/16, then Live will first
quantize the clip to 1/16 notes, *before* making the timing adjustments contained in the groove file. At percentages lower than

100%, Live will move each accent only a portion of the way to the nearest 1/16. Doing this allows you to keep some of the clip's original timing before applying the groove to it.

▶ **Timing:** This is where you tell Live how much to apply the groove's timing to the clip. At values lower than 100%, the clip's accents will be moved only part of the way to the locations specified in the groove. At 0%, no timing adjustments will be made.

▶ **Random:** By increasing the Random value, you add timing randomization to the clip. A little randomness can emulate the natural timing variations that occur with live musicians. Unless you're looking to create some serious chaos, this setting is best used at lower values.

▶ **Velocity:** This setting determines how much the velocity fluctuations in the groove should be applied to the clip. Be aware that some grooves in the Library don't contain any velocity information, so changing this value won't have any effect. Note that this value can be set to negative values to invert the velocity as well. When applying grooves to audio clips, velocity creates volume fluctuations. (This is usually the case with MIDI clips as well, but that's ultimately determined by the instrument.)

▶ **Amount:** This is the Global Groove Amount. It sits at the top of the Groove Pool and is applied to all grooves in the Set. It acts as a global control for the Timing parameter in each of the grooves. Note that Amount can be set to values greater than 100% to move all Groove Timing percentages above their specified amount.

When you've applied a groove to a clip, not only does it appear in the Groove Pool, but it also becomes available to every clip in your set. To apply the groove to additional clips, just select it from the Clip Groove menu. After there are grooves in your Groove Pool, this turns into a menu.

## BEHIND THE GROOVE

If you want to examine the contents of a groove, just drag it out of the
Browser or the Groove Pool and drop it into a MIDI track. What you'll
find is that a groove file is really just a MIDI clip that Live uses as a template for timing and dynamics. Try it!

# Commit

One thing that's great about working with grooves is that they are applied in
real time as the clip plays. In other words, no direct changes to the clip itself
are made. Adjustments to the groove can be made continuously as you work
on a track, and these changes will immediately affect any clips utilizing that
groove.

However, there may be cases where you want to apply a groove to a clip in a
more permanent way. To do this, press the Commit switch directly below the
Groove menu in the clip box. In the case of a MIDI clip, this will actually
move individual notes to conform to the groove and apply any necessary
changes in velocity. For audio clips, Live creates Warp Markers to apply timing variations and a volume envelope to create changes in dynamics.

## ANALYZE THIS

Want to create your own grooves for use with Live's Groove Engine? Just
drag an audio or MIDI clip into the Groove Pool. Live will analyze the
clip and create a new groove file based on the timing and dynamics of
the clip. If you want to save this new clip to the Library, right-click in
the Groove Pool and select Browse Groove Library. Now, you can drag
the groove from the pool into the Browser, and it will be saved for use in
future Sets.

# 6

# Tracks and
# Signal Routing

One of Live's often unsung features is its incredibly flexible routing. If you're just getting started as a producer, you may not have use for everything described in this chapter right away. However, if you're coming to this chapter with some experience, I predict you'll enjoy how easy it is to route multiple MIDI tracks into one instrument or record from one track to another.

In the following pages, we'll be exploring some track types that haven't been discussed yet (such as Groups and returns) and looking at some interesting uses for regular audio and MIDI tracks. We'll also take a look at ReWire, which is a brilliant utility for sending audio between different applications and synchronizing their sequencers.

A lot of the techniques presented here involve use of the mixer's Input/Output section, so make sure to visit the View menu and have it displayed when following along. Figure 6.1 shows an audio and a MIDI track with this section shown, so make note of the chooser names, since I'll be referring to them quite a bit.

**FIGURE 6.1**

To be a routing ninja, you need to know your way around the In/Out section.

*Source:* Ableton

## ARRANGEMENT TIP

Because the height of Arrangement tracks can be flexibly adjusted, the In/Out menus can become hidden. As you resize the track smaller, the input menus will be hidden first, followed by the output menus. If you don't see the menu you're looking for, resize the track until they appear.

# The Master Track

The Master track is created automatically and cannot be deleted. By default, all tracks route their output to the Master (see Figure 6.2), where they get mixed together. It also serves as the final stop to process the sound before it gets sent out to the speakers. For example, it's common to sweeten a final mix by adding some compression and EQ to the Master track. (That said, until you're an experienced engineer, it's probably best to leave the Master track empty when producing.)

The Master is a lot like an audio track, but it has a few important differences. For example, instead of clip slots, the Master track contains Scene Launch buttons, which are described in Chapters 3 and 4. This track also has some special controls in the Mixer and In/Out sections, which we'll take a look at next.

**FIGURE 6.2**

Your entire mix will pass through the Master track before heading out to the speakers.

*Source:* Ableton

When audio leaves the Master track, it goes to the output specified in Master Out. This can be any enabled output on your audio interface (see "Audio" in Chapter 2, "Getting Live Up and Running"). Just make sure that your monitors (or the sound system) are connected to the output specified in Master Out, and you're all set.

Above Master Out is Cue Out, which specifies the output that will be used for previewing, cueing, and the metronome. Next to the Master's volume slider, you'll find the Preview/Cue volume knob, which adjusts the volume of Cue Out.

By default, Cue Out will be set to the same outputs as the Master Out, and for many studio setups this is just fine. However, if you select unique outputs for your Cue Out, a number of possibilities arise, most of which are useful for performance. For example, by sending Cue Out to the headphone output of your audio interface, you now have the ability to preview files in the Browser or hear the metronome without those signals going out of the Main Out and into the sound system.

Another thing that happens when Cue Out and Master Out are set to different values is that the Solo/Cue switch is activated. Click on it to select either Solo or Cue. When Cue is active, the Solo buttons on the audio tracks will turn to Cue buttons (headphone icons). When you press a Cue button, Live will route that track to the Cue output, so you can hear it through your headphones.

Bear in mind that Cue works independently of the volume fader. In other words, clicking Cue does not stop the signal from going to the Master (or wherever else you may be sending it). In a DJ setup, you'd need to keep the track's volume fader down in order to cue a song without sending it out to the dance floor.

# Return Tracks

By default, there are two Return tracks in a new Live Set. You can add more (up to 12) by choosing Insert Return Track from the Create menu. Return tracks are lettered (A–L) instead of being numbered, and can be shown or hidden under the View menu. You'll probably find these tracks mostly useful for effects processing, but you may discover other uses for them as well.

Return tracks don't host clips. Instead, the signal is routed to them using Send knobs (see Figure 6.3). You don't have to do anything to create a Send knob; they are added automatically every time a Return track is created. Sends can be hidden or shown independently of Return tracks, so visit the View menu if you don't see them on your screen.

*. . . to send signal to a Return.*

*Turn up a Send . . .*

**FIGURE 6.3** Each Return track has a corresponding Send knob in every track.
*Source:* Ableton

Let's say you have a drum loop playing on Track 1. If you turn send A all the way up, the drum loop will now be sent at full volume to return A, while still playing out of Track 1. In this case, the result will be to double the volume of the drum loop, since it will now be playing out of two tracks. Obviously, that's not a very interesting result. However, if you put effects on return A, you can route any signal through these effects by turning up send A. For a full discussion of using effects on Return tracks, see "Insert vs. Send/Return" in Chapter 7, "Using Effects and Instruments."

By default, sends are *post-fader.* This means that they pass signal to the returns *after* the track's volume control. So turning down a track's volume by 6dB will also turn down the signal being sent to any Return tracks by 6dB. With the volume fader all the way down, the returns will be silent as well. As shown in Figure 6.4, a send can be configured *pre-fader* instead, which means that the send is completely independent of the volume fader and will pass the signal, regardless of the track's volume.

**FIGURE 6.4**

Sends can be set to either pre- or post-fader by using these switches in the Master track.
*Source:* Ableton

Under the Options menu, there's an item called *Solo in Place*, which is checked by default. For most applications, you'll probably want to leave it this way. With Solo in Place enabled, you'll be able to solo a track without muting any Return tracks that receive a signal from it. With it disabled, soloing a track causes all returns to be muted.

Finally, note that one of the options for a track's Output Type is Sends Only. This is an easy way to prevent the signal from going to the Master track, so it's only heard when a Send is turned up. This is an unusual configuration, but you may find situations where this is handy. For example, if you're working in surround sound, you'll find that the Max for Live surround panner requires the use of Sends Only mode.

### YOU SEND ME

Notice that even Return tracks have Sends, but, by default, the Sends on Return tracks are disabled. To enable them, right-click the Send knob and select Enable Send. Any Send in Live can be disabled by right-clicking it and choosing Disable Send. The Send control will now appear grayed out.

# Group Tracks

Think of a Group Track as a track that contains other tracks. The audio from the tracks within the group flow into the Group Track instead of directly to the Master (although this can be customized if you want). Unlike audio, MIDI, and Return tracks, Group Tracks are not created from the Create menu. Instead, they are created by first selecting one or more audio or MIDI tracks and then selecting Edit → Group Tracks.

One use of Group Tracks is for traditional submixing, such as you might use with drums. For example, let's say you have each of your drums on an individual track. In this case, it's very helpful to be able to adjust the volume of all of the drums simultaneously, as well as to be able to process the drum mix with some compression. Group Tracks make the process incredibly easy.

Not only do they simplify submixing, but Group Tracks offer other advantages as well. First, notice the fold/unfold switch shown in Figure 6.5. This makes it easy to save screen space whenever you're not working with the tracks within the group. And, of course, since this is Live, there's also a twist for live performance—Group Launch buttons, which can be used to launch a row of clips contained within a group. Group Tracks also contain Stop buttons that can be used to stop all clips in the group.

If you ever want to add an additional track to a group, just drag the track until it is adjacent to the other grouped tracks. Conversely, tracks can be removed from groups by dragging them away. Also, be aware that if you delete a Group Track, all of the tracks within it will get deleted as well. If you want to ungroup the tracks within a group, right-click on the title bar of the Group Track and select Ungroup from the context menu.

When tracks are grouped, their Output Type automatically changes from "Master" to the name of the Group Track, as seen in Figure 6.5. If a track is

**Figure 6.5** Group Tracks contain audio and MIDI tracks.
*Source:* Ableton

routed somewhere other than Master before grouping, its output routing will be left alone, and it won't pass through the Group Track.

As of Live 10, it's possible to nest Group Tracks. Just use the Group command on one or more Group Tracks to see this in action. If your Sets start to get really complex, nested groups can simplify mixing and speed up your work-flow. Figure 6.6 shows an example of using groups within a drum group.

**FIGURE 6.6**

This is what Group Tracks look like in the Arrangement View. The PERCUSSION and HIHATS groups are contained within the DRUMS group.

## ARRANGEMENT KEYS

In the Arrangement View, Group Tracks can be folded and unfolded using the left- and right-arrow keys. Use the S key to fold all groups.

# Audio Routing

If you explore Live's Input Type and Output Type menus, you'll discover that tracks can receive or send audio to other tracks. For example, you could create an audio track that records the output of another track while you launch clips and tweak effects.

In Figure 6.7, you'll see the input of Track B has its Input Type set to Track A. In the Input Channel chooser below, you'll see three options: Pre FX, Post FX, and Post Mixer. These options allow you to choose where in the signal path the audio is routed from or *tapped.*

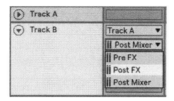

**FIGURE 6.7**

Track B is configured to record from Track A. The Input Channel menu gives you the power to tap the signal with or without effects.

*Source:* Ableton

▶ **Post Mixer:** The signal is tapped after it is processed by any effects and passed through the mixer. Any changes to panning or volume made in the mixer affect the signal.

▶ **Post FX:** The signal is tapped after the effects in the Track View but before the mixer. Changes to panning or volume made in the mixer do not affect the signal.

▶ **Pre FX:** The signal is tapped directly before any effects or mixing.

# Submixing and Multing

In Figure 6.8, pay attention to the Output Type choosers, and you'll see the "source" tracks are routed into an audio track called *DESTINATION*. This is commonly known as a *submix*. You may notice that all I've done is to manually create the routing behavior of a Group Track—several tracks are mixed together before being sent to the Master. Unlike Group Tracks, however, this method makes it easy to record the submix. Just click Arm and start recording in the destination track to create a new audio clip from the submixed tracks.

Notice that the track DESTINATION has its input menus sent to Ext. In 1/2. That means that in addition to the three "source" tracks, it will also monitor hardware inputs 1 and 2. While this is a great example of Live's incredible

**FIGURE 6.8**

Three tracks, all routed to a single destination. The track called DESTINATION is a regular old audio track. Some DAWs make you use special tracks for this sort of thing, but not Live!

*Source:* Ableton

flexibility, this is the sort of thing that can create problems in the real world. To prevent DESTINATION from listening to the hardware inputs, just change its Input Type to "No Input" like the other tracks in Figure 6.8.

*Multing* is a recording engineer abbreviation for multiplying—sending a signal to multiple destinations simultaneously. It's conceptually the opposite of submixing. Instead of sending multiple sources to one destination, you're sending one signal to multiple destinations. This is done by creating a new audio track and setting the Input Type to another track in the set. In Figure 6.9, there are three destination tracks receiving the signal from a single source. Notice that the source track still passes the signal directly to the Master, due to its Output Type setting.

**FIGURE 6.9**
The three "destination" audio tracks are all receiving the signal from the track called SOURCE.
*Source:* Ableton

Whether you are submixing or multing, bear in mind that you must either arm the destination track (if its Monitor status is Auto) or set its Monitor status to In. Otherwise, the signal will not be passed through. Review the "In/Out" section in Chapter 3, "Live Interface Basics," for more information on monitoring.

# Resampling

Another handy option you'll find in the Input Type menu of every audio track is Resampling (see Figure 6.10). Selecting this input allows you to record a new clip from the output of the Master track. This is a quick and easy way to grab audio from whatever is going on in Live at the moment. Mute tracks you don't want to record, or solo the tracks you want to be recorded and go! When you are resampling into a track, its output is automatically muted to avoid feedback.

**FIGURE 6.10**
Resampling makes it possible to record from Live's main output.
*Source:* Ableton

Because Live's mixer operates at 32-bit, you may want to consider recording at 32-bit when resampling. This way, you'll capture all of the information coming out of the mixer, even if there's clipping. (Visit the Record/Warp/Launch tab of the Preferences screen to set recording bit depth.)

# Virtual Outputs

Some of Live's built-in devices and some third-party plug-ins have multiple virtual outputs, which can be useful in a variety of ways. For example, perhaps you're using Impulse (Live's basic drum instrument), and you want to send each drum to a separate track for individual processing. Or maybe you're using a multitimbral instrument like Native Instruments' Kontakt, which can load multiple instruments simultaneously. Virtual outputs make it easy to monitor or record each sound separately.

They're easy to miss, however, unless you know where to look. Whenever you load an instrument with virtual outputs into a MIDI track, the virtual outputs will become available in Input Type menus for the audio tracks in the Set. Let's take a look at an example using Impulse.

Take a look at Figure 6.11. You'll see a track containing an Impulse drum kit (Grinder Kit) along with a few audio tracks. Each of these tracks has its Input Type set to Grinder Kit, while the Input Channel for each audio track is set to an individual drum. With these inputs selected, the drums will be sent to the individual audio tracks instead of the Impulse track. You can now place different effects on each drum or record the drums to separate audio clips (or both!).

When you are working with plug-in devices, there will typically be an additional step where you must configure the plug-in to send different sounds to different virtual outs. Consult the plug-in documentation for more information.

**FIGURE 6.11** When Input Type is set to a track containing an instrument with virtual outputs, Input Channel will display the individual outs.
*Source:* Ableton

## SUPERGROUP

After you have created separate tracks to process the virtual outputs of an instrument, it is often helpful to group them together by using a Group Track. This way, you get the best of all worlds: individual tracks for each sound, a track for group effect processing and volume adjustments, and the ability to fold all the tracks into the space of a single track.

# External Outputs

So far, every technique discussed here has to do with routing signals to various destinations within Live's mixer. It's also possible to route tracks directly to physical outputs on your interface. To do this, select Ext. Output as a track's Output Type and set Output Channel to a specific output.

One simple scenario for routing to external outputs is DJing with Live using a standard DJ mixer. In Figure 6.12, you'll see two tracks configured to send their outputs to tracks 1/2 and 3/4, respectively. By connecting these two stereo pairs to channels on a mixer, you can mix and cue just like you would if you were using two turntables or CD players.

**FIGURE 6.12**

Send tracks to individual outputs on your audio interface to mix using a hardware mixer.
*Source:* Ableton

## NAME GAME

If you're using external outputs extensively, consider naming the outputs to make life easier. Visit the Audio tab of Live's Preferences and click Output Config to do this.

# Advanced MIDI Routing

Just as audio signals can be routed between tracks so can MIDI signals. All of the core concepts of routing are covered in the previous audio routing section, so you may want to read through that before digging into these MIDI techniques.

In some cases, the MIDI routing process is very similar to that of audio routing. For example, to send a MIDI signal to multiple tracks, simply create additional MIDI tracks and set their Input Type to the track sending MIDI, as seen in Figure 6.13.

**FIGURE 6.13**
The three tracks to the right will all receive MIDI from Track MIDI 1.
*Source:* Ableton

Using this configuration, you could program clips in Track MIDI 1 and have them trigger instruments in all four tracks. (A similar result can be produced using Instrument Racks, but some prefer this technique.)

Routing multiple MIDI tracks to a single instrument is a bit different than its counterpart in the audio world—submixing. In Figure 6.14, you'll see a track called *MIDI 1* configured to send signal into a track called *Synth*. Notice that there are two choices in the Output Channel menu. The first is the track's input (Track In), while the other is an input that feeds directly into the Operator instrument in the track.

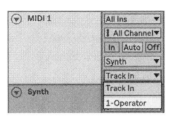

**FIGURE 6.14**
This configuration allows you to pass MIDI directly into the Operator on Track MIDI 1.
*Source:* Ableton

If Track In is selected, you'll have to make sure the Synth track is monitoring the input (Monitor = In, or Monitor = Auto and the track is armed). When you are monitoring the input, any clips playing in the Synth track will be ignored. On the other hand, if Operator is selected, the monitoring status is ignored, which means that the Synth track can have clips triggering Operator while the MIDI 1 track feeds MIDI into Operator as well.

Sound complicated? Well, yes, it is a little. This does allow for some interesting programming techniques, however. For example, you could have a four-bar legato bass loop playing in the Operator track while occasionally triggering additional notes from a second track to create slides and variations.

Just like instruments can have multiple virtual outputs, some have multiple inputs. For example, if you repeat the above experiment with a Drum Rack in the source track instead of an Operator, you'll see that the Output Channel menu allows you to route the MIDI to a specific drum within the Rack. This same technique can be done with some plug-in devices as well. If you're working with a plug-in with virtual inputs and outputs, your best bet may be to program it using the External Instrument device, which is explained in Chapter 8, "Live's Instruments."

# ReWire

These days, most music applications are incredibly powerful and don't have any serious limitations that would prevent you from using them to create a piece of music from start to finish. However, every program has its strengths, and some producers find it useful to use different programs for different things. For example, you might create some loops in Reason and have them play alongside your song in Live. Or perhaps you're working on a Pro Tools session and you want to take advantage of Live's warping features or built-in instruments.

All of these things can be done by importing and exporting audio between the programs, but sometimes it's easier to use ReWire, which allows you to link together multiple pieces of music software. With this technology, audio and MIDI stream seamlessly from one program into the other, and the transports and tempos of the two applications are linked, making them act like one mega-program.

For the most part, ReWire is very transparent to use. You don't need to install or configure it separately, and it launches automatically when needed. Its behavior is determined by the order in which you launch your music applications and how you route signal within the applications themselves.

# Masters

In any ReWire setup, there is always one program designated as the *ReWire master*. The ReWire master is the program that will be communicating with the computer's audio hardware and will accept audio streams from other ReWire applications. When a ReWire-compatible application is opened, it checks to see if any other ReWire-compatible applications are already running. If not, it gets designated as the master. Therefore, always launch the program you want to be the master first.

# Slaves

All ReWire-compatible programs launched after the master will be designated *ReWire slaves.* Slaves don't actually communicate with the computer's audio hardware at all. Instead, their audio outputs are routed to the ReWire master application. Since the audio is being passed through the master application, you will not hear the slave application unless you configure the application's internal routing properly. The exact method for doing this varies from application to application. In Live, the process is very simple and will be explained below.

# Using ReWire with Live

Live can act as both a ReWire master and a ReWire slave. Not all programs have the capability to function in both modes. For example, Pro Tools can only function as a ReWire master. Propellerhead's Reason can only be used in Slave mode. So if you wanted to use Live and Pro Tools together, Pro Tools would be the master and Live would be the slave. If you wanted to use Reason, Live would be the master and Reason would be the slave.

## Using Live as a ReWire Master

When Live is used as a ReWire master, its operation is essentially identical to when it's being used without ReWire. The main difference is the routing. You'll need to configure Live to receive audio from the slave application, and you may need to send MIDI into the slave as well.

To receive audio, create an audio track and set its Input Type to the slave application, as seen in Figure 6.15. What you select in the Input Channel depends a bit on how you have the slave application configured. By default, Live will select the slave application's main stereo output. ReWire supports up to 256 virtual outputs, which can be used if you want to route individual instruments from the slave into different tracks in Live.

**FIGURE 6.15**

Here outputs 1 and 2 from Reason are being used as inputs for an audio track.

*Source:* Ableton

After you have selected the ReWire source for a track, you can record the audio from the slave application as a new clip or simply monitor the source. ReWire synchronizes the programs, so clicking Play in Live will cause the parts from the slave to play right along in time. Just bear in mind that, while ReWire is itself very light on system resources, running multiple audio applications can be very taxing on CPU and RAM.

ReWire can also be used to send MIDI from the master to the slave. This allows you to control compatible applications the way you would control a virtual instrument in Live. Select the ReWire application in Output Type and the specific device in Output Channel (see Figure 6.16). Because this example uses Reason 10, the device preset names are shown in the Output Channel menu. Other applications will show the device name instead.

**FIGURE 6.16** These three MIDI tracks are being routed to three different instruments in Reason. They can now be programmed and automated using the power and convenience of Live's clips. *Source:* Ableton

Bear in mind that a destination channel will be listed only if there are devices or elements in the Slave application that are active and able to receive MIDI messages. For example, if you load an empty rack into Reason, there will be no output devices listed in the lower box.

Not all ReWire slave applications are capable of receiving MIDI input from the master application. If a program is not able to receive MIDI, it will not be listed as an available output destination in the MIDI track.

Remember, in order to hear the results of your MIDI messages sent to the slave, you'll need to have an audio track set up to monitor the return signal from the slave. So instead of the MIDI track outputting the audio (as would happen when a virtual instrument is loaded onto a MIDI track), you'll need another audio track to hear the results. This means that the MIDI info leaves on one track, and the audio returns on another.

### EXTERNAL INSTRUMENTS—INTERNALLY

The External Instrument device handles sending MIDI to a ReWire application and receives the audio back from that application in the same track. It's as easy as dropping an external device into a MIDI track and configuring it, using the same settings you would for a ReWire track. For a complete explanation of External Instruments, see Chapter 8.

# Using Live as a ReWire Slave

The exact steps for opening Live as a ReWire slave depend partly on the master application you use. In some cases, you may need to enable ReWire channels in the master application before Live is launched; otherwise, Live may not open in Slave mode. Be sure to check the master application's manual for recommendations on how you should do this. The only hard and fast rule, though, is that the ReWire master must be launched before Live. When Live launches as a slave, you'll see this noted on the splash screen during launch.

When using Live as a slave, you'll notice many subtle differences in available options throughout the program. The first thing to be aware of is that Live will be sending audio to and receiving MIDI from the master program instead of your audio and MIDI hardware.

Another difference will be the available output routings for audio in the mixer. When looking at the Master Out and all of the individual track Output Type menus, you'll find that the list is populated with ReWire busses instead of the outputs of your audio interface. These are the pathways that lead from Live into the master application. By default, Live will send all of its audio out of the Mix L/R bus. If you want, however, you can send different tracks into different busses and have the master application receive these on different tracks.

Note that ReWire also gives you the capability to access Ableton's built-in instruments from the master application. However, note that this will not work with plug-ins, which cannot be loaded into Live when in Slave mode.

Let's look at how to set up Pro Tools to run with Live as a slave. (The procedure for setting up ReWire varies from host to host, so consult your sequencer's documentation if you're working with a program other than Pro Tools.) First, start Pro Tools and open a new session. Then insert the Ableton Live ReWire plug-in on an Audio, Aux, or Instrument track and select Mix L – Mix R, as seen in Figure 6.17.

Now you are ready to work with Live. Go ahead and open the application; you should see the message "Running as ReWire Slave" in Live's splash screen as it starts up. Looking over at the Master track in your Live Set, you'll see that the master output is set to Mix L/R, the same input we selected in Pro Tools.

**FIGURE 6.17**
Configuring a track in Pro Tools to receive ReWire input from Live.
*Source:* Ableton

Even before there is sound coming out, you'll be able to see ReWire at work. Notice that pressing Play in either Live or Pro Tools causes both sequencers to start running, and that changing the tempo in Pro Tools causes Live's tempo to change as well. Now you can drop some clips into Live or open an existing Set in Live, and you'll hear Live's Master output through Pro Tools.

If you want to control Live's instruments from Pro Tools, there are a few additional steps. First, create a MIDI track and place one of Ableton's instruments on it. Next, create a MIDI track in Pro Tools. (If you haven't done so already, the order of the steps isn't important here.) Set the output of your MIDI track in Pro Tools to the Live track, as seen in Figure 6.18. That's it!

If you want to route tracks from Live directly into individual tracks in the host, just select a ReWire bus for a track's output in Live and create a track in your host to receive audio via this bus. Figures 6.19a and 6.19b show how to do this in Pro Tools.

**FIGURE 6.18** Any instruments loaded in Live will show up as valid outputs in the Master application.
*Source:* Ableton

**FIGURE 6.19A** Choose a ReWire bus as the output for a track in Live.
*Source:* Ableton

**FIGURE 6.19B** Receive audio from the same ReWire bus on a track in Pro Tools.
*Source:* Ableton

# 7

# Using Effects and Instruments

Gone are the days when having an arsenal of effects and instruments meant owning piles of keyboards, stomp boxes, and Rack units, labeled with tape and connected with miles of cable. Every piece of gear needed for the music production process, from the first drum beat to the last dab of reverb, now exists in software form. Sure, there's still lots of hardware out there that is fun to use and sounds great, but for the most part it's no longer a necessary part of making great music.

## Device Types

In this chapter, we'll be getting acquainted with how software effects and instruments, generically referred to as *devices,* are used in Live. Some devices are *built-in,* meaning they come with Live and can't be used directly within any other music program. Others are *plug-in* devices, meaning they are made by companies other than Ableton, and are designed such that they can be used in just about any music program you've got.

Instruments are just what they sound like: devices for *creating* sound. These fall into two categories: *synthesizers* that generate sound and *samplers* that play back audio files and don't have the ability to generate sound from scratch. If you're new to this realm, these two types may sound very different, but in fact they have much more in common than you may think. Both use similar sets of sound-shaping tools (such as filters) and modulators (such as envelopes) for designing sounds. Instruments can only be used in MIDI tracks.

Effects come in two flavors: Audio and MIDI. Audio effects are the most common type and can be used in any type of track, processing the audio coming from audio clips or the sound coming out of an instrument. Audio effects are used in a wide variety of ways: to remove unwanted frequencies (EQ), to create the sound of a room or a stadium (Reverb), or to mangle a sound into something radically different (Frequency Shifter). MIDI effects can only be used in MIDI tracks. They transform a performance *before* it reaches an instrument. This could be turning a single note into a chord (Chord) or turning a chord into a melodic pattern (Arpeggiator).

This chapter will also give you the lowdown on Racks, which are used for combining multiple devices into an easy-to-use bundle. If you're a beginner, you'll primarily interact with premade Racks from the Library, and you'll enjoy how they provide instant tweakability, while hiding the complexity within. For more advanced users, Racks are a bottomless pit of wonder, offering endless possibilities for creative routing and customization.

For a complete reference of every built-in device in Live, see Chapters 8, "Live's Instruments," 9, "Live's Audio Effects," and 10, "Live's MIDI Effects."

# Using Devices

Devices are accessed from the Browser (see Figure 7.1), as described in Chapter 3, "Live Interface Basics." The Audio Effects, MIDI Effects, and Instruments views are dedicated solely to Live's built-in devices. Sounds is a special view that shows all available Instrument (and Instrument Rack) presets organized by type, while Drums is a hybrid view that is used for accessing both Drum Racks and drum samples. The Plug-ins view displays any

**Figure 7.1**
Devices are accessed from any of the categories shown on the left. Sounds (highlighted above) displays Instrument and Instrument Rack presets.
*Source:* Ableton

third-party effect or instrument devices you've installed on your computer. Max for Live devices are like built-in devices because they can only be used in Ableton Live, but they are also like plug-ins because additional devices can be downloaded and added to your collection.

With a few exceptions that will be covered later in this chapter, devices function identically, regardless of whether they are built-in, plug-in, or Max for Live. Just bear this in mind as you read through the chapter. Unless otherwise specified, any reference to an effect or instrument applies to all types.

# From Browser to Track

Adding a device from the Browser is easy. There are several different ways to load devices onto a track, all of which work identically in both the Session and Arrangement Views.

1. Drag a device from the Browser and drop it anywhere on a track, as shown in Figure 7.2.

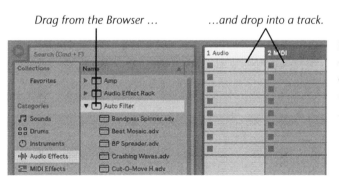

*Drag from the Browser …*        *…and drop into a track.*

**Figure 7.2**
Click and drag a device from the Browser to a track.
*Source:* Ableton

2. Select the destination track by clicking on it and then double-click the desired device or plug-in shown in the Browser.

3. Double-click the title bar of a track to expose its Device View; then drag and drop the device directly into the Device View (see Figure 7.3). When you are loading effects, the benefit of this method is that you can drop the device directly into any position in the effects chain.

**FIGURE 7.3** By dragging devices straight into the Device View, you can insert them at any point in the chain that you want.
*Source:* Ableton

4. Instead of dragging the device out of the Browser, click on the triangle to the left of the device to reveal its presets. Now, drag or double-click the preset instead of the device. (There's more on presets below).

There's no fixed limitation on how many effects you can place in a track. The only limitation is your CPU power (and your sanity). Instruments, on the other hand, have a very serious limitation: there can only be one in any MIDI track. When you add an instrument to a MIDI track that already contains one, the new instrument replaces the old one. (Spoiler alert! In the section on Instrument Racks, I'm going to tell you how to put more than one instrument in a MIDI track, but for now, just go with it.)

**THE BIG PICTURE**

You'll quickly discover that it's very easy to add enough devices to a track so that they can't all be seen at one time. When this happens, the devices will simply scroll off to the right. At the lower right-hand corner of your screen, you'll see a miniaturized image of all of the devices in the track, with a black rectangle indicating the devices that are currently in view. Just like in the Arrangement View, you can slide the rectangle around to view different parts of the device chain.

My favorite trick for keeping devices in view, however, is folding them. Just double-click in a device's title bar, and it will collapse sideways, taking up a fraction of the screen space that it did before. It's easy to keep your devices folded and just unfold the one you're working with at the moment.

# Inside the Device View

As first mentioned in Chapter 3, the Device View is the name for the area in which devices appear. If you want to become a device master, you'll need to know your way around the Device View. In case you've forgotten, remember that you can always get to the Device View by double-clicking in a track's title bar or by using the Shift+Tab keyboard shortcut.

## Activate/Deactivate and Edit

Every device has a circular Device Activator switch in the upper left-hand corner, which can be used to deactivate or *bypass* the device (see Figure 7.4). When deactivated, instruments produce no sound, and effects pass the signal through unchanged. When you are using effects, it's often important to bypass a device temporarily so that you can hear exactly what's going on with

**FIGURE 7.4**

Bypass devices by clicking the circular switch in the upper left. Also note the standard editing commands available in the context menu.

*Source:* Ableton

the sound. Also bear in mind that a deactivated device uses no CPU power, so this can also be a useful technique when trying to determine if a particular device is overloading your system.

Clicking in the title bar of a device selects it and allows you to use commands from the Edit menu. (Also, note that once a device is selected, you can select the adjacent devices using the left- and right-arrow keys.) Cut, Copy, and Paste can be used on devices, as can Duplicate. The Rename command works as well, allowing you to give a descriptive name that specifies how a device is being used. Finally, if you decide you want to remove a device permanently, just click in the title bar to highlight it and press Delete.

## Signal Flow

It's critical to understand that, once added to a track, effects process any signal passing through the track. A common misunderstanding is to think of putting an effect "on a clip." That's not how it works. When a clip plays back, its signal passes through every device in the Device View before arriving at the mixer. Therefore, the effects will transform the signal for *every clip in the track*.

Signal flows through the Device View from left to right. In the case of effects, this simply means that the output of a device is passed on to the next device to the right, and so on. This is an important point because the order that effects are placed in can have a big impact on the final result. To change device order, just click on the title bar and drag the device to a different position. Make sure to experiment!

MIDI tracks can host MIDI effects, instruments, and audio effects, which make them a bit more complex than audio tracks, which can only host audio effects. MIDI effects always appear to the left of the instrument (since they process the MIDI before it reaches the instrument), while audio effects appear to the right (since they process the audio coming out of the instrument).

Take a close look in the Device View, and you'll notice a small level meter in between each device. Audio effects have an audio level meter before and after the device, which helps you track how the effect may be changing the signal's gain. MIDI effects display a dotted meter that shows the presence of MIDI data. Some MIDI devices can perform MIDI "filtering," which blocks some MIDI messages, so if your MIDI data is disappearing, these meters can help you determine where the problem is.

Finally, instruments have a MIDI meter to the left and an audio meter to the right, showing you MIDI coming in and audio flowing out (see Figure 7.5). It's possible to have a situation where an instrument is producing no signal (a sample playback device with no sample loaded, or a synthesizer with all its oscillators turned off, for example), so this is another case where these handy meters can save you some headaches when diagnosing a signal flow problem.

**FIGURE 7.5**

There are meters to either side of each device to show the signal flow. Notice the dotted meter to the far left shows MIDI data entering the Drum Rack. To the right of the Drum Rack, there's an audio meter showing sound exiting the Simpler and entering the Redux effect.

*Source:* Ableton

## MIX IT UP

The question often arises, what do you do if you only want an effect on a certain clip and not on the others? The simple answer is to put the clip (or clips) on a separate track and add only the effects appropriate to those clips.

It's also possible to turn effects on and off temporarily by automating an effect's Device Activator (also known as the "Device On" parameter). This can be a very useful technique, but still it's often easier (and less confusing) to simply use a separate track to provide special effects where needed.

# Insert vs. Send/Return

There are two primary ways that audio effects are used. The most common method is to use the effect as an *insert*, which means you insert it directly into the path of the signal you want to process. If you drop an effect into an audio track, MIDI track, or Group Track, you're using it as an insert. The other way to get an effect into your mix is to put it on a Return track.

One of the big differences between these two methods is the relationship of the processed (*wet*) signal to the unprocessed (*dry)* signal. When an effect is used as an insert, the wet signal replaces the dry signal, unless the effect has a Dry/Wet knob for blending the two signals together. For example, if you place an EQ on a track and turn a few knobs, you're no longer hearing the unprocessed signal at all, which makes sense: the reason you use an EQ is to transform the sound such that it contains more of the frequencies you want and less of those you don't.

On the other hand, when you use a reverb or delay effect, you're typically looking to keep the dry signal intact and *add* the ambience that the effect provides. This means that when a reverb is used as an insert, the Dry/Wet knob is extremely important, since it will determine not just how much of the effect you hear, but how much of the original signal you hear as well.

This approach has a particular problem. As you increase the Dry/Wet knob toward 100%, you're not just adding effect, you're simultaneously *decreasing* the amount of dry signal. Sometimes, it's important to be able to set the level of the dry signal, and then independently adjust the level of the effect. For example, if you want to put a large amount of reverb on a snare drum, you typically don't want to turn down the level of the drum itself, you just want to crank up the reverb and leave the drum alone! Enter the Return effect.

When an effect is used on a Return track, you *add* the processed signal to the unprocessed signal and gain the flexibility that comes with having dry and wet on separate tracks. For time-based effects such as reverb and delay, this is a perfect scenario. With other effects, such as EQ, this approach rarely makes sense, since the goal is to replace the unprocessed signal with the processed one.

Sends and returns are covered in detail in the "Return Tracks" section of Chapter 6, "Tracks and Signal Routing," if you need more information.

# Using Return Effects

To get started with this method, add an effect to a Return track, just like you would with any other track. To get signal to flow through the effect, turn up the associated Send knob on the track you want to process. For example, place the Reverb device on Return A and turn up Send A on your snare drum track to add some reverb to the snare (see Figure 7.6). How much you turn up the Send determines how much signal is sent to the Return and how much of the effect is added. Keep in mind that the Send knob does not *divert* signal to the Return track—it *copies* the signal to the Return track. This means that the output volume of the source track will stay the same, regardless of the Send knob position.

There's a Send knob on every track, which you can adjust to add varying amounts of effects to any track. For our snare drum example, you might crank the Send up high to add a dramatic effect, while turning it to a low level on the hi-hat track for a subtle ambience. This is not only convenient, but it's also CPU efficient. Plug-in reverbs in particular can be very demanding on your processor, and using many instances can place an unnecessary burden on your computer. Using the Send/Return approach allows you to share one device between many tracks.

There's one important caveat to observe when placing effects on returns: *always set the effect to 100% wet.* If the effect has a Dry/Wet knob, turn it all the way up. If the effect has an independent Dry control, turn it all the way

**FIGURE 7.6**
Return tracks are particularly handy when working with reverbs and delays. In this example, there's a Reverb on Return track A. Notice Send knob A in the Snare and Keys tracks. More reverb will be added to the Keys track because the send is turned up higher.
*Source:* Ableton

down. Do whatever it takes to ensure that the effect on the Return track is outputting *only processed signal.* The unprocessed signal is unnecessary, since it's still being output from the original track. If you allow return effects to pass any unprocessed signal, you'll get the undesirable and confusing result of increasing the volume of the unprocessed signal whenever you turn up a Send.

### PRE OR POST?

On the right side of the mixer, there is a button labeled Post for each Send knob. These buttons determine whether the Send knobs take their signals *pre-fader* or *post-fader.* Post-fader is the default setting for each track, which causes the amount of signal sent from the Send knob to vary based on the track's volume slider. If you're fading down a vocal part that is sending to a reverb, the amount being sent to the reverb will also diminish, causing it to fade out as well.

The pre-fader position (click the Post button to turn it to Pre) causes the Send level to remain the same, even if the track's volume is adjusted. This is particularly handy when using compression in a Return track (a technique called *parallel compression*). Since compressors behave very differently depending on the level of the input signal, it's handy to have independent control over the volume of the send and the track.

You'll see that the Return track itself also has Send knobs. This allows you to output a portion of the returned effect to another Return. The Return track can also send back into itself, allowing you to create feedback loops (watch your volume!). Because of the feedback risk, the Sends on Return tracks are disabled by default. If you right-click on a Send, you can enable it from the context menu.

### DUB STYLE

There's loads of fun to be had with delay effects in Return tracks. For example, place a Ping Pong Delay in Return A, with a fairly high Feedback setting. Now, momentarily crank the Send knob up and down for various tracks in your song to create dramatic effects on individual drum hits or other musical phrases. Use this technique as a live performance effect, or record the Send movements as automation in the studio.

# Plug-Ins

While Live offers an impressive collection of devices right out of the box, you may also want to use plug-in effects and instruments from other manufacturers. Live supports the VST and Audio Units (Mac OS X only) plug-in standards, allowing limitless expansion possibilities for your virtual studio.

Plug-in effects and instruments are not separated into multiple views as they are with the built-in devices. To tell them apart, notice that plug-in instruments have a small piano keyboard in their Browser icon, while effects do not (see Figure 7.7). Audio Units are automatically organized by manufacturer, while VSTs can be manually organized by creating folders in the VST plug-in folder. (This can't be done in the Browser, so you'll have to use your computer's file management system.)

**FIGURE 7.7**

The piano keyboard lets you know that Kontakt 5 is an instrument. Guitar Rig 5 is an effect.

*Source:* Ableton

Unlike built-in devices, plug-ins use a separate window to display their parameters. When you load an external plug-in, Live displays a generic X-Y object in the Device View (see Figure 7.8), the axes of which can be set to any of the plug-in's parameters via the menus below. Clicking the wrench icon opens up the plug-in's custom graphical interface. Next to the wrench is an unfold switch that will reveal a panel showing generic sliders for the plug-in controls. There's more about this panel in the "Remote Controlling Plug-In Devices" section of Chapter 11, "Remote Control."

**FIGURE 7.8**

Plug-ins show up as generic placeholders. On the left there's a VST instance of Reaktor. The Rough Rider to the right is an Audio Unit.

*Source:* Ableton

## *Warnings*

By using a third-party plug-in, you are incorporating a new piece of program code into Live. Usually, this is nothing to worry about. However, a buggy plug-in can malfunction in all sorts of ways. In the worst cases, this could mean outputting high-volume digital noise or causing Live to crash. Just because a plug-in works well in another host is no guarantee that it will behave the same way within Live. There's nothing to be afraid of, though. Download and experiment to your heart's content. Just be sure to test at low volumes, save your work often, and never *ever* try out an untested plug-in on a gig!

If Live determines that a plug-in has caused a crash, it will offer to disable the plug-in so that it doesn't happen again. However, there may be cases where you need to do this manually. This is a simple matter of removing the plug-in from the plug-in folder. (See "File/Folder" in Chapter 2, "Getting Live Up and Running," for more information on plug-in locations.)

# Managing Presets

Most effects and instruments can produce a wide variety of results. Some devices (Redux, for example) have limited functionality and a small set of parameters to match, while others (like Operator) have so many parameters that even experienced users may be endlessly surprised by the sounds that can be produced. To improve the usability of complex devices, we have *presets:* a collection of parameter settings that can be instantly loaded to configure the device for a particular sound.

Knowing how presets are loaded, managed, and created is important for producers of every skill level. At first, you load a device's presets to become familiar with what it can do and get up and running quickly. Once you've gained some expertise with programming the device (or you've stumbled on something cool sounding through experimentation and dumb luck—my favorite method), you can save your sound as a preset for easy recall later.

## Managing Presets (Built-In and Audio Unit)

For Live's built-in devices, all preset management is done via the Browser. Just click the triangle to the left of the device icon to reveal the device's presets, often categorized for easy browsing (see Figure 7.9). These presets can be

**Figure 7.9**
Unfold devices to reveal their presets. This image shows some of the Bass presets for the instrument Analog.
*Source:* Ableton

added directly into tracks, as explained earlier, or added by hot-swapping them into an existing device (see the "Hot-Swapping" section).

Audio Unit presets are a little different. Just like built-in devices, there's a triangle for unfolding the device, but you won't see any presets here until you create some yourself. Factory presets for AU devices are accessed through the plug-in's GUI. Consult the manufacturer's documentation for more information on this. To save your own AU presets, you can either use the plug-in's preset management interface, or you can save them into Live's Browser, as explained below.

There are two ways of saving your own presets, using the Save Preset button or dragging devices from the Device View into the User Library. The Save Preset button is the floppy disk icon located in the upper right-hand corner of the device. Clicking this button causes a new preset to appear in the User Library (see Figure 7.10). Type in the name that you want and press Enter to confirm or Esc to cancel. If you make further edits to the preset and press the Save Preset button again, just press Enter without typing a new name to overwrite the preset with your new settings.

When the Save Preset button is used, the preset is placed into a folder dedicated to that particular device. If you modify an Instrument preset based on a factory preset, it will be placed into a subfolder corresponding to the preset's category (i.e., Bass or Experimental). Presets saved this way will appear

**Figure 7.10**
When you save a preset, it goes to the User Library. You can create folders to organize them however you want.
*Source:* Ableton

under the related category in the Sounds or Instruments View of the Browser. If you want to categorize a preset you made from scratch, just drag it into the appropriate subfolder after saving it.

Some people prefer to use their own organizational system. You can right-click in the User Library and select New Folder to create as many folders as you like; then drag around the presets just like you would in your computer's file management system. To save a preset directly to a custom folder in the User Library, just grab the device's title bar, drag it to the User Library, and drop it in the folder of your choice.

Presets saved outside of Live's predefined categories will appear in a special category called "Others" in the Sounds and Instruments Views of the Browser.

### DEFAULT PRESET

If you right-click in the title bar of a built-in device, you'll see an additional way to save a preset: the Save as Default Preset command. If you select this, the device's current settings will be saved and used whenever another device is added to a track.

## Managing VST Presets

VST presets aren't managed in the Browser. These presets are stored in VST bank files (.fxb) or preset files (.fxp), which can be saved and loaded from within the interface of the plug-in, or from Live as shown in Figure 7.11. VST presets can be saved anywhere on your hard drive. If you want to save them with the factory presets for the plug-in (many vendors install a "User" folder for this purpose), consult the manufacturer's documentation to locate this folder.

Open an effect bank. —
Save the current effect bank. —

**FIGURE 7.11**
VST preset management tools. Whether or not there are presets in the preset menu depends on the plug-in's manufacturer.
*Source:* Ableton

# Hot-Swapping

There's an icon containing two arrows in a circle that you'll find in the title bar of every device and in a few other spots within certain devices as well. This is the Hot-Swap button, which is used for loading device presets, swapping out devices, and loading content into Drum Racks, Simpler, and Impulse. Hot-Swap mode is entered by clicking the icon or by pressing Q on your keyboard. To exit Hot-Swap mode, you can press Q (or ESC) or click on the X that appears in the title bar of both the Browser and the device being swapped.

## Device Swapping

In the upper-right corner of every device, you'll find a Hot-Swap button (see Figure 7.12a). When activated, the Browser will jump to the available presets for that device (see Figure 7.12b). Double-clicking on a preset or highlighting a preset and pressing Return will load it into the device. The biggest advantage to this feature is being able to change presets or devices using only the keyboard. Use the up- and down-arrow keys to navigate in the Browser, the left- and right-arrow keys to open/close folders and switch views, and finally Return to load the sound.

Swapping isn't limited to loading presets—you can also swap out one device for another one of the same type. So, for example, you could replace a Filter Delay with a Reverb, or a built-in synth-like Operator with a plug-in synth such as Massive.

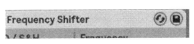

**FIGURE 7.12A**

The Hot-Swap button is just to the left of the floppy disk Save icon.

*Source:* Ableton

**FIGURE 7.12B**

The Browser in Hot-Swap mode.

*Source:* Ableton

## Content Swapping

Hot Swapping can also be used to load content into Impulse, Simpler, and Drum Racks. To reveal the Hot-Swap button, float your mouse over a sample slot in Impulse, a pad in a Drum Rack, or the sample display in Simpler. The Q shortcut doesn't work to swap samples in these devices (you'll end up swapping the device or preset instead), so you'll have to use the mouse. Once you're in Hot-Swap mode, everything works the same, except that the Browser will only display sample files.

In a Drum Rack, Q can be used to swap out an entire preset or just the contents of a pad. To swap out a pad, highlight it first and then press Q. You can highlight a pad by clicking on it or by using the arrow keys to navigate between pads. You can also use the D key to toggle between highlighting the Drum Rack itself and the last selected pad. This way, you can swap out drum kits or build an entire Drum Rack from scratch using only the keyboard.

When swapping pads, the Browser allows you to select either sample files or instruments (either built-in or plug-in). Drum Racks are relatives of Instrument Racks, which are used to host other devices. Instrument Racks are covered in detail later in this chapter, while Drum Racks are covered in Chapter 8.

# Racks

Racks allow multiple devices to be grouped together to create a custom "superdevice" that can be treated as if it were a single device. There are Racks for each of Live's device types: Audio Effect Racks, which contain audio effect devices, MIDI Effect Racks for MIDI devices, and Instrument Racks, which can contain not only instrument devices, but also MIDI and audio effects. In some ways, Racks are just like other devices: there's an Activator switch in the upper-left corner, which bypasses every device in the Rack, a Save button for saving the Rack as a preset, and a Hot Swap button for selecting a different preset or device.

Live comes with numerous preset Racks, and there are many available from third-party content developers as well. Racks presets are explored just like any other type of preset in the Browser. For example, to browse for audio effects, just unfold Audio Effect Rack (in the Audio Effects view), and you'll

see various effects organized by type. Instrument Racks appear in two different areas of the Browser: under Instrument Rack in the Instruments View and
also in the Sounds View.

If you're looking for information on Drum Racks, you'll find this topic covered in detail in Chapter 8.

# Rack Basics

Racks have three parts, which you can reveal or hide as necessary: Macros
Controls, Chain List, and Devices. Use the buttons at the left edge of the Rack
to hide or show the different sections (see Figure 7.13).

Show/Hide          Macro          Chain List                    Devices
Switches          Controls

**Figure 7.13**  A fully expanded Instrument Rack.
*Source:* Ableton

When working with preset Racks, you'll primarily interact with the eight
Macro knobs, which allow you to tweak selected parameters of the devices
contained within, without having to understand the details of how every
device works. To create your own Racks (or modify presets beyond what the
Macros will allow), you'll need to work with the Chain List and the individual devices as well.

A chain is a lot like a track in that it has basic mixer controls: volume, pan,
and an activator switch (see Figure 7.14). Just like a track, a chain can contain
multiple devices, which process audio in series from left-to-right. However,
the Chain controls (volume, pan, etc.) process the signal *last*, even though
they appear to the left of the Devices. When a Rack has multiple chains, they
operate in parallel, a concept I'll explain next.

**FIGURE 7.14**
A chain has all the mixer controls of a track.
*Source:* Ableton

The Rack's devices show up to the right of the Chain List. Bear in mind that you can only view the devices for one chain at a time. For Racks with multiple chains, click on the chain you want to edit and its devices will appear in the Devices area.

To create a Rack from scratch, drag the Instrument Rack, Audio Effect Rack, or MIDI Effect Rack from the Browser into a track. As you can see in Figure 7.15a, there's not much to look at in an empty Rack. You add devices to the Rack by dropping them directly into the Rack's Chain List or Devices area. When a device is first added into a Rack, a chain is automatically created.

**FIGURE 7.15A**
An empty Audio Effect Rack with the Macro, Chain, and Device areas exposed.

## GROUP IT

Often, the easiest way to create a Rack is by using the Group command (see Figure 7.15b). This command is used on devices that have already been added to a track. Click in the title bar of a device and then select Group from the Edit menu. The device is now contained within a Rack.

To group multiple devices into a Rack, select them all by Shift-clicking their title bars before using Group. To remove a Rack and leave its individual devices in the track, highlight the Rack and select Ungroup from the Edit menu.

**FIGURE 7.15B**

The Group command will create a new Audio Effect Rack and place these two devices inside it.

*Source:* Ableton

# Chains

When adding additional devices to a Rack, you can drop them into the Devices area or into a chain in the Chain List. However, you can also create a new chain by dropping a device into the *drop area* of the Chain List. In Figure 7.16, this is the part of the Chain List that reads "Drop MIDI Effects, Audio Effects, Instruments or Samples Here."

**FIGURE 7.16**

A layered Instrument Rack utilizing two built-in instruments and a VST instrument. All three instruments will play simultaneously when MIDI input is received. The chain controls are used to balance the levels of the chains and pan them left or right.

*Source:* Ableton

Chains are processed in *parallel,* which means that the incoming signal is split and passed to each chain independently. In other words, if you have an Effect Rack with five chains, then you have five *copies* of the incoming signal going to five different device chains. In the case of Instrument Racks, this means that you can create layered sounds by simultaneously triggering multiple instruments, processing each instrument with different effects.

This means that even if you're a novice sound designer, you can create really interesting sounds just by layering multiple presets together. In fact, Racks can contain other Racks, so you can even use this technique to combine multiple Rack presets. If this has you rubbing your hands together and cackling like a mad scientist, you've got an idea of how powerful this is. (If you're not, don't worry—head to the laboratory for some experimenting, and you will be soon.)

## EMPTY CHAINS

Chains can also be created manually by using the Create Chain command in the context menu of the Chain List. This is handy for creating an empty chain. This might not sound useful at first, but in Audio Effect Racks it can sometimes be very useful to have a chain that passes the dry unprocessed signal to blend with the effects in the other chains.

With layered Racks, the mixing features of the Chain List become particularly important. This is where you'll balance the levels of each layer and use the Activator and Solo switches as you work to help zero in on different parts of the sound. The chains for an Instrument Rack can also be viewed directly within the Session View. The title bar of a track containing an Instrument Rack will have an Unfold button next to the track name. Clicking this reveals the Chain Mixer, a mini-track for each chain in the Rack (see Figure 7.17). Click in the title bar of any track in the Chain Mixer to display the devices for that chain in the Device View. This can be quite handy when managing complicated Racks.

**FIGURE 7.17**
The Chain Mixer showing a Rack containing chains named Saw, Fifths, and Ambience. The chain called Ambience contains another Rack (!), so it can be unfolded as well, to show the chains within.
*Source:* Ableton

# Macro Controls

With the potential to include a large number of devices, a large Rack can become cumbersome to navigate. The Macro Controls address this issue by giving you a set of eight freely mappable controls.

To assign Macro Controls, click the Map button at the top of the Rack (see Figure 7.18a). Clicking this button highlights every controllable parameter of every device in the Rack and switches the Browser into mapping mode so it displays all current mappings for the Rack. Controls can also be mapped to Macros using the context menu shown in Figure 7.18b.

**FIGURE 7.18A**

In Map mode, you can select a device parameter and then click the Map button below a Macro Control to assign it. Notice that the Saturator's Drive control is already mapped.

*Source:* Ableton

**FIGURE 7.18B**

You can map controls without entering Map mode by using context menus.

*Source:* Ableton

Click a parameter and then click on the Map button under one of the Macro Controls to assign it. (If you click on a control that's already assigned, the button will read Unmap instead.) Just like MIDI controllers, a Macro knob can be mapped to control many parameters simultaneously. For example, you could control the filter cutoff of all of the synths in an Instrument Rack with a single knob.

While in Map mode, the Browser displays all of the mappings for the Rack, as seen in Figure 7.19. This is handy when designing complex Racks, and also allows you to edit minimum and maximum values for the mapped parameter. For example, in Figure 7.19, you could adjust the Min and Max values for

**FIGURE 7.19**
In Map mode, the Browser displays mappings. You can edit minimum and maximum values here, or right-click and select Invert Range to swap Min and Max.
*Source:* Ableton

the Saturator's Drive, so it only ranges from –12 to +12dB. Bear in mind that you can set Min to be *greater* than Max, thereby inverting the behavior of the Macro Control so that it turns the value down as you turn the knob up.

After making your Macro assignments, click the Map button in the Rack's title bar to exit Map mode.

### IN CONTEXT

It's possible to edit Macro Control assignments without ever entering Map mode. Just right-click on the device parameter you want to map, and you'll see a full set of mapping commands in the context menu.

# Zones

Racks can be further customized with Zones, which allow you to dynamically activate and deactivate chains or even crossfade between them. For example, you could create a multi-effect Rack that allows you to switch between effects with the turn of a knob, or create an Instrument Rack that routes different note ranges to different instruments. There are three zone types: Chain Select, Key, and Velocity. The Chain selector exists in every type of Rack, while Key and Velocity only pertain to Instrument Racks.

## The Chain Selector

Above the Chain List, you'll see a button marked *Chain*. Click on this to expose the Chain Select Editor. This editor consists of two sections: the Chain selector, a vertical orange bar at the top that can be dragged horizontally, and the Zone Editor that allows you to create a map of active chains. The position of the Chain selector determines which chains will be active. If there is a Zone directly below the Chain selector, the associated chain will be active; otherwise, it will not.

By default, the zones for each chain are lined up at the far left of the editor, with the Chain selector directly above (as seen in Figure 7.20). If you grab the Chain selector and drag it to the right, the Rack will immediately go silent. Zones can be moved by grabbing them from the center and dragging, and resized by dragging at the edges. (The mouse pointer will turn into the bracket-shaped "trim" tool that you see when resizing clips in the Arrangement.)

**FIGURE 7.20**

Click the Chain switch to reveal the Chain Select Editor at the right.

*Source:* Ableton

If the Zones are arranged as seen in Figure 7.21, the Chain selector can be used to switch between chains by dragging it across the top of the editor. The Chain selector can be MIDI-mapped or mapped to a Macro knob so that you can select chains without having the editor open.

**FIGURE 7.21**  In the configuration shown, only one chain will ever be active at a time (since none of the Zones overlap). With the Chain selector in its displayed position, the Saturator chain will be active.
*Source:* Ableton

It's also possible to have Zones fade in and out as the Chain selector is moved. To create fades, hover the mouse over the edge of a Zone until it turns into a bracket and then move it upward slightly until the small bar running along the top of the Zone is highlighted. Click and drag to create a fade as seen in Figure 7.22.

**FIGURE 7.22**
Fades can be used to increase or decrease the volume of a chain gradually as the selector is moved. With the Chain selector in the position shown, the top chain is turned almost all the way down, while the chain below is near full volume.
*Source:* Ableton

# Key & Velocity

Instrument Racks feature two additional Zone editors for further customization: Key and Velocity. These Zones are accessed by the buttons marked Key and Vel directly above the Chain List. Key Zones are used to activate chains based on the incoming MIDI note, while Velocity Zones will activate chains based on incoming MIDI velocity.

Key Zones are handy for creating performance presets (left-hand triggers a bass sound, right-hand triggers piano), while Velocity Zones allow you to create expressive sounds, adding or switching layers as the keys are struck harder. These Zones are moved, resized, and faded just like the Zones in the Chain Select Editor, so make sure to read the preceding section if you haven't already.

Across the top of the Velocity Zone Editor (see Figure 7.23), you'll see numbers from 1 to 127, representing the incoming velocity. The Zones below are used to specify which chains will be active for a given velocity range.

In Figure 7.23, we are using Velocity Zones to filter the MIDI data coming into the Rack and determine which instrument it will trigger. In this example, velocities over 79 trigger both Massive and Operator at full volume, while

**FIGURE 7.23**  In this example, the Operator chain only sounds when the velocity is over 40, and only reaches its full volume at velocities over 80. The Massive chain sounds at all times, regardless of velocity.
*Source:* Ableton

velocities of 1–39 trigger only Massive. The volume of Operator will vary for velocities from 40–80.

Across the top of the Key Zone Editor is a piano keyboard representing the incoming MIDI note (see Figure 7.24). The Zones below are used to specify which chains will be active for a given note range. In Figure 7.24, you'll see a Rack configured so that the bottom three octaves of the keyboard trigger an acoustic bass sound, while the remainder of the keyboard triggers piano.

When you're done working with Zones, click the Hide button to hide the editor.

**Figure 7.24** Key Zones in action. The lower range of the keyboard is directed to the top chain, while the other chain handles input from the rest of the keyboard's range.
*Source:* Ableton

# Freeze and Flatten

Devices use CPU power. Some use more than others, but overall it's just a fact of life. For the most part, the usage of CPU power is managed pretty efficiently. For example, a virtual instrument won't tax the CPU unless it's playing. Not only that but it will use less CPU power to play one note than it will to play 10 notes simultaneously. However, even with a powerful computer, you'll still encounter situations where your computer is struggling to keep up with all the devices you're using. The Freeze function will help you manage these situations.

Freeze works by temporarily rendering a track's output to an audio file. A frozen track uses much less CPU power, but is limited in how much it can be edited. Let's take a look at how this works.

The easiest way to freeze is to right-click in a track's title bar and select Freeze Track from the context menu. You'll have to wait a moment while Live processes the audio—obviously, tracks with long clips (or a large number of clips) will take longer. When finished, the track will look more or less the same. You'll see all the original clips and devices, but key editing features are turned ice blue to indicate that they are "frozen" and not editable. In the Arrangement View, you may notice that frozen clips are longer than the original clips. This is typically due to a reverb or delay effect in the track. The longer frozen clip shows that the effect tail has been rendered as well (see Figure 7.25).

**FIGURE 7.25**

A frozen track in the Arrangement View. The clip is longer than the original audio, indicating an effect tail. Right-clicking on a frozen track reveals the Unfreeze Track and Flatten commands in the context menu.

*Source:* Ableton

What happens behind the scenes is that Live disables all of the clips and devices in the track and plays back the temporary audio files instead. All standard editing functions, (Cut, Paste, Duplicate, Consolidate, etc.) and most track controls (output routing, volume, pan, etc.) still work, but most detailed editing (such as changing device or clip parameters) is impossible. Adding new devices to frozen tracks is prohibited as well.

If you need to tweak frozen parameters, you can unfreeze the track (again, right-click the track and select Unfreeze Track) to restore the track to its original state immediately. You can now use the track as normal and refreeze the track when you're done.

### CAN'T FREEZE?

Be aware that there are a few cases in which tracks can't be frozen, and you'll get an error message explaining why the track can't be frozen. If you get an error because you're using a sidechained device (such as Compressor), you can work around this by first grouping the track you want to freeze (see Group Tracks in Chapter 6) and moving the sidechained device to the Group Track. Alternately, you can render unfreezable tracks by using Resampling or track-to-track recording, as explained in Chapter 6.

Next to Unfreeze Track, you'll also see the Flatten command, which is used to commit to the frozen version of the track. Flatten converts the frozen track into a standard audio track and populates it with the temporary audio clips that were created when the track was first frozen. Now you can edit and tweak the audio to your heart's content and even add new effects for further sonic exploration.

### DRAG IT

Sometimes you may want to get your hands on some of a track's frozen audio without flattening the track. To do this, just drag any frozen audio or MIDI clip to an existing audio track. The frozen audio becomes a standard audio clip, ready for editing or effects processing. To leave the original frozen clip in place, Alt(Option)-drag the clip, or use the Copy and Paste commands.

Dragging a frozen clip to the Drop Area creates a copy of the original frozen track.

## Delay Compensation

Just as all devices use CPU power, all devices generate latency. When a signal passes through an effect, it takes the device a small amount of time to perform the processing, and the result is a slight delay. By default, Live compensates for this delay, so it's not something you usually have to worry about. However, because there are rare cases where delay compensation can cause sync problems, it can be turned off by unchecking Delay Compensation under the Options menu. In the rare cases where Live cannot automatically compensate for the latency generated by a plug-in, you can manually compensate using Track Delay (see Figure 7.26).

**FIGURE 7.26**

In this example, the Track Delay feature is being used to make the track play 20ms early. Track Delay can also be adjusted creatively, making a track "rush" or "drag" a little bit.

*Source:* Ableton

When Live is compensating for devices that generate large amounts of latency, you may find that virtual instruments respond sluggishly, and any audio signals you monitor are noticeably delayed. Check Reduced Latency When Monitoring under the Options menu to compensate for this.

# 8

# Live's Instruments

Live features nine virtual instruments: Impulse, Simpler, Operator, Wavetable, Sampler, Analog, Electric, Tension, and Collision. Impulse and Simpler come free for all Live users, while the others are included in the Live Suite or must be purchased separately.

Under the Instruments View of the Browser, you'll actually see 12 items, three of which aren't exactly instruments, but are included in the same category nevertheless. Drum Racks and Instrument Racks both work in conjunction with other virtual instruments to make customized meta-instruments, ranging from the very simple to the mind-bogglingly complex. External Instrument is a handy utility for easy integration of hardware instruments and multitimbral plug-ins.

Live's instruments are a deep topic that an entire book could be devoted to. Instead of endlessly listing every parameter of every device, I've made an effort to draw attention to the most important aspects of each instrument to help you through the hardest part of the learning curve. Bear in mind that sound design and synthesis are subjects that go far beyond the discussion of any individual instrument. That said, you'll often make the most progress by learning one instrument that you really enjoy, rather than trying to become an expert at everything. Each instrument you learn will make the next one easier. I do most of my deep programming on just a few synths, and I work with presets on the others.

# Common Properties

Before getting into a discussion of each individual instrument, it's important to mention some concepts and functionality that are common to all instruments. If you're new to sound design, this may be a lot of information to take in without looking at a specific instrument. Experiment as you go.

## Filters

Filters are in the business of cutting and boosting frequencies. While an EQ such as Live's EQ Eight is often used as a scalpel, the filter in a synthesizer or sampler tends to be used like a machete. The hallmark of a really great mixing EQ is how well it can improve a sound without drawing attention to itself; synthesizer filters are beloved for their prowess at aggressively transforming whatever is passed through them.

With the exception of Electric, all of Live's instruments contain a choice of filters. The two primary characteristics of a filter are its *type* and *slope*. Some instruments also let you choose a filter *circuit*. The circuit is a secondary property of a filter. Ableton has modeled the behavior of some some famous hardware filter designs to provide additional sonic coloration. If you're new to sound design, don't worry about circuit too much; master the basic settings first.

**FILTER**

In modern audio vernacular, the term *filter* usually refers to the filters like the ones we're discussing in this section. However, in a more general sense, *filter* can mean any circuit that changes the spectral balance of an audio signal. This means that you'll sometimes see the term *filter* used in other ways. For example, the individual bands of EQ Eight are referred to as *filters*, even though they have some important functional differences from instrument filters.

# Filter Type and Cutoff Frequency

Filter types are displayed a few different ways, depending on the instrument. You'll see them shown by name, by abbreviation, or by icon as seen in Figure 8.1. The filter type and *cutoff frequency* together determine the range of frequencies that will be affected by the filter. The knob to adjust cutoff frequency will be labeled Frequency or Freq; in devices with an X-Y filter display, the cutoff frequency runs across the X-axis.

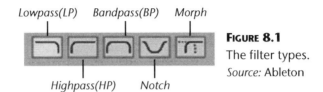

Lowpass(LP)    Bandpass(BP)    Morph

Highpass(HP)    Notch

**FIGURE 8.1**
The filter types.
*Source:* Ableton

The filter types are as follows:

▶ **Lowpass:** Cuts frequencies above the cutoff frequency, allowing lower frequencies to pass through. The lowpass is the king of all synthesizer filters—many analog synths only have a lowpass filter.

▶ **Highpass:** Cuts frequencies below the cutoff frequency, allowing higher frequencies to pass through.

▶ **Bandpass:** Cuts frequencies above and below the cutoff frequency, allowing a narrow band of frequencies to pass through.

▶ **Notch:** Cuts frequencies immediately surrounding the cutoff frequency, allowing all other frequencies to pass through.

▶ **Morph:** Cuts an adjustable range of frequencies by combining two filter types. For example, a bandpass/highpass combination aggressively cuts the frequencies below the cutoff, while those above the cutoff are more gently attenuated.

The lowpass is the king of all synthesizer filters—many analog synths only have a lowpass filter. This includes timeless legends like the Minimoog. One of the most fundamental synthesis techniques is starting out with a bright, complex sound and using a lowpass filter to reduce the high frequencies.

When highpass filters were introduced to synthesizers, it was in addition to lowpass filters, not instead of them. Before dedicated bandpass filters were commonly available, a bandpass effect was created by using a lowpass and a highpass filter in series. Analog and Wavetable both have two filter stages, so you can create multifilter sounds easily. If you're using one of the other instruments and you want more than one filter, you'll have to use an effect such as Live's Auto Filter.

The Morph filter is a really interesting beast. Its exact behavior is controlled by the Morph control—adjust it to determine which filter types are combined in what ratio. Don't worry if it takes some time to wrap your head around the morphing filter; once you're really solid on the basic filter types, it will start to make sense. The notch filter is a very different animal than the other filter types, as it tends to produce a very subtle effect. To really hear a notch filter in action, modulate the cutoff frequency. (Modulation is covered next.)

## Slope and Resonance

All of the filter types come in both 12 and 24dB/Octave variations. These numbers refer to the severity or slope of the filter. The higher the number, the more steeply the filter reduces frequencies. Generally, this means a more intense or aggressive effect, especially with high resonance values. Slope isn't labeled on the instruments. Instead, it appears as switches labeled 12 and 24, or as part of an abbreviation such as LP24 (24dB/Octave lowpass filter).

Resonance (usually labeled *Res*) controls how much the frequencies at and immediately around the cutoff frequency are boosted. The effect of boosting a narrow band of frequencies just before they are sharply reduced is an essential part of many classic synthesizer sounds. When the resonance is cranked up, moving the cutoff frequency creates the instantly recognizable "filter sweep" effect. Use some caution, however. With very high resonances, it's possible to create peaks so intense that they can damage your speakers (or your ears). Keeping the volume low during experiments is highly recommended.

## Circuit and Drive

There's a famous saying, "writing about music is like dancing about architecture" (attributed to many, but most credibly to humorist Martin Mull). Writing about different filter designs has a similar problem. All the terms used to describe different filters are highly subjective: smooth, warm, nasty, juicy, and the like. To make things even more confusing, these terms rarely apply to all uses of a particular filter design. For example, a "warm" sounding filter can start to sound decidedly "nasty" once it's driven past a certain point.

The Drive control is critical when getting to know the sound of the different filter circuits. The circuits are based on analog filter designs; each one responds to input gain differently producing overdrive and changes to the frequency response. Resonance is an important factor as well. The circuits all have slightly different filter shapes to begin with, and these differences are exaggerated when the resonance is boosted. Of the circuit types, PRD is the only one prone to creating unpleasant clipping with high resonance. The other filter types have a limiting component that will create sonically pleasing distortion instead of driving the output into the red.

The circuit types are:

- ▶ **Clean:** A basic digital filter. The Drive control is not available for this filter type.
- ▶ **OSR:** A filter based on the rare OSCar synthesizer.
- ▶ **MS2:** A filter based on the legendary Korg MS-20.
- ▶ **SMP:** A hybrid filter based on characteristics of MS2 and PRD circuits.
- ▶ **PRD:** A filter based on the Moog Prodigy.

If you want to read more about filters, check out the "Auto Filter" section in Chapter 9, "Live's Audio Effects."

# Modulation

*Modulation* is just a fancy term for changing something. For example, instead of saying that you got a great sound by repeatedly changing the filter frequency, you can impress your friends by talking about your awesome filter modulation. Modulation always has a source and a destination. The destination is the parameter being changed. The source could be an instrument's built-in envelope or LFO, or it could be a standard MIDI message, such as velocity or pitch bend.

In many of Live's instruments, you'll find numeric boxes that are used to specify modulation amounts. For example, in Figure 8.2, you'll see a box below marked Vol<Vel. This box is used to specify how much a note's velocity will affect the instrument's volume. At zero, every note will come out at the same volume, regardless of how hard you bang on your MIDI controller. As you increase this value, you'll find the instrument starts to behave like a piano—the harder you strike a key, the louder the output. You'll find that 50% is a good value to start with, but you should experiment and adjust to your taste and playing style.

**FIGURE 8.2**

Modulation boxes like the one shown here are used to route a modulator to the parameter they sit near. This example shows the very common routing of MIDI velocity to output volume.

*Source:* Ableton

You'll see similar boxes all over the place in Live's instruments, because velocity can be mapped to many parameters other than volume. For example, turning up the value of a Vel. box located near filter controls will increase the cutoff frequency as the velocity increases.

Figure 8.3 shows Analog's filter section. Here we see that the cutoff frequency has three modulation sources: LFO 1, Key, and Env. Turning any of these to a non-zero value engages modulation. The greater the value, the greater the depth of the modulation, and the more it deviates from its original value. Key is used to make the modulation respond to the pitch of the input note—the higher the note, the more the cutoff frequency will increase. The LFO and Env controls are used to apply modulation generated by the built-in LFO and envelope sections.

**FIGURE 8.3**

Many instrument parameters can be modulated by multiple sources simultaneously. However, when you are learning, it's best to start with one at a time.

*Source:* Ableton

To fully understand these last two, you'll need to know a bit more about these types of modulation sources, which will be explained next. There are other modulation types I'll be mentioning as well, and it can be a lot to absorb. Don't worry—as long as you understand the basic principle of assigning a destination to a source, you'll eventually get it all. Start simple, take your time, and experiment.

# LFOs and Envelopes

All of Live's instruments contain LFOs and envelopes for generating modulation (see Figure 8.4). While they vary a bit from instrument to instrument, they all have many things in common.

LFOs (Low Frequency Oscillators) are typically used to generate repetitive modulations, such as vibrato, tremolo, and the rhythmic "wobbles" heard in electronic music. All of Live's instruments have a selectable waveform to determine the shape of the LFO. Sine waves produce the smoothest effect, while sawtooth and square waves can be used to generate modulations with more rhythmic aggression. At the bottom of each instrument's wave menu is a random LFO style, sometimes referred to as *noise* or *S&H* (sample and hold).

All of Live's LFOs can be synchronized to the current tempo or set in Hertz (cycles per second). For Hertz, click the button marked Hz, or to synchronize, click the button marked with a musical note. The Rate control will update to display either cycles per second or note divisions, depending on the mode you select. Offset changes the overall position of the LFO, which is particularly useful in synced mode. For example, a 1/4 note LFO could be offset 180 degrees so the peaks occur in between every beat instead of directly on them.

LFO                    Envelope

**FIGURE 8.4**
Below the waveform, you'll see that Simpler's LFO can be assigned to Volume, Pitch, Pan, and Filter. To the right is the amplitude (aka volume) envelope.

Envelopes are used to create modulations that begin when a note is pressed and conclude when it is released. Most of Live's instruments have envelopes for volume, filter frequency, and pitch. Depending on the instrument, there may be additional envelopes or assignable envelopes that can be used to control any parameter you want. If you're new to working with envelopes, the volume envelope is the one you should master first.

Most of the envelopes you'll encounter use the traditional four-stage design: Attack, Decay, Sustain, and Release (ADSR). Some instruments have additional envelope stages, which will be explained in the individual instrument sections. However, if you're not sure how these work initially, don't sweat it. Just focus on the ADSR, and you'll be fine.

Here's a brief explanation of how a volume (or amplitude) envelope works. Once you've wrapped your head around this, you'll have no trouble understanding the other envelopes, as long as you're willing to be patient and do some experimentation.

As soon as a MIDI note is received, the Attack stage begins. This stage determines how long it takes the sound to reach its full volume. Turned all the way down, the note will sound instantaneously, while high Attack values will cause the note to fade in slowly. The Release stage happens as soon as the note is released. This stage determines how long it takes for the note to fade to silence once you release it. When turned all the way down, the note will be silenced immediately, while long values will cause it to linger on long after you've stopped playing your keyboard.

Decay and Sustain work in conjunction with each other. Decay specifies how long it takes for the volume to reach the Sustain level. The trick here is to understand that Decay is a measurement of time, while Sustain is a parameter value (in this example, volume). To best understand how this works, turn Sustain all the way down. This means that the Sustain level is *silence*. Now you can use the Decay control to adjust how long it takes for the note to decay to silence. Once you've got a grip on this, try setting Sustain to –12db, Decay to 50ms, and Attack all the way down. This creates a percussive transient every time you play a note, since the first 50ms of the note is 12dB louder than the note's sustain.

In some instruments, you'll see a Loop menu with the envelope controls. When Loop is set to a value other than None, the envelope will repeat. This makes the envelope behave more like an LFO. Of the Loop modes, Trigger deserves special mention because it isn't a loop. When Trigger is selected, the entire envelope occurs whether or not the note is held down. This was implemented with percussion sounds in mind. A quick tap on a pad plays the entire drum sound; you don't have to hold down the pad.

Some LFOs and envelopes have an R (retrigger) switch. This switch determines whether or not each MIDI note will restart the LFO or envelope from its starting point. For example, for a pad with long evolving envelopes, you would probably want to turn Retrigger off so you can hold notes down, and have any additional ones you add pick up the envelope at its current position.

# Global Parameters

All of Live's instruments use a handful of common commands, such as polyphony and pitch bend range, that aren't specific to the instrument's particular synthesis or sampling style. So instead of covering them with each instrument, I'll start out with this handy reference that can be applied to all of them. Just bear in mind that each synth does not have every single one of these parameters.

▶ **Detune:** Makes a fine pitch adjustment, to a maximum of 50 cents (one-half of a semitone).

▶ **Error:** Introduces a random amount of tuning variation to each note (as might happen with an unfretted string instrument, like a cello).

▶ **Glide:** Same as Portamento (see below). For instruments that offer a choice between Glide and Portamento, use Glide to get the classic monosynth glide described below, and Portamento for polyphonic operation.

▶ **Pitch Bend:** Controls how much the instrument will respond to pitch bend messages. Adjustable from 0 for no response at all to 12 or 24 semitones, depending on the instrument.

▶ **Portamento:** Causes each note to slide into the next at a rate determined by the Time parameter. For the classic portamento behavior of old monosynths, set Voices to mono when enabling this setting. With Legato enabled, only notes that overlap will slide together. The Proportional setting will automatically adjust the portamento time so that larger intervals slide longer than shorter ones.

▶ **Priority:** Determines how the instrument handles the maximum number of voices (set by the Voices parameter) being exceeded. When more notes are sounded than Voices permits, Priority will tell the instrument which notes to prioritize (and which to cut off): High (cuts off the lowest notes first), Low (cut off the highest notes first), or Last (cuts off the oldest notes first).

▶ **Semi or Transpose:** Transposes the entire range of this instrument in semitones.

▶ **Spread:** A simplified version of Unison (see below) that creates a detuned stereo output.

▶ **Stretch:** Allows the adjustment of the instrument's temperament. Increasing this value will change the tuning such that higher notes are slightly sharper and lower notes are slightly flatter, which for pianos can result in a more natural and brilliant overall sound.

▶ **Unison:** Duplicates the final output of your instrument. Unless used in conjunction with the Detune or Delay parameters, all this does is make the signal louder. Slight detuning will create a chorusing effect, while larger values can be used to create strange, out-of-tune harmonies. Delay increases the effect by delaying the unison layer up to 100ms.

▶ **Voices:** Controls how many notes can sound at once. Reducing the number of voices will save CPU power. When set to Mono (one voice), any note played will cut off any currently playing note. This is useful for emulating the behavior of classic monosynths.

# Impulse

Impulse is Live's basic drum instrument (see Figure 8.5). Where Drum Racks offer endless flexibility, Live's more limited Impulse offers instant usability due to its sparse controls and simple design.

**FIGURE 8.5** The clean and crisp Impulse interface sports eight slots for samples. Click a slot to edit its parameters below.
*Source:* Ableton

# Sample Slots

The upper portion of Impulse is made of eight square sample slots, each of which can hold one sample, and can be triggered via MIDI or with the mouse. When you hover the mouse over a slot, a Play button is revealed, along with a small rectangular Mute switch on the left, and a Solo switch to the right. To load a sample, drag an audio file from the Browser into one of the slots. You can also load samples by using the Hot-Swap button in each slot, or you can even drag in audio clips directly from Session or Arrangement.

Each slot has a full set of editing controls, but you can only edit one slot at a time—the knobs below are used to edit the currently selected slot. In other words, before editing a sample, you must first click on the slot containing it.

The MIDI notes assigned to trigger the eight cells are the white keys between C3 (middle-C) and C4 (one octave above middle-C). However, when you're editing the MIDI data of a clip playing Impulse, the normal piano keyboard will be replaced with the names of the samples assigned to each note.

### HAS ANYBODY SEEN MY KEYS?

If you're using a small MIDI controller or the computer keyboard keys, you may find yourself bashing away on the notes but hearing nothing from Impulse. This frequently occurs when the keyboard has been transposed to the wrong octave. With Impulse, any notes outside the range C3 to C4 are ignored.

If you're using the computer keyboard for MIDI input, the *Z* and *X* keys will transpose the keys. When transposing the keyboard, you'll see the current key range listed at the bottom of the screen. To transpose the range of your MIDI controller, consult its documentation.

Note that slot 8 (the farthest to the right) has one parameter that none of the other slots has: the Link switch. This links slots 7 and 8 together, so they cannot play at the same time. This is typically used for open and closed hi-hat samples, which classic drum machines (and actual drum sets!) do not allow to play simultaneously. When enabled, triggering slot 7 or 8 will immediately cut off the sample playing in the other slot.

## Start, Transpose, and Stretch

Now that you know how to trigger the samples, let's look at how to change the sound using the playback parameters offered in Impulse. The first section of controls affects the sample itself: it can be tuned, time-stretched/shortened, and have its front-end cut off. Pitch can be randomized or modulated by input velocity. The Soft button performs a fade at the beginning of the sample to soften its attack.

Transpose works as you'd expect, raising or lowering the pitch of the sample. Stretch is a bit more interesting, and is used to elongate the sample or shorten it. Long stretch times generate some weird artifacts, so make sure to experiment with this one and try it out while adjusting Transpose as well.

The Mode button changes the stretching method. In Mode A, Impulse waits a brief moment before stretching in order to ensure that the stretching doesn't distort the attack of the sound. For punchy drum sounds, this is especially important. Mode B, on the other hand, begins stretching the instant the sample starts to play. Ableton recommends Mode A for sounds that are lower in pitch, such as kick drums, and Mode B for higher-pitched sounds like hi-hats.

Turning up Start causes the sample to play back from a position later in the file. This can be used creatively to chop off the beginning of a sound, or to correct for empty space at the beginning of a sample file.

The Soft button is somewhat related to the Start dial in that it affects how Impulse plays the beginning of the sample. When Soft is off, Impulse simply plays the sample the instant it is triggered. When Soft is turned on, Impulse will perform a short fade-in. The result is that the attack of the sample is softened without changing the length of the sound. If you try this with the kick drum, you'll hear that the "snap" at the beginning of the sound is softened, while the beefy punch of the drum remains.

Notice that Transpose and Stretch can both be modulated by velocity, while Transpose also has a Random modulator beneath it. Turn this up to apply pitch randomization to the sample. A small amount of this can add subtle life and variation to an otherwise static sample.

## Saturation

The Saturation section is the simplest to use of the five controls in Impulse. Engage the Sat button and turn up the Drive to achieve overdriven percussion sounds. Small amounts of distortion can be helpful when you need to add some edge or aggression to a sample, while large amounts can mangle a sound beyond recognition. Give it a try!

## Filter

Click the Filter button to engage this section. The Mode menu is used to select the filter type, while the Freq and Res knobs set the cutoff and resonance. Notice that the resonance can be randomly modulated, just like Stretch. Note that the filter is applied after the saturation stage. This is because distorting a sound can yield some unwieldy high harmonics, which you may want to tame with a low-pass filter.

## Volume, Pan, and Decay

This section is used to set the output level (Volume) and stereo position (Pan) for each individual sample. The Decay knob shapes the tail end of a sample. If the button below the Decay knob is in Trigger mode, the Decay knob will dictate the fade-out time from the moment the sample is triggered. It doesn't matter how long you hold the pad or key that is triggering the sample—the decay time will always be whatever value is specified by the Decay knob. This is classic drum machine behavior.

In Gate mode, the fade-out won't begin until a MIDI Note Off message is received (when you lift your finger off a key). With long decay values, you may not notice any difference between these two modes. But with short values, it becomes more obvious. For example, try using Gate mode with a Decay time of 50ms. You'll find that this allows you to create variations in your drum parts by editing the length of the MIDI notes. Try making some snare hits longer than others or varying the length of hi-hats to keep things interesting. In Trigger mode, this won't work—all the hits will be reduced to a 50ms blip, regardless of the note length.

At the bottom of this section, you'll find buttons marked M and S for muting or soloing the current slot.

### Global Volume, Time, and Transpose

The Global section contains a master Volume knob, plus master Time and Transp (transpose) knobs. These last two knobs function just like the Transpose and Stretch knobs described previously, except that they apply to the entire kit. Time and Transpose can produce some really interesting effects that aren't easily created with Drum Racks—make sure to experiment!

# Simpler

When it comes to quick sample playback and manipulation, nothing is simpler than Simpler. However, don't be fooled. Simpler offers a wealth of creative possibilities within its humble interface, including a powerful beat slicing mode.

# Overview of the Interface

Simpler's main interface is organized around two tabs: the Sample tab, used for controlling sample playback, and the Controls tab, where you'll further shape and modulate the sound. For basic sampling, you'll probably never need to leave the Sample tab (see Figure 8.6).

**Figure 8.6** Simpler is the go-to instrument for quick and easy sample playback.
*Source:* Ableton

To load a sample, drag an audio file from the Browser, or an audio clip from the Session or Arrangement View, and drop it on Simpler. Since Simpler is designed to hold just one sample, any new sound dragged into the instrument will replace the previous one. The sample you load into Simpler can be triggered from any MIDI note. C3 (middle-C) will trigger the sample at its original pitch, while higher and lower notes will transpose the sample up or down.

### MULTISAMPLE MODE

When using Simpler presets, you may find the sample display window empty, reading "Multisample Mode" instead. This is the result of a clever Ableton hack that allows Simpler presets to be created in Sampler, which allows multisampling. If you own Sampler, you can get under the hood and fully edit these presets by right-clicking in Simpler's title bar and selecting Simpler → Sampler.

Along the bottom of Simpler's interface are controls for adjusting the filter, LFO, and amplitude envelope. For more information on these, see the "Common Properties" section at the top of this chapter.

## The Sample Tab

The majority of the Sample tab is taken up by a display that shows the sample's waveform. You can zoom in or out by clicking on the waveform and dragging up or down with the mouse. You can also drag left or right to navigate through the sample. Right-click in the display for additional options like Crop and Reverse.

Along the left edge of the Sample Display are three playback modes: Classic, 1-Shot, and Slice. Each of these modes has different controls for sample playback. Classic Mode is a polyphonic mode that allows you to loop the sample and play multiple notes simultaneously. Use this mode to play melodies, chords, and sustained or looped sounds. Of the three playback modes, it's the only one with Attack, Decay, Sustain, and Release controls for the amp envelope.

1-Shot and Slice are specialized modes typically used for triggering drums or shorter samples. Both of these modes have a simplified amplitude envelope offering two modes, Trigger or Gate. When Trigger is selected, the sample will play to the end, even if you release the note. In Gate mode, the sample will stop playing whenever you lift your finger off the keys or pads.

Instead of the ADSR controls for the amp envelope seen in Classic mode, 1-Shot and Slice mode have Fade In and Fade Out controls. Fade In determines how long it takes for the sample to reach full volume after it is triggered, while Fade Out controls how long it takes to fade to silence.

## Classic Mode

Along the bottom of the waveform display, you'll see the basic parameters for sample playback: Gain, Start, Loop, Length, and Fade. Any changes you make to these values will be shown graphically in the display above. There are also two important parameters that can only be set in the display: the absolute start and end points. These are represented by two flags, which should look familiar from the Clip View (see Figure 8.7).

When Start is set to 0%, playback begins from wherever you've placed the (right-pointing) start flag in the Sample Display. Length specifies how much of the sample can be played. When this value is set to 100%, playback can continue as far as the (left-pointing) end flag in the display.

**FIGURE 8.7**
Simpler can only play back the audio enclosed within the start and end flags. The audio that gets played and looped is determined by the Start, Length, and Loop controls.
*Source:* Ableton

Enable the Loop switch to activate the Loop and Fade parameters. Loop specifies how much of the sample will loop, expressed as a percentage from the end (as specified by Length). Fade applies a crossfade to the loop's connection points to smooth out any pops you may encounter when the sample starts over. When the Snap switch is turned on, Simpler automatically helps to prevent these pops by forcing the start and end points of the Loop area to snap to a zero crossing in the waveform.

Although it might not be apparent at first, some of the controls in this section are extremely expressive to adjust during sample playback. For example, altering the loop length and start positions on the fly can change the timbre and tone of the sample in wild and wonderful ways.

To the right of the Loop and Snap switches are the Voices menu and R (retrigger) switch. Voices determines the number of notes that can play back simultaneously. When the retrigger switch is turned off, one note struck multiple times will trigger the sample multiple times, using more than one voice instead of retriggering the same voice. Typically, this setting only affects sounds with longer amplitude envelope release times, and it can generally be left on.

## 1-Shot

1-shot mode is the simplest of the three modes (see Figure 8.8). It's ideal for drums or short samples that don't require elaborate control over sample playback. Trigger is the standard playback mode for playing drums using pads or keys. When triggering a kick drum, you typically want to hear the entire kick drum sample every time without worrying about the length of the MIDI note triggering it. However, if you're playing a longer sample, Gate mode may be a better choice because it makes it easy to vary how long the sample plays back for.

**FIGURE 8.8**

1-Shot mode is perfect for drums and short samples.

*Source:* Ableton

## Slice

Slice mode splits the sample into smaller samples by placing "slice markers" throughout the sample (see Figure 8.9). Each slice is triggered by a separate key or pad on your controller. This is especially useful with drum loops or song samples, because you can play each slice of the beat in any order, creating new and interesting combinations. The first slice is triggered by the note C1. Each subsequent half-step up triggers the next slice.

**FIGURE 8.9**
Each slice is triggered by a different MIDI note.
*Source:* Ableton

Slice markers can be created or deleted by double-clicking, or moved by dragging. To place slice markers automatically, select one of the four options in the Slice By menu. Three of these four options have secondary parameters, which appear to the right of the menu. The options are as follows:

- ▶ **Transient:** Slice markers are placed at transients (short, high amplitude parts of the sample). As the Sensitivity value is increased, more slice markers are created.

- ▶ **Beat:** Slice markers are placed at the beat division chosen in the Division menu. Because this mode depends on Simpler analyzing the sample and determining its tempo, you may not get accurate results when using material without a clear time reference.

- ▶ **Region:** Slice markers are spaced equally between the start and end flags. Adjust the Regions control to change the number of slices.

- ▶ **Manual:** No slice markers are created. Place slice markers where you want them. Select Clear Slices from the context menu to remove all slices and start over.

The Playback parameter determines whether playback will be Mono (only one slice at a time can be played), Poly (multiple slices can be played simultaneously), or Thru (playback continues past the current slice, all the way to the end flag).

## Warping

On the right-hand side just below the Sample Display, you'll find the Warp controls. With the Warp switch turned on, the sample's timing and pitch can be adjusted independently, similar to audio clips. When Warp is off, Simpler increases or decreases the playback speed of the sample to change the pitch. Below the Warp switch, you'll find a menu containing the same six Warp modes available in the Clip View (as explained in Chapter 5, "Clips").

If you're working with rhythmic material, you can keep it in sync with Live's tempo by doing the following. First, set the desired length of your sample with the start and end flags. Then click the Warp Region button, which will display Live's guess of the number of bars or beats the sample should be time-stretched to fit.

To make sure the sample is playing back at the same tempo as your Live Set, turn on the metronome and play the sample on your controller in time with the metronome. In some cases, the Warp engine may have analyzed the sample as half or twice as fast as the desired tempo. If so, click on either the Halve Tempo (:2) or Double Tempo (*2) button to make it play back at the correct speed. Halve Tempo will play back the sample twice as fast and Double Tempo will play it twice as slow.

# The Controls Tab

Click on Simpler's Controls tab to reveal an additional page containing a full set of controls for the filter, LFO, envelopes (filter, amplitude, and pitch), and a handful of global parameters. Or, if you want to view all of Simpler's controls at once, click the unfold switch in the left corner of the title bar. This opens the expanded view, which moves the sample controls above the Device View.

The filter section can display either an X-Y controller for cutoff frequency and resonance or the filter envelope (as seen in Figure 8.10). To hear the filter envelope in action, set Envelope Amount to a non-zero value—positive or negative values are allowed. This setting determines how much the cutoff frequency will deviate from its original value.

Envelope Amount

On/Off Switch

Show Filter
Envelope

**FIGURE 8.10**
When the filter envelope is shown, you can still adjust basic filter settings using the controls below.
*Source:* Ableton

At the far left, you'll see square on/off switches for the filter envelope and the filter itself. Keep an eye out for other on/off switches throughout the Controls tab. They are very handy for checking your sound with and without modulation.

To the right of the Filter section is the LFO. Below the waveform display, you'll see percentage boxes that are used to assign the LFO to modulate volume, pitch, pan, and filter cutoff. The LFO speed can be modulated by adjusting Key. As the Key percentage is raised, higher-pitched notes will have a faster LFO speed. Turn up the LFO's Attack time to have the LFO gradually fade in instead of starting immediately when a key is pressed. Try this out with pitch modulation to introduce vibrato after you've held a note for a moment.

The right side of the Controls tab looks a little different, depending on the playback mode. In 1-Shot and Slice mode, the pitch envelope is displayed. In Classic mode, you can choose to display the amplitude envelope or the pitch envelope, as shown in Figure 8.11. (1-Shot and Slice both have simplified volume envelopes controlled by the Fade In and Fade Out knobs.) The pitch envelope can be adjusted by dragging in the graphical display or by adjusting the numeric ADSR controls to the right. Don't forget to adjust the Amount control. If you leave it at zero, the pitch envelope won't have any effect.

FIGURE **8.11**
In Classic playback mode, you'll have to click the Pitch switch to show the pitch envelope. Below, the controls for the amplitude envelope are visible at all times.
*Source:* Ableton

At the bottom of the display are a handful of parameters explained in the Global Parameters section earlier in this chapter. Of special interest is the Ran → Pan (random pan) control. When this is turned up, a new position in the stereo field is chosen every time a note is triggered.

# Operator

Operator is a very flexible instrument that allows you to use three different types of synthesis to craft your sounds: FM, subtractive, and additive.

## Overview of the Interface

Because Operator is a deep and complex synth, it does not display all of its controls at once. Many of the parameters have been consolidated into the center window of the interface (see Figure 8.12).

**FIGURE 8.12**  The Operator interface has two sections: the center window (the display) and the eight sections surrounding it (the shell).
*Source:* Ableton

Looking at the interface, you'll see a large center window, called the *display*, surrounded by eight sections, collectively referred to as the *shell.* The shell sections are (clockwise from the lower-left corner): Oscillator A, Oscillator B, Oscillator C, Oscillator D, LFO, Filter, Pitch, and Global. If you click on one of these sections, the display will change to show its associated parameters. Try it—click anywhere within the Oscillator A section. The display will show a graphic envelope, as well as a myriad of values below it. If you click on the Pitch section, a different set of information will be shown in the display.

Ableton has placed the most tweakable parameters of Operator into the shell so that you can access them at all times. The more intricate details are neatly tucked away within the display. If you'd like, you can even hide the display, leaving only the shell exposed, by clicking the fold switch in the upper-left corner of the interface.

# Creating and Shaping Sounds

So how do you operate Operator? As you're about to see, Operator can pull off both subtractive and FM synthesis, and it has some additive synthesis features as well. Because Operator is very powerful and FM synthesis is pretty complex, this section kicks off with a lot of technical info. If at any point you get burnt out on the technical stuff, feel free to jump ahead to the "FM in Action" section and refer back as needed.

## The Algorithm

Click on the Global section in the shell. (This is the area in the lower-right corner containing the Volume and Tone controls.) The global parameters will now be shown in the display (see Figure 8.13). If you've been clicking around through the other sections in Operator, you'll notice that this display is different from the others. Across the top are various groupings of colored squares, each of which is an algorithm.

While the term *algorithm* may conjure up images of mind-bending formulas, you'll be pleased to know that Operator provides a simple way to visualize an algorithm using the assortment of colored squares in the display. By default, the upper-left algorithm will be active (its squares are solid colors, as

**Figure 8.13**
The global parameters of Operator. The algorithms run across the top. Look in the lower-right corner of this image, and you'll see that the currently selected algorithm is shown in the shell.
*Source:* Ableton

opposed to outlines). Notice that the colored letters in the oscillator section to the left are the same colors as the squares in the algorithm's display. The colored squares are therefore a map, or flowchart, of how the oscillators interact with each other.

You can read an algorithm from the top down, but starting out it's easier to read from the bottom up. If you look at this first algorithm starting at the bottom, you'll see that the bottom square is yellow. Looking at the left side of the shell, you'll see that yellow corresponds to oscillator A. You'll also see that there is a little yellow line extending downward from this square. This line shows that oscillator A will be outputting a signal that you can hear.

If you look at the next block above A, you'll see a green square (oscillator B). This block has a line extending downward from it, too, but it connects to oscillator A instead of being an output. This means that the waveform created by oscillator B will be used to change the frequency of oscillator A, which is output to your speakers. In this arrangement, oscillator B is called a *modulator*, and oscillator A is a *carrier*.

Knowing this information, you can now see what parts oscillator C and oscillator D play in this algorithm: They are additional modulators. Oscillator D will modulate oscillator C, which modulates oscillator B, which modulates oscillator A—the carrier.

Now look across to the right. The eighth algorithm over is shaped like a box. When you select this algorithm, you will see the familiar arrangement of oscillator B modulating oscillator A. The difference this time is that oscillator C is now a carrier. You will hear the waveform it generates, modulated by oscillator D. You can think of this as a dual-FM synth where you can create two unique waveforms simultaneously, which can be used in layers to thicken your sound, or to create two independent sounds that interplay with each other.

The next algorithm to take special note of is the horizontal arrangement at the far right. When using this algorithm, you will no longer be using any of the oscillators as modulators—they'll all be sent directly to the output. In this, each oscillator will output its own unique waveform, which can be mixed together and filtered, very much like a classic analog synth.

Below the algorithms is the routing matrix, which gives you enormous modulation flexibility. We'll discuss this after we've gone over more of the basics of Operator.

## The Oscillators

Leave the algorithm set to the default vertical arrangement and click on oscillator A in the shell. The algorithms in the display will now be replaced with an envelope and additional parameters. These are all of the control parameters for operator A. By default, each operator is set to produce a sine wave with instantaneous attack and release. Try playing a few notes to hear this for yourself.

In the shell, all you can set is the tuning and volume of the oscillator. (You can also click the colored ABCD buttons to turn the oscillators on and off.) Tuning and volume have a tremendous impact on the sounds resulting from FM synthesis, so these controls have been made easily accessible. Tuning has two modes: Variable and Fixed. The Variable setting (the default) causes the operator to change frequency, based on the notes you play. The Fixed setting (enabled by clicking the Fixed box of an operator) causes it to ignore incoming note information and will instead sound at the specific frequency that you set in the shell.

When in Fixed mode, the two tuning options will be Freq and Multi, which stand for frequency and multiplier, respectively. The operator's frequency is determined by multiplying the Freq by the Multi value. If the frequency is 100Hz and the multiplier is one, the resulting frequency will be 100Hz

(100Hz × 1 = 100Hz). If the frequency is 245Hz and the multiplier is 10, the operator's frequency will be 2,450Hz.

When in Variable mode, the oscillator frequencies are no longer shown. Instead, you are presented with Coarse and Fine adjustments, which express the operator's frequency as a ratio of the base frequency. An operator with a Coarse setting of 2 will sound an octave higher than one with a Coarse setting of 1. An operator with a Coarse setting of 0.5 will sound an octave lower. You can use the Fine adjustment to create ratios that are fractions, such as 1.5 (Coarse 1, Fine 500) or 2.25 (Coarse 2, Fine 250).

Tucked away in the display is a parameter named *Wave*. The option below it is currently set to Sin—a sine wave. Click on Sin to open a menu with all of the available wave shapes. Try out a few of them to hear how they sound.

The saw and square waves have multiple shapes, denoted by a number after the name. The number in the waveform name tells you how many harmonics were used to create the wave shape. In the case of Saw3, only three harmonics were used: the fundamental, the second harmonic, and the third harmonic. As a result, the Saw3 waveform still resembles a sine wave more than a sawtooth wave. As you go further down the menu of waveforms, you'll see saws with greater numbers of harmonics. Saw64 uses 64 harmonics to generate the sawtooth wave, and sounds like a traditional analog sawtooth, while D signifies a digital sawtooth—the brightest of the bunch. This same numbering scheme is true for the square waves as well.

## The Oscillator Display

Once you dig into FM synthesis with Operator, you'll find that the various algorithm/waveform/tuning options offer a wide array of wild and complex tones. But there's even more flexibility available. Operator also allows you to edit the built-in waveforms visually by graphically adding and subtracting harmonics.

Above the Envelope display, click on the box marked *Oscillator*, next to the box marked *Envelope*. This changes the display to show you the harmonics of the waveform being used for the currently selected operator. If Sine is selected from the menu below, you'll see exactly one bar all the way to the left of the display. This tells you that the wave is composed of a simple fundamental pitch with no higher harmonics. Now try selecting Saw3 from the menu. This is the sawtooth wave we discussed earlier, composed of only three harmonics. With Saw64, you'll see harmonics cascading across the display, illustrating the complex sound of a true sawtooth wave.

After you have a basic understanding of what you're looking at here, things get really interesting. When your mouse floats above the harmonics display, it turns into a pencil, allowing you to freely alter the wave's harmonics. Try it—start slowly, increasing or decreasing the right-most harmonics to make the sound brighter or darker. Then go crazy with it, drawing or deleting harmonics as you please. Notice that as you do this, the waveform display below changes as well, and the Wave menu now reads User.

This makes for a truly overwhelming number of options for programming this synth. If you're new to Operator, it might make more sense to get a handle on simple FM before you start building all sorts of custom waveforms. However, the mad scientist in you may win the day and demand a purely experimental approach to sound design. That's OK, too!

## FM in Action

Enough talk, already. It's time to hear what all of this sounds like. Load up an Operator in its default state and play a note—you should hear a single sine wave. You are hearing oscillator A by itself. Now, while holding the note, turn up the level of oscillator B. As you do this, you will hear the sound of oscillator A change. This is because oscillator B is modulating oscillator A, resulting in what are called *side bands*. Oscillator A becomes more and more brilliant (more upper harmonics) as you increase the level of operator B, increasing the modulation amount. If you turn oscillator B back down again, oscillator A will revert to a sine wave.

Conceptually, this is the opposite approach seen in traditional subtractive synthesis where one starts with a bright complex wave, such as a sawtooth, and then removes high harmonics with a low-pass filter. With FM synthesis, you can actually start with a harmonically simple sound like a sine and add high harmonics by adding modulation.

For your next experiment, turn up oscillator B again and then play with the Coarse knob. The result will be another constant tone, but one with a different harmonic structure. As you turn up the Coarse knob, you will be changing the frequency ratio between oscillators A and B in whole numbers (for example, 1 to 2, 1 to 3, 1 to 8, and so on).

Things start to get strange, however, when you begin to change the Fine adjustment. Hold a note and slowly increase the Fine setting. With a small change, the sound will go "out of tune," and with a large change will become "without tune." This is because the frequencies of the modulator and carrier are no longer at a musically coherent (whole number) ratio. Next, try switching oscillator B into Fixed mode and play some notes. As you play across the range of the keyboard, you'll get constantly changing inharmonic modulations, which are the result of the modulator staying at a fixed pitch while the carrier's pitch changes.

But enough math for now. If you want to explore the principles behind FM synthesis further, there are many scholarly works on the topic. For now, all that's important to know is that messing with fine-tuning or switching modulators into Fixed mode moves you out of the realm of the melodic into sci-fi weirdness, synthetic percussion, and all-out mayhem.

### A HIDDEN MODULATOR

While the Operator algorithms select which oscillators will be modulators for others, there is another hidden modulation you can perform as well. Click on an oscillator's section to show its parameters in the display. If it's not currently being modulated by any other oscillators, you'll notice that the Feedback parameter becomes enabled. This uses the output of the oscillator as a modulation input for itself. If you start with a sine wave and turn the Feedback parameter up to 50%, the result will be nearly identical to a sawtooth wave. If you have a waveform other than sine selected, the result will be extremely strange. Try it out!

## The Envelopes

Each oscillator has its own volume envelope. Not only that, but the Filter and Pitch sections also have their own envelopes, as does the LFO. That's seven envelopes for a single voice!

You heard in the previous experiments how the volume of a modulator would affect the timbre of the carrier. Therefore, using an envelope to change the volume of a modulator will allow you to change the harmonic content of a sound as it plays, like using a filter envelope in subtractive synthesis.

Continuing on with the experiment we started earlier, crank up Oscillator B to full volume and modify its volume envelope so that it decays to silence very quickly. The sound now has some motion to it—it has an aggressive attack that quickly decays into the fundamental sine wave. This is because oscillator B plays at full volume when you strike a note, but it quickly fades out after the initial attack. This is what creates the harmonic complexity at the beginning of every note.

The remaining parameters in the display for an oscillator govern how velocity and keyboard range will affect the oscillator's pitch and level. For starters, the Vel parameter will modulate the oscillator's volume based on velocity—positive values will cause the operator to increase in volume as you play harder, while negative values will attenuate the operator the harder you play. If you use this setting on a modulator, it will have a similar effect to applying velocity scaling to a Filter Envelope in subtractive synthesis. The harder you play, the more FM modulation will result, thus causing a brighter sound. The Key parameter will cause the operator to play louder or softer (depending on the value you use) as you move into the higher registers of your keyboard.

## The LFO

Moving to the right side of the Operator interface, you'll find the LFO section right at the top. On a synthesizer, an LFO is used to create repetitive automations for other parameters of the synth. On a subtractive synthesizer, LFOs will often be used to modulate the filter cutoff or the volume. The LFO of Operator can do this and much more.

To activate the LFO, turn it on with the little box to the left of its Waveform menu in the shell. Once active, you'll see all the parameters appear in the display. Pay close attention to the four lettered boxes matching the oscillators. By default, these are all turned on, and the four oscillators will all have their pitches modulated by the LFO. To get a feel for what you can do with this LFO, try turning off the routing to your carrier oscillator(s) and route the LFO to the modulators only.

An interesting feature of Operator's LFO is that it's not relegated to low frequency (slow speed). The LFO's range can be adjusted with the tiny dropdown menu next to the wave shape. The options are *L* for low-frequency mode, *H* for high-frequency mode, and *S* for sync. In high-frequency mode, you can run it at audio rate, thus making it act as another modulator for your FM experiments.

## The Filter

Coaxing your desired tone from an FM synth is not easy, especially for beginners. However, generating a complex waveform with FM is easy. The filter allows you to treat this complex FM waveform as the starting waveform for subtractive synthesis, taking advantage of the simplicity a classic filter offers. Thanks to Operator's FM capabilities, your arsenal of waveforms is nearly limitless.

Like the LFO, the filter must be turned on before it will have any effect. Do this by clicking the box just to the left of the Filter-Type menu. You'll see the center display spring to life with color, indicating that the filter is active. The filter contains the same six-parameter envelope as the operators and LFO that will modulate the Filter Cutoff frequency. The amount of envelope modulation is set with the Envelope parameter. The other parameters in the display determine how key position and velocity will affect the filter.

Operator's filter also includes a saturator/waveshaper (found in the display). The Shaper menu offers you four types, two of them being classic saturation (Soft and Hard), and two being more unusual digital-sounding effects (Sine and 4-bit).

## The Pitch Settings

Below the Filter section is the Pitch section, which contains an envelope, as well as some other unique pitch-related controls. To make the pitch envelope work, you'll have to switch it on using the switch at the left and turn the Pitch Env dial. You can use both positive and negative values here, so it's possible to reverse the effects of the envelope.

As with the LFO, you can choose which oscillators will be modulated with the pitch envelope. Often, it's not necessary to modulate all the oscillators.

Of course, if you don't modulate them all, you might get inharmonic results. However, this can be desirable on the attack of a sound, such as when making drum sounds.

**CUT IT SHORT**

Make sure to explore Operator with your mouse's right button—it's jam-packed with all sorts of shortcuts. For example, the Frequency knob's context menu includes a Play by Key option that configures the filter to track the keyboard perfectly, while the oscillator display has an Export AMS option that exports a custom user waveform to an audio file with an .ams extension that can be used as a sound source for Sampler.

In the display of this section, you'll find the Glide setting, which is explained in the "Global Parameters" section at the top of this chapter.

## The Global Settings

The last section of Operator contains Global Settings for the instrument. You're already familiar with the algorithms contained there, but there are still a few more things you should know.

First, the Time control. This knob adjusts the speed of all of the envelopes in Operator simultaneously. You can slow them down dramatically or speed them up to a point where you hardly notice them. This is a great tool for performing final tweaks to a sound you've mostly finished designing. It's also a great dial to tweak on presets or automate to add expressiveness to a sound.

To the right of the Time knob is the Tone knob, which is a handy way to tame high frequencies. Sometimes, a sound will sound OK at one pitch, but may sound harsh when played an octave or two higher. This is because FM synthesis is capable of producing extremely high overtones, which may sound unpleasant. Grab the Tone knob to get this under control.

Within the display for the Global Settings, below the algorithms, is Operator's routing matrix. This setting allows many different parameters to be modulated in a variety of ways, making this synthesizer dramatically more powerful than it was before.

The first item to notice here is located in the "Connection B" column and is marked *Pitch*. This is the Pitch Bend range, which is explained in the "Global Parameters" section.

Running vertically along the left side of the display are the various modulators that Operator can respond to: Velocity, Key, Aftertouch, Pitch Bend, and Mod Wheel. The menus and numeric values that appear across each row are for routing these modulators to specific parameters. For example, let's say you want the velocity of incoming notes to control the overall volume of Operator. To do this, just set Connection A in the Velocity row to Volume and set Amount A to specify how velocity sensitive you want the volume to be (70% is a good default value). Now, what if you want the velocity to control the waveshaper, too, so as you play harder, the notes also become more distorted? No problem: just set Amount B to Shaper Drive and set the amount as desired. Get the idea? You can use any of these five modulators to control two different parameters of your choice simultaneously.

Below the routing matrix, you'll see seven more parameters. The three parameters on the right are used to set the pan position of Operator's output, along with Key and Random modulator amounts. The Interpolation and Antialias controls are mostly there for backward compatibility with older versions of Operator, which did not have these settings. Leaving them on results in a smoother, more polished sound, at the cost of a slightly higher CPU load.

# Sampler

Sampler is Simpler's big brother: a fully featured multisampling instrument with a full complement of modulation, filtering, and mapping options. Although Live has powerful sampling functions in Simpler, Sampler expands on these capabilities by introducing support for multisampling, as well as a wide range of sound-design and modulation options.

Looking at the Sampler interface, you'll see that its functions are organized into a number of different tabs: Zone, Sample, Pitch/Osc, Filter/Global, Modulation, and MIDI. Let's have a look at each of these and see how they work.

# The Zone Tab

Unlike Simpler, Sampler can hold many samples at once. This makes it possible to do many things. You could create a bank of favorite kick drum samples and switch between them quickly, or create an intense layered pad from many different samples.

Yet another technique is called *multisampling.* Instead of simply transposing a single sample up or down the keyboard, multisampling uses many samples to capture the sound of an instrument at multiple points in its frequency and dynamic range. Setting up the intricate sample mapping required to accurately re-create the sound and feel of a complex acoustic instrument like a violin is an advanced topic that we can't really cover here in any depth. That's OK; the world is full of great multisampled presets such as Live's Grand Piano.

Clicking the Zone tab brings up Sampler's Zone Editor. It's used to map samples across key and velocity ranges, and it appears above the main Sampler interface, as seen in Figure 8.14. The Zone Editor opens in its own special window, directly above the Track View.

On the left side of the Zone Editor is the sample layer list. All of the individual samples belonging to a given instrument will appear here, referred to as *layers.* For very large multisampled instruments, this list might be hundreds of layers long. (Note that selecting any layer by clicking it will load its sample into the Sample tab for examination.)

The Zone Editor actually contains three different editors: Key, Velocity, and Sample Select. Figure 8.14 shows the Key Zone Editor, which is displayed by selecting the Key switch above the list. Samples are triggered only when incoming MIDI notes lie within their key zone. By default, the key zones of newly imported samples cover the full MIDI note range. In other words, unless you edit the zones, all layers will be triggered simultaneously.

Zones can be moved or resized by clicking and dragging in the middle or from their right or left sides. Zones can also be faded in or out by clicking and dragging the narrower small line above. This makes it easy to set up smooth crossfades from zone to zone.

**FIGURE 8.14** Ableton's Sampler unfolds to show a layer/zone editor. These samples are assigned to different ranges of the keyboard. If the zones overlap, multiple samples will be triggered by the keys in the overlapping zones.
*Source:* Ableton

The Velocity Zone Editor is used to trigger samples according to velocity range. The top of the editor is numbered from 1 to 127, the full range of MIDI velocities. Edit the zone length for any layer to limit its playback to certain velocities. If you want to read more about Velocity Zone editing, check out the Racks section of Chapter 7, "Using Effects and Instruments." The behavior of Zones in Simpler and Racks is nearly identical.

The last option is the Sample Select Editor, which is shown by clicking the Sel switch. This is a very Ableton touch, and works like the Chain Selector in an Instrument or Effect Rack. As the sample selector is moved from left to right, it enables the sample in the range shown in the editor. In the example shown in Figure 8.15, the selector can be moved to enable one of the layers shown.

**FIGURE 8.15** By using the Sample Select Editor, you can have loads of different samples at your fingertips just by turning a knob on your MIDI controller.
*Source:* Ableton

## AUTO ZONE

If you drop a lot of samples into the Zone Editor, the zone editing can be tedious. If you need to spread zones out across the editor, right-click and select Distribute Ranges Equally to save some time.

# The Sample Tab

The Sample tab is where you can set the playback characteristics of individual samples. A large part of this tab is devoted to displaying the waveform of the sample you currently have selected (see Figure 8.16). The name of the sample is displayed below in the Sample drop-down chooser box. You can select a particular sample to edit by clicking it in the Zone Editor window, by using this chooser, or by clicking the Hot-Swap button next to the chooser, which will take you to the Browser and show you a list of samples used in the current instrument.

At first glance, the Sample tab appears similar to the display of Simpler, and it serves a similar function. However, Sampler gives you different options to control how each of your samples plays back and loops. Note that the settings

**FIGURE 8.16** The Sample tab.
*Source:* Ableton

in the Sample tab will affect only the sample (or multiple samples) currently selected in the Zone Editor.

▶ RootKey sets the reference pitch for the current sample. When a given sample is triggered by an incoming MIDI note matching the RootKey, it will be played back at its original pitch. MIDI notes higher or lower than the RootKey will transpose the sample accordingly.

▶ Detune makes fine adjustments to the sample tuning, +/–50 cents.

▶ Volume adjusts sample volumes individually.

▶ Pan adjusts the left-right position of individual samples.

▶ The Reverse button causes the entire multisample to play backward when triggered. In this case, sample playback begins from the sample end point and proceeds backward to the sample start point.

▶ When the Snap button is engaged, the start and end points of your sample will snap to the waveform zero-crossing points in order to avoid clicks or pops in playback.

To the right, the rest of the controls in the Sample tab work together with the Global Volume envelope in the Filter/Global tab to determine how your samples should be played back.

The Sample Start setting determines where the playback of the sample will begin when triggered, while the Sample End setting determines where playback will end.

## Sustain and Release

The Sustain and Release modes are selected with the various arrow buttons located at the center of the area below the sample display. These determine how sample playback works during their respective phases of the ADSR volume envelope.

There are three Sustain modes: On (single arrow), Loop (double arrow), and Loop Back and Forth (bidirectional arrows). When On is selected, the sample will play from beginning to end, until either it reaches the Sample End or the volume envelope (on the Filter/Global page) comes to the end of its release stage, whichever comes first.

With Loop enabled, the sample will play from the beginning until the loop end, at which point it will revert to the loop start and continue looping. Loop Back and Forth differs only in that when it reaches the loop end point, it will play backward until it reaches the loop start. Toggling the Link button automatically sets the sample start to the same point as the loop start and prevents them from being set to separate values.

Activating one of the looped Sustain modes also allows you to modify the Release mode, which determines what will happen during the release phase. When set to Off, the sustain loop simply continues through the release phase of the volume envelope. When set to On (single arrow), however, the sustain loop is disabled during the release phase, and the sample plays through to the end point.

Selecting one of the loop modes enables the Release Loop (notice the second loop brace to the right—refer to Figure 8.16), a separate loop with an end point fixed to the Sample End value. With either Loop (double arrow) or Loop Back and Forth (bidirectional arrows), the sustain loop is deactivated during the release phase, allowing the sample to play through to the end, at which point it loops back to the Release Loop point, until the end of the release phase.

Sustain Loop Crossfade (labeled *Crossfade*) sets fades at the loop boundaries in order to smooth out the loop. You can also use Sustain Loop Detune (labeled *Detune*) to make small adjustments in pitch as desired.

The Interpol (interpolation) control lets you decide which algorithm you want Sampler to use when transposing samples. You can choose from No, Normal (the default), Good, Better, or Best Interpolation. Your choice here can have a significant impact on the overall quality of sound coming out of Sampler, but you also need to remember that selecting Better or Best will increase the hit on your CPU.

You can engage the RAM mode switch if you want to load the entire multisampled instrument into your computer's RAM instead of streaming it from disk in real time (the default mode). This can be used to alleviate any disk overload problems you encounter when using Sampler, but if you have many samples loaded into RAM, this will eat up your available memory quickly and affect the performance of your computer/software adversely. (By default, Sampler will load only the beginning of each sound into memory at first and then stream the rest of the sound from your hard drive as it plays.)

The next tabs include a number of controls that shape and modify the sound of your samples. Let's look at what you can do with them.

# The Pitch/Osc Tab

The Pitch/Osc tab (see Figure 8.17) contains a range of controls for Sampler's modulation oscillator and pitch envelope, which are used to modulate the audio output from the playback in the Sample tab.

**FIGURE 8.17** The Pitch/Osc tab.
*Source:* Ableton

## The Modulation Oscillator

The upper part of the Pitch/Osc tab is occupied by the controls for Sampler's modulation oscillator. This oscillator makes no sound of its own, but it is used instead to modify your samples via frequency or amplitude modulation (FM or AM). You can toggle between these two modes using the FM and AM buttons on the left side of the interface. To hear the modulation oscillator in action, start with the parameters on the right. Crank up the Volume, select a waveform from the Type menu, and adjust the Coarse and Fine parameters. The functionality of these controls is identical to those in Operator, so make sure to read up on FM synthesis in the Operator section of this chapter if you need more information.

If you use the modulation oscillator for amplitude modulation, the modulator affects level instead of pitch. However, when amplitude is modulated at extremely high rates, it produces effects unlike anything you might expect. Turn on the Fixed switch and set Freq to a very low value to produce a tremolo effect. Crank up Freq past 40Hz, and you'll start to hear weird sound-bending harmonics. Think of AM as a strange cousin of FM; once you've got a handle on FM, it's pretty easy to work with.

The Modulation oscillator's control interface features an image of an envelope at left, showing the ADSR envelope stages for the oscillator. If you select a long attack time here, then the effect of the oscillator will fade in slowly. You can change the envelope settings by moving the breakpoints of the envelope itself or by adjusting the values in the boxes to the right.

## The Pitch Envelope

The lower part of the Pitch/Osc tab contains an additional set of controls for a separate pitch envelope. There is a graphical display for editing, as well as numerical controls. This envelope can be used to create pitch changes in your samples. The setting just to the left of the envelope, labeled *Amount*, will adjust the total amount of pitch-shifting effect in semitones.

# The Filter/Global Tab

The Filter/Global tab (see Figure 8.18) contains the controls for Sampler's powerful morphing filter, as well as a Global volume envelope. Both of these affect the master output of Sampler.

**FIGURE 8.18** The Filter/Global tab.
*Source:* Ableton

The Filter section contains all the usual goodies explained in the "Common Properties" section of this chapter. Of special notice is the Shaper below. This offers the same distortion/waveshaping modes offered by Operator, with the additional option of changing its position in the signal path. Click the arrow directly above the Shaper switch to apply waveshaping before or after the filter. Try this out, and you'll see this is no small distinction. Just changing the order of operations here has a big impact on the sound.

The volume envelope is a global envelope; it will affect how the final output of Sampler is heard. You have standard Attack, Decay, Sustain, and Release controls here, as well as an Initial setting that allows you to specify the volume at the moment the envelope is triggered.

Also notice the small handles in the graphical display, in between those representing the ADSR values. These can be dragged to change the envelope shape from linear to exponential. When dragged, you'll notice the controls below refresh to show numeric values for the slope you're drawing.

In the lower right-hand corner, you'll see the R (retrigger) switch. When the retrigger switch is turned off, one note struck multiple times will trigger the sample multiple times, using more than one voice instead of retriggering the same voice. Typically, this setting only affects sounds with longer amplitude envelope release times, and it can generally be left on.

# The Modulation Tab

The Modulation tab (see Figure 8.19) gives you four different modulation sources you can use to continuously modulate and change nearly any parameter in Sampler. There is a modulation envelope here, as well as three separate LFOs and a familiar range of controls.

The left-most section of this tab is the interface for the auxiliary envelope, which can be used to apply ADSR modulation to a variety of Sampler's parameters. It can be switched on by using the Aux button on the left edge of the interface. If you click the drop-down choosers labeled *A* and *B* at the bottom of this part, you will see a long list of other parameters in Sampler. Any of these can be selected as a destination to be modulated by the envelope. The A and B choosers enable you to select two simultaneous modulation targets to be affected.

**FIGURE 8.19** The Modulation tab.
*Source:* Ableton

There are three LFOs here you can also use to modulate a wide variety of parameters in Sampler. The first one, labeled LFO1, has four particular global parameters: Volume, Filter, Pan, and Pitch. The other two, LFO2 and LFO3, can be freely assigned to a list of parameters in Sampler; just as with the modulation envelope, the A and B choosers enable you to select two simultaneous modulation targets to be affected by each LFO.

# The MIDI Tab

I'm sure you won't be surprised when I tell you that the MIDI tab (see Figure 8.20) is the place where you set up MIDI modulation routings for Sampler. Here, you can use various MIDI parameters as modulation inputs and use them to affect various parameters in Sampler. Let's look at how to do this.

The interface here allows you to take the MIDI input from a number of specific parameters. The MIDI parameters available as sources for modulations are listed along the left-hand edge of the tab, including Key (pitch), Velocity, Off Vel (release velocity), Aftertouch, Mod Wheel, and Pitch Bend. Any of these input sources can be mapped to two different modulation destinations

**FIGURE 8.20**

The MIDI tab. As shown, the modulation wheel will control vibrato, and velocity will affect the filter cutoff frequency.

*Source:* Ableton

simultaneously, using the Destination A and Destination B drop-down choosers. You can set the amount of modulation with the Amount A and Amount B controls. By routing the Velocity parameter to control volume, you can make your samples play back more loudly or softly when those channels receive higher or lower MIDI velocity messages, or, for example, when you play harder or softer on your MIDI controller keyboard. (Note that you can also do this with the Vol<Vel control on the Filter/Global page.)

## Importing Third-Party Instruments

As mentioned previously, if you already own any collections of multisampled instruments in AKAI, GigaStudio, Apple ESX24/Garageband, SoundFont, or Kontakt format, you can import these into Sampler for easy access in Live. To import a third-party instrument preset into Sampler, locate the file in the Browser and drag it into Live. If this doesn't work, you may be able to open the preset by dragging it from the Browser and dropping it onto Sampler. You can see all of your imported instruments in the User Library under Sampler/Imported.

Some more complex multisampled instruments will be converted to Instrument Rack presets using multiple instances of Sampler in order to better translate the sound of the original. For most multisample formats, Live will import the audio samples into the User Library. However, in the case of Apple EXS24/GarageBand formats, Live will create new Sampler presets that reference the original WAV or AIF sample files. This means that they will not work if you remove the original WAV or AIF samples. (However, Live's File Manager also offers the option to collect and save these external samples into the Library, if desired.)

# Wavetable

Wavetable is Live's newest, and possibly its most fun instrument. It combines a powerful sound engine capable of a wide array of sounds with the most streamlined interface Ableton has come up with yet. To get a quick look at the power of Wavetable, open the expanded view by clicking the unfold switch in the upper left-hand corner. By default, the expanded view shows the envelopes and LFOs. Drag the top edge of the expanded window upward to expand it even further and show the oscillators. It may seem intimidating because there's so much going on, but fear not. You don't need to use everything all at once.

# The Oscillators

Forget about the rest of Wavetable and plan on spending some time getting to know the oscillators (see Figure 8.21). The range of sounds that can be produced by these guys is amazing. The core of the oscillator is the wavetable. Each wavetable is a series of waveforms. By adjusting the wavetable's position, you seamlessly fade from one wave to the next. When you select a wavetable, you're selecting a range of timbres; by adjusting the position, you're selecting a timbre from within that range.

*Wavetable
Categories    Wavetables*

**FIGURE 8.21**
The Wavetable oscillators are a sonic playground.

*Position*

*Effect Mode*

Start out by navigating the wavetable menus, selecting a category from the menu on the left and a wavetable from the menu to the right. Play a few notes or record a MIDI clip and sweep the Position slider up and down to get a sense of the range of tones each wavetable can produce. Don't go too fast when changing the position—small moves can produce some very interesting sonic variations.

Select an oscillator effect from the Effect Mode menu to take the sound palette even further. To the right of the menu are two percentages that you'll adjust to fine-tune the effect. (They change their names depending on the mode). Adjust Pulse Width (PW) and Sync (in Classic mode) or Warp and Fold (in Modern mode), and you'll find these effects transform the harmonics in a pleasing way that's virtually idiot proof.

FM mode is a bit more unwieldy, unless you're looking to create inharmonic madness, in which case it's decidedly wieldy. Crank up Amount (Amt) to 50% so you can hear the frequency modulation in action. As you adjust the Tune parameter, you'll hear that with a few exceptions (such as 50% and 80%), some very out-of-tune harmonics are introduced. However, with Amount being set very low (close to 1%), a wide variety of Tune settings can be used without obscuring the original pitch.

Select the Osc 2 tab to layer a second oscillator, if you dare. Adjust the Semi and Detune (Det) controls to detune the oscillators in semitones or cents. To the left of the wavetable controls, you'll see the sub oscillator section. Turn on the Sub switch to add low frequencies to the sound and adjust the Gain, Tone and Octave controls as desired.

# The Matrix

The modulation matrix is where you assign the functionality of Wavetable's three envelopes and two LFOs (see Figure 8.22). By default, you'll see three modulation targets running down the left side: Oscillator 1 Position (Osc 1 Pos), Amp, and Pitch. Additional modulation targets are added automatically. Every time you click on a control, it appears on the left side of the matrix. If you assign modulation to the control, it remains in the matrix. Otherwise, it disappears and is replaced with the next control you click on.

Drag up or down in the matrix to assign positive or negative modulation. Double-click on an existing assignment to remove it. Notice in Figure 8.22 that both of the modulations are affecting parameters of Oscillator 1. This is

**FIGURE 8.22**

As shown, LFO 1 is modulating the position of oscillator 1 and LFO 2 is modulating the pulse width.

where I suggest you begin as well. The position and effect parameters produce harmonically rich variations; the movement produced by modulating them is a hallmark of wavetable synthesis. Small modulation amounts can produce really exciting results, so take your time.

Along the bottom are two global controls. Use the Time control to speed up or slow down all envelopes and LFOs. Adjust Amount to change the overall amount for all modulations assigned in the matrix.

Click the MIDI tab to reveal the MIDI modulation matrix. Nearly identical to the standard modulation matrix, this view makes it possible to route standard MIDI messages to any parameter of Wavetable. This matrix contains columns for Velocity, Note, Pitch Bend, Aftertouch, and Mod Wheel. Unlike Live's other instruments, Wavetable has no dedicated controls for pitch bend range and volume<velocity. These adjustments are made in the MIDI matrix, as seen in Figure 8.23.

**Figure 8.23**

As shown, velocity (Vel) is routed to overall output level (Amp). The pitch bend range has been set to two semitones by routing the pitch wheel (PB) to Pitch with a modulation amount of 2. The mod wheel (Mod) will control the position of oscillator 1 (Osc 1 Pos).

# The Modulators

In expanded view, you can see all five modulators at once (see Figure 8.24). If you're using the standard view, you can edit one modulator at a time in the Mod Sources tab.

In most respects, the modulators are just like those of Live's other instruments, as explained in the "Common Properties" section of this chapter. In the LFOs, the Shape control is of particular interest. Its exact function varies depending on the wave shape selected above. For example, when the square wave is selected, Shape adjusts the pulse width; when triangle is selected, it skews the shape until it becomes a saw wave. Make sure to try negative values as well as positive.

**FIGURE 8.24** Envelope 3 and LFO 1, as shown in the expanded view. In the upper-right corner of Env 3 is the envelope's loop menu. Above the LFO waveform, you'll see the Attack (A) control, which is used to make the LFO fade in.

Next to Shape, there's an Amount control that reduces the amplitude of the LFO. This is here to give your modulations an abundance of flexibility. If the LFO is only modulating one target, adjusting Amount is the same as adjusting the modulation amount in the matrix. But if it's modulating several targets, it provides an easy way to change the depth of all modulations with a single control.

# The Filters

Wavetable has two filters shown in Figure 8.25. They are identical to the filters described earlier in the chapter, but because there are two of them, some unique possibilities arise.

*Filter 1 On/Off*     *Filter 2 On/Off*

*Filter Routing*

**FIGURE 8.25**
Wavetable has two filters with flexible routing.
*Source:* Ableton

The Filter Routing determines the signal path for the filters. In Serial mode, the output of filter 1 is sent to filter 2. This is the simplest mode, useful for classic two-filter techniques. For example, a lowpass and a highpass filter can be combined to create a bandpass with a completely customized shape. Or, crank up the drive of a lowpass filter and then process that signal with a second lowpass filter to control the overtones created by the overdrive.

In Parallel mode, the output from the oscillators is split and sent to both filters at once. This is a powerful setting that can take a little getting used to. For example, combining a highpass and a lowpass no longer creates a bandpass effect because each filter adds back the frequencies subtracted by the other. That said, this routing can create some effects that would be impossible otherwise, such as two bandpass filters set at different frequencies. In Split mode, oscillator 1 is sent to filter 1 and oscillator 2 is sent to filter 2. This makes it possible to create layered sounds as if you were working with two separate synthesizers.

# The AAS Instruments

The remainder of Live's built-in instruments are developed in partnership with Applied Acoustic Systems, a software company that specializes in modeling technology. Physical modeling concerns itself with creating mathematical equations that imitate or "model" the behavior of real-world acoustical events. Three of these synthesizers—Collision, Electric, and Tension—are based on familiar physical processes: hammers hitting tone bars and guitar picks plucking strings, for example. Analog, on the other hand, models behavior that goes on under the hood of an analog synthesizer, so from a synthesis standpoint, it's going to be a bit more familiar.

While this may sound fairly pedestrian, get ready for a major paradigm shift if you've never worked with a physical modeling synth before. Because you'll be working with controls that model physical events, you'll need to be aware that many of the parameters affect each other dramatically. Especially in the case of Tension, it's possible to create patches that don't create any sound at all! You'll need to think more in terms of inventing and playing an instrument, rather than twiddling knobs. (Will a very smooth bow moved very quickly across a violin string with very little force produce any sound? What if you move it slowly?)

# Electric

Electric, the simplest of the physical modeling instruments, is an electric-piano emulator (see Figure 8.26). Instead of reproducing actual electric pianos through sampling, physical modeling is used instead. This means that sound is produced via mathematical equations representing the various physical aspects of the instrument itself.

Electric's interface is divided into four sections dedicated to different aspects of how an electric piano produces sound: the mallet, the metal fork that gets struck by the mallet, the damper that controls the tine's resonance, and the magnetic pickup that converts the sound into electricity. The fifth section, Global, deals with overall instrument settings that aren't electric piano-specific.

**FIGURE 8.26** Electric gives you the power to design a wide array of electric pianos.
*Source:* Ableton

# Mallet

This section controls the characteristics of the mallet, or hammer, that causes the metal fork to vibrate. Stiffness represents how hard the surface of the mallet is, so lower values will produce a gentler attack, while higher values will tend to make the sound more percussive and less full-bodied. Force is the speed at which the mallet hits the fork, with higher values tending to produce more overdrive and "growl." Since both of these controls affect how much the fork is made to vibrate, they interact with each other closely. For example, both values affect the overall volume of the sound, but in different ways. A very hard mallet hitting the fork with a small amount of force will tend to produce a hard attack, but a relatively weak overall sound. A soft mallet hitting a fork very hard will produce a much fuller sound at a similar volume to the first setting, but with a much weaker attack. Both of these parameters can be modulated by both the velocity and the pitch of incoming MIDI notes. This is where physical modeling gets interesting. It's fairly intuitive to see that modulating the force with velocity will create a real-world situation, whereby more force is applied as you strike the key harder. However, you are also given the option of making your electric piano's hammers get harder as you play louder (or softer if you want).

The Noise subsection models the noise of the hammer hitting the fork, so it also affects the attack of the piano sound. Noise, however, is independent of the tone that the fork produces. Think of it as an additional percussive attack that you can blend in using the Level control to give the sound more definition. To get a better understanding of how noise affects the sound, turn both of the Level controls in the Fork section down to 0% and play with the noise Pitch and Decay.

# Fork

Some electric pianos, such as those made by Yamaha, use actual strings to produce sound—just like an acoustic piano. The most familiar electric piano sound, however, is the sound of a hammer striking a metal tuning fork—the design of the famous Rhodes piano. The tuning fork consists of two distinct parts: a stiff metal wire (the "tine") and a tuned metal resonator (the "tone bar"). The tine is struck by the hammer, and it causes the resonator to vibrate, creating a distinct pitch.

To understand how the Tine and Tone subsections of the fork work, start by turning the Level control for Tone to 0% and the Level and Decay for the Tine to 100%. This will allow you to hear clearly only the Tine portion of the sound. It sounds very much like you might imagine a hammer hitting a stiff wire—a high-frequency "ping" with very little body to the sound. Increasing the Color control will bring out more of the higher frequencies, while reducing it will make the sound darker. The Decay control can be used to make the sound range from a short percussive hit to a drawn-out ring.

Once you have a handle on the Tine part of the sound, the Tone section is fairly self-explanatory. This is obviously the sound of the tuned resonator that produces the lion's share of the piano's tone. Again, you can get familiar with this aspect of the piano's sound by turning down the Level control in the other sections and listening to it by itself. The Decay control adjusts how long the note rings out while the key is held down, while the Release determines how long the note rings after the key is released. Don't expect to hear long release times like you would with a synth, however. Because we're modeling the behavior of a vibrating piece of metal in contact with a damper (see below), the release time is necessarily fairly short.

# Damper

In a real electric piano, the dampers control the sustain feature of a note. When a key is struck, the same mechanism that moves the mallet also moves the damper away from the fork so that it can resonate. When the key is released, the damper moves back into place, causing the tone bar to stop ringing. In the Damper section, you can control both the hardness of the damper surface and the noise made by the dampers moving back and forth.

As the Tone value is increased, harder dampers are modeled, and the damper noise becomes brighter and more pronounced. The Att/Rel knob controls whether damper noise is heard on the attack or the release of the note, with −100% being attack only, 100% being release only, and 0% being both. To hear what the Damper section is doing, it's easier if you crank the Att/Rel knob to 0% or greater so that it sounds when the note is released. The damper noise on the attack is much harder to hear since it is masked by the attack of the piano. Also, it's important to note that the amount of damper noise heard can be affected greatly by the Pickup settings.

# Pickup

Much like an electric guitar, the vibrations produced by a mallet-striking fork are converted into an electrical signal through the use of a pickup so that they can be amplified. The Pickup section customizes the design and position of the pickup, which has a huge impact on the final sound. Before looking at the knobs, you'll want to turn your attention to the pickup type (the R and W buttons in the lower left-hand corner of the Pickup section). When set to W, the pickups have the high-end bite typical of the electrostatic pickups in a Wurlitzer piano. The R setting has the pronounced mids and full low-end associated with a Rhodes piano's magnetic pickups.

To get familiar with the Symm and Distance controls, start out with Distance at 100% and Symm at 0%. Symm controls the pickup's symmetry in relation to the fork. At 50%, the pickup is centered directly in front of the tine. Moving the knob to the left moves the pickup increasingly above the tine, emphasizing the higher harmonics, while moving it to the right shifts the pickup position lower, emphasizing lower harmonics. Note the dramatic change as you sweep symmetry from 0 to 100%.

Distance controls how far from the fork the pickup is. The farther away the pickup is from the fork, the more spectrally balanced the sound will be, while moving it closer will emphasize the frequencies produced by the part of the fork it is closest to and will produce more overdrive. Adjusting the distance has a different effect, depending on what type of pickup you are using. In the case of the W pickup, decreasing the distance will increase the high-end bite and decrease the amount of bass overall. The R pickup works a little differently. First, watch your speakers and your ears, because decreasing the distance of the R pickup increases the volume of the sound. As the R pickup is moved closer, there is an overall increase in drive and intensity in the highs and mids without much low-end attenuation.

## Global

The Global section gives you control over the overall characteristics of Electric. For information on this section, see the "Global Parameters" section, earlier in this chapter.

# Tension

Tension is the most interesting and unusual beast of the AAS Ableton instruments (see Figure 8.27). As a "string-modeling" synth, it takes the modeling concepts that you saw in Electric to a whole different level. Where Electric models a specific type of instrument, Tension applies modeling generically to the entire range of stringed instruments, ranging from cellos to pianos. The many parameters offered by this instrument also give you the opportunity to create some bizarre-sounding instruments that could never exist in the real world.

**FIGURE 8.27** Tension allows you to create stringed instruments of many different types, including oddities such as a violin played with piano hammers.
*Source:* Ableton

The Tension interface is broken into several sections modeling different aspects of a stringed instrument: the Excitator that causes the string to vibrate; the Damper that reduces the string's vibrations; and the Termination, which emulates the effects of fingers and frets, the type and size of the instrument's body, the pickup for emulating electric instruments, and finally the string itself. Tension also features a second page of parameters for the filter and other aspects of the instrument not related to string modeling.

Note that each section has an on/off switch next to the section name, allowing you to bypass a set of parameters completely. While you are learning how to use Tension, it's going to be helpful to turn off other sections while learning a new one. It's a necessary evil (or benefit) of modeling that many parameters closely interact with each other. For example, a bow that is applied to a string with very little force will only produce sound if the bow is moved very slowly. There are many such interactions in this instrument.

# Excitator

This section deals with one of the most fundamental aspects of any stringed instrument: the physical relationship between the string and the object that "excites" it into motion. Here you can choose to use a bow, a piano hammer, or a plectrum (pick) to get your sound going. Depending on the Excitator you choose from the menu, you'll be presented with different parameters for defining the object you've chosen and the way that it's used. With this section turned off, you'll probably get no sound at all out of Tension, although it is possible to create sounds that consist of damper noise and the string's decay.

For a bow, you'll first see the parameters for Force (how hard the bow is pushed against the string) and for Friction (the amount that the bow material naturally resists the string). Velocity determines the speed at which the bow is moving, while Position moves the bow all the way from the string's end (0%) to its midpoint (50%).

Hammers have a totally different set of parameters. You can adjust the mass and stiffness of the hammer, followed by the speed at which it hits the string (Velocity) and the hammer's location (Position). The final control, Damping, controls the stiffness of the mechanism that brings the hammer into contact with the string. At higher values, the action is very "springy," so the hammer bounces right off the string, allowing it to vibrate loudly. At lower values, the hammer action is very stiff, muting the string somewhat as it lands firmly upon it.

Hammer (bouncing) simulates a hammer that is dropped onto the string and allowed to bounce multiple times. Again, here you see a complex interaction of forces. Generally speaking, the velocity is going to have the largest effect on how much the hammer bounces, with low values producing little volume, a series of rapid bounces that can become as subtle as a slight buzz, and the highest values emulating the behavior of a hammer dropped from a very great height, producing a long trail of bounces with several seconds between the initial attack and the first bounce.

A plectrum is a fancy name for a guitar pick. It has the same set of parameters as a hammer, with the exception of protrusion, which replaces mass. Protrusion specifies the amount of the surface of the pick that comes in contact with the string. Lower values mean just the tip of the pick is being used to pluck the string, while higher values use more of the pick and result in a louder sound.

# Damper

The Damper section controls how the string is made to stop vibrating. In the case of a piano, it emulates the behavior of the felt dampers coming into contact with the strings when the key is released (and the sustain pedal is off).

In the case of a guitar, the damper could be the guitarist reducing the pressure on the string with the fingering hand or using the palm of the strumming hand to mute the strings.

Looking at the Damper's controls, you'll see that they are the same as those of the hammer in the "Excitator" section. This makes sense, because the sound produced by the damper is affected by all of the same qualities—the overall mass, the stiffness of the damper's surface, the velocity with which it comes into contact with the string, and its position along the length of the string. The final control, Damping, determines how stiff the damper mechanism is.

# String

Here is where you'll set the properties of the string itself. The Decay and Ratio work closely with one another. The Decay setting controls both the string's initial decay time (right after the attack) and the release time (after the key is released). With Ratio set to 0, the string's decay will begin after the note is struck and continue to decay naturally, regardless of how quickly the key is released. At 100, the note will decay naturally as long as the key is held down, but will cut off abruptly as soon as the key is released. To get a better sense of this, set Decay to a high value and then experiment with different Ratio values, making sure to test each value with both a long key press and a short one.

The Key value can also be used to control how much note pitch will modulate the decay time. The trick here is that since you're modeling real-world strings, lower notes will always decay longer than higher ones. (Just imagine what happens when you hit the lowest note and the highest note on a piano with the sustain pedal on.) The Key control modulates this natural behavior. So by raising this value, you can make the higher notes ring longer and the lower notes ring shorter than they usually would. Lowering the Key value will exaggerate the instrument's natural decay behavior.

The Inharmonic and Damper controls both affect the tone of the instrument in dramatic ways. Inharmonic controls how much the upper partials of the string are out of tune with the harmonic series. As opposed to a theoretical perfect string that produces a perfectly pure tone, strings in the real world have inharmonic qualities. Depending on the Excitator you are using, you'll notice different effects from increasing this value. With a bow, the upper frequencies of the sound will become more like noise, whereas a hammered string will simply begin to sound more out of tune with itself as the higher harmonics are detuned.

# Termination and Pickup

Termination applies to stringed instruments that are fingered. In other words, an individual string is "terminated" or ended on one of its ends by a finger, and possibly a fret, as opposed to a piano or a dulcimer, where the strings are fixed between two pegs and tuned to the desired pitch.

The Finger Mass refers to the force that is being applied with the finger. At lower values, the pitch becomes less distinct as the string is terminated in a less stable fashion. If Fret Stiffness is increased with a low Finger Mass setting, you will hear the string buzzing against the fret, much like it did during your first guitar lesson. With a low Fret Stiffness, you'll generally get a less distinct pitch from the string—unless, that is, you increase the Finger Stiffness to compensate for the lack of clear frets on the neck.

Switching on the Pickup section changes the sound from that of an acoustic instrument to the output of a magnetic pickup. The Position control changes the location of the pickup. At 0, the pickup is placed at the string's termination point, much like the bridge pickup on an electric guitar. As the value is increased to 50, the pickup is moved closer to the midpoint of the string, more like an electric guitar's neck pickup.

# Body

The Body serves two purposes in the creation of the modeled string instruments. First, the instrument body acts as an amplifier of the strings' vibrations, which can add additional fullness and a longer decay to the sound. The Body also filters the frequencies that it radiates, further coloring the final sound.

To get an understanding of the different body types, try experimenting with different ones, first setting High and Low Cut to 0 and setting the Str/Body ratio to 100 (all body sound, no direct string sound). Turning up the Decay as well will tend to exaggerate the effect of the body and make its effects even clearer. As you might expect, a piano body offers the smoothest response across the frequency spectrum, while the violin body tends to bring out the higher frequencies more. Next to the Body Type menu, there is a menu to select the size, ranging from extra small to extra large. Larger body sizes tend to make the instrument sound more diffuse and farther away, while smaller sizes make the instrument sound closer and more present.

## Filter/Global

The Filter section is located on Tension's second page of parameters and consists of a multimode filter that can be modulated with both an envelope and an LFO. In addition to the common filter types, you'll also find a formant filter (F6 and F12 in the Filter menu), which is a filter modeled on the resonance of the human vocal tract. Adjusting the resonance of this filter sweeps through the vowel sounds A, E, I, O, U and is capable of producing some very powerful resonant frequencies, so be prepared to lower the output volume, or you may find yourself running into some nasty distortion. Below the Frequency and Resonance controls, you'll find additional controls to specify how much you want these values to be modulated by the envelope and the LFO.

# Analog

Analog is Ableton's take on a classic subtractive synthesizer (see Figure 8.28). Two oscillators and a noise generator feed two filters and two output amplifiers. There are two independent LFOs that can be used to modulate nearly any aspect of the sound, and each module has its own envelope section as well. So much has been written about the principles of subtractive syntheses that instead of covering all of this ground for the millionth time, we're going to focus most of our energy in this section on what makes this little synth unique.

**FIGURE 8.28** Analog is a powerful analog-style subtractive synthesizer.

Analog's interface is similar to Operator in that it is divided into a series of modules that surround a center window that will be updated to provide additional parameters for whichever module is currently selected. Again, here we will use the terminology *shell* to refer to the basic controls in the outer ring of the interface and *display* to refer to the center window.

The modules for Analog are as follows: two oscillators, a noise generator, two filters and amplifiers, the LFOs, and finally the Master. Clicking anywhere in any of these modules will change Analog's display to show its envelopes, LFO routing, or any other parameters that may apply. Finally, also note that the name of each section (for example, Osc1) is also a switch that can be used to turn the module on or off.

## Oscillators and Noise

The oscillators are where the sound begins. In the Osc modules, you can select the shape of the waveform, adjust its volume and tuning, and set whether it gets routed to Filter 1, Filter 2, or both. The default value for filter routing is 50/50, meaning the signal is split equally between both filters. Dragging up or down in this control will show the ratio of how much signal is distributed to each filter until the display reads F1 (Filter 1 only) or F2 (Filter 2 only), at which point the signal is no longer split between the two filters.

With the Osc1 or Osc2 module selected, the display contains controls for adjusting the oscillator's pitch, pulse width, and optional Sub or Sync oscillator. The graphical display on the left displays the pitch envelope, which is used to make the oscillator's pitch rise or fall into its target pitch. This display corresponds to the Pitch Env Initial (the starting pitch) and Time (how long it takes to reach the final pitch) controls, seen to the right. Below, you can determine if the pitch is to be modulated by the LFO. The LFOs are "hardwired" to their corresponding oscillators—Osc1 can only be modulated by LFO1, and Osc2 can only be modulated by LFO2.

The Pulse Width section is only enabled when a square wave is selected as the waveform shape. Try sweeping this from 0 to 100, and you'll hear the tone go from being narrow and pinched to big and fat. Modulating the Pulse Width with the LFO is a great way to add some subtle movement to your sound. Note that unless the LFO is actually switched on, the LFO modulation amount will be disabled.

Hidden within each Oscillator module is a second oscillator that can be controlled via the Sub/Sync section. When Mode is set to Sub, an additional note will sound one octave below the pitch of the main oscillator. The volume of the Sub tone is set by the Level control. If you want some real nastiness, however, try setting Mode to Sync. When set to Sync, the additional oscillator is not heard directly. Rather, it is used to control the main oscillator by forcing it to restart from the beginning of the waveform for each cycle of the Sync oscillator. This changes the harmonic content of the main oscillator, with the pitch and intensity increasing as you increase the Ratio (the frequency of the sync oscillator).

Finally, in between the two oscillators is the Noise module, a sound generator that produces white noise. Noise has many uses—not only in producing percussion sounds, but also for adding a bit of extra attack or texture to an otherwise dark sound. All of the controls for Noise are located in the shell. The filter routing works just like it does for the oscillators, and the Color control is a simple low-pass filter that can be used to reduce the high-frequency content of the noise.

# Filters and Amplifiers

After the sound wave leaves the Oscillator module, it proceeds on to the filters. While filters are an essential part of most sounds, strictly speaking they do not need to be used. Both Filter modules can be turned off, and Analog will work just fine. Which filter will be used to shape your sound is determined by the filter routing in the Oscillator modules.

While the two filters are essentially identical, they do have a few subtle differences. Both have menus for selecting a filter type and the usual frequency and resonance controls. The first difference between the two is that Filter 1 has a control called To F2, which can be used to send the output of Filter 1 to Filter 2. This gives you the option of running the two filters in series (one after another) instead of in parallel. To fully understand what is possible here, it's also important to understand that the filters and the amps are hard-wired to each other—in other words, Filter 1 is passed to Amp 1 automatically, while the same holds true for Filter 2 and Amp 2. So, even if you route Filter 1 to Filter 2, it will still be going to Amp 1.

Let's look at an example. For starters, we'll assume that you have both filters and both amps turned on, and that both of your oscillators are routed to Filter 1 only. Filter 1 is set to send 100% of its signal to Filter 2. This causes the output of Filter 1 to be sent both to Amp 1 *and* Filter 2, because the "To F2" control is a send—it taps the signal and passes it to the second filter without interrupting the signal flow to Amp 1. This means that if you want to truly hear the filters operate in series, you need to turn Amp 1 off completely. Now the signal will flow from Filter 1 to Filter 2 to Amp 2 and then on to the master output. If you leave Amp 1 turned on, you'll hear a combination of the output of Filter 1 along with the output of Filter 1 and Filter 2 running in series.

Filter 2 features a Slave switch, which allows its cutoff frequency to be controlled from Filter 1. With Slave enabled, the Frequency control of Filter 2 controls the difference between the two cutoff frequencies. This could be used to create a dual filter with two peaks that are always the same distance apart. Then, whenever Filter 1 is modulated, whether manually or by an LFO, Filter 2 will follow it.

With either of the filters selected, Analog's display will display options for the envelope (see below), as well as a few other options. Selecting a drive mode will cause the filter to overdrive, with the Asymmetrical modes tending to create a more harmonically rich-sounding distortion and the Symmetrical modes being a bit on the nastier side. The Freq Mod and Res Mod sections specify how much the filter's frequency and resonance are modulated by the LFOs, the pitch (Key), and the envelope. The display looks nearly identical when the Amp modules are selected, the only difference being there is no Drive control, and the Modulation section applies to Volume and Pan.

# Filters and Amp Envelopes

Since the envelope sections for the filters and the amplifiers are identical in design, we'll discuss them both together. The envelope is an ADSR (Attack, Decay, Sustain, Release) envelope that can be adjusted either by dragging the breakpoints in the graphical display or by changing the values in the numerical display to the right. In the numerical part of the Envelope display, you'll see one special value in addition to the usual ASDR values: Sustain Time. The standard Sustain value is a decibel level—the volume that the note sustains while you hold the key down.

In the numerical part of the Envelope display, you'll see one special value in addition to the usual ADSR values: Sustain Time. Unlike Sustain (which specifies level), Sustain Time specifies the length of time over which the level will decay, even if the note is held down. By default, Sustain Time is set to "inf," which makes the envelope behave like a standard ADSR envelope— the Sustain level is maintained as long as the note is held down.

At the far right of the envelope display, you'll see the Loop menu, which creates some very interesting variations to your sound. By selecting one of the Loop modes, you'll be telling Analog to repeat a part of the envelope instead of playing it through from start to finish. AD-R will repeat the Attack and Decay portions of the envelope until the key is released, while ADR-R will repeat the Release portion as well. This makes it possible to use the envelope as more of an LFO, cycling through a series of values. When ADS-AR is selected, the envelope works normally until the key is released, at which point the Attack portion repeats before the Release, which could be used to create an additional swelling or short attack at the end of each note.

Looking to the left, there are a few switches above the graphical display that are worth mentioning. First, the Linear and Exponential switches are used to control the type of slope that occurs between the envelope's breakpoints. Linear slopes are increments or decrements in value that change at a constant rate over the time of the envelope segments (which is a fancy way of saying they are straight lines!). Exponential slopes start out as straight lines but curve more dramatically toward their destination point as they get closer.

Because exponential curves tend to approach their target value very quickly before curving, they sound shorter than linear envelopes. The Legato switch may take a moment to understand, but it's well worth it. When enabled, instead of the envelope starting over every time a new note sounds, the envelope will continue if the two notes overlap. In other words, if a new note is played while another is held down, the new note's envelope will start at the existing note's envelope position instead of beginning from the attack phase. Finally, the Free switch can be used to bypass the Sustain portion of the envelope. Since the envelope will now jump from the decay to the release phase, it will always be the same, regardless of how long the note is held. The most common example of a Free envelope is a percussion sound—a short attack and decay phase immediately followed by a release.

## MAKING FILTER ENVELOPES WORK

If you're finding that adjusting the filter envelope isn't doing anything, it's probably because you haven't entered a value in either of the envelope (Env) fields for the filter. Unlike the volume envelope (which works automatically), you have to specify how much the filter envelope should be modulating the filter's frequency or resonance, or it won't do anything at all! In the display, enter an envelope amount under Freq Mod or Res Mod to specify how much the filter should be modulated by the envelope. Bear in mind that the frequency or resonance value shown in the shell is the starting value for the filter. The Env field can then be set to a positive or negative value to indicate whether the envelope should be increasing or decreasing that value as the envelope plays.

# LFO

The two LFOs are completely independent of each other and can be used to control a variety of other parameters, as discussed in the previous sections. The only control here is the Rate, since the LFO amount is controlled within the module that it is being used to modulate. The rest of the controls for the LFO are located in the center window.

Use the Wave and Width selectors to control the shape of the LFO. When the Triangle wave is selected, the Width control can be used to change the wave shape to ramp up or ramp down. With Rectified selected and Width at 50%, the LFO is a square wave, while modulating Width in either direction changes the pulse width. Retrig (the R switch) controls whether or not the LFO starts over (is "retriggered") with each key press.

Offset is used to adjust the phase of the wave. With a tempo-synced LFO, this could be used to move the peaks of the wave that occur before or after the beat. Delay will wait a specified length of time after a keypress to begin the LFO, while Attack will cause the amplitude of the wave to fade in over the amount of time specified.

## Global

Most of Analog's Global parameters are covered in the "Global Parameters" section, earlier in this chapter, but a few things warrant special attention. The first switch in this section turns Vibrato on or off. Vibrato is a simple LFO that modulates the pitch of the oscillators. Only two controls are available here: the Amount, which controls the depth of the modulation, and the Rate, which controls the speed. The last switch in this section is marked "Gli" for Glide. For information on Glide, refer to the "Portamento" section, earlier in this chapter.

At the left-hand side of the display, you'll see some colored boxes. These are Quick Routing schemes, which can help speed the process of setting up a new patch. Unlike the similar-looking algorithms in Operator, these short-cuts are just timesavers—all they do is set the filter routing and turn the amplifiers on and off. For example, clicking on Quick Routing 4 (in the lower right-hand corner) sends both oscillators into Filter 1, the output of Filter 1 into Filter 2, and turns off Amp 1 so that only the output of Amp 2 is heard.

# Collision

Collision takes the concept of designing percussion sounds to a whole new level (see Figure 8.29). Just as Tension can be used to create either familiar stringed instruments or otherworldly beasts, Collision is just as much at home producing the sound of a marimba or, let's say, a hybrid hand drum/metal tube with a decay of 25 seconds!

**FIGURE 8.29** Collision: Ableton's percussion powerhouse.
*Source:* Ableton

Before getting too deeply into the unique details of Collision, I recommend that you at least read over the section on Electric. It's a far simpler instrument that covers some of the important concepts of physical modeling, and since an electric piano is essentially a percussion instrument, it's particularly relevant here. Tension also contains some important concepts that we'll be discussing here, too. In particular, Tension uses the concept of a designable Excitator—namely, an object with changeable characteristics that is used to strike a resonating object. In the case of Tension, the struck object is some sort of string. In Collision, it's a variety of different objects associated with different kinds of percussion instruments. For the initial experiments here, find the menu in the Resonators section that contains the different resonator types and set it to Plate.

The first similarity to Electric that you'll notice in Collision is the presence of percentage boxes marked Key and Vel (sometimes K and V to save space), located below a number of the controls. These are here to map the controls so they follow the velocity of the incoming MIDI messages or the pitch. Negative values are allowed here as well, so you can have controls change in inverse proportion to velocity and key.

# Excitators

The Excitator section of Collision is broken into two parts: Mallet and Noise. Mallet is fairly straightforward. Looking at the far left, you'll see Volume and Stiffness. Stiffness controls the relative softness or hardness of the mallet. You'll find that as you increase it from 0%, the sound generally gets louder and brighter up until around 60%, after which the sound continues getting brighter, but the overall loudness is decreased as it starts producing fewer low harmonics. The Volume control simply controls the overall level of the Mallet excitator. The only reason this is needed is because there is a second, entirely independent excitator, and you may need to balance the relative levels of the two. For now, just make sure that it is turned up loud enough for you to hear Collision's output clearly.

Moving over to the next column of knobs, you'll see Noise and Color. *Noise* refers to the sound that is made by the mallet coming into contact with the resonating object. So, for this to make sense, you have to think of the sound as containing two distinct sounds—the initial impact of the objects colliding, followed by the resonance of the struck object. Like the Mallet's Stiffness control, the Noise parameter tends to decrease low harmonics and overall volume above 60%. Try this experiment: Park the Stiffness and Color controls at about 50% and Noise at 0%. Slowly increase the Noise control until you can start to hear a flinty "chiff" sound in the initial impulse. Now, turn down the Stiffness. You'll hear the fundamental pitch of the resonator get less distinct and the noise component of the sound will become much clearer and more noticeable. Next, sweep the Color control back and forth, and you'll be able to clearly hear how this adjusts the harmonic content of the noise.

The next section over is the Noise excitator, which can be turned on by clicking in the box next to the word *Noise*. This is a slightly strange beast because, while it acts as a physical object that causes the resonator to vibrate, it does not have any real-world counterpart. Rather, it's an imaginary object that consists only of a burst of noise. It can be used in conjunction with, or instead of, the Mallet excitator. Just bear in mind that you must use one or the other if you want Collision to produce any sound at all.

For now, turn off the Mallet excitator so that you can hear the Noise section on its own. You'll find that this produces a similar sound to the Noise control you worked with previously, but it is far more customizable. When you first turn it on, you may not notice much sound coming out. If this is the case, increase the Volume control and also have a look at the Filter section immediately to the left. As you increase the cutoff frequency of the low-pass filter (using either the graphical or the numeric display), you'll be able to hear the noise more clearly, and you'll also notice the sound of the resonator getting brighter as well. The Filter section contains your basic filter types, along with an LP+HP filter, which combines a high-pass and a low-pass filter to produce a very flexible bandpass type filter.

What makes the Noise section really interesting is the envelope below. By adjusting the phases of the ADSR envelope, you can create a completely different palette of sounds as a long, sustained noise signal vibrates the resonator, more like a bow than a mallet or stick. Try increasing the Attack to one or two seconds, and you'll hear what I mean. Also, take a look above the Envelope display, and you'll see that there's a percentage box marked E below the Filter display. This applies the envelope to the filter frequency as well. If you need more info on ADSR Envelopes, brush up on them in the sections on Simpler and Analog.

# Resonators

Continuing over to the right, you'll get into the Resonators section, which has the biggest impact on the overall sound. First, you'll come to the pitch section, which contains some controls that should be relatively familiar. *Tune* controls the overall tuning of the instrument in semitones, while *Fine* tunes Collision in cents (100ths of a semitone). Notice that below the Tune knob it is mapped 100% to Key, which makes it fully responsive to the notes on your MIDI keyboard. Adjusting this value will allow you to make some more unusually tuned instruments. For example, with Key set to 50%, a movement of a semitone on your keyboard will only produce a change of a quarter tone in Collision, and so on.

The pitch envelope controls determine whether or not Collision reaches its target pitch immediately after it receives note input, or if it slides into the final pitch. Time determines the length of the slide, while Pitch controls how much higher or lower the initial pitch is than the target.

If you're new to synth programming and really want to get a handle on this instrument, this would probably be a good time to stop reading for a bit and make sure that you really know how to get around the controls we've dealt with so far. The rest of the controls in the Resonator section are very important because they're going to introduce a lot more complexity, and it's often easier to digest this sort of material in chunks.

The next section determines the physical properties of the Resonator, in other words, the primary component of the instrument itself. If you've followed along with the previous experiments, this would be a good time to switch back to the Mallet excitator and turn the Noise section off, just to keep things simple. The easiest aspect of the Resonator to set is the type, which is specified in the menu you set to Plate at the beginning of this section. Six of the resonator types fit into three categories: beams, planes, and cylinders. There's also a string type resonator, which in terms of its parameters is identical to the beams.

Beams are not what get emitted from your light saber—instead, think of the beams in your ceiling. These are the bars that you strike when playing a xylophone or vibraphone. Marimba is simply a special type of beam that has a deep arch cut out from the bottom. Membrane and Plate are two types that I'm describing as planes because they are both thin, flat surfaces—Membrane being a flexible material stretched tightly, such as a drum head, and Plate being flat pieces of metal. Finally, Tube and Pipe are both cylindrical objects, the only difference being that Pipe is open at both ends, while Tube is closed.

The controls below vary somewhat, depending on the type of resonator you've selected. The simplest resonator is Tube, so let's look at that first. The only controls available here are Decay and Radius. Decay is common to all the resonators and is probably the simplest to understand: this is how long it takes for the resonator to decay to silence. Radius determines the width of the Tube and has a major impact on the high harmonics produced. A low radius produces a subtle subby sound that could sound great layered in with a kick drum or bass sound. Switching over to Pipe, you may not notice much of a difference in the sound. The only difference in the controls available here is Opening, and when this control is at 100%, it's nearly identical to Tube. As you decrease Opening from 100%, you'll hear a high-frequency buzzing in the sound get louder and more complex.

For all of the other resonator types, the Radius control is replaced by Material. While this control represents a different physical property, in practice, it is very similar. Going from low to high values takes you through a range of tonal possibilities from dark and deep to extremely bright. You'll also notice that when selecting a resonator other than the two cylinders, the Quality menu becomes enabled. This feature controls how complex the harmonics generated by Collision are and therefore the CPU usage.

The remaining physical property controls are as follows:

▶ **Ratio:** This control only exists for the Membrane and Plate types and controls the overall shape and size of the resonator. Higher values produce much more complex harmonics and produce a less distinct pitch. This control interacts heavily with the Quality menu, which determines how complex the overtones can get.

▶ **Brightness:** Acts like a master tone control. Low values heavily favor low harmonics and can produce some serious volume, so watch your ears!

▶ **Inharmonics:** This is a pitch control for the overtones produced by the resonator. The most important thing to know about this control is that it is extremely sensitive (especially with Quality set to Full) and sometimes produces unexpected results. Try adjusting this control using your arrow keys, 1% at a time.

▶ **Listening:** Labeled ListeningL and ListeningR, these controls are easiest to understand if you think of them as controlling the placement of a pair of microphones being used to record your virtual percussion instrument. They both affect the tonal characteristics of the sound and the stereo field. When they are set to the same value, you'll get a mono sound, while adjusting them to opposing values gives you a much wider sound.

▶ **Hit:** If you've ever played drums, you know that they produce a very different sound, depending on where you hit the skin. The Hit control moves the point of impact from the center to the edge as you increase its value. This produces a minimal change for all of the resonators except Membrane and Plate.

▶ **Bleed:** Increasing the Bleed mixes in more of the unprocessed sound of the Excitator. With Quality set to full, this doesn't have much impact since the Excitator tends to get lost in the harmonics. With Quality set to basic, however, turning this value up can create some very interesting timbres.

The only other controls that you may find unfamiliar here are the Structure switches, which brings us to an important aspect of Collision. You actually have two resonators (selectable via the tabs at the top of the interface) to work with when designing your sound. Structure determines whether the output of Resonator 1 will be sent to Resonator 2 for further processing (1>2), or if both resonators will act in parallel as if they were being struck simultaneously by the same Excitator (1+2).

By default, Resonator 2 is turned off, so you'll have to click on its on/off switch in the tab if you want it to be used. Also, you can edit both resonators simultaneously by clicking the link icon in between the two tabs or make both identical by using the Copy button above the Ratio control. Be aware that using both resonators (especially when running in series) can produce some serious gain, so be careful when you turn on Resonator 2.

## The LFO and MIDI Tabs

You may think of LFOs as primarily being useful for giving motion to sounds like strings and pads. But for designing traditional percussion sounds, LFOs offer some interesting options. For example, with Retrig off and a nice slow Rate, you can use an LFO to modulate a resonator's Pitch or Hit parameter, so that every time you strike a note, it has a slightly different quality.

The LFO and MIDI sections of Collision are very similar to those of Sampler, although the MIDI mapping implementation for Collision is much simpler. Please refer to the "Sampler" section, earlier in this chapter, for a further discussion of these controls.

# Drum Rack

For many of us, Drum Racks are one of the best things to happen to drum programming in a long time. A Drum Rack is an Instrument Rack that is customized for … drum roll, please … programming drums. While Drum Racks have much in common with standard Instrument Racks, they have a number of unique features. We'll focus on those features in this section.

What's particularly interesting about Drum Racks is that they have no built-in synthesis or sample playback capabilities. As opposed to powerful, complex plug-ins like Battery and Stylus RMX, a basic Drum Rack is incredibly simple. The beauty of the Drum Rack is that it can be powerful and complicated, but it doesn't have to be. Instead of having to deal with piles of features from day one, you get to decide how involved your Drum Racks are. When you're learning, you can keep them simple. As you get more comfortable, you can turn them into programming monsters using Macros, nested Racks, effects, and MIDI devices.

## Pads and Chains

When an empty Drum Rack is dropped onto a track, it appears as 16 pads, each one displaying the name of the MIDI note it is mapped to (see Figure 8.30). While only 16 pads can be displayed at a time, there are actually 128 pads available—one for each possible MIDI note. The grid to the left of the pads shows an overview of all 128, while the black square highlights which 16 are in view. Drag the square to show a different group of pads.

**FIGURE 8.30**

An empty Drum Rack.
*Source:* Ableton

Creating a basic drum kit with a Drum Rack is easy. Just drop a drum sample from the Browser onto any pad. Once you've dropped the sample, the pad will be updated to display the sample name instead of the note name. A play button for previewing the sample will appear, as will mute and solo switches. To see what's going on under the hood, you'll need to look at the Chain List and the Devices of the Rack (see Figure 8.31). The buttons for showing these are to the left side of the pads and look and function identically to those on a standard Instrument Rack. It's also possible to display the Device View by double-clicking on a pad.

**FIGURE 8.31** Our new Drum Rack with chains and devices shown.
*Source:* Ableton

First, notice the far right-hand side of the Rack. As I mentioned a moment ago, Drum Racks have no built-in sample playback capability, so here you'll see that Ableton's solution to this is to automatically create a Simpler when a sample is dropped onto a pad. The Simpler offers loads of options for tweaking the playback of the sample, so this is an excellent solution. There's no reason, however, that you need to use the Simpler to play back your samples, nor is there any reason that your Drum Racks need to be based on sample playback. You can just as easily drop a synth onto a pad and use synthesis to create your drum sounds.

After you've picked out some samples or synths and gotten a basic drum kit together, you can start customizing your sounds with effects. Drop a Saturator into your snare chain to add some extra bite, or a Velocity device into your hi-hat chain to generate some random velocity variations. See where this is going? Your Drum Racks can become completely customized beasts with features that can rival any drum program out there. Your imagination is really the only limit.

It's also important to note here that a pad isn't limited to triggering only one sampler or synth. Want to create a sound that consists of several layers of samples, or synths, or both? No problem. You can create a layered sound in one step. Simply drag samples or devices to a pad while holding down Cmd (Mac) or Ctrl (PC). Live will automatically create a nested rack with one chain for each sample or device (see Figure 8.32). Triggering the pad will play all of the chains simultaneously.

**FIGURE 8.32**

Here's a chain in a Drum Rack that triggers both a kick drum sample and an Operator for some layered madness.
*Source:* Ableton

## MIX IT UP

As your Drum Racks grow in size and complexity, you may want to use the Chain Mixer, which is accessed by clicking the triangular "unfold" button located in the title bar of the track containing the Drum Rack. This feature (explained fully in the "Racks" section of Chapter 7) can make navigating a complex Drum Rack much easier.

# Advanced Settings

Whenever the Show/Hide Chains button is highlighted, a few buttons that are unique to Drum Racks appear in the lower left-hand corner (see Figure 8.33).

The first button shows additional Input/Output options for the chains. With this turned on, you can view the routing options and choke groups for each chain. The next two buttons, marked S and R, are for viewing the sends and returns. (Yes, Drum Racks have their own Send/Return bussing system!) The last button is an arrow icon called Auto Select, which makes it easy to find and view the chain you want by automatically highlighting the chain for the last pad that was triggered.

Input/Output

Sends

Returns

Auto Select

**FIGURE 8.33**

These buttons give you access to some custom features of Drum Rack chains. They are only visible when the Show/Hide Chains button is highlighted.
*Source:* Ableton

# MIDI Routing

When the Input/Output section is in view, it's possible to adjust the MIDI routing of the chain, as shown in Figure 8.34a. The Receive menu specifies what MIDI note triggers the chain. This is determined automatically when you drop a sound source onto a pad. If you change this value, you'll see the change reflected in the pad display. In other words, if you've dropped a sample called Kick1 onto pad C1 and then change the MIDI Receive for this chain to D1, you'll see Kick1 jump to that pad. Each pad is hardwired to its note and location.

The Send setting is much more flexible. Here you can choose what note is sent to your sound source. By default, it's set to C3, which is the Simpler's default root note. So a C3 will play back the sample at its original pitch. Modifying this setting could be useful if you want to use a pitched sine wave as part of a kick sound. Change the Send note so that the pitch matches the key of your song.

# Choke Groups

Occasionally, it's necessary to configure some of the sounds in your kit so that playing one stops or "chokes" the other. The classic use for this is hi-hat. With a real-world drum kit, you cannot have an open and closed hi-hat sound happening at the same time. Whenever the closed hi-hat plays, the open one should stop immediately, and vice versa.

If you've used Impulse, you may already know that it has one choke group hardwired to cells 7 and 8. Just press the Link switch on pad 8, and the two pads automatically choke each other when played. Drum Racks offer the flexibility of 16 different choke groups, which can be assigned to any group of pads. To set up the choke group, choose a choke group number from the Choke menu and assign it to all of the sounds you want included in the group (see Figure 8.34a). It doesn't matter which number you use—just make sure to use the same number for each sound. Now triggering any of the sounds in the group will automatically cut off any of the others.

# Sends and Returns

To use the built-in sends and returns of a Drum Rack, you first have to create a return chain. First, show the returns by clicking the button marked R at the lower left-hand corner of the Drum Rack. Now you can drag an effect in to create a new chain. After you've created a return chain, you can show the sends by clicking the S button. Now you can dial in as much of an effect as you want for each drum individually (see Figure 8.34a).

You can also right-click in the drop area and select Create Chain to create an empty return chain. Why would you want an empty return chain? Let's say you have a reverb on Return track A in Live's Mixer. You want to add a bit of this reverb to the hi-hats in the Drum Rack. To do this, just create an empty return chain and send the hand claps to it. Then, in the Audio To menu of the Return Chain, set the output to Return track A, where your reverb is located (see Figure 8.34b).

**FIGURE 8.34A**

In this example, the open and closed hi-hats are both assigned to Choke group 1. Notice also the "Send-a" column, which shows that the open hi-hat is being sent to the Ping Pong Delay.
*Source:* Ableton

**FIGURE 8.34B** In this example, take a look at what's going on in the Audio To menus. The hi-hats are both routed to "b Hat Group" where they can be processed as a group. "a Main Reverb" routes its signal to Return A in Live's mixer.
*Source:* Ableton

Return chains can also be used to create subgroups of sounds in the Drum Rack. For example, you might want to route hi-hats to one return chain and snares and claps to another. This makes it easy to make volume adjustments for groups of sounds and to process them with effects like compression and EQ. This technique is shown in Figure 8.34b. A return chain called *Hat Group* has been created, and this return chain is selected in the Audio To menu of both hi-hat sounds.

### EXTRACTION TEAM

Once you're finished programming your drums, you may want to split each drum out to its own individual track. To do this, just right-click in the title bar of a drum in the Chain Mixer or the Chain List and select Extract Chains. Now you've got a new track with just that one drum and a new MIDI clip containing just the part for that drum. This technique is particularly useful if you need to render each drum to an individual audio track for mixing in another program.

# External Instrument

External Instrument allows you to control an external synth from a MIDI track and make it behave like a virtual instrument track. Make sure to read through this section even if you don't have any hardware instruments. This device is also useful for anyone who uses instruments via ReWire, or plug-ins with multiple virtual outputs, such as Native Instruments Kontakt.

Before the External Instrument device was introduced, sequencing external MIDI synthesizers always required two tracks: a MIDI track to control the synth and an audio track for returning the audio from the synth. Not only does External Instrument allow this entire setup to be done with one track, but it takes advantage of Live's delay compensation as well.

After dropping External Instrument into a MIDI track, use the MIDI To menus to specify the port to which your hardware is connected (and the MIDI channel, if necessary). Arm the track for recording and play a few notes—the hardware should register the MIDI input. Next, make sure that your hardware is connected to an input on your audio interface and select this input in the Audio From menu (see Figure 8.35). Voila! You should now begin to receive audio into the track.

As mentioned earlier, you can use this device to make working with some software instruments easier as well. Any multitimbral instruments in the Set will appear in the routing menus as if they were hardware (see Figure 8.36). Instruments accessible from any currently loaded ReWire slave application will also appear here. To use these instruments with the External Instrument device, just configure the MIDI To and Audio From menus to the virtual ports on your software instruments.

### FREEZE!

When it's time to record the audio from External Instrument into the Set, use the Freeze command. Live is smart enough to know when you're freezing a track that's communicating with external hardware, so it invokes a real-time process to record the audio through your soundcard's inputs.

**FIGURE 8.35** This External Instrument device is configured to send MIDI to an external synth and to receive audio from the synth through inputs 3 & 4. *Source:* Ableton

**FIGURE 8.36** External Instrument can also transmit MIDI and receive audio from multitimbral plug-ins, such as Maschine, and ReWire applications, such as Reason. *Source:* Ableton

# 9

# Live's Audio Effects

**W**hat are audio effects? Ranging from subtle mixing tools to extreme sound manglers, effects are used in every part of the music production process. A delay may be an integral part of a synthesizer sound, a distortion unit may be used to give a snare drum some extra bite, and equalizers and compressors may find their way onto nearly every track in a song during final mixdown. In this chapter, I'll discuss all of Live's effects, giving some tips as to how each might be used along the way. But don't take my word for it, using effects is all about experimentation. So get in there and make some noise!

## EQ and Filters

The first batch of effects we'll dive into are the filters and equalizers (EQ for short). These types of signal processors are used to attenuate (reduce in volume) and amplify (increase in volume) only specific frequency ranges within an audio signal. Engineers will use filters and EQs to finely craft the frequency distribution of the tracks in a song, resulting in beautiful, rich, and detailed final mixes. Of course, these tools can also be used to radically reshape sound, creating unique effects in their own right.

# EQ Eight

A parametric EQ is a powerful frequency-filtering and timbre-shaping tool. While many hardware and some software mixers have some type of equalization available on every channel, you will need to add an EQ plug-in manually to a track anytime it's needed in your Live project.

The goal when using an EQ is to either boost or diminish certain audio frequencies in order to overcome problems arising from poor recordings, to reduce muddiness from overlapping frequencies in other sounds, or to emphasize certain characteristics of the sound to make it cut through the mix.

### OVERSAMPLE

For the highest sound quality in the high-frequency spectrum, right-click in the title bar and select Oversampling from the context menu. This feature causes EQ Eight to process at a higher sample rate internally, resulting in fewer artifacts at the cost of slightly higher CPU usage. To make Oversampling the default, right-click in the title bar after turning it on and select Save as Default Preset from the context menu.

The frequencies are often referred to as *lows, mids,* and *highs* or other subdivisions such as *low-mids* or *high-mids.* High frequencies are found in the register called *treble* and are shown on the right-hand side of the EQ's display, while low frequencies are referred to as *bass* and appear on the left. Low-mids, mids, and high-mids make up the middle section of the sonic spectrum. Live's EQ features a built-in spectrum analyzer to help you visualize the frequency content of your sounds, which can be incredibly useful when your ears need a little help. Live's EQ Eight features up to eight adjustable bands, or filters, each of which can be enabled or disabled individually (see Figure 9.1).

Each filter can be used to cut or boost frequencies ranging from 10Hz to 22kHz, using one of a variety of different filter types. Each filter can be turned on or off using the eight switches running vertically across the bottom of the interface. Above each on/off switch is a menu for selecting a filter type.

**FIGURE 9.1**
Live's powerful eight-band EQ. In this example, only four bands are in use. Turning off the bands you're not using saves CPU power.
*Source:* Ableton

The filter types, from top to bottom in the menu, are as follows:

▶ **Low-cut (12db & 48dB):** Also known as a high-pass filter, it aggressively removes frequencies below the specified frequency. For this filter type, Q adjusts the resonance (how much the cutoff frequency is emphasized or reduced). Gain has no effect for this filter type. The −48dB/octave version appears with "x4" next to the icon, indicating that its slope is four times as steep and reduces the frequencies below the cutoff much more dramatically. Using these to remove unnecessary low frequencies from as many tracks as possible can really clean up your mixes.

▶ **Low-shelf:** Reduces or boosts all frequencies below the specified frequency. With a low Q setting, the gain change will be a gentle linear slope. At high Q values, the change becomes more drastic, and you get an additional emphasis around the filter frequency. (For example, if you're cutting with a high Q, you get a boost right above the filter frequency and the greatest gain reduction directly below it.) A low-shelf is a great way to make a broad boost or cut to the low frequencies without excessive coloration. When boosting, you may want to combine with a low-cut to keep the lowest frequencies under control.

▶ **Bell:** A parabolic-shaped boost or cut of a given range of frequencies. For this filter type, the Q adjusts the bandwidth of the filter—how much the adjacent frequencies are affected. This is where the most surgical adjustments in a mix occur. Use caution with high Q values in the high frequencies, as they can sound harsh. With low frequencies, however, you can get much more aggressive with the Q without concern.

▶ **Notch:** Like a bell curve with extremely high Q and extremely low gain, Gain has no effect for this filter type. It's especially useful for removing problems such as resonant room frequencies.

▶ **High-shelf:** Same as low-shelf, but acts on high frequencies. A little high-shelf boost can be a great way to add sparkle to tracks without coloring the sound too much.

▶ **High-cut:** Also known as a *low-pass filter*, it removes high frequencies. High frequencies can be less forgiving when it comes to aggressive cutting, so unlike low-cut, this filter has more of a tendency to sound like an "effect," especially with high Q values. For a more natural sound, try using a shelf or a bell first to see if you can accomplish the desired result.

To adjust the specific frequency that a filter acts on, you can work directly in the graphical display or the knob to the upper left. Experiment for a moment, and you'll see these are just two different ways of doing the same thing. You'll also find that when you click on the filter numbers along the bottom, the knobs refresh to show you the parameters for whatever filter you click.

Perhaps the most important power that EQ holds is its ability to preserve headroom in a mix. By reducing less important frequencies in a sound or cutting frequencies that conflict with other instruments, you end up with mixes that sound louder and clearer. For instance, if the meat of a sound is in the bass, such as a bass guitar or synth, you may want to reduce the high-frequency content of this sound to make space for your singer's voice and your drummer's hi-hat.

In this case, you'd use the EQ to reduce the highs and possibly to boost the lows in the bass track. Conversely, you can often benefit by using a high-pass filter on vocals and other instruments that don't have a lot of low-frequency content. Especially when working with voices and real instruments, there are often unwanted low frequencies, such as rumble from air conditioners and the like, doing nothing but consuming headroom and muddying up your mix. In addition to solving problems, EQs can also do a lot to sweeten certain sounds. Using a high-shelf to boost 10k can help acoustic guitars sparkle, and a bell to boost 60Hz can give a weak kick the extra power you're looking for.

## DOUBLE STACK

For aggressive cuts, boosts, and effects, you can stack EQs by assigning the same parameters to two or more filters. For example, you could use two –12dB low-cut filters both set to 150Hz and a Q of .75 to create a –24dB/octave filter—right in between the two built-in filter slopes.

Along the right side are a variety of useful controls. The spectrum analyzer in EQ8's Display can be turned on or off, and the headphones (Audition mode) switch can be used to listen to *only* the filter you're currently adjusting. Click and drag a filter in the graphical display to hear this feature in action. You may find it useful for zeroing in on the frequency you want to boost or cut.

Next in line is the Mode menu. Stereo is the standard mode for all stereo and mono signals. L/R differs from Stereo in that it allows you to equalize the left and right channels of a source separately (as seen in Figure 9.2). Select L in

**Figure 9.2** Here's EQ Eight in its expanded view. Notice that the device is now in L/R mode. While you can see both EQ curves simultaneously, you can only edit whichever band is shown in the Edit switch.
*Source:* Ableton

the Edit switch to EQ the left side; then press Edit again to switch over and EQ the right side. Bear in mind that L/R mode can be used to create stereo effects on mono sources by EQing left and right differently. M/S mode allows you to separately EQ the "middle" of a mix (material that is purely mono) and the "sides" of a mix (material that is purely stereo).

Adaptive Q is a feature inspired by the behavior of some classic analog EQs. It causes the Q to change automatically when adjusting the gain of bell and shelf filters. (It has no effect on the other filter types.) The theory is that the more you boost, the more desirable it is to narrow the range of frequencies you're boosting to avoid dramatic changes in the overall gain of the signal. Bear in mind that you can achieve the same results with or without this feature turned on. You may, however, find that it makes the operation of the EQ more intuitive and musical.

The Scale control is an ingenious bonus that changes the gain of all EQ bands simultaneously. So if you've created the perfect EQ curve but decide that you've laid it on a bit thick, you can scale it back a bit and apply less EQ over-all. The Scale control goes all the way up to 200%, so you can use it to increase the effect as well.

Finally, the Gain control should not be overlooked. Remember that boosting and cutting frequencies changes the overall gain of your signal. If you're doing a lot of boosting, then you may need to bring down the gain to avoid clipping. Conversely, cutting the frequencies you *don't* like, and then boost-ing the gain of a signal is often the best way to bring out the qualities you *do* like.

In the upper left-hand corner of EQ Eight, you'll find a triangular "unfold" button. Clicking on this yields dramatic results! As you'll see in Figure 9.2, this gives you a giant graphical display to work with and a full set of controls for each filter below.

**KICK ME! (PART 1)**

Many people will add bass to get a kick drum to cut through a mix. The end result is that you end up feeling the kick more (your subwoofer will really be bumpin'), but it still sounds muddy because it is occupying many frequencies used by other instruments in the mix.

To get that punchy, clear tone that really cuts through, try using a bell filter with a high Q setting to cut frequencies in the 150 to 400Hz range. To find the frequency you want to cut, first boost the band and sweep it up and down while listening carefully for the kick's most resonant frequency.

The kick now occupies its own space (the low frequencies where you feel it and the high frequencies where you hear it) and cleans up the sonic image. (The range from 150Hz to 300Hz can be extremely problematic in many mixes.)

# EQ Three

The DJ-style EQ Three is concerned only with three frequency bands: lows, mids, and highs. As you can see in Figure 9.3, the EQ Three has three main dials: GainLow, GainMid, and GainHi. The frequency range of these dials is determined by the FreqLow and FreqHi knobs at the bottom of the effect. The GainMid knob will boost or cut all the frequencies between FreqLow and FreqHi. The GainLow will adjust all the frequencies below FreqLow, and the GainHi knob will handle everything above FreqHi.

Because this device is modeled after a DJ mixer, you'll find that when turning the Gain knobs down, they eventually reach infinity, meaning the frequencies are completely cut. If you want, you can use the kill switches (labeled L,

**FIGURE 9.3**

Lows, mids, and highs are under your complete control with EQ Three.
*Source:* Ableton

M, and H) located below each Gain knob to toggle that frequency range on and off with ease.

The 24 and 48 buttons determine the slope, either –24dB/octave or –48dB/octave, at the edges of the frequency bands. This setting will be most apparent when using the kill feature of the EQ Three on a full song. For example, drag a whole song (an MP3 with lots of bass) into a clip slot and place an EQ Three on the track. Click the 48 button, place the FreqLow control at 200Hz, and kill the low band—you'll hear the bass disappear from the song. Now try clicking the 24 button. You may notice that you can hear a little more bass.

The EQ Three is a handy performance tool, but doesn't have the same sound quality as EQ Eight. And because it's modeled on mixer circuitry, it even affects the sound with all the controls at their default. If you need the particular functionality this device provides, but want the sound quality of EQ Eight, look in the Performance & DJ folder under Audio Effect Rack in the Browser. You'll find a Rack called *EQ Three Rack*, which provides similar functionality, but is built using EQ Eight.

### SONIC JIGSAW PUZZLES

Try placing three different drum loops on three different tracks, each armed with an EQ Three. Then isolate the bass in one track, the mids in another, and the highs in the remaining track. You'll now have one hybrid beat consisting of kicks, snares, and hi-hats from different loops. Try swapping or automating the kills for other rhythm combinations.

# Auto Filter

The Auto Filter (seen in Figure 9.4) is a virtual, analog-style filter with four classic filter types (high-pass, low-pass, bandpass, and band-reject) and a morphing filter. Each of these can be controlled via the effect's X-Y controller and modulated by an envelope and any of seven different low-frequency oscillator (LFO) shapes. As you may have gleaned from the EQ Eight explanation, suppressing certain frequencies allows you to carve out specific problems or overcooked frequencies. Like Live's EQs, Auto Filter can be used to carve out problematic frequencies, but it also shines as a creative effect capable of a wide variety of sounds.

**FIGURE 9.4**

Live's Auto Filter device. If you've just been reading so far, you really need to get up and try this one.
*Source:* Ableton

## Filter Type

Running along the bottom of the graphical display are five icons for selecting the Auto Filter's type. They are, from right to left: low-pass, high-pass, band-pass, notch, and morph.

Low-pass simply means that the low frequencies pass through the filter, but nothing else does. For instance, if used on an entire song, the bass guitar and kick drums will be audible, although a little dull-sounding due to the lack of highs. Some sounds may disappear completely, such as small cymbals or shakers. Conversely, a high-pass filter will allow shimmering cymbals and sparkly guitars and synths to pass, but will suppress basses and any other instruments in the lower frequency range. How low is up to you.

Band-pass filters are basically high-pass and low-pass filters put together; thus, only frequencies falling between the two filters will pass, sounding similar to a telephone at times. Notch filters work opposite of bandpass—only audio lying outside of the cutoff frequency can pass. With the Morph SVF filter, a Morph knob appears to the right. Use this knob to flow between the four classic filters.

For more information about filter types, circuits, and slopes, refer to the Filters section in Chapter 8, "Live's Instruments."

## Frequency and Resonance

To get going with Live's Auto Filter, select a filter type—Low-Pass is a good starter—and then click and drag the X-Y controller to dial in Frequency (X-axis) and Resonance (Y-axis). Or, if you prefer, use the Frequency and Resonance knobs to the right of the display.

Increasing the Resonance control will increase the intensity of the filter by boosting the frequencies around the cutoff, while lowering it will cause the filter to roll off more smoothly. If you really crank up the Resonance, you can get some very intense effects as you move the filter frequency. This can sound great, but be sure to watch your volume!

## LFO

To the right of the X-Y controller is the LFO, which can be used to modulate the filter frequency. The Amount knob controls the amplitude of the modulation, while the Rate controls its speed. Next to the Amount knob is the Shape menu. These waveforms are fairly self-explanatory—the sine wave at the top creates smooth changes, while the square wave creates choppy ones. The best way to get a feel for the different waveshapes is to crank up the Amount, add a bit of resonance, and listen. The bottom two waveshapes are random (sample and hold): the first one generates separate random values for the left and right channels, while the second one is mono.

When the Phase control is set to 180 degrees, the LFO will generate opposite modulations for the left and right channels, creating a stereo effect. In other words, as the frequency of the left channel is increased, the frequency of the right channel is decreased. Increasing or decreasing the Phase will bring the phase relationship of the left and right LFOs closer together until eventually they become identical.

The Rate control can be adjusted in Hertz by clicking the Hz switch, or it can be synchronized to the tempo by clicking the switch with the note icon. Depending on which you select, there are different options available for the Phase control. When Rate is set to Hertz, two switches appear near the Phase knob. When the lower switch is clicked, the Spin knob appears. Spin changes the speed of the left and right LFOs relative to each other, creating a swirling effect. When Rate is set to tempo sync, the Offset knob appears. This can be used to create some interesting rhythmic effects. As you increase the Offset, you shift peaks and troughs of the LFO off the beat instead of right on it.

## Envelope

The Envelope knob determines how much the input signal's volume will modulate the filter frequency. This type of modulator is commonly known as an *envelope follower* because it creates an envelope that "follows" the signal's amplitude. Positive values cause the filter frequency to be turned up, while negative values turn the frequency down as the volume increases.

The effect can be fine-tuned by using the Attack and Release controls. Attack determines how long it takes for the frequency to reach its maximum value, while Release determines how long it takes for it to return to its original value. Crank the Envelope knob to get familiar with these controls. Short Attack and Release times will tend to give you a funky, clucking effect because you'll get more of the filter sweep for each note. Longer times will tend to make the effect more subtle since it takes longer for the filter to open up, and it tends not to release all the way back to its original value before opening again.

## Quantize Beat

The Quantize Beat parameter affects filter modulation (generated either by the LFO or the envelope) by forcing the filter frequency to change in tempo-synchronized steps. The steps are specified in 16ths ranging from .5 (32nd notes) to 16 (1 bar). To get a feel for what this Quantize Beat does, load it on to a track with a sustained pad and configure the Auto Filter, as shown in Figure 9.5. You may have to adjust the frequency so that you hear a nice up-and-down sweep. Now try clicking the On switch a few times. As it goes on and off, you'll hear the modulation go from a smooth sweep to a choppier sound. This is the sound of the filter frequency jumping to a new value once every 16th note. Now you can experiment with other Beat values and play with the Phase as well.

## Sidechain

In Figure 9.5, you may have noticed the Sidechain section of the Auto Filter to the left of the Envelope section. This section is only displayed if you click the small triangle in the title bar.

Sidechaining refers to having an audio source, other than the one you are currently processing, trigger the envelope for an effect. In other words, in the case of the Auto Filter, you can have the envelope follow the dynamics of any track in Live, instead of following the dynamics of the signal that you are processing with the Auto Filter. Let's take a look at how this works.

**FIGURE 9.5**

Specify a sidechain input to have the envelope of your Auto Filter follow a different audio source.

*Source:* Ableton

If you tried out the Quantize Beat example earlier, you'll want to keep working with the same sustained pad for this example, too. We'll also need another track to serve as the sidechain source. This can be an audio or a MIDI track, but it should output something percussive with strong transients. Now, in the Sidechain section, set the Source to the percussion track, as seen in Figure 9.5. Also, make sure that the LFO Amount is set to 0. There's no reason you can't use the LFO at the same time, but for learning purposes, it's best to keep it simple.

Now, play back both clips and slowly raise the Envelope control. As you do this, you'll hear the filter on the pad begin to rise and fall with the hits in the drum loop. If you're not getting enough of an effect even with the Envelope control cranked, you can increase the Gain to feed more signal to the Sidechain. The Dry/Wet knob controls how much the sidechain signal is mixed with the direct signal before it is sent to the envelope. In the current example, a setting of 50% would mean that the envelope would follow the dynamics of a 50/50 blend of the drum loop and the pad. At 0%, the sidechain is bypassed completely.

## PRE OR POST?

In the sidechain example earlier, you may have noticed that the sidechain source is set to Pre FX (refer to Figure 9.5). This is because we want to trigger the envelope with the beat before it gets to the effects or the mixer. By using either the Pre or Post FX setting, you can mute the sidechain track in Live's Mixer and still have it reach the sidechain input. This way, you can get the rhythmic envelope without having to hear the drum loop.

# Dynamic Processing

In the audio world, dynamics refers to the volume or amplitude of a sound. More specifically, it refers to the *change* in volume of a sound. The sound of a drum kit can range from quiet ghost notes on a snare drum to the thundering sound of the kick drum and toms, and it is therefore considered to have more dynamic range than a distorted guitar, which usually plays at a more consistent volume.

It therefore makes sense that dynamic processors would alter the volume of signals passing through them. But why would you want to do this? Like EQing, dynamic processing can be used to compensate for problems arising in the recording process. It can also be used to control the natural peaks that occur during live vocal performances, to exaggerate the transients in a part, or for a variety of creative effects.

## Compressor

Compression can add clarity and power to your mixes if done properly. Done wrong, it can suck all the life from what was once a brilliant track. For audio engineers, compression is one of the hardest things to learn to use properly and is one element that separates the big fish from the little guppies. Live 10 includes a great-sounding, very flexible compressor.

Compressor offers three unique views for visualizing the way it changes a signal's gain. Before getting into the nitty-gritty of compression, let's get familiar with the interface. The three possible views are selected via the icons that run along the bottom of the device (see Figure 9.6).

**FIGURE 9.6**
Live's Compressor offers three unique views, selected with the buttons shown here.
*Source:* Ableton

The views are as follows:

- ▶ **Collapsed (default):** The most compact of all the views, showing simple meters for Threshold, Gain Reduction (GR), and Output Gain. Threshold and Output Gain are adjusted using the slider attached to the right side of the meters. In this view, the Lookahead and Envelope controls cannot be adjusted.

- ▶ **Transfer Curve:** This view differs from the Collapsed View only in that the Gain Reduction meter is accompanied by an X-Y grid displaying the relationship of input signal (the horizontal axis) to output signal (the vertical axis). Dragging the yellow dot horizontally adjusts the Threshold, while dragging it vertically adjusts the Ratio.

- ▶ **Activity:** This view is a scrolling representation of how the gain of the signal changes over time. The input signal is represented in gray as peaks and valleys along the bottom, while the gain reduction is shown as a jagged orange line across the top. Note that Threshold and Ratio are adjusted using number boxes at the top when using Activity View.

## Compression Basics

In brief, a compressor is a device that will automatically turn down the volume of sound passing through it. To explain this concept, let's use a simplified example. What if you could buy something that would turn down the TV whenever something loud came on? It would keep the commercials at the same volume as the TV show, and it would also keep loud things like car explosions from blasting your neighbors awake in the middle of the night. Enter the compressor.

To get our imaginary TV compressor to work, there are a few settings you have to choose. The first one is called *Volume Trigger.* You set this one to the volume where the box should start turning down the volume. You set this to a point just slightly louder than the TV show you're watching. Most of the time, the compressor won't do anything. However, if a loud commercial comes on, it will engage the Volume Trigger, and the compressor will kick in.

The next control you're supposed to set on this thing is the Turn-Down Amount. When the compressor engages as a result of the Volume Trigger being exceeded, the volume will be turned down by the Turn-Down Amount. Setting this to infinity makes the compressor turn down the volume to match the Volume Trigger. Thus, the commercial is turned down to the volume of the TV show.

The third setting is the Turn-Down Time. This setting sets the time that the compressor takes to turn down the volume after the commercial starts. If this value is set to a long time, like five seconds, the compressor will take five seconds to turn down the volume when the commercial comes on. The point here is to cut the volume on the commercial the moment it comes on, so you set the time to 10ms. Now, the commercial is turned down within 10ms of coming on.

The last value is Turn-Up Time. This is the opposite of the Turn-Down Time where you specify how long it should take for the compressor to turn the volume back up again after the commercials are over. You don't want to miss any of the dialogue when the show starts, so you set this to 10ms as well. But this causes an unforeseen problem: any time the commercial announcer's voice dips below the Volume Trigger—even just trailing off at the end of a word, the volume shoots back up to its original level causing low-level sounds, such as breaths, to become unnaturally loud. Therefore, you set the Turn-Up time to one second. This way, the announcer's voice will stay down until the end of the commercial, at which point it will fade back to full volume over one second.

So that's it. You've now mastered the compressor. It turns down commercials that exceed the volume of your TV show within 10ms and then returns the volume to normal one second after the commercials are over. Nice.

If you've looked at a compressor at all, hardware or software, you know that I replaced the real names of the controls with fake names in the example above. Here's the decoder: the *Volume Trigger* is really the *Threshold* control. The *Turn-Down Amount* refers to the *Ratio*. *Turn-Down Time* and *Turn-Up Time* refer to *Attack* and *Release*, respectively. You will see all of these controls on Live's Compressor, shown in Figure 9.7.

**FIGURE 9.7**

Live's Compressor, shown here in Transfer Curve view.

*Source:* Ableton

While a compressor's main task is making loud sounds quieter, engineers often employ compressors as part of a technique for making sounds louder. Compressors make the dynamic range of audio smaller, so the overall level can be higher. Imagine that you have some audio that ranges from −30dB to 0dB. Because its loudest peak is at 0dB, you can't turn it up without clipping. However, if you compress the audio such that every peak over −10dB is reduced to be no greater than −10dB, you can then raise the level of the whole signal by 10dB. Now you have audio that ranges from −20dB to 0dB, resulting in a much greater perceived loudness. When the Makeup switch (explained later) is enabled, this process of raising the level to compensate for reduced gain is automated.

## Threshold, Ratio, Attack, and Release

Compression is useful in a variety of situations, but keeping peaks under control is by far one of the most common. (In electronic dance music, side-chain compression actually may be the most common of all tasks.) Some parts, such as drums and vocals, have many very short peaks, called *transients*, while others (such as a synth part with resonant filter modulation) may have peaks that occur more slowly. Knowing how to compress a sound is all about knowing what result you're trying to achieve

How do you properly control peaks? First, you need to identify the volume at which you want to start compressing, which is done with the Threshold.

To do this, set the Ratio to the maximum, reduce the Attack to its minimum, and set the Release to 500ms. With the Threshold at its default, play the signal and watch the Gain Reduction meter to see if any compression occurs. If not, start to move the Threshold downward until you notice the Gain Reduction meter starts to respond. This means that you've found the

Threshold at which some of the transients are loud enough to trigger gain reduction. As you keep moving the Threshold slider downward, the Gain Reduction meter will begin to respond more often and will also show a greater amount of attenuation.

If you keep reducing the Threshold, there will come a point where nearly every element of the sound you're compressing, the transients and the quieter tones, will all be beyond the Threshold, thus causing the Compressor to work nonstop—always in some state of gain reduction. Back off the Threshold to a point where only the peaks are triggering the Gain Reduction meter.

The Ratio control determines the amount of compression expressed as a ratio of the input volume to the output volume. For instance, a 2-to-1 compression means that when a sound goes over the threshold by 2dB, you will hear only a 1dB increase at the output. And 4-to-1 would mean that for a 2dB increase, only a .5dB change would occur at the output. You may also notice that for high Ratio settings and low Thresholds, the sound may become muffled or muted as a result of the volume squashing what is going on. On the other hand, extreme gain reduction, sometimes called *overcompression*, is also useful as a special effect.

Compressor's other two controls, Attack and Release, determine how long it will take for maximum gain reduction to occur after a sound crosses the Threshold, as well as how long it will take for the sound to return to its original level after the sound has dropped below the Threshold. With a high Ratio and low Threshold, slowly turn up the Attack, and you'll start to hear more of the sound's natural transients passing through. Typically, a small amount of attack time (5 to 10ms) is best for retaining some sense of dynamics. When used on drums, Attack times that are less than 5ms can produce some interesting effects, but you run the risk of squashing the natural transient in a way that makes the sound dull and lifeless. Use it cautiously. Longer attacks are often used with horns, bass, and other sounds that naturally have more gentle transients.

A compressor's release is typically less noticeable when long. A long release time means that the compression backs off slowly after the signal level has dipped back below the threshold. Typically, a short release time will cause compression to engage and disengage repeatedly, and a listener will be more apt to hear the repeated contrasts (sometimes referred to as *pumping* or *breathing*) and low-frequency distortion. Short release times can be a cool-sounding effect for drums and other dynamic material, so make sure to experiment.

The Auto switch just below the Release knob enables a "program dependent" release—meaning the release time is adjusted automatically based on the material that passes through it. This setting is particularly well suited when compressing an entire mix, since there may be several different types of peaks that cause gain reduction, all of which sound better with different release times. This is also the type of release built into the famous LA-2A compressor, which is legendary for sounding great on vocals, even when applying large amounts of compression.

## Knee, Lookahead, Release Envelope

The Knee control is called such because it adjusts the point in the compression graph where the line bends—ergo, the "knee." As the Knee is increased, the bend in the line rounds out. What this represents is the Ratio and the Threshold becoming more dynamic and gradually applying gain reduction as the signal approaches the Threshold.

Especially with high ratios, the sound produced by compressors can be harsh and unnatural. This effect is partly caused by a compressor leaving a signal completely unprocessed and then slamming on the gain reduction every time the Threshold is passed—a behavior known as *hard-knee compression*. By increasing the Knee, you can specify a range of decibels below the Threshold over which gain reduction should be applied. In other words, with a Threshold of –10dB, a Ratio of 10:1, and a Knee of 10dB, a small amount of gain reduction will occur to signals hitting –20dB (the Threshold minus the Knee value). For signals between –20dB and –10dB, an increasing amount of gain reduction will be applied until the full Ratio of 10:1 is reached for signals exceeding –10dB. The result of this "soft-knee" compression is that the dynamic structure of the Compressor's output is closer to the original signal and a more natural sound is produced.

Next to the Knee, you'll see a menu marked *Look*, which sets the Lookahead. Because analog compressors respond to audio in real time, there is a limit as to how quickly they can respond to a peak. In this digital realm, this limitation can be overcome by having the gain detector "look ahead" at the audio to determine exactly when to act. By increasing the Lookahead amount, you can increase the Compressor's accuracy in responding to fast transients and also generate some extreme compression effects impossible with analog compressors.

The Release Envelope (marked *Env*) can be set to either Logarithmic or Linear. In Linear mode, the results you get are a bit more effect-oriented. Use it when you want something to sound compressed. It's great at getting a squashed, overcompressed sound, and it can really make a drum loop pop out. It should be used sparingly and deliberately—too much of it is harsh sounding. Logarithmic release is a more refined-sounding mode and can be used to shape transients with a greater degree of transparency.

### KICK ME! (PART 2)

After you've used the EQ Eight to dial in a nice kick drum tone, place a Compressor on the track. You'll use the Compressor to shape the amplitude of the kick sound, similar to using an ADSR envelope on a synth. To get started, adjust the Threshold until every kick drum hit is triggering some gain reduction.

Set the Ratio to 10:1 and then try adjusting Attack from .01 slowly up to about 20ms. As you adjust it higher, you'll hear more of the "click" of the drum's initial attack. Use lower settings to tame the click for a more mellow sound. Turn the ratio up to make the effect more dramatic or down to smooth it out.

Start with the Release all the way up. As you lower it, you'll hear the low-frequency sustain of the kick become more exaggerated. You may want to use a high release time to control a boomy kick, or a low value to add some extra thump. If the release is too long, the compressor will never release, and it will just sound like you turned down the volume of the kick track.

## Compression Modes

On the right side of the Compressor, you'll see three different compression modes: Peak, RMS, and Expand. In Peak mode, the Compressor will respond to any signal that goes over the threshold, whereas RMS responds more slowly and will have less effect on transients. The advantage to RMS is that when applying compression to complex sources, such as an entire mix, you may not always want an overall gain reduction in response to an individual transient. However, since RMS will allow transients greater than the threshold to pass straight through, it's not well suited to anything where you need very accurate control, such as drums.

Expand is a different beast entirely. This mode exactly inverts the Compressor's behavior from reducing the gain of high-level signals to increasing them instead. Expansion is useful when working with signals that may sound lifeless due to a dynamic range that is too small, such as a signal that was initially recorded with too much compression. (There's a limited amount that this can help, though, so don't record with a lot of compression unless you really know what you're doing.) Additionally, upward expansion can sometimes help with recordings made in unpleasant-sounding rooms. By exaggerating the volume of the peaks, it's possible to effectively turn down some of the room reflections.

## Makeup, Output Gain, and Dry/Wet

If you've been experimenting with the Compressor, at this point you've probably noticed that even though you're applying all sorts of "gain reduction," the signal isn't getting softer—in fact, it may actually seem louder. This is due to the Makeup switch (in the upper right-hand corner) being activated. It's automatically compensating for the amount of gain reduction being applied to the peaks and bringing up the overall level of the signal. While this works nicely, there might be times where you just want to turn down errant peaks without bringing up the overall level. To do this, just turn off Makeup. Whether or not it's turned on, you can always tweak the output level using the Output control.

Dry/Wet is a handy control for blending some uncompressed signal into the Compressor's output. For everyday mix tasks where controlling the peaks in a signal is the goal, this knob should stay at 100% (no dry signal). However, when using the Compressor with more extreme settings, this control has enormous potential. When using compression as an effect, you may love the squashed sound you get but find there's a big downside in terms of lost transients and natural tone. With Dry/Wet, you can dial some of the original sound back in to complete the sonic picture.

## Sidechain

Expanding the Sidechain section (see Figure 9.8) reveals a powerful set of controls for shaping your sounds. When the Sidechain switch is enabled, the gain detector listens to the source specified in the Audio From menus, instead of the signal being processed. This external source can be the output of a track or any source that Live's routing system can access. For example, you could use the top menu to specify a track containing a Drum Rack and the second menu to pick the kick drum chain within the rack.

A classic use of sidechain compression is to use the kick drum to trigger gain reduction in the bass track, to solve the problem of competing frequencies in the low end of a mix. If you're not sure what this means, try it out: load the Compressor onto a bass track and set its Sidechain Audio From menu to the kick drum track. You'll immediately see the device begin responding to the kick drum signal instead of the bass.

**FIGURE 9.8**

The Compressor is shown here in Activity View, with its Sidechain section open. The Sidechain section features an EQ, so you can trigger compression using only certain frequencies of the Sidechain source.

*Source:* Ableton

## PUMP IT UP!

In much of contemporary electronic music, sidechaining signals to the kick drum is an essential part of the sound. You'll hear this technique used to create dramatic pulsating effects, sometimes called *pumping*. Not strictly used on bass, pumping can be used to give rhythmic energy to pads, leads, percussion, and even effects like delay and reverb.

Insert the Compressor onto a track and set its Sidechain source to the kick. Set the Mode to Peak, Ratio to maximum, Attack to minimum, Knee to 0dB, and Env. to Linear. Now, with audio playing back, reduce the threshold until you're seeing and hearing some very intense gain reduction. The Release control is where you'll fine-tune the effect. Crank it up to somewhere between 200ms and 1s. In this range, you get an audible swelling in between each kick drum hit. The exact value you'll use depends on the tempo of the song, how busy the kick part is, and the feel you're going for. Once you've got the hang of this, you can fine-tune the other settings to taste.

But what if your kick drum is already mixed into a drum loop? We can work with that! After you've set the sidechain input to the track that your drum loop is on, enable the EQ section. Now, solo the bass track and click the headphones icon (Sidechain Listen) directly to the left of the EQ switch. Now, you're hearing the Sidechain source (the drum loop) instead of the bass track. Select the low-pass filter and bring the frequency down until most of the other drums disappear. Then you can turn off Sidechain Listen and tweak the Compressor controls until you get the desired amount of gain reduction. You can even adjust the Dry/Wet mix and boost the Sidechain Gain control so that you're getting compression triggered by both the kick and the bass.

The Sidechain EQ can also be used without an external Sidechain source. In this case, an EQed version of the input signal triggers gain reduction. This technique is frequently used for de-essing, which is the process of softening the sharp "sss" sound that occurs in vocal parts. By filtering out all the lower frequencies or boosting the sibilant frequencies (often 5kHz and higher), you can force the Compressor to respond only when a strong "sss" escapes the vocalist's lips. Typically, this will require some careful tweaking of the Threshold and a very fast attack.

# Gate

Where compressors focus on reducing volume spikes above a certain threshold, gates help turn down low-level signals beneath a certain threshold. Gates are a tool for reducing background noise, microphone bleed, and undesirable reverb decay. They are also a creative tool for chopping up audio loops and creating wild rhythmic effects by using the sidechain. Figure 9.9 shows Live's Gate effect.

**FIGURE 9.9**

Live's Gate effect.

*Source:* Ableton

A Gate effect operates just like it sounds. Certain audio can make it through the gate, while other audio cannot. The minimum level to get through the gate is set by the Threshold slider. Any incoming sound quieter than the threshold will cause the gate to close, thus attenuating the signal. Once the gate opens, it remains open until the signal goes below the Threshold value *minus* the Return value. In other words, if Threshold is –10dB and Return is 5dB, the gate will open for signals above –10 and stay open until the signal goes below –15.

To get a feel for this, set Return to zero and adjust Threshold until only the highest peaks of the signal come through. At some point, you'll discover a phenomenon called *chatter* where the gate opens and closes rapidly as the signal crosses back and forth across the Threshold. Increasing the Return will stop the chatter and impart a more natural sound to the gating.

The Attack, Hold, and Release settings determine the rate at which the gate opens and closes. For instance, a very short attack will make the gate open quickly when the threshold is exceeded, sometimes resulting in harsh, audible clicks.

Similarly, the Hold and Release functions affect how long the gate remains open after the signal has fallen below the Threshold. Hold is a fixed minimum amount of time the gate must stay open, while Release is the speed at which it closes. The Flip switch turns the gate upside down—only signals *below* the threshold will get passed. While not often the most practical thing, the Flip switch can be used to generate some interesting glitchy effects on your beats, and can be very effective when used in conjunction with the Sidechain.

Floor is the amount of gain reduction applied when the gate is closed. When used as a corrective tool for microphone bleed or noise reduction, you may need to experiment with less gain reduction to get natural-sounding results. When Gate is being used as an effect, try turning this all the way down for the most dramatic effect.

The Sidechain opens up loads of creative possibilities for the gate. Its settings are identical to those described in detail in the "Compressor" section in this chapter. For an interesting experiment, try the Auto Filter sidechain example (involving a sustained pad and a drum loop) with the gate. By opening and closing the gate using a beat, you can turn the pad into a chopped-up rhythm part.

# Glue Compressor

This compressor takes its odd name from a common piece of audio engineer-speak: namely, the ability of compression to make a mix sound "glued together." This difficult-to-describe quality refers to the final result sounding like a cohesive whole, while still being composed of clear and carefully delineated elements. One of the most famous compressors for achieving this result is the master buss compressor found in SSL consoles, the compressor on which Glue is modeled (see Figure 9.10).

**FIGURE 9.10**

The Glue Compressor brings a bit of big console sound to Live's sound palette.

*Source:* Ableton

All of the basic controls found in the Compressor are the same here, with the exception that the output Gain knob is called *Makeup* and the Attack, Release, and Ratio settings are limited to the same values found on the original hardware. (Make sure to read the "Compressor" section if you need a briefing on the basic functionality of this device.) The Glue Compressor is optimized for dealing with complex sources, like a drum buss or an entire mix, and it models the circuitry of the analog device on which it's based, and thus is capable of producing some sonically pleasing color. With the Soft switch enabled, the device's grit and color are maximized, as an additional waveshaping algorithm is used to limit peaks and produce subtle distortion.

One control unique to the Glue Compressor is Range. This setting gives you the ability to limit the amount of compression applied to an absolute value. For example, setting range to –10dB means there will never be more than 10dB of gain reduction applied, regardless of the Threshold and Ratio settings. This is very handy when using this device on a buss or an entire mix, because in these cases it's often desirable to use very small amounts of gain reduction—sometimes a maximum of 2 or 3dB.

The unfold switch in the title bar can be used to expose the Sidechain controls. These work just like those of the Compressor, so review that section of this chapter for more information on this topic.

# Limiter

Ever notice that when you complete a mixdown of your music, it's still not nearly as loud as commercial tracks that you've bought? This is because after the mixdown phase, most tracks go through a separate mastering process to balance the overall frequency characteristics and also to increase the overall loudness of the track. For a number of years, competing for loudness became such an obsession with many artists and labels that it was dubbed the *loudness wars*. Live's built-in tool for boosting loudness is Limiter (see Figure 9.11).

Live's Limiter is the simplest of all of the dynamics processors. It simply prevents the signal from ever going above the volume specified by the Ceiling parameter. In traditional audio engineering terms, a Limiter is typically a compressor with a ratio of 10:1 or greater, although it's not an exact term.

**FIGURE 9.11**
Live's Limiter is great
for getting your songs
a few dB hotter or
aggressively controlling
the peaks of any signal.
*Source:* Ableton

When you see a "brickwall limiter" device, such as this one, its ratio is fixed at infinite, meaning that the signal is never allowed to exceed the threshold.

The Limiter has no threshold control. That's because the Ceiling functions as the threshold. If your Ceiling is set to –1dB, and you feed it a signal that contains no peaks above –1, then the Limiter will have no effect. To apply limiting, you would simply increase the Gain control until the signal begins to exceed the Ceiling. Then you'll see the Gain Reduction meter begin to flash, and you'll hear the overall level of the signal become louder without ever clipping. As you continue to increase the gain, you'll start to get some distortion and will eventually destroy all of the dynamics in the signal, so listen carefully and go easy if in doubt.

The Release knob can be used to fine-tune the Limiter's release characteristics, but for most applications, Auto will work just fine. Lookahead functions like a simple Attack control. At lower values, it responds faster to peaks, which results in more limiting but also a potential increase in distortion. This is always the trade-off with increasing gain through limiting. The more you apply, the less dynamic and more distorted the signal becomes. To find the right amount, it's a good idea to put on some headphones and crank up the gain until you can hear distortion; then back off until you've found an acceptable level.

The switch marked Stereo should generally be left alone unless you don't mind messing with the stereo image of the material you're working with. In Stereo mode, a peak in either channel will cause gain reduction to occur on both sides, preserving the stereo image. By changing this to L/R, you can treat each side separately.

# Multiband Dynamics

If you're still wrapping your head around what dynamics processors do, then you may want to spend more time with Live's basic Compressor and Gate before digging into the Multiband Dynamics device (see Figure 9.12). If you're already a seasoned engineer, then you're certainly familiar with the power of this type of processor. This section assumes that you know the basics of compression and gating, so make sure to read through the "Compressor" and "Gate" sections if you need to brush up on these concepts.

**FIGURE 9.12**

Live's Multiband Dynamics.
*Source:* Ableton

Essentially, a multiband compressor (the most common type of multiband dynamics processing) is what you get if you breed an EQ and a compressor. For example, in the case of the EQ Three, the signal gets split into three different bands, each of which has its own volume control—one for turning each of the bands up or down separately. In the case of a multiband compressor, each of the bands gets its own dynamics processor, capable of automatically turning the volume of that band down, depending on the volume of that band in the input signal. For the Multiband Dynamics device, Ableton has created a processor that is capable of both upward and downward compression and expansion, which means that each band can be automatically turned either down or up in response to the signal going either above or below a given threshold. There's an awful lot of functionality packed into this relatively small interface.

In the case of Live's Multiband Dynamics, the three bands are laid out from top to bottom instead of left to right. Each band has its Activator and Solo switches, while the high and low bands each have an On/Off switch, which can be used to make the device use just two bands or even one band (in which case it's not a multiband processor at all).

Below each of the On/Off switches, you'll also see a number box for specifying a frequency. These are the crossover points for the device, and they define the exact range of frequencies that each of the bands controls. So you'll see that the High frequency band includes everything above 2.5kHz by default, but by changing this value, you can easily make the High band include only frequencies above 5kHz. The Mid band then handles everything below 5kHz down to whatever frequency is specified for the Low band.

As you play a signal through this device, you'll see meters in the center display for each band, showing the volume of the signal. The clear blocks at the far left and right of the display are a graphical representation of the Threshold and Ratio settings. The left-hand block is used to display settings for either upward compression (making a signal louder when it dips below a given threshold) or standard expansion (making a signal quieter when it dips below a given threshold), which is similar to gating. The right-hand blocks make settings for upward expansion (making a signal louder when it exceeds a given threshold) or standard downward compression.

In any of these cases, the threshold is set by dragging the edges of the boxes left or right, making them longer or shorter, and the ratio is specified by dragging up or down anywhere within the boxes. You'll see that, depending on the direction you drag, the box turns either orange or blue. Blue signifies ratios of greater than 1, which means gain reduction, while orange signifies ratios of less than 1, meaning there will be a gain increase when the threshold is crossed. To view these values numerically, click the B (for Below) or A (for Above) in the lower right-hand corner of the display. *Below* shows you the settings for the left-hand block, while *Above* shows the ones on the right. The T (for Threshold) will adjust the Attack and Release times.

In practice, multiband processors are often used in mastering. For example, you might want to gently compress the low end of a dance track for more tightness and focus, while giving the mids a more aggressive squeeze so they don't get painful at high volumes. When you're learning to use Multiband Dynamics, don't be afraid to turn off the Activator switch for two of the bands and just focus on one. For example, if you've got a part that sounds too crisp, but EQing it makes it sound too dull, try turning the mid and low bands off and see if you can get what you want by applying a little compression to the top.

Multiband Dynamics also features a Sidechain section, which functions just like that of the Compressor, except that it lacks an EQ section. Refer to the "Compressor" section in this chapter for more information.

# Delay Effects

Ableton's Delay effects group may just be the company's most creative effects ever. Each effect features solid tools for both assembling new rhythmic variations and creating innovative textures with repeated long sounds. While many of the delays have some similar controls, each delay is also somewhat specialized and has some unique features. As you explore them one by one, don't be afraid to do lots of experimenting and get lost in your own creativity.

## Simple Delay

While you may think we are starting simple, Live's Simple Delay is still a formidable stereo, tempo-syncable delay, with a rhythmic beat-division chooser (see in Figure 9.13).

Looking at the device, you can see two separate beat-division choosers—one for the left channel and one for the right. Each boxed number represents a multiple of the 1/16-note delay time. For instance, choosing a 4 would mean a four-1/16-note delay, or a full 1/4-note hold, before you would hear the delayed note sound. An 8 would be two beats, and 16 would be four beats—typically, an entire measure. In either of the beat-division choosers, you can select 1, 2, 3, 4, 5, 6, 8, or 16 for your delay multiple.

**FIGURE 9.13**
Live's Simple
Delay plug-in.
*Source:* Ableton

This beat dividing works only if the Sync switch is enabled for that channel (right or left). *Sync* means that the delay is set to synchronize with the song tempo (beats per minute). Next to the Sync switch is the offset percentage, which is used to adjust the delay time by a fractional amount. Use this to add a little slop or even approximate a triplet feel, if your delays are sounding too strict.

With Sync disengaged, you can manually set the delay time from 1 to 300ms by adjusting the Time value.

### DOUBLE WIDE

Any signal can be given stereo width by using an easy delay trick. Set both the left and right sides of a Simple Delay to Time mode and then set the left delay to 1ms and the right to 20ms. Next, set the effect to 100% wet. It will sound as if the center has dropped out and the signal is coming only from the sides. To further customize this effect, experiment with different delay times and Dry/Wet settings.

The Dry/Wet knob determines how much of the delayed sound versus original sound you hear. At 50%, the delayed signal is at the same volume as the original. A 100% Wet setting means that you will no longer hear the original sound, only the delay effect.

Feedback controls the duration and intensity of the effect. By increasing the percentage of Feedback, you raise the effect's signal output to its own input. Feedback will radically shape the delay, from a slapback echo (short delay time, low feedback) to a wild echo chamber.

### ALL WET

When devices are used in a Return track, set the Dry/Wet setting to 100% wet. Since the original source sound is audible through Live's Mixer, there is no need to route any dry signal through the effect.

# Ping Pong Delay

Ableton's Ping Pong Delay (see Figure 9.14) plays a game of stereo tennis with your sound by serving it up from left to right. In looking at this device, you may notice that many of the controls are similar to the Simple Delay covered earlier. Like Simple Delay, Ping Pong Delay is a stereo delay with built-in tempo synchronizing capability, and it sports the same beat-division chooser boxes, as well as the same Dry/Wet and Feedback controls; however, Ping Pong Delay is a little more creative in terms of what frequencies actually get repeated. You will find a bandpass filter, complete with an adjustable X-Y controller axis to adjust both the cutoff frequency and the width of the frequency band (the Q). You can select between 50Hz and 18kHz and a Q from .5 to 9dB.

**FIGURE 9.14**

Live's Ping Pong Delay bounces a signal from left to right.
*Source:* Ableton

Notice that the same Sync and delay time boxes are also present in Ping Pong Delay. When Sync is activated, Ping Pong Delay will rhythmically synchronize your audio delays from left to right, according to your beat-division chooser. Once you deactivate Sync, you can set the delay time manually from 1 to 999ms.

Next to the Sync switch is a tiny little button labeled *F*. This is the Freeze button. When active, it will cause the Ping Pong Delay to repeat indefinitely without fading away and without adding new audio into the loop. Therefore, you can "freeze" what is repeating by activating this button. When you deactivate it, the delay will continue to decay and repeat as normal.

# Filter Delay

Next in Live's group of delay effects is the powerful Filter Delay. This effect is actually three delays in one: one stereo delay and two mono delays—one on each stereo channel. Individual delays can be toggled on and off via the L, L+R, and R boxes on the far left, seen in Figure 9.15. Similarly, each high- and low-pass filter can also be switched on and off via the box labeled On (default setting) in the upper left-hand corner next to the X-Y controllers.

**FIGURE 9.15**
Live's very flexible Filter Delay. Notice that the L+R input is disabled in this example, causing the device to produce completely independent results for the left and right channels.
*Source:* Ableton

The Filter Delay device is made up of three individual delays, each with its own filter. The X-Y controllers work in the same way as the Ping Pong Delay. The Y-axis determines the bandwidth (Q), while the X-axis shifts the frequency. Each delay also features its own beat-division chooser with tempo-syncable delay times.

On the right-hand side of the plug-in, you will see Feedback, Pan, and Volume controls specific to each delay. Each feedback control will reroute the delayed signal back through that delay's input (just like all Live delays). Each delay's Pan knob can be used to override its default setting. For instance, if you pan the L delay (top delay) to the right side (with the top Pan knob), you will hear it on the right.

Instead of a Dry/Wet knob, the Filter Delay has separate Volume knobs for each delay. The unaffected signal level is controlled with the Dry knob, located in the lower right-hand corner. For a 100% wet signal, turn the Dry setting to –inf dB.

**IN TRANSITION**

Right-click in the title bar of the Simple, Ping Pong, or Filter delays to reveal the Transition Modes: Jump, Fade, and Repitch. Select Repitch and play with the delay time while passing a signal through. As the delay time changes, you'll hear the raising and lowering of the delayed signal's pitch, just like you would with a tape delay or analog delay unit. Jump works almost identically to the default Fade mode, but it allows the production of digital artifacts created by changing delay times. Fans of a glitchy digital sound palette may like this mode.

The Input switches at the far left are used to turn the delays on and off, while the On/Off switches next to the filter can be used to enable or disable filtering of the signal. These options make the Filter Delay the most customizable of Live's delay units.

# Echo

Introduced in Live 10 Suite, Echo is Live's newest and most flexible delay. Similar to Live's other delay devices, Echo includes adjustable delay time with tempo sync, feedback, and a filter. In addition, this powerful delay has built-in reverb, three selectable stereo modes, modulation, dynamics control, and adjustable character.

**FIGURE 9.16**

Echo is Live's newest delay device. Create beautiful-sounding delays, offset delays per channel to make interesting rhythms, control delay volume, or creatively mangle your delays with modulation.

*Source:* Ableton

## Delay Time

Like Live's other delays, Echo's delay time can be synchronized to your Set's tempo (Sync) or specified in milliseconds (Time). Above the Sync/Time switches are Left and Right knobs to adjust the delay time. Between these knobs is the Stereo Link switch. When enabled, it links the left and right channel delays so they are identical. When deselected, you can set a different delay time for each channel.

In Sync mode, there is a menu below the Sync switch for choosing the beat division: Notes, Triplet, Dotted, and 16th. When Notes is selected, the delay time is exactly the value shown by the delay time knobs above, while Triplets or Dotted will adjust the delays to play back triplet or dotted values respectively. When 16th is selected, the delay time is specified in a number of 16th notes. For example, if the delay time is set to 4, a repeat will occur every four 16th notes, otherwise known as a *quarter note*. This is the same as selecting 1/4 in Notes mode, but with the flexibility of being able to switch easily to odd delay times like 3/16 or 5/16 without having to change modes.

Below the Sync modes are the Delay Offset boxes. Adjusting Delay Offset will increase or decrease the delay time in very small amounts. Use this to make your delays push forward or lag behind the beat a little, or to create a swing effect. The offsets for the left and right channels can be changed independently, so you can create interesting rhythms, or add a sense of space to your delays by setting different percentages on each side.

## Feedback

Like the other delays, Feedback determines how long the delay repeats continue. However, Echo brings an added twist by allowing values over 100%. Once feedback hits 100%, the repeats continue indefinitely. Over 100% they increase in volume over time and eventually begin to distort, simulating the out-of-control feedback effect possible with some hardware units. After you've got an infinite feedback loop going (make sure that your speakers aren't too loud!), play around with the delay time, filter, or character controls discussed later in this section.

Next to the Feedback knob is the Invert switch, which inverts the delayed signal's phase. When used with very short delay times, this can have a big impact, sometimes smoothing out the delay into a reverb-like effect, and sometimes causing the repeats to choke out rapidly even with longer feedback times.

## Channel Modes

To the right of the center display, you'll see the Channel Mode switches: Stereo, Ping Pong, and Mid/Side. These change how your delays will sound throughout the stereo field. When the Stereo switch is selected, the delays are played back exactly as specified with the Left and Right delay time knobs. With the Ping Pong switch enabled, the delays go back and forth from left to right sides, creating a ping-pong movement across the stereo field. In Mid/Side mode, the original sound will play in the middle and the delays will shoot out to the left and right sides, creating an airy and spacious feel. To dictate how wide these two stereo modes sound, adjust the Stereo Width knob. As you adjust it below 100%, the repeats will move toward the center, while values above 100% will exaggerate the stereo spread.

## Reverb

If you'd like to add space to your delays, Echo offers built-in reverb, which is adjusted using the three controls directly above the Channel Mode switches. To add some reverb, crank up the Reverb knob. Next, choose the location of the reverb in the signal path using the Reverb Location menu below. Pre adds reverb to the original sound before the delays occur. Post adds reverb after the delays, typically producing a more ambient effect that sounds less like a conventional delay. Feedback adds reverb to the feedback loop—a pretty wild-sounding effect in which the delays blur together to create a lush effect. Be careful with high percentages of feedback and reverb, because it can get out of hand easily! The Decay amount is where you select how long you'd like the reverb to ring out. The higher the percentage, the longer the reverb will decay time.

## Input and Output Gain

In the bottom-left corner, you'll find the Input Gain knob. While this may seem like an odd control for a delay effect, it's an important part of Echo's hardware-emulating design. As this knob is turned up, you'll hear the delay repeats become more distorted, just as they would in many prized hardware studio delays or delay pedals. This added grit can fatten up a sound, or provide a sense of separation between the dry sound and the delay repeats and for increased clarity in a mix. As the distortion increases, so does the volume of the repeats, so you may need to use the Dry/Wet knob to compensate.

The D switch (Clip Dry) processes the dry signal through the input gain as well. This has two effects: the dry signal is distorted just like the repeats, and the relative level of the dry signal and the delayed signal is maintained. With Clip Dry disengaged, the delay repeats can easily end up much louder than the dry signal.

Located to the right of the center display, the Output knob is available to adjust Echo's final output level. If you're driving Echo hard by cranking up the Input gain (which you probably will be!), it will typically be necessary to reduce the output gain to compensate.

## Echo Tab

Click the tab marked *Echo* to reveal the Echo Tunnel. This is Echo's visual display of the delay and feedback over time. Horizontally, the image depicts the stereo field from left to right. The yellow semi-circles depict each delay from the top/outside to the bottom/inside of the tunnel over time. Notice that clicking and dragging vertically in the Echo Tunnel display will change the delay time.

Below the tunnel is the filter section. Click the Filter toggle button (right-pointing triangle) on the bottom left next to the Filter On/Off switch and a graphical display will open. This display shows the bandpass EQ that is applied to the delay repeats. Adjust the range of the filter with the high-pass (HP) and low-pass (LP) frequencies. Both frequencies have adjustable resonance (Res), which can be adjusted directly or by clicking the yellow nodes and dragging vertically.

Removing low frequencies keeps the repeats from getting too muddy, while cutting highs will affect how noticeable or "forward" the delays sound in the mix. Boosted resonance is great for special effects and vintage vibes. To turn off the filter completely, click the square switch next to the word "Filter."

## The Modulation Tab

The Modulation Tab offers controls to impart subtle movement to your delay repeats or add extreme pitch variations and intense filter sweeps (see Figure 9.17).

**FIGURE 9.17**

Crank up the Mod percentages to hear the Modulation Tab at work.

The first thing you'll notice is the waveshape of the modulation oscillator. Change the modulation waveshape using the icons located below the selected shape, or click and drag vertically on the main shape to change the modulation rate. By default, the rate is synchronized to Live's tempo. Turn the Sync switch off to set the modulation speed to a frequency between 0.01 and 40Hz. The higher the frequency is set, the faster the modulation speed will be. Phase Offset is available if you'd like the modulation to be offset between the left and right channels.

In order to hear the modulation, you have to choose what you'd like to modulate: the delay time, the filter, or both. To do this, you'll adjust the percentages labeled Mod. Raise the Delay percentage, and you'll hear the delay time start to fluctuate, or raise the Filter percentage to hear the filter's cutoff frequency change. The X4 switch next to the Delay percentage increases the modulation depth by four times. This mode is not subtle and will tend to produce wild warbling and insane glitches!

Next to the Mod controls is an envelope percentage marked *Env*. Increasing this applies an envelope follower to the modulation amount. This means that, as the input signal gets louder, the modulation amount increases. The higher the Env setting, the more the modulation amount changes in response to the level of the signal.

## The Character Tab

The third tab in Echo is the Character Tab, which contains parameters that adjust dynamics and add creative artifacts to your sound. Each section has a main on/off switch in the upper left-hand corner and two parameters for adjusting the sound.

### *Gate and Ducking*

The gate is used to eliminate quieter sounds. (If you are new to gates, please review the previous section on Gate in this chapter). Because the gate only processes the delay repeats, this can be used to create great effects. For example, putting delay on a drum loop can easily become overwhelming, but the gate can get things under control by silencing the delay on all but the loudest drum hits.

With Threshold all the way down, the gate won't have any effect. As you bring it up, you'll start to hear repeats disappear. By default, the gate closes instantaneously when the signal falls below the threshold, which tends to create a dramatic, choppy effect. By increasing Release, you can have the gate close slower, so the repeats are silenced more gradually.

Ducking turns down the volume of the delays when the dry signal exceeds the threshold. This can be very effective for maintaining the clarity of a melodic instrument or lead vocal even when using long delay tails. Because the delays are automatically turned down in response to the dry signal, they are most noticeable when the original signal pauses, ducking into the background when it comes back in.

The lower the Threshold value, the more the delay repeats will be suppressed. Release determines how long it takes for the repeats to return to full volume after the signal drops below the threshold. How fast you want to set the release time may be determined by the overall busyness of the signal. For example, if you're ducking the delay on a sparse melody, a short release time may be jarring because the repeats will noticeably jump in volume when the melody pauses. A longer release will be smoother and gentler.

### Noise, Wobble, and Repitch

Noise emulates the noisy sound of some analog units. As the amount is turned up, more noise is added to the signal. Amounts over 50% get *very* noisy and can be used to turn the Echo into a stand-alone sound design device. Get some noise going, crank up the feedback, and then mess with the delay time or other parameters. The Morph control changes the tone of the noise. Automating it can create some wild effects!

Wobble comes from the world of analog tape delays. Because of their mechanical nature, tape delays could be very inconsistent causing the pitch and time of the delays to wobble as the tape speed varies. Try adding a small amount of Wobble to create a chorus effect, or a large amount to sound like the tape drive is broken. Morph moves between different types of modulation, varying modulation rates and degrees of inconsistency.

When Repitch is enabled, you'll hear the pitch vary as the delay time changes. When disengaged, the pitch stays the same.

# Grain Delay

Grain Delay is among Live's more complex and creative effects. The Grain Delay is the same as Live's other delays in that it has many of the same controls: Delay Time, Feedback, Dry/Wet mix, and Beat Quantize settings. While the other delays we've seen so far had a filter at the input stage, the Grain Delay has a granular resynthesizer instead. The basic concept is that Grain Delay dissects audio into tiny grains, staggers the delay timing of these grains, and then opens up a toolbox full of pitch, randomized pitch, and spray controls for some far-out sound design results. While all the common delay controls exist in this device, the lion's share of the Grain Delay interface (seen in Figure 9.18) is taken up by a large parameter-assignable X-Y controller.

**FIGURE 9.18**
Live's Grain Delay can take audio apart, altering the structure and pitch before replaying the sound.
*Source:* Ableton

## Frequency

This is the second parameter in the delay interface, but its setting affects all the others, so I'll explain it first. In the Grain Delay, small grains of sound are dispersed quickly. The Frequency setting determines the size and duration of each grain that will be subsequently delayed and can range from 1 to 150Hz. The default setting of 60Hz means that each second of incoming audio is divided into 60 grains. This means that a low setting creates a large grain, while higher Frequency settings create smaller grains. High-frequency settings (lots of small grains) will help keep sounds with rhythmical timing, such as drum loops, intact through the resynthesis process. Low-frequency settings will sound more natural for long sounds, such as textures and pads. If you are having trouble getting a desirable setting out of the Grain Delay, set the frequency to 150 and work backward from there.

## Spray

The Spray parameter roughs up the sound, adding noise and garble to the delayed signal. This setting will allow the Grain Delay to choose a random delay offset amount for each grain. If the Frequency setting above is a high value, the effect of Spray will be more pronounced, as there are more grains to randomize every second. The delay time for Spray can range from 0 to 500ms. Smaller values tend to create a fuzzy-sounding delay effect, while a larger Spray setting will completely take apart the original signal.

## Pitch versus Random Pitch

Like the Spray parameter, Random Pitch tends to throw sound around. The amount of randomness can range from 0 to 161 in terms of intensity (0 being the lowest intensity). The plain old Pitch parameter ranges from 12 to –36 half steps, while allowing for two decimal-point interim values. In other words, fine-tuning a delayed signal's pitch to an actual, discernible tone would be best suited for the Pitch control; trying to eliminate, destroy, or add movement to a pitched signal is the strength of high Random Pitch values. You can use Pitch and Random Pitch in tandem for some robotic and wild pitch modifications. As with the Spray control, the higher the Frequency setting, the more pronounced the Random Pitch effect will be because there are more grains to be resynthesized.

## Putting Grain Delay to Use

Now that you have some idea of just what kind of mischief the Grain Delay is up to, it's time to get familiar with using Grain Delay's X-Y interface. The parameters it controls are selected by clicking one of the boxes located along the side and bottom.

Along the X (horizontal) interface, you will see the boxes for Delay Time, Spray, Frequency, Pitch, Random Pitch, and Feedback. The vertical Y-axis can be set to control Spray, Frequency, Pitch, Random Pitch, Feedback, and Dry/Wet controls. To set feedback to be controlled by the Y-axis, simply click on the vertically aligned box labeled *Feedback* just above the Dry/Wet setting. To enable the X-axis to control the delay time, click the Delay Time box in the bottom-left corner.

Now you're ready to manipulate these controls graphically. Vertical moves affect the Y-axis, while horizontal moves alter the X-axis.

### SHIFT MY PITCH UP

One of the more straightforward applications for the Grain Delay is to provide an echo at a pitch different from the original track. Leave the Spray and Random Pitch values at 0 and choose your delay time normally. If the Pitch value is at 0, the Grain Delay will be working like the Simple Delay in that it delays only the incoming signal. Change the Pitch setting to transpose the echo to a new note. For example, choosing a Pitch setting of 12 will cause the delayed signal to come back an octave higher than the original. This can be fun on vocal parts.

# Reverb

While Ableton's Reverb device may not seem like a delay, it's from the same time-based effect family. Reverberation occurs when sound bounces off a surface, usually many surfaces, many times. In the process of reflecting, the original sound dissipates, becoming diffuse and eventually disappearing altogether. Depending upon the shape and reflective qualities of the room, certain frequencies will be more pronounced than others in the reverberated sound, or *tail*.

The number of controls may seem daunting, but as we step carefully through the signal path, you will see that it all makes sense. Before we get carried away, take a quick look at Figure 9.19.

**FIGURE 9.19**

Live's feature-laden Reverb plug-in.

*Source:* Ableton

## Input Processing

The first link in Reverb's signal chain is the Input Processing section. Here you have on/off selectable Low- and High-Cut filtering, as well as a Predelay control. The Low-Cut and High-Cut X-Y interface allows you to trim your input's frequencies before they are reverberated. Similar to Live's other delays, the X-axis shifts the frequency of the cut (50Hz to 18kHz), while the Y-axis changes the bandwidth (.50 to 9.0). You can also turn each filter off by deselecting its yellow illuminated box. I recommend spending some time playing with this filter each time you use this effect. Think of these filters as altering the acoustic characteristics of a room. For instance, a concrete room may not reproduce low frequencies as well as an acoustically engineered studio room. Each room will favor completely different frequencies.

Also, check out the Predelay control for adding milliseconds of time before you hear the first early reflections, or delayed sound, of the forthcoming reverberation. Larger rooms generally have longer Predelay times since the first reflection takes longer to occur in a large space. Predelay is very useful for preserving the definition of the sound you're adding reverb to. Even with longer decay times, you can crank up the predelay to prevent the original sound from becoming too wet or buried by the effect. While the Predelay can range from .50 to 250ms, to simulate a normal-sounding room, the Predelay works best below 25ms.

## Early Reflections

Early reflections are the first reverberations heard after the initial sound bounces off the walls, floor, or ceiling of the room—yet they arrive ahead of the full reflection, or tail. At times, they sound like slapback delays or mushy portions of the whole reverberated (diffused) sound. The Reverb houses two early reflection controls: Shape and Spin. Spin's X-Y interface controls, Depth (Y-axis) and Frequency (X-axis), apply a subtle modulation to early reflections. Results may range from shimmering highs to whirligig panning flourishes. For quicker decay of early reflections, try increasing the Shape control gradually toward 1.00. Lower values will blend more smoothly with the normal reverb diffusion.

## Global Settings

In Reverb's Global settings section, you can select the quality level of the reverb: Eco, Mid, or High. The three settings will demand small, moderate, and large processor power, respectively. You may also determine the size of the imaginary room via the Size control, which ranges from .22 (small/quiet) to 500 (large/loud). A Stereo Image control selects from 0 to 120 degrees of stereo spread in the reverberation. Higher values will be more spread out, while lower ones approach a mono sound.

## Diffusion Network

The Diffusion Network is by far the most complex-looking area of the Reverb effect. These controls help put the final touches on the actual reverberation that follows closely behind the early reflections. From here, you will be able to decorate and control the finer points of the reverberated sound. To begin with, High and Low shelving filters can further define your imaginary room's sound. By shaving off the highs, for instance, your room may sound more like a concert hall or large auditorium, while brightening up the diffusion (raising the high shelf) will approximate a "bathroom" reverb. Similar to X-Y interface-controlled filters, each filter's X-axis determines frequency, while the Y-axis controls gain. Turning these filters off will conserve some system resources.

Beneath the High and Low shelving controls, you will find the Reverb's Decay Time setting, which ranges from an extremely short 200ms to a cavernous 60-second-long tail. Long reverbs are mesmerizing but can make audio sound muddy and jumbled if used profusely.

To test the coloring and sonic quality of your Reverb, you can use the Freeze control. Any time you press Freeze, Reverb will hold and reproduce the diffusion tail indefinitely. When Flat is activated, the low- and high-pass filters will be ignored. In other words, your frozen Reverb tail will contain all frequencies. An active Cut command prevents further audio from being frozen, even if it is passing through the Reverb. The second X-Y interface in the Diffusion Network, labeled *Chorus*, can add subtle motion or wobbly effect to the overall Reverb tail diffusion. When not in use, deactivate the Chorus button to save system resources.

The final section in Diffusion Network controls the density (thickness) and scale (coarseness) of the diffusion's echo. The Density control ranges from .1% (a lighter-sounding reverb) to a 96% rich and chewy reverb, while Scale can run from 5% to 100%, gradually adding a darker and murkier quality to the diffusion. A high Density setting will diminish the amount of audible change made by Scale controls.

## Output

The Output section is the final link in the Reverb signal chain. At this stage, just three knobs, Dry/Wet, Reflect Level, and Diffuse Level, put the finishing touches on your masterpiece. Dry/Wet controls the ratio of original, unaffected sound to affected, reverberated sound that you hear coming from the effect's output. The Reflect Level control knob adjusts the amplitude (level) of the early reflections specified in the Early Reflections box, from −30 to +6dB. The louder you make the early reflections, the more you will hear an echo of the true sound (which will sound even more like a slapback delay as opposed to a reverb).

In similar fashion, the Diffuse Level controls the amount of Diffusion Network level in the final Reverb output. A low diffusion level will diminish the reverb tail, while a high amplitude of Diffusion Network will increase the overall presence of the effect.

# Modulation Effects

The term *modulate* simply means "to change," so by itself, it doesn't really tell us much about what these effects do. Generally speaking, when we speak about modulation effects, we are talking about ones that are driven by an LFO, such that an inherent part of the effect is the sound of it changing over time. Make sure that you're clear on the role of the LFO in the Auto Filter and Auto Pan effects, and you'll have a much easier time understanding the ones in this section. That said, some of these effects also produce quite useful results without using the LFO section at all. As usual, carve out some time to explore each one fully.

## Chorus

When you listen to a group of people singing a chorus, each member of the group has slightly different timing and intonation, even if they're singing the same words with the same melody. The result is a large and lush vocal sound achieved by the variations in all of the voices.

The Chorus effect attempts to re-create this phenomenon by taking the input signal, delaying it by varying amounts, adding a touch of random Pitch Shift, and then blending the results with the original. In other words, Chorus effects assume that two sounds are better than one. It is common to run synthesizers, guitars, vocals, and strings through a chorus. The doubling, or even tripling, effect of a chorus makes solo voices sound more powerful, takes up more space in a mix, and therefore sounds more "present."

Live's Chorus (see Figure 9.20) features two parallel delays that can be set for .01 to 20ms or linked by activating a tiny equal sign (=).

**FIGURE 9.20**

Live's Chorus effect. Note the tiny equal (=) sign between the delays. This button syncs the two.

*Source:* Ableton

## Delays 1 and 2

The effect's first delay will always be active when the Chorus is on. To adjust the delay's timing, slide the fader. The adjustable Highpass filter knob bypasses chorusing low frequencies, which can often become muddier and less defined when doubled. The definable range is 20Hz to 15kHz. Delay 1 can be used on its own or in parallel with Delay 2.

Chorus's Delay 2 can add even more thickness and intensity to your sounds. Delay 2 can run in two separate modes, Fix and Mod, and can be bypassed by selecting the top visible button labeled Off. Fix mode will force Delay 2 to the timing specified by its slider. Mod mode will allow the delay time to be modulated by the effect's Mod source.

## Modulation

The Chorus's Modulation section is where the effect gets its movement. This section controls a sine wave oscillator (an LFO), which can be used to change the timing of the two delays. Whether you are going for completely unrecognizable new sounds or just looking for a little more stereo spread, you will want to spend some time fiddling (click-dragging) with the Modulation X-Y controller. Horizontal moves change the modulation rate from .03 to 10Hz, while the vertical axis increases the amount of modulation from 0 to 6.5ms. So if Delay 1 is set to 1ms, and you have a modulation amount of 1ms, the LFO will continually change the delay time between 0 and 2ms. The modulation rate changes the speed of the LFO from subtle movements to bubbly vibrations. You also have the option of typing in values by simply clicking on the box, typing a number within the allotted range, and pressing the Enter key.

The LFO will modulate both delays in stereo. This means that the delay times used for the right and left channels will be different, which increases the stereo intensity of the effect. This also means that if both delays are being modulated, there will be four different delay times at any given moment. How's that for fattening up a sound?

If you are looking for radical sonic redesign, the *20 button multiplies the Chorus' LFO rate by 20. While this may not sound great all of the time, the *20 multiplier will push the envelope of the dullest of sounds.

## Feedback, Polarity, and Dry/Wet

For increased intensity, the Feedback control will send part of the output signal back through the delays. The more feedback you elect to add, the more robotic and metallic your sounds will become. The positive and negative polarity switch determines whether the signal being fed back to the delays is added to or subtracted from the new input signal. To hear the greatest contrast between the two polarities, you should use short delay times and increase the Chorus Feedback. The results are often frequency and pitch related. For example, a low-frequency sound becomes a high-frequency sound, a pitch may shift by as much as an octave, and so forth. Finally, the Dry/Wet control determines the amount of original versus chorused signal going to output.

# Phaser

The Phaser (see Figure 9.21) introduces phase shifts in specific frequencies of a sound. It creates a smooth sense of warmth and motion, popular on psychedelic rock guitars and "loungy" electric pianos. Thanks to some unorthodox controls, Live's phase shifter can create some very cutting sounds as well.

**FIGURE 9.21**
Starfleet Command requires that you be equipped with a Phaser at all times.
*Source:* Ableton

## Poles, Color, and Mode

The Phaser uses a series of filters to create phase shifts. The Poles control sets the number of filters, or notches, that are used in the Phaser. If you use a lower number of poles, the Phaser effect will not be as pronounced as when you use a larger number of poles.

The button below the Poles knob sets the mode for the Phaser. The button toggles between Earth and Space. This switch adjusts the spacing of the notch filters, but that's not important. What you need to know is that when *Earth* doesn't provide an intense enough effect for you, it's time to move to *Space.* The Color control will further change the overall tone when Earth mode is active.

## Frequency and Feedback

The large X-Y area in the middle of the Phaser is for adjusting the center frequency and the feedback amount. Move the dot on the screen left and right to adjust frequency (or use the number box in the lower-left corner). Vertical movement will adjust the feedback (whose number box is in the lower-right corner). You normally won't find a feedback control on a typical Phaser, but it's a control that Ableton added to its Phaser to help emphasize the Phase effect.

## LFO and Envelope

Phaser's LFO section is used to modulate the Frequency parameter automatically. This section is a duplicate of the LFO found in the Auto Filter. You'll use the Rate control to set the LFO's speed either in relation to the current tempo or freely in Hertz. The relation of the left and right LFOs is set with the Phase/Spin controls on the bottom right. Finally, the LFO's overall influence on the Phaser frequency is set with the Amount knob on the top right.

Like the LFO, the envelope is identical to the envelope follower you'll find in the Auto Filter device. It works by using the volume of the incoming signal as a means to modulate the frequency of the Phaser. The speed at which the envelope follower responds to changes in input volume is governed by the Attack and Release knobs. Use the top knob (Envelope Amount) to increase the envelope's influence on the Phaser frequency.

# Flanger

The Flanger bears an extremely close resemblance to the Phaser, both in design and use (see Figure 9.22). A flanger works by taking a sound, delaying it by a continuously changing amount, and blending it back with the original sound. This introduces constructive and destructive interference between various frequencies in the sound, producing a characteristic comb filter effect. The Flanger has a much more metallic edge than the Phaser. Its sound can become quite abrasive with high feedback settings, as you'll see in a moment.

**FIGURE 9.22**

In the old days, flanging involved playing two identical recordings on tape machines and then touching the flanges of one of the tape reels to subtly shift the timing of the two recordings. Live's Flanger makes the same effect easier and cheaper to achieve.

*Source:* Ableton

## Hi Pass Filter

As mentioned previously, the Flanger will make a copy of the input signal and mix it back in with the original after a brief delay. Often, this can produce inharmonic (unpitched) results, which can make melodic parts "muddy." To alleviate this effect, you can pass the input signal through a Hi Pass filter. When the delayed signal is mixed back in with the original, the flanging will take effect only on the higher frequencies, leaving the lower frequencies intact.

## Delay and Feedback

This looks quite similar to the X-Y control in the Phaser, doesn't it? Functionally, it's the same—horizontal movements adjust the delay time, while vertical movements increase the Feedback. Because the Flanger uses a delay, there will be a pitch to the effect, which is related to the Delay Time parameter. As the delay time is shortened, the pitch will seem to rise. When you crank up the Feedback, the pitch will become even more pronounced.

## Envelope and LFO

These two sections are identical in functionality to those of the Phaser and Auto Filter, except they modulate the delay time of the Flanger. To push things to the max, switch the Feedback polarity of the Flangers by clicking the small + button next to the Feedback number box in the bottom-right corner of the X-Y control. By default, the LFO is set to 100% to create the classic "swoosh" that flangers are known for.

# Distortions

This brings us to the third group of Ableton's devices: the Distortion effects. Whether you are looking to add fuzz, edge, dirt, brightness, buzz, growl, or even warmth to your sounds, distortion can create some incredibly diverse results. While each of these effects can quickly and drastically alter your audio content, taking time to learn the ins and outs of these babies can take your mixes to a whole new level. Note that Saturator, Dynamic Tube, and Pedal have a high-quality mode to reduce aliasing artifacts in high-frequency sounds. This mode is turned on by right-clicking in the device's title bar and selecting Hi Quality from the context menu. There's only a small CPU hit for using this feature, so it's generally recommended to turn it on.

# Overdrive

Overdrive is the simplest of Live's distortion effects. Instead of trying to be the most flexible effect, Overdrive focuses on the sound created by driving analog equipment past the point where it can reproduce the signal cleanly ("overdriving" it). As the term is usually used to signify, Overdrive (see Figure 9.23) produces a warm, harmonically rich effect that is useful on a wide

**FIGURE 9.23**
Overdrive: warm-sounding and easy to use.
*Source:* Ableton

variety of sources. Even at high settings, it does not produce the harsh clipping that Saturator is capable of.

The heart of Overdrive is the Drive knob: turn it up to get more distortion. There are two different EQ adjustments as well: the bandpass filter above, which is applied to the signal before the drive circuit, and the Tone knob, which adjusts the tone post-drive. This gives you a lot of flexibility. For example, cutting some lows with the bandpass filter may clean up the mud that you might get from distorting a bass, while the Tone knob can be used to control any harsh-sounding artifacts that the Drive circuit adds to the signal.

To further customize the sound, use the Dynamics and Dry/Wet controls. Dynamics is a simple compressor—high values preserve the original dynamics of the sound, while low values increase the compression. Don't underestimate the importance of the Dry/Wet control. In the previous example about cutting lows, you would use this control to make sure that you added in enough of the dry signal to compensate for the low end that you've removed from the overdriven one.

# Saturator

If you like the sort of effect produced by Overdrive, but you need something more programmable, Saturator is where you'll turn next, as shown in Figure 9.24. This effect not only has a variety of analog distortion models, but it is also capable of producing digital clipping and has a flexible waveshaper.

**FIGURE 9.24**

The Saturator: Subtle edge or gateway to destruction.

*Source:* Ableton

## Waveform Display

The top of the Saturator interface is dominated by the large waveform display. Manipulating the controls below the display will give you insight into how the effect modifies your signal by looking at the resulting curve.

You can choose six different modes of signal shaping using the drop-down menu below the display: Analog Clip, Soft Sine, Medium Curve, Hard Curve, Sinoid Fold, and Digital Clip, each with its own distinct characteristics.

The Waveshaper mode allows flexible control of the waveform through the following six parameters:

▶ **Drive:** Not to be confused with the Drive knob (see below), determines the amount of influence of the waveshaping effect.

▶ **Curve:** Adds harmonics to the signal.

▶ **Depth:** Controls the amplitude of a sine wave superimposed over the distortion curve.

▶ **Lin:** Alters the linear portion of the shaping curve.

▶ **Damp:** Flattens the signal, acting as a sort of super-fast noise gate.

▶ **Period:** Determines the density of the ripples in the sine wave.

These controls are specific to the Waveshaper and are not available in other modes.

## Drive

On a dynamic distortion unit such as this, the Drive knob is where you'll demolish your sound; you'll find this to the left of the waveform display. The higher the Drive amount, the more the input signal is amplified. This forces more of the signal into the distortion range, slaughtering the sound at high levels. Depending on the mode, you may find that a loud signal creates distortion without turning up the Drive control at all. If you're getting too much distortion, you can reduce the Drive to a negative value.

Below the Drive, you'll see the DC offset switch, which removes extremely low frequency problems typically caused by a faulty soundcard or other hardware. This low-frequency distortion is usually inaudible until processed with an effect that increases gain, such as the Saturator.

## Color

When the Color toggle switch is on, the four controls below it also become active. These controls are similar to the tone controls on a guitar amp. The Base knob will increase or decrease the amount of bass distorted by the effect. The last three knobs set a high-frequency EQ with specs for frequency, width, and depth (gain).

## Output

As you increase the Drive amount, you will increase the volume of the distortion, often to the point of overpowering other instruments in your mix. Pull the Output down a bit to bring the sound back where it should be. A Dry/Wet control here sets the amount of effect being heard. When the Soft Clip button is activated, an additional instance of the Analog Clip curve will be applied to the final output.

# Dynamic Tube

The Dynamic Tube effect models the distinct "saturated" effect that the vacuum tubes in amplifiers can have on audio (see Figure 9.25). It doesn't really sound like most distortion effects. It can provide some extremely subtle effects, somewhere between compression and distortion, while its more aggressive settings sound like equipment malfunctioning!

This effect allows you to choose between three different tube models: A, B, and C, with C being the most distortion-prone tube and A being the cleanest of the bunch. With Bias set at 0, tube A won't produce any distortion at all. It can, however, produce some very "hot" sounding compression. Raise the Bias and tube A will cause the signal to "break up," producing bright harmonic distortion on louder sounds.

**FIGURE 9.25**
The Dynamic Tube saturation effect.
*Source:* Ableton

To get familiar with Dynamic Tube, try it out on a drum loop. Sweep the Tone knob to both of its extremes, and then listen to what happens when you bring Envelope down to −300%. With a negative Envelope value, less distortion is produced for louder sounds, bringing back more of the loop's original punch.

The Tone control determines what frequencies (higher or lower) are most affected by the tube-distortion effect, while Drive sets how much of the incoming signal is routed through the tube. Setting the Drive control higher will result in a dirtier output.

The Bias control works in conjunction with the Drive control. It determines how much distortion the tube is capable of producing. As you turn this up to the top, the signal will really start to break apart into dirty, fuzzed-out noise. You can modulate the Bias control with the Envelope controls at right. The higher the setting of the Envelope knob, the more the Bias setting will be influenced by the level of the input signal. You can use the Attack and Release knobs to adjust how quickly the envelope reacts to the input.

# Pedal

Pedal is Live's newest distortion device. Inspired by classic guitar pedals, it includes three types of distortion: Overdrive, Distortion, and Fuzz (see Figure 9.26). A built-in EQ makes it easy to dial in the desired frequencies. Use Pedal to gently warm up your sounds or give them that filthy edge you are looking for. Whether you use it to add drive to synths and beats, fullness to your vocals, or fuzz to guitars, Pedal is an impressive-sounding and flexible distortion unit that adds character and energy to your sounds. Note that Pedal is only available in Live Suite, not the Standard or Intro versions of Live.

**FIGURE 9.26**
Live's Pedal device brings guitar pedal edge to your sounds.
*Source:* Ableton

Choose between the three distortion models with the OD (Overdrive), Distort, or Fuzz switches. Turn up the Gain knob to increase the amount of distortion. Unlike some other distortion devices, turning up the gain does not cause the overall volume to get louder, so you won't have to use the Output knob to get the volume under control. That said, adding distortion can make a signal sound louder in a mix (even if the meters say the level hasn't changed at all), so you may find the Output knob comes in handy anyway.

The OD setting gives a subtle warmth or fullness to your signal, which can be great with just about any sound, including vocals. With Distort, you'll get an edgy, crisp, and energetic distortion. But if you're looking for a raucous, heavy buzz, Fuzz is your setting.

A three band EQ is available below the switches, where you can set the amount of Bass, Mid, or Treble. This is handy because distortion can radically alter the sonic characteristics of the signal. Turn down the treble to decrease harshness, or boost the mids for a thick, aggressive tone. Below the Mid knob, there's a switch to adjust the specific frequency range of this knob. Move to the left if low mids are what you're after or to the right for high mids.

When selected, the Sub switch adds sub bass frequencies. This is useful to fatten up a bass or kick that might otherwise lose low frequencies when distorted. Although turning up the Gain knob doesn't add level to the output signal, boosting EQ and using the Sub switch will. If the sound is clipping, use the Output knob to compensate. Finally, try using the Dry/Wet knob to add in some dry signal. This can be a great way to improve clarity, even when using heavy distortion.

# Erosion

Erosion uses an unusual method for sonic degradation. By rapidly modulating a very short delay time, strange distortion artifacts are created. The modulator can be Noise, Wide Noise, or Sine, as seen beneath the X-Y interface (pictured in Figure 9.27).

Depending upon which mode you currently have active, Erosion will use either a sine wave or a noise generator to modulate a very short delay. The only difference between the two noise modes is that Wide Noise uses a separate noise generator for each channel, resulting in a stereo effect.

**FIGURE 9.27**

Live's Erosion device window, primarily taken up by its unusual X-Y field.

*Source:* Ableton

To control the degree of Erosion's effect on a sound, move along the Y-axis to change the level of the modulation signal and the X-axis to control the frequency. For Wide Noise, the Width can be adjusted by holding Alt (Option) while dragging vertically. In my experience, the most consistently pleasing results are achieved using the Sine modulator. Try cranking up Amount and automating Frequency for some glitchy goodness.

# Redux

While you're digging into tools for sonic decimation, you will definitely want to check out Live's Redux device. Redux is a bit-depth and sample-rate reducer that can make even the prettiest of guitars, or anything else for that matter, saw your head off (see Figure 9.28). Of course, results need not be this drastic if you are capable of restraint. In fact, reducing the fidelity of a sample is like a tip of the hat to old Roland, Emu, and Akai 8- and 12-bit samplers—or even old 2- and 4-bit computer-based samples. (Commodore 64, anyone?)

The controls for Redux are split into two tidy sections, with a Bit Reduction knob and On/Off switch on top and a Downsample knob and Hard/Soft switch on the bottom. The default position for Bit Reduction is 16-bit (off). As you reduce the bits, you will hear an increasing amount of noisy grit infect the sample. Anything below 4 bits causes a dramatic increase in gain, so use

**FIGURE 9.28**

Live's Redux is a talented bit-depth and sample-rate reducer.

*Source:* Ableton

caution. The numerical setting will indicate the bit depth (for example, 8 = 8-bit, 4 = 4-bit). Extremists can try trimming it down to 1-bit, but be warned: this gets LOUD!

When it comes to sample-rate reduction, the settings are a little more inexact. In Hard mode, downsampling will stick with whole integers such as 1, 2, and 3 (up to 200) for dividing the sample rate, while in Soft mode you can adjust from 1 to 20 to the nearest hundredth of a point (1.00 or 19.99). A setting of 1 means you are not hearing any sample-rate reduction—oddly, the higher the number, the lower the resulting sample rate.

For a quick course, spend a minute perusing the Ableton Redux factory presets, such as Old Sampler and Down 2.66. These will give you a basic template to work from. Also, while you are in Playback mode, try toggling between Hard and Soft Downsampling with different settings for a cool effect.

# Vinyl Distortion

The imperfections of vinyl have actually become quite lovable these days. Whether you are missing the dust pops and crackles of an old record or the warped vinyl sound of a record left out in the sun, vinyl has a certain retro charm. Although CDs and digital recordings are great, they are hopelessly clean and free of these impurities. Of course, Ableton thought about this, too, and as a result, we have Vinyl Distortion (see Figure 9.29).

Vinyl Distortion is divided into three separate sections: Tracing Model, Crackle, and Pinch. While the controls for Tracing Model and Pinch look identical, each section generates a totally different sound. Note that the Soft/Hard and Stereo/Mono switches are also a part of the Pinch effect. If Pinch is off, these controls will remain grayed out (inactive).

**FIGURE 9.29**

Live's Vinyl Distortion effect hopes to make you miss your turntable just a little bit less.

*Source:* Ableton

Tracing Model adds a subtle amount of harmonic distortion to your audio as a means of simulating wear and tear on vinyl or an old stylus. To adjust the intensity of the distortion, increase the Drive by moving the yellow circle along the Y-axis (which ranges from 0.00 to 1.00). Adjust the frequency of the harmonic on the X-axis (which ranges from 50Hz to 18kHz) or input a value manually by typing in the box. To adjust the size of the bandwidth you are affecting, hold down Alt (Option) and click-drag forward or backward on the yellow circle.

The Pinch section of Vinyl Distortion is a more drastic and wild-sounding distortion at the input level. The resulting richer stereo image is from Pinch's 180 degrees out-of-phase harmonic distortions. Like the Tracing Model, you can increase the intensity of the distortion through the Y-axis. The X-axis will configure the frequency range. You will want to pay special attention to the Soft/Hard boxes to the right of the X-Y interface in the Pinch section. Soft mode is engineered to sound like an actual dub plate (acetate), while Hard mode will sound more like a standard vinyl record. Also, the Stereo/Mono switch applies to the Pinch effect only.

No vinyl simulator would be complete without a vinyl pop and crackle effect. Crackle provides two simple controls: Volume and Density. Volume is obviously the level of the hiss and crackle in the mix. Density adds a thicker amount of noise to the output. Note that you will hear the crackle and hiss whether Live is in playback mode or not.

# Miscellaneous

This last section of devices covers Live's more esoteric and hard-to-classify plug-ins. Some of these could have been squeezed into other sections of this chapter, but they are all unique enough that it made sense to give them their own section.

## Amp and Cabinet

Amp and Cabinet are two completely independent effects designed by the modeling wizards at Softube. While they can certainly be used separately, they are designed to go hand in hand. Amp models the signal path of several classic guitar and bass amplifiers, while Cabinet reproduces the sound of a variety of speaker cabinet and microphone combinations. These two effects are included with Live Suite only.

Guitar amplifiers and speaker cabinets (both real and virtual) have long been part of many engineers' sound-shaping toolkits. While Amp and Cabinet are certainly useful for processing direct-recorded guitars and basses, they are also great for applying distortion and unusual EQ characteristics to a wide variety of sources. When you're having trouble getting a sound to find its unique place in a mix, sometimes these devices provide just the color and edge you need.

## Amp

The most important control in this device is the Amp Type selector, which offers the following modes: Clean, Boost, Blues, Rock, Lead, Heavy, and Bass (see Figure 9.30). As you'll discover quickly, each of these modes sounds radically different from one another. Run a signal through Amp and try them out. You'll know pretty quickly which of these works for the sound you're trying to process, if any. As you move from left to right, the models tend to produce more distortion until you get to Bass, which is a clean model optimized for bass guitar, but may produce good results on a variety of sources.

Once you've picked a model, experiment with the Gain control. Decrease it if you want a bit less distortion and crank it up to hear the amp model at its most aggressive. Adjusting Gain will change the overall volume of the signal; use the Volume control to compensate for this. The Bass, Middle, and Treble controls adjust the lows, mids, and highs respectively, with Presence acting as a high-frequency adjustment for added sparkle. The Presence knob varies quite a bit in the various amp models, so make sure to experiment.

**FIGURE 9.30**

Are you ready to Rock?

*Source:* Ableton

# Cabinet

In the real world, the signal coming out of a guitar amplifier is almost always passed into a speaker cabinet, where its output is then captured by a microphone. In the virtual world of Live, you can achieve this same effect by placing the Cabinet effect after Amp.

When Amp is run on its own without Cabinet, you'll notice that it produces some very intense treble frequencies (just like a real guitar amp would). One of the first things you'll notice when adding Cabinet to the signal path is the taming of these intense high frequencies and the imparting of a mellower characteristic to the sound (see Figure 9.31).

**FIGURE 9.31**

Amp's best buddy, Cabinet.

*Source:* Ableton

The first parameter for adjusting the sound is the Speaker menu. The configurations in this menu follow the convention <number of speakers> × <speaker size>. So, for example, 4 × 10 means a cabinet with four 10-inch speakers in it. Selecting a speaker configuration is much more art than science, although you may notice that the 12" speakers reproduce a bit more low end than the 10" ones. The 4 × 10 Bass cabinet reproduces the most high-end sound of the bunch, as it models a style of bass cabinet that contains tweeters for delivering crisp highs.

The next adjustment is the microphone type and placement. Condenser microphones tend to capture more high-end sounds and a more balanced sound overall, while Dynamic mics are known for their focus and punch when used on speaker cabinets. Placement has a big impact on sound as well. Off-Axis placement tends to capture more low-end sounds, while Far placement emulates recording the speaker from across the room, capturing room reflections and a sense of space.

## Output

Finally, both Amp and Cabinet allow stereo or mono operation via an Output switch and have a Dry/Wet knob for blending the unprocessed signal with the output. Be aware that both devices are relatively CPU-hungry, and running them in stereo doubles the required resources.

# Drum Buss

Another one of Live's newest additions is the mighty Drum Buss, a robust and powerful drum effects processor. Whether you want to warm up your drums, add energy or character, or push them to ultimate massiveness, Drum Buss combines characteristics of a variety of devices. It provides distortion (see Figure 9.32) along with compression, the ability to shape transients and dampen high frequencies, as well as create and tune deep-sounding subs that add volume and body to your sounds.

**Figure 9.32**
Drum Buss sounds amazing on your drum group, but try it on anything you want.
*Source:* Ableton

## The Input Stage: Drive, Trim, and Comp

On the left-hand side of Drum Buss, you'll see the Drive knob. Raise its percentage so that overdrive is applied to the incoming signal. There are three selectable distortion types: Soft, Medium, or Hard. The Soft setting is the smoothest and subtlest of the three. It's good for adding fullness to nearly any sound, not just drums. Try it out on a synth or bass, for instance. Medium has a slightly harder and brighter edge, with added overtones and limiting. Hard features a bass boost and huge-sounding clipping.

You may find that Drum Buss distorts even when Gain is set to 0%. Use the Trim control to reduce the input level to reduce the distortion. The Comp switch below adds a fixed compressor to the input. This can add energy and volume while keeping the dynamic range under control. If the compressor is flattening out the signal too much, pull down the Trim value a bit.

## The Shaping Stage: Crunch, Damp, and Transients

Now let's get into the nitty-gritty. Raising Crunch increases distortion focused in the mid to high frequencies. The Damp knob is used to reduce high frequencies (which can get very intense when a lot of distortion is used). Turn it to set the frequency at which high-frequency damping will begin.

The Transient knob boosts or cuts short the high-amplitude attacks known as *transients*. (For example, when a snare drum is hit, the loud crack when the stick first hits the skin is the transient.) Turn the knob to the right and you will hear the attacks become louder and crisper. This may help drums and percussion stand out better in a mix. Because the Transients function operates specifically on mid to high frequencies, you'll notice that it shapes more than just the attacks. At high settings, you may notice the decay of snare drums (or other sounds with a lot of high-frequency content) getting elongated. Conversely, low values can make drums sound very dry and staccato. It's an unconventional control that requires experimentation!

## The Enhancer: Boom, Freq, and Decay

If you're looking to add a deep-sounding sub to your kicks, this is the place. Crank up the Boom knob, which enhances the low end of your sounds. Then tune the boom to your song using the Frequency knob, which can be adjusted from 30Hz to 90Hz. As you turn Frequency, keep an eye on the small oval-shaped button below. It displays the closest musical pitch to the frequency you've dialed in. Click on this button (it's called *Force To Note*), and Frequency will jump to the closest exact pitch. To hear the enhanced sub by itself, click the headphone switch to the right of Force To Note.

Decay determines how long the sub rings out. A long decay may sound huge and powerful, but just make sure it's not creating too much mud at the bottom of your mix and dial it back if necessary. The Bass meter to the right shows the overall low-frequency level. You'll notice that low-frequency enhancement produces excessive gain at some frequencies, and this meter will help you visualize it.

## Output and Dry/Wet

The Output meter displays the level, and it has a small slider for adjusting it. If the processed audio sounds too effected, use the Dry/Wet control below to blend in some dry signal. Don't be afraid to create over-the-top effects with Drum Buss and then get them under control with Dry/Wet. It's a favorite effect-processing technique of many engineers and producers.

# Auto Pan

Auto Pan is a conceptually simple but surprisingly powerful device. It will automatically pan the position of the track from left to right in cycles. It does this by alternately turning down the volumes of the left and right sides of the channel. When the left side is turned down, the sound will be heard from the right, thus making it sound as if the track were panned to the left. The mixer's Pan control is not affected at all.

The Auto Pan interface is split into two sections. The top section contains a graphical representation of the volume pattern being applied—for display purposes only. The Auto Pan is adjusted by using the knobs and buttons on the lower half of the interface.

## Amount and Rate

When the device is first loaded, it will have a flat line through the middle of its display, and you will hear no effect. The reason you hear nothing is because the Amount knob is set to 0%. As you turn this knob up, you'll hear the sound begin moving left and right. The higher you set the Amount knob, the "wider" the left-to-right movement will be.

As you increase the Amount knob, you'll also see the graphic begin to change on the Auto Pan interface. When the Amount reaches 100%, you'll see two sine curves representing the left and right channels. What these curves tell you is that when the left channel is at full volume, the right channel will be at its lowest volume (see Figure 9.33). As the left channel drops in volume, the right channel will rise and vice versa. The button below the Amount knob will switch the left and right Pan assignments (Normal vs. Invert).

**Figure 9.33**
By looking at the picture in the Auto Pan window, you can see the relationship of the left and right channels over time.
*Source:* Ableton

The Rate will change the speed of the left-right motion created by the Auto Pan. You'll see that as you turn up this knob, not only does the left-right speed increase, but you'll also see the graphic waveform change in kind. The rate can be set in either cycles per second (Hz) or divisions of the beat (the musical note button).

## Phase and Shape

Next on the list of Auto Pan controls is the Phase knob. If you move this knob while watching the waveform graphic, you'll see that this knob adjusts the phase relationship of the left and right curves, or the position where the waveforms start. When set to 180 degrees, the two curves are out of phase, meaning one channel is at full volume while the other is silent. If you twist this knob down to 0 degrees, the two curves will now be in sync (you'll see only one curve), resulting in the left and right channels changing volume in sync. The Auto Pan will no longer pan the signal from left to right—it will simply turn the volume of the whole signal up and down. This is where the Auto Pan device begins to function beyond what its name implies, and it becomes a tremolo or "chopper" effect.

Below the Phase knob, you'll find either the Phase and Spin buttons (when in Hz mode) or the Offset knob (when in Beats mode). These controls work identically to their counterparts in the Auto Filter, so review that section if you need the details on how they work.

The last knob on the Auto Pan is the Shape knob. As this knob is turned clockwise, the waveform will slowly morph into a square wave. When set to 100%, this will cause the Auto Pan to flip-flop the audio between the left and right channels—there will be no motion through the center. Of course, setting this knob at an amount less than 100% will allow you to hear some of the left-right transition.

In real terms, we use this knob to make the pan "stall" at the left and right extremes. Sometimes, even though the Amount knob is set to 100%, it doesn't sound like the sound is fully panning from left to right, especially when being mixed in with the other parts of the song. This is because the sound is panned fully left and right for only an instant before the Auto Pan begins to pan it back again. Turning up the Shape knob results in flat lines at the top and bottom of the waveform, causing the pan motion to sit at these extremes for a moment before panning back to the other side. The result is a more pronounced panning motion that can be heard best over an entire mix.

The final controls of the Auto Pan are the Waveform Selection buttons that control the shape of the modulation, just like in other LFOs you've encountered in Live. The last button in the lower right is for a random waveform where the volumes of the left and right channels are changed at random. When this mode is selected, the Phase knob changes to a Width knob and adjusts the left-right deviation of the randomness. When set to 0%, the random pattern will influence the left and right volumes identically, resulting in random changes to the sound's volume. When set to 100%, the difference between the left and right volumes will increase, resulting in random panning patterns in full stereo.

## CHOP IT UP

When Phase is set to 0 degrees, the Auto Pan will simply turn the volume of the sound up and down. Try this out: load an entire song onto a track and use Auto Pan. Set its Rate to 1/8, shape to 100%, Phase to 0 degrees, Offset to 270 degrees, and Waveform to sine. As you increase the Amount knob, you'll begin to hear the track volume jump up and down in 1/8-note steps in sync with the song. Turn up Amount to 100%, and you'll have chopped the song into tiny slices!

For a really crazy effect, try slightly altering the Phase knob. When the two waveforms are just slightly out of phase, you'll hear each strobe zip across your speakers as one side is turned on just slightly before the other.

# Beat Repeat

Glitch-heads, rejoice! Ableton brings you the Beat Repeat device (see Figure 9.34). Now you can produce the classic beat-stutter with the push of a button, or even cause repeats to happen randomly.

Note: If you are brand new to Beat Repeat, try starting out by creating a MIDI clip of a very simple drumbeat or even just a basic high-hat pattern. After you've placed Beat Repeat on the same track, play the clip to hear the effects of the device.

**FIGURE 9.34**
Th-Th-Th-This
dev-v-v-v-ice is
sw-ee-ee-ee-ee-t!
*Source:* Ableton

## Grid and Variation

You set the size, or length, of the repeated segment with the Grid knob. Turn on Repeat and try tweaking this knob. You'll hear the Repeat size change in real time—an awesome effect for remixing. The No Trpl button will ignore the triplet values when scrolling through the grid sizes, which is handy if you want to keep the rhythmic repeats simple and straightforward.

The Variation knob just to the right of the Grid knob introduces randomness to the grid size. When set to 0%, the grid will always be what you've set with the Grid knob. As this value increases, Live automatically changes the grid, based on the mode selected in the pop-up menu below the knob. When you select Trigger in that menu, Live gives you a new grid size anytime you start the Repeat function. It will hold the grid size until you stop or retrigger the Repeat. The 1/4, 1/8, and 1/16 settings will change the Grid setting at the specified time interval. The Auto setting will change the grid size after every repeat. This can get really hairy, as you can have a single repeat of 1/64 followed by a repeat of 1/6, followed by 1/16, followed by 1/2, and so on. The results are truly unpredictable!

## Offset and Gate

These two knobs determine when an automatic repeat will start and how long it will last. When Offset is set to 0, the repeat will start the instant it is called by the Interval and Chance knobs. If you turn this knob clockwise, you'll see it count up in 1/16 notes—with the knob turned up halfway, the value will be 8/16. This means that the Beat Repeat won't start until the third beat of the bar. You'll also see the Repeat markers move in the display as a visual aid.

The Gate knob sets how long the repeats will last once triggered. If set to 4/16, the repeat will last for a quarter note. If set to 8/16, the repeats will last for half a bar. Therefore, using Offset and Grid, you can specify any location in the audio to repeat, as well as how long to do it.

## Chance, Interval, and Repeat

In its default state, Beat Repeat's Chance parameter is set to 100%, which means that repeats will be generated every interval. With interval set to 1 Bar, you'll hear repeats once per bar. If you set Chance to 50%, there will only be a 1-in-2 chance that the Beat Repeat will trigger.

It's also possible to set the Chance knob to 0% and trigger the repeat effect manually using the Repeat button. Try this out. As soon as you click Repeat, you're off to the races. Click the Repeat button again to turn it off, and the regular beat will resume. Obviously, this button is named appropriately.

## Mix, Insert, and Gate

These three buttons control the output mode of the Beat Repeat. The default is Mix mode, in which you'll hear the original drumbeat while the repeats occur—the two are being mixed together. In Insert mode, the original drumbeat is silenced whenever repeats are occurring. The final mode, Gate, always silences the original signal and only outputs the repeats. This mode is useful when you've placed the Beat Repeat on a return track, a technique that's especially useful if you want to add effects to the repeats but not the original signal.

## Volume and Decay

The Volume knob sets the volume of the repeated sounds. Note that the first repeat is always at the original volume. I like to decrease the volume a little bit so that the music comes back in heavier after the repeat. It's almost necessary to turn this down when you're using small grid sizes because the repeats become so fast that they start to make a tone of their own.

The Decay knob will cause the volume of each consecutive repeat to be quieter than the first. This means that your repeats will slowly (or quickly) fade away to silence each time you trigger Repeat.

## Pitch

The Pitch controls can be used to introduce pitch shifts into your repeats. The Pitch knob will simply transpose the repeated sound down by the specified number of semitones. As you adjust the pitch, you'll see the repeats change color in the display. The Pitch Decay knob works similarly to the Volume Decay knob, except that it makes the pitch drop further and further with each consecutive repeat. It's possible to make the repeated sound drop so low in pitch that it becomes inaudible. This is a neat tool to use in conjunction with the Volume Decay because you can make your repeats drop in pitch and fade away at the same time.

## Filter

Beat Repeat has a flexible bandpass filter for processing the repeats. It's similar in design to the filter in the Ping Pong Delay. Click the Filter switch to engage it and choose a specific frequency range for the repeats. This can give your repeats a lo-fi sound in comparison to the normal part. You can even change the filter frequency and width in real time for even more animation.

# Corpus

Corpus is the effect version of Collision (see Figure 9.35). It's included when you buy Collision (or the Live Suite). The majority of the effect is identical to Collision, so we'll be focusing on the aspects that differentiate it here. Like Collision, this effect is only included with Live Suite.

**FIGURE 9.35** Corpus processes any sound source you want using Collision's resonators. The Sidechain section at the left allows you to control the pitch of the resonators via MIDI.
*Source:* Ableton

The main difference between Collision and Corpus is that there is no Excitator section. This is because the effect uses the input signal to get the virtual resonator vibrating. The area that would be used for the Excitator is instead filled by an LFO, which controls the pitch of the resonator. For more information on how Ableton's LFOs work, please consult the "Auto Filter" and "Auto Pan" sections of this chapter.

What makes Corpus really interesting is its Sidechain section, which is displayed by clicking the triangular unfold switch in the title bar. Unlike the other Sidechain sections we've looked at, this one uses a MIDI track as its source, because Corpus can receive MIDI notes to control the pitch of the resonators. So, for example, I could use Collision to produce some unusual resonance on a synthesizer sound and use the synth's MIDI part to make sure that the resonance is perfectly tuned to every note played by the synth. To get this working, pick a MIDI track from the menu in the Sidechain section and then click the Frequency switch to enable it.

Since the Sidechain makes this device behave like a hybrid effect unit/ synthesizer, the other controls in the Sidechain section are very synth-like. Last and Low determine how Corpus responds to multiple MIDI notes being input simultaneously, with Last tuning the resonator to the pitch of the last-played note or Low choosing the lowest note. Pitch Bend determines how much the resonance can be controlled by pitch bend messages.

At the bottom of the Sidechain section is the Off Decay switch, which causes the resonators to stop resonating when Note Off messages are received via MIDI. When turned on, the speed with which the resonators are silenced is controlled by the percentage box below. When off, the Decay controls the resonator decay, without regard to the length of the incoming MIDI notes.

Looking to the right past the LFO controls, you'll notice that the pitch controls are slightly different than Collision. If you're using the Sidechain, you'll see Transpose and Fine controls, which can be used to change the resonator pitch relative to the Sidechain input. Otherwise, there's just a Tune control. In either case, you can use Spread to detune the left and right channels.

# Frequency Shifter

The Frequency Shifter is a powerful effect capable of creating subtle modulation or massive sonic deconstruction. This device, shown in Figure 9.36, can do ring modulation and frequency shifting, so it's like two effects in one.

Since this effect can change pitch so dramatically, it often works well on sources where it is not important to retain a specific tonality. Make sure to give it a workout on drums and percussion, or send a sine wave through it to create some fun alarm-type sounds. Alternately, you can put a really subtle amount on a synth pad or lead to add complexity and motion.

**FIGURE 9.36**

The Frequency Shifter—not for the faint of heart!

*Source:* Ableton

Frequency shifting adds a fixed amount in Hertz to the incoming signal, producing strange inharmonic sounds. Start out by adjusting the Fine knob (leave Frequency alone). Try creating a shift of about 3Hz and pull the Dry/ Wet down to 50% to hear some really cool phasing effects. Clicking the Wide switch will give the effect stereo depth, as it raises the pitch in the left channel while lowering it in the right. (You'll also notice that it changes the label of the Fine switch to Spread.) Now move on to the Frequency control. This one requires very little explanation—it's not a subtle effect!

Switching into Ring mode changes the effect to ring modulation, which involves both adding and subtracting a fixed amount, resulting in a slightly different but still bizarre-sounding effect. Higher Frequency settings will get you all sorts of robotic bleeps. Lower Frequency below 8Hz or so and a rhythmic pulse effect will occur. In Ring mode, the Drive control can be enabled to add distortion to the signal. Use the numeric box to dial in the right amount. The LFO is used to modulate Frequency automatically. It is nearly identical to the LFO in the Auto Filter, with the exception that the Amount knob is labeled in Hz so you know exactly how much the LFO will vary the frequency.

# Resonators

Similar to Corpus, when a sound is fed through the Resonators, it causes a set of virtual resonators to start vibrating, or creating a tone at their set pitches and volumes (see Figure 9.37). Even though this effect has quite a few controls, it's conceptually much simpler than Corpus.

**FIGURE 9.37**

The Resonators device will start generating pitches based on an input signal.

*Source:* Ableton

To begin, crank the Dry/Wet mix knob fully clockwise to isolate the sound of the resonators. Turn off the Input filter (in the upper left-hand corner) so a full-range sound is feeding the device. Adjust the settings for Resonator I first, using the Note knob, since the other four resonators base their tones and pitches on the first. You'll see that you have control of Decay (top left) of the resonators (best heard on sparse percussion tracks), as well as the Color (bottom left).

After the first resonator's root note is set, engage the other resonators and use the Pitch knobs to set their frequencies relative to the first. This makes it simple to create chords using multiple resonators; then you can transpose them all using the first resonator's Note knob.

Resonators II and III and Resonators IV and V can be panned apart from each other by increasing the Width knob. This can help create a lush tonal pad that blends well with a mix. You can also use the input filter to remove frequencies that may be overpowering or saturating the resonator banks. The Gain knobs are used to achieve a blend between the various resonators, allowing you to emphasize certain pitches over others.

# Spectrum

Spectrum isn't an audio effect, but it does process audio (see Figure 9.38). Instead of changing the sound that passes through it, Spectrum generates a real-time display of the audio's frequency content. This can be very useful for isolating problematic frequencies or for helping you learn more about the important frequencies in various sounds, thus improving your mixing skills.

**FIGURE 9.38**
Spectrum is here to help you visualize your sounds.
*Source:* Ableton

As of Live 9, the EQ Eight includes a built-in spectrum analyzer, so this device may get a bit less use. Nevertheless, it provides some additional flexibility the EQ version doesn't have, so it's worth knowing a bit about.

The display represents frequencies horizontally from low to high and amplitudes vertically. By default, the amplitude range is set to Auto, which can be a little confusing. In Auto mode, the decibel range shown automatically adjusts to the overall volume of the material being monitored, so the display may jump around a bit. If you're new to the Spectrum device, I recommend turning off the Auto switch (in the lower left) and instead specifying a range of 0 to –100dB. Once you get a feel for this, you can adjust the range to your liking.

The Graph setting can be used to switch the display between Bins (a series of vertical lines) or Line, which traces the overall frequency curve. The Bins look awfully pretty but can be quite distracting, so you may prefer Line instead. Max causes the display to maintain a constant line representing the peak value for every frequency. This is a very useful feature and generally recommended.

For most uses, the rest of the controls never need to be adjusted. The Refresh value can be increased to decrease CPU load, and the Avg value can be turned up if you're less interested in monitoring individual peaks and want to focus on the average spectral content of a signal. In the upper-left corner of Spectrum, you'll find an unfold switch that will super-size the display.

# Utility

The humble Utility, shown in Figure 9.39, never generates much excitement, but it is a very handy device with a variety of audio tools. Some of the features seem so simple that you may not realize how they'll be useful until the day you stumble into a circumstance where you need just that thing.

**FIGURE 9.39**

Utility is a nifty little problem solver.

*Source:* Ableton

## Phase

The topmost switches allow you to invert the phase of both the left and right channels separately. This comes in handy to correct phase problems when combining multiple recordings of the same source (such as when multiple microphones are used). Inverting one channel of a stereo signal can create a very wide sound, but be careful that it also works in mono (see following section).

These switches are also useful if you ever need to check whether or not two audio signals are identical. When two identical audio signals are played back fully out of phase with each other, they cancel each other out and the result is silence. To try this out, place the same audio file on two tracks and insert Utility on one of the tracks. Hit play, engage the L and R phase switches, and poof! The signal vanishes.

## Channel Mode, Width, and Mono

The Channel Mode menu gives you control over which portion of a stereo signal is utilized and the option of swapping the left and right channels as well. Let's say you have a stereo file and you want to use only the left channel. Setting this menu to Left outputs the left channel on both sides, as if it were a mono signal.

Width is useful because it allows you to change the balance of the "middle" (purely mono information) to the "sides" (information that is unique to the left and right channels). A setting of 0% Width provides a mono signal. As you raise Width, the sides will increase in volume. The Width control goes all the way up to 400%, which will make the side signal four times as loud, so watch your output levels!

Right-click on Width and select Mid/Side Mode from the context menu to change this knob into a Mid/Side balance control. This mode adjusts the balance of the middle and the sides, unlike Width, which only changes the side level while leaving the middle static. At 200%, the center will completely disappear, leaving only sides.

Click the Mono switch to sum the left and right channels to a mono signal. Try this on the Master track to hear how your mix sounds in mono. You may find that some sounds vanish due to phase issues or discover EQ problems that weren't obvious in sounds panned left or right. Use the Bass Mono switch to convert bass frequencies from stereo to mono. Synth bass sounds are often programmed with some stereo spread, which sounds great on the higher frequencies, but can cause real issues with the bottom of a mix. Dial in the cutoff frequency in the box below or leave it at its default 120Hz, which works well for most situations. Click the Headphone audition switch to hear only the affected bass frequencies.

## Mute, Gain, Balance, and DC

Mute and Gain are just what they sound like: a button for silencing the signal and a button for level control. They are useful to have in device format because they allow you to place these functions anywhere in any signal path. For example, many producers avoid using automation on the Mixer's volume control and automate the Gain knob on a Utility device instead. This leaves the Mixer volume as a final stage where overall volume adjustments can be made without disturbing the automation. DC is a high-pass filter for removing extremely low frequencies below the audible range. Balance is a simple pan control.

# Vocoder

Vocoders have a long and storied history. Originally popularized in the 1970s by artists from Kraftwerk to ELO, the Vocoder is famous for its ability to create talking synthesizers and singing robots by applying the complex envelope of a human voice to any sound source. Throughout the years, many other applications have been discovered for Vocoders, and Ableton has used these developments to create a very useful, modern implementation of this classic effect (see Figure 9.40).

A Vocoder deals with two different signals: the Modulator and the Carrier. The effect is created by splitting the Modulator (a vocal or any other signal you choose to run through it) into an array of narrow frequency bands and

**FIGURE 9.40**
Live's amazing
Vocoder.
*Source:* Ableton

then analyzing the amplitude of the individual bands in real time to produce an envelope that can be applied to another sound, known as the *Carrier*.

In Live's Vocoder, the Modulator is the signal being produced by the track into which the Vocoder is inserted. So, if you were to drop a Vocoder into a vocal track, the clip playing on that track would be the Modulator. The Carrier is selected from the menu in the upper-left corner of the effect.

The options are as follows:

▶ **Noise:** This setting uses a built-in noise oscillator to generate the output signal. The X-Y controller below modifies the sample rate and density of the noise to produce different colors. This setting is particularly good for producing percussive sound effects.

▶ **External:** This is the setting you use for classic Vocoder effects. Specify another track to use as the source, such as a synth pad, and the vocal on the carrier track will appear to be "singing" the synthesizer sound.

▶ **Modulator:** The most unusual of the bunch, this setting uses the modulator signal as the carrier. This allows you to create some very unusual effects by manipulating the other controls such as Depth, Range, and Release. Or you can use this mode to use Vocoder as a powerful EQ.

▶ **Pitch Tracking:** In this mode, a monophonic oscillator tunes itself to the pitch of the carrier signal and produces a wave chosen by the switches below. The accuracy of the tracking will vary greatly, depending on the source material, with polyphonic material producing some very unpredictable results.

At the top of this section is the Enhance switch, which can be used to restore high frequencies that get lost during the vocoding process. At the bottom section of the interface are the Unvoiced controls, which help the Vocoder handle unpitched aspects of the sound, such as consonants. To deal with the fact that these sorts of sounds may not produce an audible result in the Vocoder's output, a noise signal is synthesized to compensate for this. To activate this feature, turn up the Unvoiced knob to the desired level and adjust the Sensitivity until it responds to the Modulator properly. When it's all the way up, the Unvoiced synthesizer no longer responds to these sounds and produces a signal continuously.

The center display is where you can really get into the nitty-gritty aspect of manipulating the filter bank. The mouse becomes a pencil when it's held over the graphical display and can be used to suppress a particular band partially or fully. When Carrier is set to Modulator, you can use this technique to use the Vocoder as a powerful filter.

The first control along the bottom of the display is Bands, which controls the number of bands used to analyze the Modulator. More bands mean more accurate analysis and a more natural-sounding output, which may or may not be what you want. (What's "natural" about a singing synthesizer anyway?) Range specifies the upper and lower limits of the bands and can be used to remove any excess frequencies at the extremes. BW stands for bandwidth and controls the width of each filter. At values other than 100%, the filters either have gaps between them or overlap each other, producing a variety of interesting effects. Use your ears.

The Gate control can be used to clean up the Modulator signal by suppressing any bands below the threshold. By default, no gating occurs, as its setting is –inf. Level is a volume control for the effect output. Use this in conjunction with Dry/Wet to get the perfect blend.

Depth determines how dynamic the resulting effect is. By default, the volume envelope of the modulator is applied to the carrier. This control can be turned down to reduce the dynamic range of the output signal or increased to exaggerate it. The Attack and Release controls can be used to further shape the volume envelope. Note that the Release control goes up to a whopping 30 seconds and can be used in conjunction with the Noise carrier to create some really intense builds.

Finally, the Formant knob can be used to alter the frequencies of the filters that get applied to the carrier signal. This can be used to create some unusual frequency shifting effects, or can be used to change the perceived gender of the modulator when the voice is used.

This effect has so many uses that it's well worth spending some time with it. Try using the Noise carrier to add some extra snap and depth to a snare drum sound, use a drum part as the modulator to create a rhythmic synth part by using a pad as the carrier, or try that same drum loop Pitch Tracking mode to generate some unusual melodic material. The possibilities are literally endless.

# External Audio Effect

External Effect is in a class by itself. Instead of processing audio, it provides a flexible insert point for interfacing with external hardware.

Using effect boxes in your Live productions has never been easier. Insert an external effect device in a track and select the inputs and outputs your processor is connected to, as seen in Figure 9.41. Audio from the track will now be routed through your external device. Then you can use the Gain knobs to adjust levels to and from the device. What's really cool, though, is that there is a Dry/Wet knob for blending the send and return signals. This means that you don't have to mess with the Mix control on an external effect. You can just leave your effects set up with a direct signal at 0% and make fully recallable adjustments of the Dry/Wet balance from within Live.

**FIGURE 9.41**

The External Audio Effect shown above will route audio through whatever hardware is connected to input and output #4 on your audio interface.

*Source:* Ableton

The remainder of the controls in the External Audio Effect device deal with timing issues. The Phase switch inverts the phase of the returned signal to correct phase cancellation problems that could occur when blending dry and processed signals. The Latency control compensates for delay incurred by routing the audio to and from the hardware device.

The benefits here become obvious quickly. If you have enough I/O on your audio interface, you can keep external processors connected and create presets for them. Not only can you quickly access your hardware in this fashion, but you can also insert your hardware devices anywhere in a device chain or a Rack.

# Looper

Ableton creating an effect called *Looper* may sound like a strange and redundant thing. After all, isn't Live already known for being a looping monster? Well, Looper was designed to deal with the fact that folks who record loops on the fly using instruments or voice have some very specific needs that haven't always been addressed by Live. Lots of people have used Live in this way over the past few years, but it's often required various hacks and workarounds to get it to behave more like some of the popular hardware loopers. Rather than exhaustively documenting every single feature of Looper (the Looper section in Live's manual is outstanding), I'm going to focus here on taking you through a few practical experiments so that you can really understand what this device is all about.

To get started with Looper, drop it into an empty audio track and focus on the extra large button called the *Multi-Purpose Transport* (see Figure 9.42). It starts by displaying a Record icon. Arm the track for recording (or set Monitor

**FIGURE 9.42**

If you're a fan of hardware loopers such as the Loop Station, you're going to have a lot of fun with Looper.

*Source:* Ableton

to In) and spend a moment picking a tempo in your head. Do not start play-back in Live; just click the large button while simultaneously starting to count your tempo into a microphone ("1,2,3,4…"). After a bar or two, click the button again. Once you've done this, you should notice a few very interesting things. First, Live's sequencer is now running, and you should hear the loop of your counting. Take a look at Live's master tempo and turn on the metro-nome. Live has set its tempo by the length of the loop you just recorded. Pretty cool!

Now, take a look at the big Multi-Purpose Transport button and the small row of icons just above it. The small icons will always tell you what mode you are currently in. Right now, you'll see a highlighted plus sign letting you know you're in Overdub mode. Any additional sounds you make will get added to the loop. The big button is displaying a Play icon. Clicking it will take you into Play mode and stop the overdubbing. Clicking it repeatedly will toggle you back and forth between Play and Overdub, allowing you to either add additional layers to your recording or just listen to playback. Finally, double-click the large button, and Looper will stop playback without stopping Live's sequencer.

So, without digging too deeply into this device's options, you should get a pretty good idea of how powerful this baby is right out of the box. If you haven't already guessed, the big reason for putting so much functionality into one button is to make it really easy for instrumentalists to control it via MIDI. Just map a single footswitch control, and you're ready to begin recording improvised loop odysseys with no further configuration. If you make a mis-take as you go, just hold down the footswitch for two seconds to Undo (or Redo). When stopped, holding the button for two seconds will clear out Looper completely.

The configuration options are many. Before these next experiments, stop the sequencer and click the Clear button to empty out Looper. Now, let's say that you want the second press of the MultiFunction Transport to take you into Play mode, instead of directly into Overdub. Scan your eyes over to the right where you'll see "Record <x bars> Then <+>". Click the plus sign. You'll see it change into a Play icon, and you're done. Or try changing "x bars" to "2 bars." Now you can start up Live playing back a click or a drum loop, and a single-click of the big button will record for two bars and jump automatically into the next mode.

Just below, you'll see a menu labeled *Song Control.* Imagine that you want a double-click to stop not just the Looper but also all clips playing back in Live. Change this menu to Start & Stop Song, and you're all set. With one foot-switch, you can begin recording a loop, automatically have Live start playing back prerecorded loops in time with your loop, overdub additional layers, and then stop the entire song!

By now, you may have also realized that some of Looper's functions are quantized just like clips. That's what the Quantize menu below the Multi Function Transport is for. This is very useful because it can be used to make sure that loop recording or playback starts at the beginning of the bar. The Quantization menu also affects the behavior of the Double and Half Speed buttons.

Next to the Speed knob, you'll notice up- and down-arrow buttons. These are used to double or halve the speed of your loop, a very common feature on looping pedals. Like these hardware devices, changing the speed of a loop also changes the pitch (just like a clip in Repitch mode). You'll see this reflected by the Speed knob—its value is displayed in semitones. It's possible to make all sorts of crazy loop textures by recording elements at different speeds. Record a guitar loop, drop it by an octave, and overdub a new layer over that. Now raise them both by two octaves and press the Reverse switch. Add additional material before returning to the original speed and pressing the Reverse switch again. Rinse and repeat.

If you want to change the length of your loop without changing the speed, use the ÷2 and x2 buttons above. Since there are a couple of "gotchas" with these, back up the loop you've created first. Just click and drag from the Drag Me area of Looper and drop into a clip slot. Now, while your loop is playing back in Looper, use x2 to double the length of the loop, which duplicates the loop and allows you to overdub new phrases twice the length of the original loop. Using ÷2 cuts the loop length in half and throws away the rest of it. Bear in mind that using x2 now will not restore the loop. It just duplicates the newly truncated loop. Also be aware that Live's Undo command cannot be used to back out of these commands. You have to use the Looper's Undo instead, which only has one level of undo. Fortunately, you can drag the clip you made from the loop back into Looper and get right back to where you started.

I'm pretty confident that there are many uses for Looper that have yet to be discovered. Spend some time experimenting and see what you come up with.

# 10

# Live's MIDI Effects

**M**IDI effects allow you to alter MIDI data before it reaches its destination. A MIDI effect can be used by itself on a MIDI track whose output is some external MIDI sound device or before a virtual instrument in the Device View.

MIDI data passes through the MIDI effect, which then passes the altered MIDI on. Note that MIDI effects do not change the sound that comes *out* of an instrument the way audio effects do. Instead, MIDI effects change the notes coming *in* to those instruments.

## Arpeggiator

Since we are discussing the MIDI effects in alphabetical order, we get to start with the coolest MIDI device of them all, the Arpeggiator (see Figure 10.1). Arpeggiators came into existence in the early days of monophonic synthesizers. *Monophonic* means "only able to play one note at a time." When synthesizer technology was in its infancy, that's all you could hope to get out of a synth—just one note at a time. This isn't much of a problem if you're playing a lead or melody part. The trouble arises when you try to play a chord, which a monophonic synth is incapable of. The solution devised was an Arpeggiator that would quickly play all the notes you held on the keyboard in series or

**FIGURE 10.1**

The Arpeggiator on this track is creating instant sequences from the MIDI notes it receives.

*Source:* Ableton

other repetitive patterns. As a result, even though the notes don't play simultaneously, you can "hear" the chord being played because the notes are played in such quick succession.

Drop Arpeggiator into a MIDI track, press a key on your MIDI keyboard, or just use the computer keyboard to play a note. A steady stream of eighth notes comes out. Now try holding down two notes. Instead of hearing both notes playing eighth notes, Live will play each of the notes alternately. Now try holding three notes. Live will play each of the three notes in series and repeat.

There are many ways to tweak the performance of the Arpeggiator. You can change the note order employed by the Arpeggiator, the speed at which the notes are played, the length of each note, and the quantization in relation to the grid of the current Set.

# Style

The Style drop-down menu is used to select the note-order pattern employed by the Arpeggiator. The default setting is Up, which means that the Arpeggiator plays each of the held notes in sequence starting from the lowest note and working up to the highest before repeating. The Down option is the exact opposite—the Arpeggiator starts with the highest note and works down before repeating. The UpDown and DownUp patterns are simply hybrid patterns made from the individual Up and Down patterns. The UpDown style will make the Arpeggiator play up the note sequence and then back down again before repeating. The DownUp style does the opposite. The Up & Down and Down & Up modes are the same as the UpDown and DownUp modes, except that the top and bottom notes of the scale are repeated as the Arpeggiator changes direction.

The Converge style works by playing the lowest note followed by the highest note. It will then play the second lowest note followed by the second highest. The pattern will continue by playing the third lowest note followed by the third highest note, and so on, until all the notes in the scale are exhausted. The pattern will then repeat. The Diverge style is the opposite of Converge, and Con & Diverge places the two patterns end to end.

The Pinky and Thumb styles are interesting in that they alternate the note order with the highest and lowest note played, respectively. For example, when using the PinkyUp mode, the Arpeggiator will play the lowest note followed by the highest note (the "pinky note"). It will then play the second lowest note followed by the highest note again. The Arpeggiator will continue to work up the scale of held notes, alternating each with the high "pinky note" until the pattern repeats. The ThumbUp mode works in the same way, except that the lowest held note (the "thumb note") gets inserted between each step of the scale.

The Play Order style is nice in that the Arpeggiator works through the scale of held notes in the exact order as you played them. For example, if you play the notes C, E, G, and A, the resulting pattern will be "C E G A C E G A C E G A…." If you play the notes in a different order, like E, C, G, then A, the pattern will be "E C G A E C G A E C G A…."

The Chord Trigger style breaks away from the traditional arpeggiator methodology in that it plays more than one note at a time. In fact, it repeatedly triggers every one of the notes you held down. The result is a stuttered chord.

The final style options are random modes that will generate unpredictable patterns from your held notes. The Random mode simply chooses a note at random from your held notes for each step it plays. In this mode, it's possible for Live to choose the same note repeatedly—it's truly random. The Random Other pattern is a little more controlled. It will create a random pattern from your held notes, play it, and then create another random pattern and play it. The result is that you have fewer repeated notes because Live will play all the notes at least once before it creates a new pattern. The Random Once pattern is like Random Other, except that it builds only one random pattern. After the Arpeggiator plays the random pattern once, it will play it again identically. The result is a new random pattern every time you play new notes, but a pattern that repeats while you hold the notes. Pretty cool, huh?

# Groove

The Groove menu is used to add a swing feel to the Arpeggiator's patterns. The intensity of the swing is determined by the Global Groove Amount value, which is displayed at the bottom of the Groove Pool.

# Hold

The Hold button will automatically latch, or sustain, the notes you play so that you don't have to continually hold notes while a pattern plays. Switch this on and try playing a chord. When you release the notes on your keyboard, the Arpeggiator will continue to play. Now, play another chord. The Arpeggiator will stop the old pattern and will start the new one when it receives your new notes.

# Offset

This dial is used to offset the start point of the Arpeggiator pattern by the specified number of steps. For example, if the style is set to Up and you play a C-major triad, the resulting pattern from the Arpeggiator will be "C E G C E G...." If you set Offset to 1, the pattern will be "E G C E G C...." The starting point of the pattern has been shifted to the right by one step; therefore, the pattern begins on the second note of the chord (E) as it plays.

# Rate and Sync

The next two parameters, Rate and Sync, are related to one another. The Rate knob is used to set the speed at which the Arpeggiator plays each step of its pattern. The default selection is 1/8 notes. When the neighboring Sync button is on, the Rate will be constrained to note values. If you turn Sync off, the Rate will now be running free of the current project tempo and will play at the exact rate specified here in Hertz. You'll find that you can get the Arpeggiator running quite fast when you turn Sync off, even to a point where the individual notes in the scale are blurred. This is a neat special effect and is also reminiscent of SID-based synth music, like that of the Commodore 64 of yore.

# Gate

This dial is used to set the length or duration of each note played by the Arpeggiator. By default, this value is 50%, which means that the notes are only half as long as the rate at which they are played. Therefore, with Rate set to 1/8, the notes are only 1/16-note long. If you set this to 25%, each note will only be 1/32-note long. This is a great parameter to tweak while the Arpeggiator is running.

# Retrigger

The Retrigger parameters can be used to cause the Arpeggiator to restart its pattern when triggered with a new note or in rhythm with your song. The default Retrigger mode is Off, which means that the Arpeggiator will never restart its pattern, even if you play new notes while the Arpeggiator is running. The pattern will only restart when you stop all notes and play new ones. If you set this to Note, the pattern will restart any time a new note is played. Therefore, if you're holding three notes and play a fourth note, the Arpeggiator will immediately restart, now including the fourth note in its pattern. The last mode, Beat, will cause the Arpeggiator to restart automatically at the rate you specify with the neighboring knob. By default, this value is set to one bar. If you hold a three-note chord while this is on, you'll hear the Arpeggiator pattern start over on every downbeat of a bar.

# Repeats

By default, Live will arpeggiate the notes you play for as long as you hold them. This is because the Repeats amount is set to Infinity by default. If you change this knob to a numerical value, the Arpeggiator will only run its pattern the specified number of times before stopping. Setting this to a low value, such as one or two repeats, and choosing a quick setting for the rate will cause the Arpeggiator to "strum" the notes of your chord. That is, they'll play quickly and then stop. This little burst of arpeggiation is reminiscent of the old video game soundtracks.

# Transposition Controls

Grouped together into a column near the center of the Arpeggiator are the Transpose controls. These parameters will allow the Arpeggiator to shift the pattern in pitch as it repeats. Start by turning the Steps knob to 1. Now play a single note. You'll no longer hear a single note being repeated. Instead, you'll hear two notes: the note you're holding, plus a note one octave higher. This is because the Distance knob is set to +12 semitones, which is an octave. By turning Steps to 1, you've instructed the Arpeggiator to shift its pitch by the Distance amount, once for each repetition of the pattern. Turn Steps up to 2 and listen to what happens. Now the Arpeggiator plays three notes for each key you press. This also works when holding multiple notes—the Arpeggiator will play the pattern once and then play it again for each step indicated, transposing by the Distance amount each time.

Now try this. Set Steps to 8 and Distance to +1 semitones. Now when you hold a single note, the Arpeggiator plays nine notes chromatically. If you hold C, the Arpeggiator will play C C# D D# E F F# G G# and then repeat. This is because the Arpeggiator is shifting the pattern (which is only the one note you're holding) eight times after it has played the original pitch, transposing it one semitone each time. Change the Distance amount to +2 and listen to what happens.

Obviously, you can create some transposition patterns that will fall outside of the key you're working in. To remedy this, there are two menus that can be used to constrain the notes to those of a selected key and mode. With the top Transpose menu, choose Major or Minor. After you make your selection, you can choose a root note with the Key menu below it. For example, set the Transpose menu to Minor and change the Key menu to D. Now press and hold D. All the notes in the resulting pattern will be transposed to the nearest note within a D-minor scale.

# Velocity

The final controls in the Arpeggiator are for modifying the velocity of notes as they play. Normally, these functions are off, which makes each note of the arpeggiation pattern sound at its played velocity. That is, if you press C lightly while striking G hard, the resulting pattern will have quiet C notes and loud G notes.

The purpose of the Velocity controls here is to create a pseudo-envelope for the volume of the arpeggiation. Of course, this can be used to modify not just volume but whatever parameter velocity is mapped to in the instrument you're using. When you turn Velocity on with the top button, the Arpeggiator will modify the velocities of the notes as they repeat. The bottom dial sets the Target velocity, and the Decay knob above it determines how long the Arpeggiator takes to modulate from the original velocities to the Target. For example, if you set Target to 10 and Decay to 1,000ms and play a note with full velocity, the Arpeggiator will reduce the velocity of each consecutive note it plays to 10 over one second. You can invert this by setting a high Target velocity and playing quiet notes—the velocity will increase to the Target over the specified Decay time.

The Retrigger button will cause the velocity scaling to restart with each new note that is added to the chord. Otherwise, new notes will be constrained to the current values of the decaying velocities.

# Chord

The Chord device (see Figure 10.2) will generate new MIDI notes at pitch intervals relative to an incoming MIDI note. This will allow one MIDI note to trigger a chord on the receiving instrument.

When the Chord device is first loaded, it will have no effect on incoming MIDI notes—they will pass straight through. As soon as you move one of the Shift knobs, it will become active. The knob sets the interval in semitones for the new MIDI note. For example, setting Shift 1 to +4 and playing a C will cause both a C and E note to be sent from the plug-in. Setting Shift 2 to +7 will create a C-major chord when you play just the C note. Playing G will result in a G-major chord (G, B, and D). You can define up to six notes to be

**FIGURE 10.2**

The Chord device builds a multinote (up to six notes) MIDI chord from one input note.

*Source:* Ableton

added to the incoming note using the dials. Just below each dial is a value that determines the velocity of the new note relative to the velocity of the incoming note. You can use this if you don't want all of the notes in the chord to be the same volume. If Shift 1 is set to .50 (50%), the E in the resulting chord will only have a velocity of 64 when the incoming C has a velocity of 127. Try slowly changing this value while playing repeated notes to hear how the additional note fades in and out of the chord.

## DANCE CHORDS

Chord stabs and pads are a staple of electronic music. Originally, these fixed chords were created by detuning some of the oscillators in a synthesizer so that they sounded at musical intervals (usually +7—a perfect fifth) against the base oscillators.

The Chord effect can be used to easily create the same effect. There are a number of chords already built for your use in the presets.

# Note Length

The Note Length MIDI effect (see Figure 10.3) can be used to change the duration of incoming MIDI note messages. This can be used to make a MIDI part sound more rhythmically consistent or automate note durations creatively. It can also be used to trigger your MIDI instruments with Note Off messages instead of Note On messages.

The Note Length MIDI effect has two trigger modes, which you can toggle to Note On or Note Off. In Note On mode, only the timing controls are active: Mode, Length, and Gate. You can use the Mode toggle button to sync the durations to the song Master tempo, or not, as you like. The Length knob selects the base length of the MIDI notes that the effect will output, and the

**FIGURE 10.3**

The Note Length MIDI effect.

*Source:* Ableton

Gate modifies this base by the percentage you select. For example, as in Figure 10.3, if Mode is set to Sync, Length set to 1/4, and Gate set to 50%, the Note Length effect will output eighth notes (half a quarter note).

In Note Off mode, this MIDI device will output MIDI note messages when you release your fingers from your MIDI keyboard. This will cause the notes to play through your MIDI instruments, and the length of the notes produced can be set using the timing controls below. You can also use three other controls in Note Off mode. The Release Velocity control determines the velocity of the output note (relative to the velocities of the notes you played on your controller), and Decay Time sets the length of time it will take for an incoming note's velocity to decay to zero. The Key Scale control can be used to alter the length of the output MIDI note messages, according to the pitch of the notes you play on your controller, from low to high. Set positive or negative values here to invert the relationship of pitch to note length.

# Pitch

The Pitch device transposes the MIDI notes sent to an instrument, resulting in a higher or lower part (see Figure 10.4). This can be very handy in a variety of situations, such as finding the best key for a singer. Let's say you have a MIDI track playing a piano accompaniment. Just drop a Pitch effect onto the track and dial in the new key.

The two values at the bottom of the Pitch device set the range of notes that can be used with the effect. If the bottom value, labeled Lowest, is set to C3, only MIDI notes C3 and higher will be allowed to enter the effect. The range value determines, by interval, the highest note that can enter the effect. So if the range is set to +12, notes C3 through C4 will enter the effect. Only after the incoming notes have passed the range test will they be transposed up or down.

**FIGURE 10.4**
Twist the Pitch knob to transpose the MIDI data passing through the effect. Easy, huh?
*Source:* Ableton

This situation may also arise when using patches on synthesizers that have splits. If you try to transpose the MIDI information out of the appropriate key zone, the synth will start playing the notes with the patch assigned to the other zone.

## TRANSPOSING DRUMS

There is a situation in which the Pitch effect will have unusual results—when transposing drum parts. Because Impulse and Drum Racks assign drum sounds to individual notes, you'll end up changing which drums play, rather than transposing the pitch of the drums. For example, if a kick drum is loaded into the first cell of Impulse and a snare is loaded into the second, MIDI note C3 will trigger the kick, and D3 will trigger the snare. If you use the Pitch effect with the Pitch knob set to +2, playing C3 will result in triggering the snare drum rather than the kick.

# Random

As the name suggests, the Random device will randomize the incoming MIDI notes. We can determine how liberal Live is with its randomization using the controls shown in Figure 10.5.

The first control in this effect is the Chance value. This knob sets the odds that an incoming MIDI note will be transposed. At 0%, the effect is essentially bypassed because there is no chance a note will be transposed. At 100%, every MIDI note will be subject to randomization. At 50%, roughly every other note will be randomized. Once a note is chosen by the effect to be transposed, it will be shifted using the rules set up with the three remaining controls. The three parameters make up part of a sort of formula that determines the transposition.

**FIGURE 10.5**

The Random MIDI device shifts the pitch of incoming notes.
*Source:* Ableton

The Choices parameter determines the number of random values that can occur. If the value is set to 3, a random number with a value of 1, 2, or 3 will be generated. This number is multiplied by the value of the Scale knob. The result is the number of semitones the MIDI note will be shifted. So if the Scale knob is set to 2, the resulting random transpositions will be 2, 4, or 6 semitones. The final variables in the formula are the Sign buttons. If Add is selected, the resulting random value will be added to the MIDI note, causing it to move up in pitch. Sub will subtract the random value from the current note. The Bi setting will randomly choose between adding or subtracting the value. The indicator lights on the plug-in panel will show when the note is being transposed up or down.

Let's run some quick examples to make sure that you understand the math behind the plug-in.

1. If the Choices knob is set to 1 and the Chance knob is set to 50%, about half the time a transpose value of 1 will be generated by the Choices knob. If Scale is set to 12 and the Sign mode is set to Add, the incoming notes will be transposed up one octave half of the time.

2. If the Choices knob is set to 4 and the Chance knob is set to 100%, a transpose value of 1 to 4 will be generated for every MIDI note. You can then set the Scale knob to 3 and leave the Sign mode on Add. In this situation, every note will be transposed (Chance at 100%) by one of the following semitone amounts: 3, 6, 9, or 12 (1[Choices]×3[Scale]=3, 2×3=6, 3×3=9, and 4×3=12).

3. If the Choices knob is set to 2, the Scale knob is set to 12, and the Sign mode is set to Sub, the resulting transposition will be either 1 or 2 octaves down (1×12=12 and 2×12=24).

Above the direction switches is an additional switch for selecting Alternate mode instead of Random mode. In Alternate mode, the effect will cycle through all of the possible values in order. So, in example 2 above, the output will be transpositions of 3, 6, 9, 12 in order, repeatedly.

# Scale

Scale allows an incoming MIDI note to be mapped to another one. You can tell the device that you want every incoming D# transposed up to E. You can also tell it that you want incoming Es to be taken down to Cs. Remapping pitches like this could be a great practical joke on a keyboard player, but it also has some very practical uses as well.

Don't play keyboards well? Don't know your scales? The Scale device will transpose all the wrong notes you play to the proper pitches for the appropriate key. This mapping is achieved with a 12×13 grid of gray squares that are laid out as piano keyboards. The columns in the grid refer to the *input* notes, while the rows refer to *output* notes.

If you look at Figure 10.6, you'll see that the bottom-left grid square is on. This means that when a C note enters the far left column, it runs into the blue indicator in the last row, which is the C output row. So, in this case, all entering C notes will still exit as C notes. The next column over is the input column for C# notes. As you look down the column, you run into the indicator light on the third row from the bottom, which is the output row for D notes. This means that when a C# note enters the Scale effect, it leaves as a D note.

Incoming MIDI notes are
fed into the columns . . .

. . . then exit on the rows.

**FIGURE 10.6**
The Scale effect lets you remap MIDI notes using a unique grid interface.
*Source:* Ableton

The Scale effect can be a bit confusing and takes awhile to get used to. Here's another way to get familiar with how it works. Play the note C and notice the lower left-hand corner light up. Now, click a different box in the leftmost column and play the note C again. What note is being output now? Just count up in semitones from the bottommost box (or turn your head sideways and imagine that you are looking at the grid as a vertical piano keyboard!).

If you've clicked four boxes up from the bottom, you'll now be hearing the note E flat.

You can use the grid to create musical scales. The pattern of indicators on the grid in Figure 10.6 is that of a major scale. Any attempt to play a black key on the keyboard will result in the MIDI note being transposed up to its nearest neighbor in the scale, since no black keys are used in C major.

## NO SCALE?

So you're just starting out and don't know all your musical scales? No problem. Ableton has included common scales in the presets of the Scale effect. You can load one and then use the Base knob to adapt it to your working key.

The Base control can be used to change the starting point of the grid. In the previous example, hanging the Base control to G will change the scale to a G major. Every key played on the keyboard will now be forced to one of the pitches in the G-major scale. Notice that changing Base also moves the piano keys so the bottom row and first column are G instead of C.

The Transpose and Range boxes do what the Pitch effect does, transposing any incoming MIDI data by a fixed value and limiting the notes that will be accepted.

## IN SCALE

The Scale effect can keep you in key, and it can also keep the results of a Random effect in key, too. If the Random plug-in is generating too many notes that are out of key, load up a Scale effect and set it to the appropriate scale. Any stray note from the Random effect will be knocked into key by the Scale plug-in.

By combining a Random and a Scale plug-in, you can make a random arpeggiator that arpeggiates the pattern of notes entering the chain.

The Fold switch will prevent Scale from outputting any notes more than six semitones higher than the input note. However, it doesn't just make these notes disappear. Instead, it drops these notes down an octave. In other words, if you've mapped an incoming D3 such that a B3 would be output, enabling the Fold switch would cause B2 to be output instead.

# Velocity

The previous four MIDI effects in Live are concerned with controlling MIDI pitch information. Velocity, on the other hand, deals with (can you guess?) velocity data. It's very much like a Compressor or Scale plug-in for velocities. The grid display is like the display used in the Scale device (see Figure 10.7). Input velocities are mapped across the X-axis (the bottom of the grid), while output velocities are on the Y-axis (the right edge of the grid).

Velocities enter on the horizontal axis.

New velocities exit on the vertical axis.

**FIGURE 10.7** The grid of the Velocity effect shows the effect of adjusting the various parameters in real time.
*Source: Ableton*

In its default setting, there is a straight line from the bottom-left corner of the grid to the upper-right corner of the grid. This means that every input velocity maps to the same output velocity.

Increasing the Drive knob will cause the line in the grid to begin to curve. This new shape shows that low input velocities (near the left edge of the grid) are mapped to higher output velocities. This will raise the volume of notes played quietly, while leaving the loud notes basically unchanged. Decreasing the Drive knob below zero has the opposite effect, causing loud input velocities to be mapped to lower output velocities. Only the loudest input notes will still leave the plug-in with high velocities.

The Comp ("Compand"—meaning Compression/Expansion) knob is like the Drive knob, except that it creates two curves instead of one. Turning this knob up past zero exaggerates the velocity curve by making quiet notes quieter and loud ones louder. Lowering the Comp knob below zero has the opposite effect, forcing more of the values to the middle of the range. Be aware that, like the Pitch effect, the Velocity effect is changing the notes fed into an instrument. Because of this, increasing the Comp knob will not make the part sound compressed as it would if you placed a Compressor after the instrument. It will merely limit the velocities sent to the instrument while the instrument continues to output an uncompressed sound.

The Random knob defines a range of randomness that can be applied to the incoming velocities. As this knob is increased, a gray area will form on the grid, showing all the possible velocities that may result from the random factor.

The Out Hi and Out Low knobs determine the highest and lowest velocities that will be output from the effect. The Range and Lowest values work like their counterparts in the Pitch and Scale effects. The Clip, Gate, and Fixed buttons determine the action taken when an input velocity is outside of the operation range set by the Range and Lowest values. In Clip mode, any velocity outside of the range will be bumped into range. The Gate mode will only allow notes with velocities within range to pass. Fixed mode will force every incoming velocity to be set to the value determined by the Out Hi knob. Finally, the Operation menu can be used to specify whether the effect should process the incoming note's velocity, release velocity, or both.

### BREATH OF LIFE

Velocity randomization can be used to add subtle variation to a programmed part. Humans can't play with the consistency of a machine, so randomizing the velocity of certain parts a small amount can make a beat sound more alive. This is especially effective on hi-hats and shakers.

# 11

# Remote Control

As briefly explained in Chapter 3, "Live Interface Basics," nearly everything in Live can be controlled via MIDI or your computer keyboard. This is referred to as *remote control*. Most of this chapter will focus on MIDI control since it's deeper and more flexible than computer keyboard control.

Because the computer keyboard can only transmit key presses, it's best suited to simple tasks like launching clips or controlling on/off switches. MIDI controllers, on the other hand, can have buttons, keys, knobs, joysticks, sliders, and X-Y pads. This can make them seem awfully complicated, but in fact most MIDI control is fairly simple. Regardless of the physical design of your hardware, most MIDI remote control is communicated with two types of data: note messages and control change (or continuous controller) messages, also referred to as *CCs*.

There are also numerous controllers on the market that can act as control surfaces for Live, which means there is no configuration required for them to work. These include devices designed for Live, such as the Akai APC40 and Novation LaunchPad, as well as numerous other devices from a variety of manufacturers. However, even if you're working with a control surface, there are going to be cases where a little customization is required and knowledge of Live's remote control system will really come in handy.

At the end of this chapter, you'll find an extended section on Ableton's own Push. This is a controller for Live that incorporates all of the functionality of a control surface, but includes Browser integration, a custom drum-programming interface, and a variety of other features that go beyond the typical controller.

# Enabling Remote Control

In order to use a MIDI controller as a remote, it must be enabled in the MIDI tab of Live's Preferences. Some supported devices can be enabled in the menus at the top, while others must be configured using the switches below. There are even cases where you may set up a single device in both areas. Let's take a closer look.

## Control Surface Setup

When a MIDI controller is natively supported by Live, it appears in the Control Surface menu, shown in Figure 11.1. When you select your controller in this menu, it can automatically implement certain behaviors known as *instant mappings.* Many control surfaces can be detected automatically by Live, so they will work from the moment you plug them in, and you won't even need to take this step. Live allows you to use up to six control surfaces simultaneously.

If your controller doesn't appear in this menu, it means it's not natively supported by Live. However, this doesn't necessarily mean it can't be used as a control surface. Some devices require additional software installation, after which the device will appear as an available control surface. Check with the hardware manufacturer for more information.

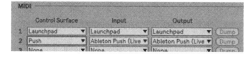

**FIGURE 11.1**

Select your controller in the Control Surface menu to enable instant mappings. The controller's Ports are usually identical (or very similar) to the controller name.

*Source:* Ableton

# Manual Controller Setup

Below the Control Surface menus is a list of the MIDI devices connected to your system. Any device that you want to use for remote control must have its Remote switch turned on. Figure 11.2 shows a device configured for remote control only.

**FIGURE 11.2**

Turn Remote on to enable remote control. Turn Track on to enable a controller for standard MIDI recording.

*Source:* Ableton

It's also possible to turn both Track and Remote on for a single device. If you've got a keyboard controller that also has knobs and sliders, you may do exactly that. As long as you avoid doing any remote mapping of piano keys and other controls that you're going to use for Track input, you'll be just fine.

You'll also find that Live allows you to select a MIDI controller in the Control Surface menu *and* enable it as a remote below. This is handy because it enables instant mappings and manual mappings on the same controller.

For example, let's say you're using an APC40, but you find that you never want to use the Arm buttons during performance. By enabling the Remote switch for its input port, you can map these buttons to whatever you want, and the instant mapping behavior will be disabled only for those buttons. If you delete the manual mapping, the instant mapping comes back—*instantly.*

## KEYBOARD CONFLICTS

Be aware that the Computer MIDI Keyboard setting (the piano keys icon in the Control Bar) turns much of your computer keyboard into a MIDI keyboard, preventing many keys from being used for remote control.

When the Computer MIDI Keyboard switch is on, Live will still allow you to map keys being used by the MIDI keyboard, but the remote mappings will not work until the Computer MIDI Keyboard is switched off. If the switch is left on, the Key switch will flash whenever a remote Key mapping is overridden by the MIDI keyboard.

# Instant Mapping

Instant mappings vary quite a bit depending on the type of controller you're using, but they fall into a few categories. Many control surfaces have basic mixer control. For example, the APC40 contains eight faders that control volume and several rows of buttons that control the Arm, Solo, and Track Activator switches. It's also very common for control surfaces to have a bank of eight knobs that will automatically map themselves to the currently selected device. This topic will be discussed in detail next.

## Device Controls

Instant mapping is especially useful when it comes to working with devices. Assuming that you already have a supported control surface selected in your MIDI preferences, click on the title bar of any device (see Figure 11.3). You will see a small hand appear, indicating that it has been mapped to the controller.

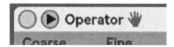

**FIGURE 11.3**

The blue hand indicates that the Operator has been mapped to the device controls of a control surface.

*Source:* Ableton

Turning your controller's eight device control knobs will manipulate the first eight parameters of the device you've selected or the eight Macro knobs if you've selected a Rack. Your control surface will also have a button that allows you to get to additional banks of eight parameters of the device, should it have more. Many control surfaces have left/right buttons for navigating to other devices in the track. If not, you can select devices using the mouse or the left- and right-arrow keys on your computer keyboard. As soon as a new device is selected, the hand appears, and the device controls map to it.

If you right-click in the title bar of the device, you will see a context menu including the option Lock to Control Surface for each of the designated control surfaces you have connected. This enables you to always control a specific device, no matter where your immediate focus is in Live.

If you want to see the details of how Ableton has mapped the controls of your particular control surface into Live, there is a Control Surface Reference in the Help View, which contains a list of all currently supported hardware devices and the details of their instant mappings.

**BE THERE NOW**

While in the MIDI map, notice that the name of the device in the title bar can be mapped just like any device parameter. This enables you to map a button on your controller that will select the device, mapping it instantly to your control surface.

# Clip Launchers

The easiest way to launch clips is to use a control surface with a clip-launching matrix, such as the LaunchPad, APC40, or Push. When a grid controller is connected and configured, a rectangle appears around the area of the Session View that is being controlled. The rectangle can only be moved from the controller, not from within Live.

The clip-launching matrix will give you visual feedback to show you the status of the clips in the Session. For example, the LaunchPad's buttons will glow yellow to indicate that a clip is loaded, green to indicate that a clip is playing back, and red to show that a clip is recording. Some controllers have different color schemes.

If multiple grid controllers are connected, Live will display multiple rectangles in different colors. Whether you want them side-by-side to control different tracks or above one another controlling different clips in the same tracks is up to you. It's a very flexible system (see Figure 11.4).

Clip launchers will *only* work if the device is enabled as a control surface. If the controller is only enabled as a remote, you'll still be able to send messages from the buttons in the matrix, but they won't control clips automatically.

| | | | | | | | | |
|---|---|---|---|---|---|---|---|---|
| ▶ Drum Kit 1 | ▶ Drum Kit 2 | ▶ Oxi Bass Rack | ▶ Three Op Ba | | | | ▶ | |
| ▶ Drum Kit 1 | ▶ Drum Kit 2 | | | ▶ Deep in Dari | | | ▶ | |
| ▶ Drum Kit 1 | ▶ Drum Kit 2 | | | | | | | |
| ▶ Drum Kit 1 | ▶ Drum Kit 2 | ▶ Oxi Bass Rack | ▶ Three Op Ba | | | ▶ Crossover S: | | |
| ▶ Drum Kit 1 | ▶ Drum Kit 2 | ▶ Oxi Bass Rack | | | | ▶ Crossover S: | ▶ | |
| ▶ Drum Kit 1 | ▶ Drum Kit 2 | ▶ Oxi Bass Rack | | | | | | |
| | | | | | | | ▶ | |
| | | | | | | | ▶ | |
| | | ▶ Oxi Bass Rack | | | | | ▶ | |
| ▶ Drum Kit 1 | | | | | | | | |
| ▶ Drum Kit 1 | ▶ Drum Kit 2 | ▶ Oxi Bass Rack | ▶ Three Op Ba | | | ▶ Crossover S: | | |
| ▶ Drum Kit 1 | ▶ Drum Kit 2 | ▶ Oxi Bass Rack | | | | | | |
| ▶ Drum Kit 1 | ▶ Drum Kit 2 | ▶ Oxi Bass Rack | | | | | ▶ | |
| ▶ Drum Kit 1 | ▶ Drum Kit 2 | | | | | | | |
| ▶ Drum Kit 1 | ▶ Drum Kit 2 | ▶ Oxi Bass Rack | | | | | | |
| | | | | | | | | |

**FIGURE 11.4** This is how the Session View might look with two different clip-launching control surfaces connected. The colored rectangles can be freely adjusted in any direction.
*Source:* Ableton

# Remote Mapping

As explained in Chapter 3, the basic process of mapping is easy. First, enter Map mode (see Figure 11.5), click the control you want to map, and then press the key or move the MIDI control you want to assign control to.

**FIGURE 11.5**
Click Key to map your computer keyboard or MIDI to map MIDI remote controllers.
*Source:* Ableton

### MULTI MIDI

In most cases, Live will allow you to map a single physical control to multiple on-screen controls simultaneously. In cases where this would cause a conflict, Live will warn you and automatically remove the old mapping before implementing the new one.

When a control is mapped to a computer key, it's labeled as seen in Figure 11.6. Live recognizes both lowercase and capital letters, most special characters, and the numbers on the numeric keypad. The only computer keys you can't map are those reserved for special purposes, such as the spacebar, Return, and Tab keys. To remove a manual mapping, enter Map mode, click on the control, and press Delete.

Let's take a closer look at what happens when you map MIDI controllers. After the control is mapped, Live displays a small box showing the MIDI channel and message that have been mapped (see Figure 11.7). When notes are mapped, Live tells you the note name. If you send a CC, you'll see the CC number after the MIDI channel.

FIGURE 11.6 The letters q and w have been mapped to the Track Activators of tracks 1 and 2.
*Source:* Ableton

FIGURE 11.7 These two volume sliders have been mapped to CC 6 and CC 8, both on MIDI channel 1.
*Source:* Ableton

When it comes to CCs, there are two types: absolute and relative. Faders and knobs often send absolute control messages. These are values from 0 to 127 and can move any control from the bottom of their range up to the top, with a resolution of 128 steps. If you're mapping absolute controllers, it's a good idea to make sure that you understand the takeover modes on the Link/MIDI tab of Live's Preferences (as explained in Chapter 2, "Getting Live Up and Running").

Relative CCs are typical of endless knobs called *encoders.* A relative control message is one that tells Live "move this value up" or "move this value down"; in other words, there's no direct correlation between the value of the controller and the value in Live. It just takes the control from its current position and moves it in one direction or another.

Remote messages come in a number of different flavors, but typically Live can automatically detect which type is being used. Whenever you map a control, the menu seen in Figure 11.8 is displayed in the lower left-hand corner of the screen. Take your time when mapping a CC—move it slowly, and Live will detect its type. If a type is detected incorrectly, you'll see the control jump around or other bizarre behavior when you try to use it. If this happens, check the controller's documentation and enter it manually in the menu.

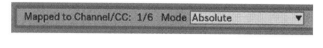

**FIGURE 11.8**

This menu shows you the type of CC your controller is sending.
*Source:* Ableton

### MIDI MESS

Bear in mind that manual mappings are not bound to a specific controller. For example, if you map the note C3 on channel 1, Live will respond to this note regardless of the MIDI controller that sends it. This is why you have to be careful when you have a lot of controllers connected. Make sure not to enable remote control for devices that you don't mean to use for this purpose. For the most complex MIDI setups, the easiest way to avoid conflicts is to have each device transmit on a different channel.

## The Mapping Browser

Whenever you enter the Key or MIDI Map mode, the Browser transforms to show you all of the current mappings. Not only does this give you a useful reference of every mapped control, but it also allows you to specify control ranges, using the Min and Max parameters. For example, in Figure 11.9, you'll see a track volume configured so that it can't go above 0dB (as opposed to its default of +6dB)—a very handy technique to avoid clipping during performance.

You can also set Max *below* Min in order to invert the behavior of a control. You may be wondering why you'd want to do this, but there are actually a few common cases. Let's say you've got a tempo-synced LFO mapped to a knob.

| C... | Note/Con... | Path | Name | Min | Max |
|---|---|---|---|---|---|
| 1 | CC 8 | 2-Drum Kit 2 \| Mixer | Track Volume | -inf dB | 0.0 dB |
| 1 | CC 6 | 1-Drum Kit 1 \| Mixer | Track Volume | -inf dB | 0.0 dB |
| 1 | CC 22 | 1-Drum Kit 1 \| Auto Filter | LFO Synced Rate | 8 | 1/64 |

Invert Range

**FIGURE 11.9** The top mappings show two volume controls limited to a maximum of 0dB. In the bottom mapping, the Invert Range context menu was used to flip the Min and Max levels.
*Source:* Ableton

By default, turning the knob up will make the LFO slower because its value is getting *higher*—you're moving from 1/32 to 1/16 and eventually all the way up to 4 bars. To a lot of folks, it makes more sense to have the LFO get faster as you turn up the knob.

# Special Mappings

There are quite a few ways that Live can be mapped that may not be apparent at first glance. For example, the Tempo control has two segments when in Map mode. The left segment is for coarse adjustments, while the right adjusts in fractions of a BPM.

Figure 11.10 shows a few areas of interest when it comes to mapping. The title bar of a track can be mapped in order to show its Track View. The clip status area can be mapped to show the Clip View for the currently playing clip in that track. If no clip is playing, this mapping won't do anything.

Map the title bar to show the track view.

Map the clip status area to show the clip view.

Relative Clip Launcher

Relative Scene Launcher

Scene Navigation Controls

**FIGURE 11.10**
A few hidden goodies in Map mode.
*Source:* Ableton

Relative clip launchers allow you to launch a clip based on the currently selected scene, but notice that these only appear in Map mode. In the Master track, you'll see some additional controls in the same row as the relative clip launchers. These are used for navigating through the scenes. The up and down arrows can be mapped to move up or down one row at a time, while the numeric box can be mapped to an encoder for scrolling through scenes.

## TWEAK THAT CLIP

You can assign MIDI and key controls to many parameters in the Clip View. Be aware, however, that mappings in the Clip View do not stay stuck to a particular clip. Instead, the assignments work on whatever clip is currently being displayed in the Clip View. Therefore, if you use a MIDI knob to transpose a clip, you can click on another clip and the same MIDI knob will now transpose the new clip.

The crossfader is another control that offers additional options when in Map mode. In Figure 11.11, you will see that the crossfader has three sections. Mapping the center section to a MIDI controller will give you access to the entire range of the fader, while the outer edges let you map the absolute left and right positions for fast cuts. This way, you can have a crossfader that is controlled by a single MIDI fader, three individual keys, or any combination thereof. Welcome to the future!

**FIGURE 11.11**

The crossfader is different than most of Live's controls in that it has three separate areas that can be mapped to MIDI controllers or the computer keyboard.
*Source:* Ableton

# Remote Controlling Plug-In Devices

Controlling the parameters of a plug-in device, such as a VST audio effect, is a little more difficult, due to the fact that each plug-in has its own unique graphical interface. Because of this, Live cannot superimpose the mapping overlay on the plug-in controls while in Map mode. To solve this problem, Ableton has included an unfold switch in the upper-left corner of the plug-in's title bar. Unfold the plug-in to reveal a generic display of the plug-in's parameters (see Figures 11.12a and 11.12b).

**FIGURE 11.12A**
Click the unfold switch to display the plug-in's parameters. If none are shown, you'll have to add them manually.
*Source:* Ableton

**FIGURE 11.12B**
After configuring the parameter display, save it so that it's there the next time you load the plug-in.
*Source:* Ableton

If the device has more than 32 parameters, no parameters will be shown, and you'll have to configure it to display the ones you want to map. To add a parameter, click the Configure switch in the title bar and click on any control in the plug-in window. A horizontal slider will appear for every control you click. (You might have to move the control slightly to get it to appear). These sliders can be mapped like any other control.

To remove a parameter from the configuration panel, just click on it and press Delete. The parameters can also be reorganized by dragging them into the order you want. When a control surface instantly maps device parameters, they appear on the device in the same order they appear in the configuration panel. Once you've got the device configured the way you want it, click Configure again to exit Configuration mode. Right-click in the title bar and select Save as Default Configuration to load this parameter configuration whenever the plug-in is used.

# About MIDI Controllers

Literally any MIDI controller can be used to control Live. MIDI devices come in different varieties best suited to different tasks, but it doesn't matter whether you've got an old MIDI synthesizer or the latest LED-encrusted behemoth—they're all compatible. What varies is the physical controls they offer and how much configuration they require.

While there's quite a bit of configuration that can be done within Live, it's important to understand that the specific MIDI messages sent by your controller can impact the results you get. Some controllers allow you to program every knob and button to send specific messages, while other controllers do not. Typically, you can expect piano keys and drum pads to send note messages while knobs and sliders (and anything that can be moved through a range) transmit control change messages.

Whether or not you need a programmable controller depends on the complexity of your MIDI setup and what you need to do with it. For example, there may be cases where you want to use several controllers and have each one transmit on a different MIDI channel to avoid conflicts. There might be a case where you want a button to be *momentary* (sends one message when the button is pushed and another when it is released) as opposed to *toggle* (sends one message when pushed and a second message when pushed again).

These are settings that are set within the controller and cannot be changed from within Live. Sometimes this is done with lots of menu diving on the hardware (read the manual carefully), and sometimes this is done with a software editor (generally a much easier task). So, if creating a highly customized performance setup is a task you need to accomplish, you should consider buying at least one controller with a good software editor, such as a Korg Nano-series controller or any of the controllers from KMI or Livid.

Some controllers require that you install separate software before you can use them with Live. Some, such as Novation's various LaunchPads, won't work at all until a driver is installed, while others will work as generic MIDI controllers right out of the box, but require additional software installation to allow control surface support with Live. Just make sure to check the manufacturer's website for the latest downloads, and you'll be all set.

# Push

Push is Ableton's own dedicated hardware controller for Live. Conceived of as an "instrument" rather than simply a MIDI controller, Push focuses heavily on the initial compositional phase: programming drums, creating parts with virtual instruments, and tweaking devices. The current version of Push hardware is Push 2, and that's the version I'll be focusing on here.

This section is meant to get you up and running with Push as quickly as possible. When you're ready to go deeper, make sure to consult the Live user manual, which will have all of the latest information on Push.

## Getting Started

Getting started with Push is easy. Press Add Track, navigate the display to select an instrument, and then press Load (in the lower right-hand corner of the display). Press Record, bang the grid buttons to play a few notes, and press Record again when you're done. Your newly recorded clip starts playing back. Take a look at Live's screen, and you'll see it in the clip grid. To record a new clip, press New. On-screen, you'll see Live select a new scene with empty clip slots ready to record into. Repeat this process and make a mess—it's the best way to learn!

A word of advice: when learning Push, check in with your computer screen regularly. Even though the ultimate goal may be to make music on Push and avoid gazing at Live, you'll get a more solid understanding of what's going on if you watch what happens to your clips and devices on-screen while working with the hardware. And remember that communication between Push and Live is two-way, so if you can't remember how to get to something on Push, just click on it in Live, and Push will update to show you the relevant controls.

The next things I'll cover are some general principles for navigating Push. These will make your next round of experiments go much faster. Figure 11.13 shows a few things you'll need to know right away. Because Push's buttons are backlit and clearly labeled, you'll generally have an easy time finding what you need. When a button goes dark, it's not relevant to the current workflow. For example, if Live already has an empty scene selected in the clip grid, the New button will go dark.

**Figure 11.13** Most of Push's functions are clearly labeled and easy to find. All of the buttons are backlit. When a button goes dark, that means that it has no functionality in the current mode. *Source:* Ableton

## Command Buttons

One important thing to know about Push right out of the gate is that many of the command buttons are designed to do one thing when pushed and another when held down. For many of the buttons on the right (Scale, Repeat, Note, Session), a single push switches Push into a new mode, while holding the button down enables the mode temporarily and returns Push to its previous state when you release it.

In the case of the buttons on the left, it's a bit different. For example, a single push of Quantize immediately performs quantization. Holding it down presents quantization options, including the option to turn record quantization on or off. Similarly, holding down Fixed Length allows you to select a predetermined length for all newly recorded clips, while a single push is used to turn this mode on or off.

## Encoders and Multifunction Buttons

The controls above and below the display have different functions, depending on the current display mode. The display mode is changed using the buttons to the right of the display: Device, Mix, Clip, and Browse.

The encoders that run across the top adjust the parameters shown in the display. Select Mix to adjust volume or other mixer parameters, Device to adjust effects and instruments, and Clip to tweak clip properties. When Browse is selected, the knobs are used to scroll through devices. When you've found the device you want to load, press the button below the word "Load"–you'll see it in the lower right-hand corner of the screen.

In Device and Mix mode, the buttons at the top of the display are used to navigate the pages of information that are available for that mode. For example, in Mix mode, these buttons select Volume, Pan, or Sends. Pick one and then use the knobs to make adjustments. In Device mode, you'll use these buttons to select a particular device for editing.

If the Device is a Drum or Instrument Rack, you'll be able to use these top buttons to select either the Rack itself or the currently selected chain. To select a different chain, hold down the button above the Rack name and use the bottom row of buttons to select a chain.

### DIVING DEEP

Because Live allows nested Racks, device chains can be very deep, and the navigation can take some getting used to. As you're learning, you may want to keep an eye on the Device View in Live. Follow the little blue hand that appears in the title bar of the devices! It's the key to knowing what Push is controlling at any given moment.

## Tracks and Clips

Navigate from track to track using the left- and right-arrow buttons on the right side. Or you can select a particular track using the buttons beneath the display (except when in Browse mode). When a track is selected, it is automatically armed for recording. New tracks are created by pushing Add Track.

Push's main button grid is used to either create clips or launch clips. To switch between these modes, use the Notes and Session buttons on the right side of the grid. In Session mode, the grid buttons represent clip slots; only the ones containing clips will light up. To move the grid, use the standard arrow buttons or use the Page/Octave arrows to jump eight tracks or scenes for each press.

In Notes mode, the grid is used to play notes or to program sequences. To cycle through the various sequencer layouts available in Notes mode, press Layout. Keep an eye on the display as you do this, and you'll see the name of these various layouts displayed. I'll be explaining drum programming in more detail later in this chapter; to learn more about the other sequencing modes, consult the user manual.

## Mixer

Press Mix to see an overview of eight tracks at a time. Press it again to see a detailed view of the currently selected track. When in the overview (Global Mix Mode), use the arrow buttons to navigate to tracks not shown. Or you can switch to Session mode and use the page arrows to jump by banks of eight tracks.

A short press of the Mute or Solo buttons on the left will mute or solo the currently selected track. Give either of these buttons a long push to convert the bottom row of multifunction buttons into mute or solo switches.

### AUTOMATE IT!

To automate device controls, press Automate (this enables the Automation Arm switch in Live) and then press Record. Automation is written from the moment you move an encoder until the moment you stop touching it. (Push's encoders are touch-sensitive.)

# Drum Programming

When a track containing a Drum Rack is selected, Push automatically switches into drum programming mode. Programming drums on Push is a lot of fun. While many controllers focus on performing drum parts using pads or step-sequencing using a grid, Push does both simultaneously.

The layout button will cycle through a few different modes: Loop Selector, 16 Velocities, and 64 Pads. 64 Pads is not a sequencer mode. Instead, it uses the 64 pads to trigger up to 64 sounds in a single drum rack. In this section, we'll be looking at the Loop Selector and 16 Velocities mode.

The top half of the pads is the step sequencer (see Figure 11.14). By default, it represents two bars with 16 steps in each bar. (Each row constitutes one-half of a bar.) This can be changed by selecting a different note division (using the 1/4 to 1/32t Grid buttons at the right), but I'd suggest starting out by mastering the 16-step grid and then venturing into the other divisions later. To add drum hits to the sequence, first push one of the Drum Rack pads in the lower left to select a drum. Then push buttons in the step sequencer to add the selected drum to a given step.

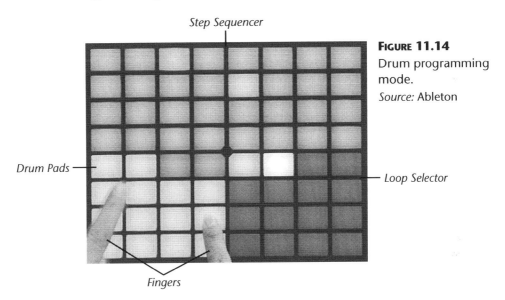

Step Sequencer

Drum Pads

Loop Selector

Fingers

**FIGURE 11.14**
Drum programming mode.
*Source:* Ableton

Hold down a step to reveal additional controls in the display. If Clips mode is selected, you can adjust velocity and note length, and move the note forward or backward a small amount by twisting the Nudge encoder. In Device and Mix mode, hold down a step and turn the encoders to create automation. For example, in Mix mode hold down a step and turn the Pan encoder all the way to the left. That one hit of that particular drum will now be panned left. In Device mode, you'll be able to automate whatever device is selected using the top row of multifunction buttons.

## DOUBLE LOOP VS. DUPLICATE

After you've created a clip, you can make it twice as long by pressing Double Loop. Duplicate, on the other hand, makes a copy of the currently playing clip and places it in the clip slot below.

To record drums live, just press Record and bang away on the pads. Whether or not your performance is quantized as you record is up to you. Hold down Quantize to display the settings for turning Record Quantization on or off. My preference is to leave quantization off while recording and then quantize after the fact, if necessary. When perfectly quantized parts are necessary, I use the step sequencer. This is a great advantage offered by having both programming approaches handy.

When you play Push using the pads, the steps will appear in the grid, even when they haven't been quantized. This is a cool feature that allows you to see how your pattern looks on the grid, even though it may not be strictly aligned with it. This creates an interesting opportunity and a potential problem. After playing a part, you can quantize an individual hit by pushing the step twice. The first push deletes the hit, and the second re-creates it, perfectly aligned to the grid. Just be aware that if you've played a note really late or early, it may appear on the step before or after the one you intended.

Using the step sequencer to edit parts you performed, however, can be tricky. What if you want to experiment with turning certain hits off, but don't want to lose the timing when you turn them back on again? Instead of deleting notes, hold down the Mute button while pushing the notes you want to remove. Hold Mute and press them again to reactivate them. (Fortunately, Push also has an Undo button so you can easily step backward if you forget this workflow.)

### QUANTIZE

A single push of Quantize will quantize the entire clip. To quantize a single drum, hold down Quantize and then press a drum pad. Voila! Only that drum gets quantized.

The only difference between Loop Length mode and 16 Velocities is the function of the lower-right set of pads. In 16 Velocities mode, these 16 pads each select a different velocity. Press a velocity pad before adding a step in the sequencer. The new step will be assigned the velocity you selected.

Loop Length mode presents a brilliant solution to a basic problem. When programming longer drum parts, you're often faced with the need to focus on an individual bar while working on its details and then jump back out to listen to the bar in context. Repeating this process over and over can be a hassle, but with the loop length grid, it's a piece of cake.

Each pad in the loop length section represents one of 16 possible bars. Pushing any of these buttons causes the clip to jump immediately to this bar. To specify a range of bars, hold one pad and then press a second. For example, pressing pad 1 (the one in the upper left of the loop area) causes bar 1 of the clip to loop. Holding down pad 5 and then pressing pad 8 creates a 4-bar loop including bars 5 through 8.

**THE TOUCH STRIP**

The touch strip is used to navigate the Drum Rack's Pad Overview. Slide your finger along it to navigate to other banks of 16 pads.

## Replacing Drum Sounds

Push makes it easy to load sounds into the pads of a Drum Rack one at a time, or to replace the entire Drum Rack with a new preset. The trick is to make sure that the right object is selected in Device mode before pressing Browse. If the Drum Rack is selected, pressing Browse will take you straight to Drum Rack presets. If the pad/chain is selected, you'll be shown drum hits and only the currently selected pad will be replaced. While in Browse mode, press different pads, and you'll see the Browser update to show you the type of sound currently contained in that pad.

# Notes Mode

When you select a track containing any instrument other than a Drum Rack, Push switches into its unique "keyboard" mode. This is Ableton's take on how to program melody or harmony using a grid instead of a piano keyboard. If you're an experienced keyboardist, this may be a mere curiosity, or it may be a fun new way to experiment. After all, you're sure to come up with some different ideas when playing a totally new instrument!

## FOOTWORK

Consider plugging a sustain pedal into Jack 1 on the back of Push. You may find that it makes the pads much more expressive and playable for melodic instruments.

Plug a footswitch into Jack 2 to control recording. A single push starts and stops recording, while a double push triggers the New command.

By default, this mode presents you with only the notes in a given scale (C major by default). Each colored pad marks the tonic (root) note of the scale. Therefore, anyone who knows a little music theory will expect to see a colored pad, followed by seven white pads, and then another colored one. And, indeed on the bottom row, that's exactly what you do see, but beyond that the pattern doesn't continue, because Ableton has taken advantage of the fact that a grid is two-dimensional, unlike a piano keyboard, which is strictly linear.

By default, notes are organized in fourths along the vertical axis and steps along the horizontal axis. This is similar to the arrangement of notes on a string instrument, such as a guitar or bass. And just like those instruments, this means that the same chord or scale can be played in a variety of locations in the grid. Play the lower four pads of the grid in order from left to right. When you get to the fourth pad, notice that the far left pad in the second row lights up as well. This means they are the same pitch. To change the note layout, press Scale and adjust the Layout and Direction parameters.

## SENSITIVE SOUNDS

If you find the pads in the grid to be too stiff or too sensitive, press Setup to reveal the Pad Sensitivity setting in the display. As you increase this value, the pads require less force to produce a high output level.

To adjust the dynamic range of the pads, adjust Pad Dynamics. Low values will cause the pads to produce values that hover around the middle of the velocity range, while higher values will produce more extreme highs and lows.

The Scales button reveals controls for selecting the key and scale of the note grid. For example, to play in B♭ Lydian mode, you would scroll to Lydian using the encoders and then select B♭ using the buttons. If you're not experienced with music theory, you can study to make sense of this, or take it as a purely experimental endeavor. If you find a scale you like, you'll be able to use this scale across any other parts you create and every other part will be in key.

For some types of music, you'll be able to select a single scale and make an entire song. However, much great music moves across keys and uses notes outside of a single key center to create harmonic and melodic interest. Fortunately, the scale display also has a button to switch from In Key to Chromatic mode, which provides a layout in which every note is included, but only the notes from the selected scale are lit. This provides an interesting perspective on scales and allows you to move outside them when necessary.

The scale display also lets you turn Fixed mode on or off. In Fixed mode, the pads always keep their original orientation, which means that the lower-right corner is always C. When you switch keys, the available notes change, but the overall range of the pads is unaffected. With Fixed mode turned off, the grid reorients itself around whatever root note you select. For example, if you select the key of G, the entire range of the pads changes, and the colored notes all become G instead of C.

One interesting way to generate chord patterns using Push is to repeatedly press the same pads while changing the key in Scale mode. If you do this in Fixed mode, you'll get subtler changes with individual notes moving a half step as necessary to stay in key. With Fixed mode turned off, you'll get very clear movement from chord to chord as you change key. For example, if you play a C-major triad (C-E-G) with the key set to C and then change the key to G, the whole chord will move up a perfect fifth (G-B-D).

# Working with Plug-Ins

If you want to use Push's device controls with plug-ins, you'll have to set them up using the Configure switch, as explained in "Remote Controlling Plug-in Devices" earlier. You may also find it useful to create plug-in Racks and configure Macro knobs, but strictly speaking this is not necessary. The controls you add by configuring the plug-in will be available to Push either way.

They'll be distributed into eight banks according to the order in which the generic sliders are displayed in Live. When configuring, drag them into the order you want. For example, if you want all of your filter controls to be in the first bank, make sure that they are the first eight parameters listed. Once you've got the plug-in set up the way you like, the "Save as Default Configuration" will ensure that the parameter configuration you like is used whenever you load.

# 12

# Playing Live ... Live

**M**ost books written about music-production software would not include a chapter like the one you're about to read. As you will discover, it's a real treat to use the same software to create your music *and* perform it. Because of its flexible control methods and instant response to user input, Live is the perfect companion for a gigging musician. Live shines in all sorts of scenarios, from DJ gigs to touring pop acts to improvisational music and theater.

Regardless of what type of musician you consider yourself to be, I recommend reading all the information presented in this chapter. Even if you never take Live on stage, you'll find that its performative nature makes all sorts of unique creative workflows possible. Many live performance techniques can be used to great effect when producing in the studio.

## Warping Songs and Long Audio Files

If you perform with Live, use Live on stage with a band, or create sample-heavy music in the studio, you'll bump into the need to warp longer audio files. While the tools are the same as those discussed in Chapter 5, "Clips," working with long audio files can present some unique challenges. There's no universal solution to address every warping need—it takes practice and experience. The good news is that for most contemporary music with big drums and steady tempos, it's not too difficult

Small errors with warping make a bigger difference the longer the audio clip. In other words, you could be off by 1/10 of a BPM when warping a 2-bar loop and never hear a problem. If it's a six-minute song, however, the first 16 bars will sound pretty good, but by the time bar 128 comes around, it will be seriously out-of-sync. Often, all you need to do is zoom in toward the end of the song, and it will be easy to see how far it has drifted from the grid. Find a clear drum hit and drag it to the grid to correct the problem.

One of the most common rookie mistakes with long audio files is *too many Warp Markers.* In some situations, this doesn't cause any big problems. In others, it can compromise sound quality or create a confusing mess. Remember, if the tempo of the audio doesn't fluctuate at all, additional Warp Markers aren't necessary to keep the audio in sync. That said, you'll sometimes encounter small tempo fluctuations in unexpected places. For example, you might encounter a techno track that's been through an analog mastering process and drifts from 127 to 127.02 BPM. In this case, you'll need a few Warp Markers to keep the song in sync.

New users also tend to get confused when working with files with no clear tempo reference. For example, maybe you're using an acapella in a remix, or you're using a synth pad as a backing track for your band. Don't start dropping Warp Markers into these files. Instead, determine their original tempo another way. In the case of an acapella, tap the tempo to the original song, or warp the song and get the tempo from the Seg. BPM box. If it's something you produced, you should already know the tempo! Type the tempo into the Seg. BPM box, and your clip will play in sync.

You may still have to adjust the clip's starting point by ear—acapellas don't always start in the right place. If you're exporting files to use as backing tracks, make your life easier and always make sure to begin the export at the beginning of a bar. For example, if the synth pad comes in 16 bars into the song, make sure there are exactly 16 bars at the start of the exported file. It can get very confusing otherwise.

If you're working with backing tracks or acapellas on a regular basis, you'll be much happier with the Auto Warp Long Samples preference turned off. Auto Warp usually doesn't know what to do with these files, and you'll waste time cleaning up the mess it makes. The same holds true for some types of music—even songs with a steady tempo and clear rhythm parts can confuse Auto Warp if the rhythms are very syncopated, or there are long introductions and interludes.

In the next examples, we'll look at scenarios that might come up when Auto Warp Long Samples is turned on. After that, I'll talk about working with this setting turned off. Obviously, these won't cover every situation you'll encounter, but they will help you think through the problem-solving process.

# Working with Auto-Warp Long Samples Turned On

Auto Warp analyzes audio and makes guesses about the length and original tempo of the file. For short, evenly timed, properly cut loops, this is a very simple process. For entire songs, it's more complicated. If you let Live automatically use Auto Warp on your songs, and the material you're working with is straightforward, it will often do most of the work for you. Don't ever assume that it will do *all* of the work for you, though. Always check against the metronome and look out for some of the common problems discussed next.

One common problem is inaccurate detection of the first downbeat of the song, often caused by an intro lacking a clear time reference. Sometimes, Live gets the tempo right, but the song is offset from the metronome and other clips. In other cases, the introduction to a song confuses Auto Warp enough that it gets the tempo wrong.

The introduction to the song shown in Figure 12.1 has no drums, and Auto Warp has gotten the first downbeat wrong. To help Live out, we're going to place 1.1.1 where the drum beat comes in, instead of at the beginning of the song. This is done by a combination of ears and eyes. Listen for the area where the beat starts in and then zoom in on that section. In this case, I've used the Scrub tool to launch the song from this section and visually located the first kick drum. This takes a little practice, but pay attention, and you'll get it.

Auto Warp thinks the downbeat is here    ...but it's really here

**FIGURE 12.1** Auto Warp has gotten the tempo correct, but the entire song is offset from the grid by a quarter note.
*Source:* Ableton

After you've located this first clear downbeat, right-click the transient marker above it and select Set 1.1.1 Here. This aligns the song to the grid as seen in Figure 12.2. The beat now starts at bar 1, and the introduction is numbered with negative bar numbers. I'm a fan of the negative bar numbers—they give an extra visual cue to tell me where the intro ends and the song kicks in. Check the song against the metronome to make sure the tempo is correct. If it's off, right-click at 1.1.1 and select Warp From Here from the context menu. (There are several different versions of this command, so refer to Chapter 5 if you need more information.)

Finally, move the start marker to the left so the clip plays back from the introduction. *Make sure that you move it back an even number of bars.* For example, if the intro is 16 bars, the start marker should be at −16.1.1.

Sometimes, you'll encounter a situation where Auto Warp gets confused and adds way too many warp markers. Figure 12.3 shows a song where this has happened. It's only in rare situations that an audio file will require this many Warp Markers. It would have to have a constantly varying tempo or have completely freeform timing. This happens to be a song that I know was recorded at a completely steady tempo (because I recorded it myself!).

**FIGURE 12.2** Once you've identified the first clear downbeat, right-click and select Set 1.1.1 Here.
*Source:* Ableton

**FIGURE 12.3**
My music seems to
have given Auto Warp
a nervous breakdown.
*Source:* Ableton

In a case like this, you're better off getting rid of all the Warp Markers and starting over. To delete Warp Markers, drag to create a selection in the editor (or use Edit → Select All) and then press Delete. Once the Warp Markers are gone, zoom in on the first beat and select Warp From Here (Straight) from the context menu. This tells Live that you know the tempo is steady, and as such, it's going to produce more reliable results. However, in this case it gets much closer, but still is not perfect.

To solve this, it may just be easier to zoom in, find a clear downbeat, and drag it to the grid. Sometimes, however, it's even easier to solve the problem by editing the Seg. BPM value. Figure 12.4 shows that Live decided the tempo for this file is 149.29. It's entirely possible that you'll be warping songs with fractional tempos, but you'll be amazed at how often just rounding up or down is all you need to do. For this song, typing in 150 does the trick.

**FIGURE 12.4**
Sometimes fractional
tempos are correct, but
with contemporary music
they often are not.

## PAINT BY NUMBERS

You might want to type a tempo into the Seg. BPM box, but find that it's grayed out. This is because Segment BPM can only be edited after you've clicked on a Warp Marker, even if there's only one in the clip.

# Working with Auto Warp Long Samples Turned Off

After importing the files, use the Tap button in the Control Bar to figure out the tempo as closely as possible. Don't turn the Warp switch on—you need to hear the clip play at its original speed while you're tapping. This process has to be done in the Session View. Try it in the Arrangement View, and you'll see that tapping causes the playback position to jump around as you tap.

Launch the clip and begin tapping along with the song using the Tap Tempo button. Since Live's Tempo display is accurate to two decimal places, you'll probably get tempos like 125.82 BPM or 98.14 BPM instead of round numbers like 110 BPM or 85 BPM.

After you've got the rough tempo, zoom in and move the Start flag to the first clear downbeat of the song. Then turn on Warp, right-click on Start, and select Set 1.1.1 Here from the context menu. Notice that the clip's Seg. BPM has been set to Live's tempo. Listen with the metronome playing, and it should sound pretty close.

From here, there are a number of ways to proceed. How you complete the warping depends on the material you're working with and what makes the most sense to you. Bear in mind that what follows is a simplified workflow. You may find yourself mixing and matching techniques to get the right results.

If you believe the audio has a completely steady tempo, you can do one of the following:

▶ Right-click on Start and select Warp Here (Straight) from the context menu.

▶ Scroll to the right in the editor, find a clear downbeat, and drag it to the grid.

▶ Round the value in Seg. BPM up or down.

If you believe the audio has tempo fluctuations, you can:

▶ Right-click on Start and select Warp From Here (Start at <x> BPM). This will use the tempo you tapped as a hint to get Auto Warp on the right track.

▶ Scroll to the right in the editor, find a clear downbeat, double-click to create a Warp Marker, and drag it to the grid. Continue to move through the clip and repeat this process.

At this point, you should be very close if not completely done. Listen against the metronome and add Warp Markers, if necessary.

Sometimes, material is really problematic—lots of tempo fluctuations and poor visual indicators in the waveform for determining rhythm. In these cases, you may have to loop a bar or two at a time and obsessively tweak to get the sound in sync. Figure 12.5 shows a four-bar loop that's close, but not quite right.

**FIGURE 12.5**

This loop doesn't play back smoothly. Notice that I've created a Warp Marker at the actual downbeat of the next bar. Once I drag it left to line up with the end of the loop, it sounds great.

*Source:* Ableton

The loop technique works like this: after tapping the tempo, adjust the loop brace around the first one or two bars of the clip and begin playback. Chances are, the loop won't play back smoothly. Examine the waveform in the area around the end of the loop and try to identify the downbeat of the next bar. Create a Warp Marker for it and drag it so that it lines up with the right-hand edge of the loop brace. Depending on whether your tapped tempo was too fast or too slow, you may have to drag it to the left or right. Once it's looping properly, add additional Warp Markers within the loop as necessary.

When you're ready to move on, click on the loop brace and press the up arrow. This will move the loop brace ahead so you can fine-tune the next section of the song.

**ANALYZE THIS**

You've probably noticed that the first time you drop a long audio file into Live, it takes some time to analyze it. Once the file is analyzed, the data gets stored in a file with the same name as the original file and an extension of .ASD. This file can also store other clip settings, such as Warp Markers. If you click the Save button in the Clip View, the current clip settings will be stored as the default for the file referenced by the clip. The next time that clip is dragged into a Set, these settings will be used.

# Performance Strategies

There are many different approaches to performing with Live. Some are highly interactive, with Live at the center of the action. There are performers who hit the stage with Push and a handful of MIDI tracks loaded with drums and synthesizers, composing music on the fly. Others rely more on audio clips, mixing and matching loops, samples, and entire songs. When Live was first on the rise, it became very popular as a DJ platform, although in recent years many DJs have returned to more traditional DJ tools like CDJs and Serato DJ.

Live also is part of many performances as a supporting player. You'll find bands using Live to play back backing tracks or trigger the occasional sample. Some musicians use Live as a host for synthesizers to be played live, while others use it as a powerful effects processor, sending vocals or instruments through Live's effects in real time.

In this section, we'll look at some performance examples. These are meant to give you some ideas and get you started. Since there are so many possibilities, you'll find that developing a performance setup is a labor-intensive process. It's hard to know if something is going to work until you try it. That's why I typically recommend starting simple, testing, and making modifications based on your experience.

Because Live is so flexible, it's tempting to go overboard when designing a performance setup. Many ideas that seem great when you're designing the setup are difficult to pull off in a performance situation. Mapping 10 effects to 10 different knobs is great until you keep grabbing the wrong knob on stage. Start simple, build over time, and practice!

# Performing in the Session View

Not surprisingly, the most interactive performance setups are focused in the Session View. When a new Live user wants to get started with performance in the Session View, I typically suggest that they start out by creating a DJ setup and then building off it. DJing is a well-known paradigm and offers a great foundation to build off. Even if you have no interest in DJing, go through this section, and you'll come away with some great ideas.

In Figure 12.6, I have set up Live's Session View like a standard two-channel DJ mixer. There are two audio tracks, each assigned to different sides of the

**FIGURE 12.6**

A simple Live Set ready for DJing. Deck A and Deck B are set to opposite sides of the crossfader. Map EQ controls, effect controls, track volumes, and the crossfader to your MIDI controller(s).

crossfader. There are EQs loaded onto each of the audio tracks and a few Effect Racks on the Master track. The EQ Three Rack (shown) and the Racks loaded into the Master track all come from the Performance & DJ folder under Audio Effect Racks in the Browser. Make sure to explore this folder as you begin creating your performance setup.

The next step is to import and warp some music. Then map some controls to your MIDI controller and go to town. Try cutting all of the low frequencies from one clip while mixing it in. Use the Sends to momentarily add reverb or delay. Go crazy with effects on the Master. This will give you a feel for working with the MIDI controller, launching clips, and using effects. Don't be shy about changing the MIDI mappings—nobody gets it right the first time. This is a trial-and-error process.

Now it's time to take it to the next level. Create an additional track for drums and a synthesizer track to play live (see Figure 12.7). If you've got Push, you might want to create a MIDI drum track and program drums on the fly. If not, keep it simple and load up some drum loops instead.

| Deck A | Deck B | 3 Cashon Kit | Drum Loops | Wavetable-Lead |
|--------|--------|--------------|-----------|----------------|
| ▶ Audiojack-Reverie | ▶ ClaudeVonStroke | ● | ▶ sm101 db bong | ■ |
| ▶ MemoriesOfTheFutu | ▶ Mobot-Slapdash | ● | ▶ Minimal House-1 | ■ |
| ▶ Wave-Solarium | ▶ Hobotech-Hobo | ● | ▶ High Hats with R | ■ |
| ■ | ■ | ● | ▶ Hats and Snare S | ■ |

**FIGURE 12.7** A few extra tracks turn a DJ set into an interactive jam session.
*Source:* Ableton

For the next enhancement, return to the DJ tracks and use the Duplicate command to make copies of the clips. Adjust each clip to start and loop in a different place. See Figure 12.8 for what this might look like. These clips will allow you to launch different parts of the song, remixing the arrangement on the fly.

| |
|---|
| ▶ Reverie-Intro-Groove1 |
| ▶ Reverie-Groove1Loop |
| ▶ Reverie-Breakdown |
| ▶ Reverie-Groove2 |

**FIGURE 12.8**
These four clips are all made from the same song.
*Source:* Ableton

## SAVE THE STACK

Once you've created a stack of clips based on a single song, you can highlight them all and drag them into the Browser to create a new Set. You could drag them into the User Library or create a folder on your hard drive and add it to Places. The next time you want to play this song, drag the Set from the Browser into your DJ Set and your stack of clips will be ready to go.

This last image gives you an idea of where you might end up if you're out to create an original live performance (see Figure 12.9). The DJ music on the first two tracks is replaced by the original grooves you've produced. Instead of being fully produced songs, these are raw backing tracks—mostly drums and bass. You'll launch these clips to lay down the groove while playing parts live, improvising with loops and using effects.

| Deck A | Deck B | Loops | Vox Samples | Wavetable-Lead |
|---|---|---|---|---|
| ▶ Rogue-DrumsOnly | ▶ Edison-IntroBass | ▶ JasonGraves_Butter | ▶ B. Fuller 1 | ■ |
| ▶ Rogue-Groove 1 | ▶ Edison-LongBuild | ▶ HY_Latin_Bossa 01 | ▶ B. Fuller 2 | ■ |
| ▶ Rogue-GrooveNoKic | ▶ Edison-FullGroove | ▶ HY_Gritty Vibe Stor | ▶ Bret & Eric | ■ |
| ▶ Rogue-Groove 2 | ▶ Edison-Groove2 | ■ | ■ | ■ |

**FIGURE 12.9** An example of how a DJ setup can morph into something new.
*Source:* Ableton

If you take the time to go through these steps, you'll begin to understand why I suggest starting simple. The possibilities expand very quickly, and you'll probably need to do a lot of experimenting to figure out what works for you. You may also find yourself spending a lot of time researching MIDI controllers as you get into performance. You could discover that you need more than one MIDI controller to do what you want, or you could decide to simplify the setup so that you only need one.

## MAKING THE SCENE

To quickly get a chunk of your Arrangement into the Session View, select a range of time in the Arrangement View; then right-click and choose Consolidate Time to New Scene from the context menu. When you return to the Session, you'll have a brand new scene with the material you selected. This can provide a great starting point for preparing a multi-track performance Set.

# Cueing and Click Tracks

Some performance setups require that you, or a member of your band, hear something that the audience does not. For example, when drummers perform with sequenced material, they sometimes use headphones and play to a click. We'll get into this subject by exploring the DJ paradigm a bit more. Once you've got a handle on how it all works, you'll be able to apply it to your particular situation without much trouble.

For traditional DJ setups, headphones are a must. The DJ needs to be able to hear the music before the audience does in order to pick the exact playback location and adjust the tempo. In Live, the tempo isn't a concern, but you might want to preview a song or loop to hear what it sounds like before mixing it in. Figure 12.10 shows how to set this up.

In order to cue or preview tracks, you'll need an audio interface with at least four outputs—two outs for the main mix and two others to feed your headphones. Many audio interfaces have assignable headphone outputs, while others have the headphone out hard-wired to a specific pair of outputs. In this case, we're assuming that outputs 1/2 will feed the headphones. Therefore, in the Master track outs, 1/2 are specified for Cue and 3/4 for Master. Connect outputs 3/4 to the sound system.

**FIGURE 12.10**
Basic settings for Live's cueing system.

Cue Out routed to headphone output of audio interface.

Master Out connected to sound system.

Solo/Cue switch set to Cue.

Click Cue to preview.

Now you're ready to cue tracks through the headphones, as shown previously. Please note that enabling Cue on a track does not remove it from the Master. You'll need to turn off the Track Activator button or turn down the volume to keep it only in the headphones. After the track is properly cued, you can bring up the volume and send it out to the mains.

Another approach is to use a dedicated cue track. This track is used to hold clips before you play them. It has its Cue switch on and Track Activator off, so any audio clip played in this track will be heard only in the headphones. Tracks like these can be used as virtual "record crates." Load all the songs you think you might want to play into the cue track. Then, after you're done previewing it, drag the clip from the cue track over to Deck A or Deck B.

In a band situation, you may need to send a click to one or more members of the band. Now that you understand the Cue output, this is easy because Live's metronome is sent out of the Cue output by default. Just turn on Live's metronome and set the Cue output to a pair of headphones.

It's also possible that you'll need to create a dedicated click track in your Set. For example, you might need an easy way for the drummer to hear exactly two bars of click before the song begins. When using the Arrangement View for backing tracks (explained later in this chapter), it's easy to place two bars of click in a track before the backing tracks start. To make a click, just select a simple percussion sound, such as cowbell or rim, and program a bar of quarter notes.

# Looping

Live lets you define loop points on the fly by using the Set buttons for the Position and Length parameters in the Clip View (see Figure 12.11). While a clip is playing, you can press Set Position to set the point where the loop begins and Set Length to set the loop's end point *and* turn the Loop switch

**FIGURE 12.11**

Map the Set buttons shown above for on-the-fly looping. Map the Loop switch, too, for enabling or disabling the loop.

*Source:* Ableton

on in one step. When you turn the Loop switch off, the clip will continue to play to the end. If you turn it back on again, the clip will jump back to playing the loop.

As you'd expect, the Set switches can be mapped to a controller, but remember: since these buttons are in the Clip View, the controller will only set the loop points for the clip that's currently being displayed. To jump to the currently playing clip from your controller, you have to map the Clip Status indicator, as explained in Chapter 11, "Remote Control."

### UNDER THE LIMIT

It can be helpful to place a Limiter in your Master track to make sure that you don't clip the outputs on your audio interface. However, it's important to make sure that you're not hitting the Limiter unnecessarily and crushing your dynamics. Dial in negative gain on the Limiter (try −3dB for starters), to give yourself some extra headroom to mix tracks and loops together. This way, limiting only occurs if something extreme happens.

# Performing in the Arrangement View

Two common uses for the Arrangement View in performance are backing tracks and dub-style mixing. (Jamaican dub is probably the most important precursor to modern electronic music, and it's well worth taking a little time to research.) The basic concept of dub mixing is this: you play back a multi-track recording of a song, processing tracks with effects and using the mixer to pull parts in and out improvisationally. In this way, a unique performance is created from a fixed set of raw material.

If you want to try dub mixing, start out by exporting files from your productions. Don't export every single track individually; export groups of tracks instead (commonly referred to as *stems*). For example, put all of the drums in one file, bass tracks in another, and so on. The Set itself can be configured very similarly to the Session View examples earlier in this chapter, but instead of launching clips, you'll be playing them back from the Arrangement. Experiment with different effects on the tracks, and make sure to use a few sends for delay and reverb.

Backing tracks are used to enhance a live performance. For some bands, backing tracks are a way of bringing a few parts from the studio on stage, while for others they may be the backbone of a high-tech show with synchronized lighting and video. Backing tracks can be played from the Session View, but this tends to work best for simpler needs, or in situations where you have a dedicated person operating Live. In this section, we'll explore using the Arrangement View for backing tracks.

Figure 12.12 shows a backing track set that was created for my band Tiny Machines. Running across the top are locators, one for each song. These are MIDI mapped for easy recall.

You'll notice there are drums for each song; they've been exported from the final mixes. The drum parts have been placed in separate tracks because when used live, it turned out that they all needed some EQ tweaks. These EQ adjustments could be resampled to fit all of the drums onto one track, but there's a different point to be made here. When you are building a live performance, it's important to have some flexibility with the backing tracks. Set things up so that it's easy to tweak individual parts, and the tracks will be part of the creative process, rather than something rigid that you're stuck with as is.

The KICK SNARE track is a MIDI track that's used to reinforce the existing drum tracks when necessary. This was added when we discovered that a couple of songs with gentle drums didn't have quite enough punch for live performance. Moving a couple of tracks up, you'll see a track called *Click*.

**FIGURE 12.12** Backing tracks in the Arrangement View.
*Source:* Ableton

This track is routed to a pair of outputs that only feeds the band's in-ear monitors. It's only needed for one song that has an ambient introduction.

Toward the bottom of the set, there's a track dedicated to bass parts. These are here primarily for rehearsal purposes. That's why all the clips are muted. If there's ever a need to rehearse without the bass player, we can just unmute these clips and get to work. PART 1 and PART 2 are for odds and ends. On one song, they are extra vocal harmonies for use when doing a stripped-down duo version of the show. In other places, they are snippets of sound effects and synthesizer parts.

Figure 12.13 shows a few ways that automation is used in the Set. G-Synths contains a Rack of different sounds to be triggered from a guitar synthesizer. The synths in the Rack are selected using the Chain Selector (as explained in Chapter 7, "Using Effects and Instruments"). The Chain Selector (which has been mapped to a Macro called *Song Selector*) is automated, so the correct synth is automatically selected when the song is played.

**FIGURE 12.13**

Automation can handle all sorts of tasks such as selecting the right instrument for a song.

*Source:* Ableton

The track AprilIN receives a send from the singer's microphone. With automation, some additional effects are added to the vocal in some parts. The track PC is used to send program change messages to other MIDI gear on stage. This is done by automating a great Max for Live device called *Dial To Program Change*. By automating the dial, presets are recalled on my pedalboard and on the Behringer X32 rack mixer we use.

Hopefully, this section has given you some ideas about the possibilities of using Live on stage. Now get in there and start experimenting!

# 13
# Live 10 Power!

In this final chapter, we'll be looking at an assortment of more advanced techniques, along with a few things that just don't fit anywhere else, such as the File Manager and Max for Live.

## Getting Your Groove On

The power of loop-based music is also its biggest problem: repetition. While repetition can be magic for keeping a dance floor moving, the "feel" can become stagnant, ultimately making music monotonous and uninspired. To combat this, it is important to understand the three heavy hitters of groove: dynamics, timing, and variation. What you'll find in this chapter are suggestions that can be used in addition to, rather than in place of, Live's built-in Groove feature.

Be aware that some of this is very subtle stuff, and it is not always immediately apparent to the untrained ear. For example, when I'm talking about dynamics here, I'm not talking about a song having a quiet section and a loud section. Rather, I'm talking about the variations in the volume of the hi-hat part over the course of a bar.

▶ **Dynamics:** Whether you're working with audio or MIDI, it's worth exploring the effect of subtle volume changes on your parts. Altering the velocity of a few MIDI notes or adding a volume envelope to tweak a couple of hits in an audio loop is one of the simplest ways to breathe life into your sound. Dynamic variations can be built into shorter loops with envelopes while working in the Session View, and then more can be added in the Arrangement View using Automation. For example, you might decide to make one hit slightly louder every eight bars.

▶ **Timing:** It's not uncommon to hear drummers and bass players talk about being "ahead of the beat" or "behind the beat." For example, the bass player may play right on the beat, while the drummer plays the 2 and 4 snare hits slightly behind. Or perhaps the drummer plays ahead of the beat, ever so slightly, rushing the snare and hi-hats while the bass player lays back. These subtleties are often what make music rhythmically compelling. It's not that you should avoid perfectly quantized rhythms, it's just that they often sound more exciting when contrasted against something that's pushing or pulling against them a little bit.

For some people, this subtlety is achieved by performing parts live to get the natural timing variation that comes with performance. For others, it's a process of surgically adjusting MIDI notes or Warp Markers ahead or behind. After clicking on a note, hold down Ctrl (Cmd) to disable the grid while dragging or just zoom in until the grid is 1/256 or smaller. It's also possible to make entire tracks rush or drag by using the Track Delay. Try starting out with values of ±10ms if you want to experiment with this.

▶ **Variation:** Some people like to make tons of variations in the Session View while composing, while others build an arrangement first and then create variations in the Arrangement View by using Split and making modifications to the separated clips. It doesn't have to be anything fancy—taking the kick drum out for a beat or two, altering a note in the bass part, and inserting a dramatic pause are just a few of the many ways you can keep things interesting. To really get busy with variation, get into the Clip Cuttin' Clinic that follows.

# Clip Cuttin' Clinic

No matter how good your programmed parts are, you'll still find ways to enhance them through creative editing in the Arrangement View. And the better an editor you are, the more fun you can also have with prerecorded loops, using them as raw material instead of just prefabricated musical ideas. While the techniques shown here are for all sorts of material, I find they are often easiest to learn with drum beats. But that said, the only goal here is experimentation and discovery, so dig in with any material you like!

Most of these techniques will be demonstrated with audio, but you'll find that many apply to MIDI as well. For techniques that are audio only, you can still try it out on your MIDI parts as long as you freeze and flatten them first.

Figure 13.1 shows a drum loop that's been cut into multiple slices using Split—Ctrl (Cmd)+E. After doing this, it's easy to rearrange the order of the slices. Use Duplicate to copy certain ones and Delete to remove others. Even if you do this randomly, many a happy accident will occur. You can even skip using the Split command. Just create a selection and then drag or use the arrow keys to move it around. If you need to bring your mashed-up beats back into the Session View, use Consolidate to make a new clip out of the slices.

Once you've sliced up a clip, there's lots of fun to be had whether or not you rearrange the slices. Try using the :2 and *2 buttons in the Clip View to double or halve the original tempo of a slice. Add crazy Warp Markers or change the transposition, and then experiment with the Warp modes to generate different artifacts. Don't forget the R keyboard shortcut to reverse selected audio. After reversing, turn off the grid and Shift+Alt (Option) drag the audio to correct any awkward-timing variations this creates. Zoom in until the grid is super fine, or hold down Ctrl (Cmd) to temporarily disable the grid.

**FIGURE 13.1**
Repeatedly split any clip. Then go crazy.
*Source:* Ableton

You can also generate variations by moving the Start marker within individual slices. To do this, select the clip and then make sure the Loop switch is turned on in the Clip View. (If it's not, moving Start and End will simply move the boundaries of the clip in the timeline). Now, move Start or even move around the loop brace, and you'll see that the clip remains in the same place in the timeline, but you're moving the audio within it. You may find that this technique is more interesting when used on slightly longer slices, since you'll get bigger chunks of the original material offset in interesting ways.

Occasionally, when working with audio clips, you may realize that it would be easier (or more fun) to manipulate the audio from a MIDI device. No problem! Just drag the clip into a Drum Rack, Impulse, Simpler, or Sampler. You can even drop the clip directly into the Track View of an empty MIDI track and cause a Simpler to be created. The clip's Start position will be used within these devices automatically.

# Harnessing Follow Actions

Follow Actions are some serious stuff. The carefully thought-out rules governing Follow Actions will allow you to do innumerable things, limited only by your imagination. Not only can they be used to enhance live performances, but they are also a wonderful compositional aid, helping you create variations you might never have thought of on your own. Check out the "Follow Actions" section in Chapter 5, "Clips," for a refresher on how all of this works.

Here are a few ideas for using Follow Actions:

▶ **Loop variations:** Here's another technique that's useful when you want a part to be very steady, but want to keep it from becoming stale. Create two (or more) loops that are nearly identical, but have subtle variations, such as an extra hi-hat or kick-drum hit. Set the first clip to trigger the second clip randomly from time to time. You'll set the second clip to retrigger the first. The result is that you get a constant beat with an additional snare hit thrown in occasionally, mimicking the way a real drummer would modify his beat on the fly.

▶ **Fills:** Follow Actions can be used to make sure that the main beat always comes back after you trigger a drum fill. Create a group of clips and make the top one the main beat. Make every clip below a drum fill. Set Follow Action A of each drum fill to "First." Each time you launch a drum fill, the main beat will be launched automatically.

Don't just try this with beats and fills; try it with other types of parts, too. Create multiple clips and treat them with different effects and parameter tweaks. Try setting them to Legato mode so that the playback position is traded off as you switch clips. It will sound like you're performing crazy processing on the part as you switch between the clips.

▶ **Legato madness:** Make a dozen or more variant clips. Set them all to Legato with a Follow Action of Any. Set the Follow Action times to something pretty short (1/8 or 1/16) and let it rip. Live will start jumping randomly between all your variations. Use Arrangement Record to capture the results and then edit together your favorite bits in the Arrangement View.

# Minimizing Performance Strain

No matter how fast and new my computer is, I always seem to find a way to tax it beyond its capabilities. While most of Live's built-in devices are pretty CPU efficient, you can bring your system to its knees by using a lot of them in Sets with loads of tracks. Third-party plug-ins are harder to generalize about. Some are very lightweight, while others can cripple your system with just one or two instances. Here are a few tips for staying on top of your CPU load.

▶ **Freeze tracks:** This feature will render everything on the track into an audio file, so effects and virtual instruments can be disabled. Simply right-click on the track's name and choose Freeze Track from the Context menu. If your computer is really struggling, select every track you're not currently editing and freeze them all at once. If you need to edit anything that's been disabled by Freeze, you can unfreeze the track, make your edits, and then refreeze it. If you can't freeze something due to a routing issue, you can always record from track to track (see Chapter 6, "Tracks and Signal Routing") or use Export Audio/Video to export a single track.

▶ **Eliminate clips using Complex mode:** Unless it's absolutely necessary to use Complex or Complex Pro, use a different Warp mode. For clips where you need it for sound quality reasons, right-click on any clip or group of clips that use Complex and select Consolidate. A new clip will be written to disk. It will sound identical (as long as you don't change the tempo), but will no longer use Complex mode.

▶ **Delete unused elements:** If you have unused tracks that have been silenced with the Track Activator, remember that those tracks may still be wasting resources. Delete them. If you're finished working in the Session and only need the Arrangement, delete *everything* from the Session. Not just the clips. Delete the scenes as well until you're down to the minimum of one empty scene. Then remove the clip's Stop buttons from the remaining scene. Use Save As to save a new version of your Set before deleting, in case you need to get anything back.

▶ **Increase your buffer:** Be aware of the impact of your Buffer Size (in the Audio tab of Live's Preferences) on CPU usage. The smaller your buffer, the higher the drain on your computer's resources will be. It's not uncommon during a final mixdown to set the Buffer Size to its maximum value to help your computer keep up with numerous instruments and effects. You can reduce it back to a smaller size later if you need lower latency.

▶ **Lower the edit density:** Sometimes simply having a large number of clips close together in the Arrangement will make it difficult for your hard drive to keep up. This can happen as a result of extensive vocal editing or from using the techniques described in the "Clip Cuttin' Clinic" earlier. Select groups of clips and use Edit → Consolidate to turn them into a single clip.

# Templates

In the File/Folder tab of Live's Preferences, you're allowed to save a default Set that's loaded whenever you start Live or select File → New Live Set. However, with all the different uses for Live, chances are that you won't be able to create a "one-size-fits-all" template to handle every situation. In this section, we'll look at a few approaches to working with reusable Sets.

One easy way to manage a collection of templates is by using the Templates folder. In your User Library, create a folder called *Templates* (if there isn't one already) and save your template Sets into it (see Figure 13.2). When you double-click to open a Set from this folder, Live will automatically open a copy of the Set and name it "Untitled." This way, you don't have to worry about accidentally editing your template.

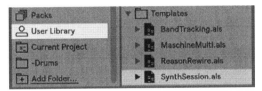

**FIGURE 13.2**

Use this folder to store your reusable Sets. Double-click to open a copy, or just drag one into the currently open Set.

*Source:* Ableton

# Drag-and-Drop Import and Export

Also, bear in mind that Sets can be imported into other Sets by dragging them from the Browser. Conversely, you can export Sets by dragging one or more tracks, or a group of clips, into the User Library or another folder in the Places area of the Browser. Using this technique, you can create a highly modular setup where useful tracks and clips can be imported at will. For example, the Sets shown in Figure 13.2 could be imported instead of opened directly. The "Band Tracking" set could be imported to instantly give you a set of tracks with the correct routing for recording.

Even if you don't create templates, bear in mind that any Set can be unfolded in the Browser, revealing its tracks and clips. This means you can grab musical elements from any Set, at any time. Be aware that unfolding large Sets is a rather resource-intensive process and may move quite slowly. If your computer stalls as you drag from the Browser, be patient. Hold the mouse button down and wait until Live shows that the imported elements are ready to be dropped.

When importing templates that contain clips, you'll discover that you have the option of dropping the clips into existing tracks or dropping them into the Drop Area to create new tracks. Remember that devices will only be imported into existing tracks if those tracks contain *absolutely no devices.* If you're not sure, just use the Drop Area. Also note that when importing Sets containing *no clips* into the Session View, you'll have to drag the Set to the title bar area, and you won't be allowed to drop it in the clip grid.

If you export a Set containing audio clips, there is a file management issue to consider. Remember that Sets only *reference* audio files, they don't contain them. Therefore, you need to consider whether you want Live to copy the audio files along with the exported Set. This is handled by the Preferences screen shown in Figure 13.3.

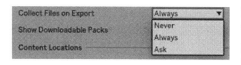

**FIGURE 13.3**
When exporting Sets and presets, Live gives you full control over whether or not all the referenced files are exported as well.
*Source:* Ableton

The advantage of exporting the associated audio files is knowing they'll always be available. For anything with original content you've created, this is generally recommended. If you're exporting a Set that relies on content from sample libraries that you're confident won't get moved, you can skip collecting the files and save some space. I generally set this preference to Ask, so I can decide on a case-by-case basis.

You will discover that when exporting to locations other than the User Library, Live automatically creates a project folder for the exported Set (unless you export it into an existing project folder). If you choose to export the audio files as well, they will be placed inside this new project. In the User Library, this is handled behind the scenes.

### CLIP TIP

If you drag a single clip into the Browser, a Live Clip is created. A Live Clip is sort of like a Set containing only one clip. It contains not only audio or MIDI but also the devices from the track.

# Defaults

In your User Library, you'll see a folder called *Defaults* (see Figure 13.4). Live uses the contents in this folder as templates for a variety of objects. When you right-click in the title bar of a device and select Save as Default Preset, a device preset file is created in this folder.

**FIGURE 13.4**

The Defaults folder lives in your User Library. Personalized defaults for devices and tracks are stored here.

There are a few other behaviors you can customize here as well. For example, inside the Dropping Samples folder, you'll find a folder called *On Drum Rack*. Configure a Simpler or Sampler any way you like and then drag it into this folder. The next time you drop a sample onto a Drum Rack, your custom configuration will be used.

The Audio to MIDI folders are used to customize the MIDI tracks that are created when the Convert to New MIDI Track commands are used. Drag instruments from the Track View into these folders, and the next time you convert audio to MIDI, the instruments you've chosen will be used in the new MIDI tracks.

## TRACK TIP

If you find that you're regularly setting the same routings or adding the same devices when you create new tracks, you can create default track settings. In the context menu of a track's title bar, select Save as Default Audio Track or Save as Default MIDI Track. The track settings are saved in the Defaults folder as an .als file.

# Working with Video

They say timing is everything. Nowhere is this more evident than in scoring music for the moving image. Whether you are adding sound effects, mood music, or creating a complete soundtrack, Live's ability to easily manipulate the timing of audio makes it a great tool for fitting sound to picture.

## Importing Video

Getting video into Live is simple: Just locate the video file you want to import in the File Browser and drag it into your Live Set. The audio will be loaded on an audio track in Live, and the video will appear in a special floating video window. Only video files in QuickTime format (.mov, .mp4, or any other format playable by QuickTime) are supported.

You can only work with video in the Arrangement View. If you drop a movie into the Session View, the clip will load as audio only. Once loaded, the video clip will look like any other audio clip in Live, except that you will see virtual "sprocket holes" in its title bar.

Video clips in the Arrangement View behave more or less just like audio clips. Thus, by dragging a video clip into the arrangement and aligning it with the beginning of the first measure, you can quickly start scoring the picture and creating a soundtrack. You can use Live's FX and audio editing tools to edit the video clip's associated audio in the Arrangement View, just like any other audio clip. (You will find that Consolidate, Crop, and Reverse operations will cause your video clip to be replaced by an audio clip.)

## The Video Window

The Video window opens automatically when you add video to the Arrangement. Start Live, and the video will follow playback. You can drag the video window around wherever you want. You can resize it by clicking on the lower-right corner, or expand it to full-screen mode by double-clicking on the video itself. If you close the Video window, it can be reopened from the View menu.

As you move clips or trim their left edge, the video window will continuously scrub through the video so you can see exactly where you are placing the audio in relation to the video. The video window also updates when you click in the editor in the Clip View, so you can place MIDI notes or Warp Markers in exactly the right place. Alternately, if you need to stretch or time-compress an audio clip to fit a video event, you may find that Shift-dragging the edges is a little easier than adjusting Warp Markers.

## Warping and Looping Video

One of the unusual things that Live allows you to do is add Warp Markers to video, just as you would with audio. Obviously, this is not something you'll be doing if you're tasked with adding audio to someone else's work, but if you're creatively experimenting with video, you can get some very cool results. Add Warp Markers and watch the video speed up and slow down as you move them around. Looping can also be used. It works just as you would expect, causing a portion of the video to repeat indefinitely.

You can also set a video clip's Master/Slave switch to Master when using Warp Markers. This will preserve the video's original timing and allow you to use Warp Markers to make important moments in the video line up with the grid in any way you choose.

## Saving/Exporting

After you have finished your new soundtrack, you will want to save your work either as a new movie or as an audio file to be turned over to a video editor. If you're just exporting audio, there are a few things to bear in mind. First, the safest bet for turning in your soundtrack to an editor is to make an audio file the exact length of the video you were given, so the start points line up exactly, and there won't be any confusion about where your sound cues go. Second, if you're exporting audio only, don't forget to mute the audio on the video track; otherwise, you'll get a file containing both the dialogue and music. The standard sample rate for digital video is 48kHz. That said, when you are creating audio for someone else's film or video project, the best policy is often to ask them the format they want.

To create a video, select File → Export Audio/Video and turn on Create Video File in the bottom section of the dialog. The menu below allows you to choose the type of video encoding you desire. If you need to customize the video settings in any way (to optimize it for Internet streaming, for example), use the Edit button next to Encoder Settings.

# The File Manager

No matter how careful you are, it's going to happen—files will get lost or misplaced, or you're going to occasionally get confused about where all those great sounds from last year's project came from. The good news is that Live's File Manager is here to help you get a handle on what's going on.

Select Manage Files from the File menu to open the File Manager. When it opens, you'll be given the option to manage either the current Set, the current project, or the User Library.

- ▶ **Manage Set:** This will present you with options and information pertaining only to the current Set. You can locate missing samples, collect external sample files into the project folder, or simply view all of the samples in your Set.

- ▶ **Manage Project:** Remember what we just said about saving multiple versions? When you've done this, using the Manage Project feature is very useful. For example, it can tell you how many external samples you have for every version of your Set and collect them into the project folder, so you can make sure that your project is self-contained for each and every version of your Set that you have saved.

- ▶ **Manage User Library:** This feature will give you information about all of the presets and samples stored in your User Library. It can be used to get things back into shape if files have gotten moved or lost.

# Manage Set

Let's take a look at what happens when you choose Manage Set. Figure 13.5 shows the window entitled Current Live Set that opens when you choose this option. Like all of the File Manager's windows, it's broken into several sections, each with a small triangle to the left that can be used to hide or show the section. The first section is View and Replace Files. Clicking the View Files button will reveal a list of all of the samples used in the Set (see Figure 13.6). The Location column next to the sample name will tell you if the file is located within the project folder, in an external location, or is missing. Clicking the Edit button to the left of the sample name will open the file in the audio editor you have specified in the File/Folder tab of the Preferences screen.

View Samples reveals the sample list, which shows you all of the samples in your Set and all of the clips that contain them. You can replace samples or open your audio editor from here.

**FIGURE 13.5**

Manage Set reveals a window with information about the locations of the files in your set.

*Source:* Ableton

**FIGURE 13.6**

You can unfold a sample to reveal all of the clips that contain it.

*Source:* Ableton

Clicking the Hot-Swap button to the left of the sample name will reveal the file's location in the File Browser. While the Hot-Swap button is highlighted, any file you double-click in the File Browser will be used to globally replace that sample in your Set. That means that any clip that is based on this sample will be updated to use the new sample. All of the other properties (such as loop points and transposition) of the clip will be retained. Another way to globally replace samples in your set is simply to drag a file out of the File Browser and drop it into the File Manager—directly onto the sample you want to replace.

Looking at the title bar of the File Manager, you'll notice a set of three Web Browser style buttons in the upper right-hand corner. You can use the Back button (the left-pointing arrow) to return to the Set Management overview. If at any point you want to return to the main File Manager window, you can use the Home button on the far right.

## Finding Lost Files

Below the View and Replace Files section of the Manage Set window is the Missing Files section (see Figure 13.5). Clicking the Locate button in this section will bring up a list of missing samples in the Set. Instead of having a Hot-Swap button next to these samples, there is a Search button, which can be used to execute a search for the file in the Browser.

The other way to replace missing samples is to use the Automatic Search feature (see Figure 13.7). What's nice about this feature is that it lets you search for all of your missing samples in one shot, instead of one at a time.

**FIGURE 13.7**

The Missing Media Files window is used to replace individual samples or automatically search for lost audio files.

*Source:* Ableton

Here's how it's done:

1. Expand Automatic Search to reveal the search options and set the Search Folder switch to Yes, unless you only want to search your project folder and the Live Library, in which case you can skip to Step 3.

2. Click the Set Folder button and navigate to the folder you want to search. Any subfolders in this location will be searched as well.

3. Set the Search Project and Search Library switches to Yes if you believe your files may be in the current project folder or the Live Library.

4. Click the Go button at the top of the window.

When the search is completed, Live will tell you how many "Candidates" (how many potentially correct files) were found and how many samples it was able to automatically replace with the candidates it found. The missing samples list will now be updated to show the replaced files, changing their location status to either Project or External. There will be two main reasons a file does not get replaced automatically. Either the missing file cannot be found at all, or more than one file has been found that matches the name of the missing file. In this case, the location will read *Candidates*, and the number of possible replacement files found will be listed in the Candidates field (see Figure 13.8).

**FIGURE 13.8** When more than one file with a matching name is found, Live needs you to intervene and pick the right one.
*Source:* Ableton

Clicking on the ? button will reveal a list of all the matching files in the File Browser. You have a few choices to determine which is the right one. First, you could simply enable the Preview button and decide by ear. Another option is to right-click on the file and select Show in Finder (Mac) or Show in Explorer (PC). Once you've found the right file, you can double-click or drag and drop as described earlier.

## External Samples

The final area of the Current Set window is the External Files section (refer to Figure 13.5). If all of your samples are already within the current project folder, this section will be empty. If not, the first Show button will allow you to view all samples that exist outside of the current project folder but that are within the main folder of other projects. Below you'll see the option to reveal samples in other locations such as the User Library.

You'll also see switches that allow you to collect (copy) these external samples into your project folder. These differ from the Collect All and Save command, in that they allow you to specify what samples should be copied into the project. You can differentiate between files that are in other project folders and files elsewhere. Once you've selected the samples you want to copy, click the Save button at the bottom of the File Manager.

# Manage Project

Manage Project contains several features that are identical to Manage Set (except that they act on all Sets in the project), so I'll just focus on the features that are different here.

The first area of the Manage Project window is the project location—it just shows you the path of the current project. After that is the Project Contents section, which tells you the number of Sets, Live Clips, Preset Files, and Samples in the project. Clicking any of the Show buttons will reveal the referenced files in the File Browser (see Figure 13.9). There's also a Missing Files section and a Locate button, just like we saw in the Manage Set window. If used here, you'll be able to locate missing files for all of the Sets in the project in one shot.

Further down the Manage Project window is the Unused Files section. When you are working on a project, it's possible to generate many extra audio files that don't end up getting used. These could be multiple takes of a live performance or earlier versions of a loop before you effected and resampled it to perfection. This section differentiates between files that were recorded into the Set, created with the Freeze command, created with the Consolidate command, and files not created by the current project. Clicking the Show button will reveal these unused files in the File Browser, where you can choose what you want to do with them.

**FIGURE 13.9**
Project Contents tells you about all sorts of different files that exist within your project.
*Source:* Ableton

## UPPER MANAGEMENT

What if you want to manage files for a project other than the one you have open? Fear not. Even though the Manage Files command opens the current project by default, there's a way to get to others without closing your current Set. Simply navigate to a project folder in the File Browser and right-click it. Select the Manage File option that appears in the context menu, and it will open in the File Manager.

Here's another trick that may save you some time. The next time you want to replace a sample, right-click the waveform in the Clip View and choose Manage Sample File from the context menu. The File Manager will open with that sample highlighted in the samples list.

Personally, this is a feature that I would only use in special cases—for example, if I needed to send a project to a collaborator over a slow Internet connection. Otherwise, disk space is cheap enough these days that I'd rather waste some disk space rather than risk losing something I need. If you're going to remove unused files, I'd recommend backing up the entire project first, extra files and all, before deleting anything. Bad things can happen. Like a lot of what I have to say, this recommendation is based on a true story!

The final section of the Project Manager is the Packing section. This section lets you create a Pack from your project. A Pack is simply a compressed archive file (much like a zip file) containing everything in the project folder. If your project uses external files, there will be a warning message to remind you that the Pack will be missing some necessary files. If your plan is to transport this Pack to a different machine, it's important to use Collect All and Save first.

# Max for Live

For many years now, Max/MSP (or just Max for short) has been a favorite of those who need to create customized audio and MIDI tools, whether they are simple MIDI patchers, software instruments, or the brains behind complex interactive multimedia installations using sound and video. In fact, before Ableton Live came along, most of the laptop performers I knew were using software built in Max/MSP! Now, this graphical programming environment integrates directly with Live. It is included with Live Suite and available as an add-on for Live Standard users.

The integration of Max with Ableton Live is one of the most innovative things to happen in music software for quite some time because it integrates a completely open-ended programming tool into a stable sequencer with a familiar workflow. With Max for Live, you'll get a powerful set of instruments and effects, plus the ability to download many additional devices from the ever-growing community of Max programmers.

If you're the programming type, you'll also be able to create devices that act just like Live's built-in devices and make tools that interact with the Live API (application programming interface). This means that you have access to the guts of Live itself, and can programmatically access things such as Live's tempo, a clip's groove properties, a current Set's track names, or nearly anything you can think of.

If all this talk of programming and APIs makes your head spin, don't worry. There are plenty of devices that come ready to use as-is, and many more that can be downloaded separately. In this next section, we'll take a look at some of the devices that come included with Max for Live and at the process of adding on devices. The programming itself is a very deep topic that goes well beyond the scope of this book, so there will just be a very brief look at this side of things.

All of the devices discussed next are found in the Max for Live view of the Browser. They are included for free if you own Live Suite, or you've purchased the Max for Live add on for Live Standard. If any of them are missing, visit the Packs page at ableton.com.

# Drum Synths

Drum samples are great. With a working knowledge of how to program Simpler, Sampler, and Drum Racks, you can get a great deal of variety out of a modest number of samples. However, there are still good reasons to work with purely synthesized drums. There is something about being able to freely shape a drum sound while pushing against the natural limitations of a particular synthesis engine that yields all sorts of satisfying results. Synthetic sounds can also be automated, and velocity can be mapped to create variations and movement that would be hard to get with sampled drums.

The latest version of Max for Live comes with a brilliant tool kit for synthesizing drums—a series of modules designed to be used in the pads of Drum Racks, each one specialized for producing a different type of sound. The drum synths are found under Max Instrument, and all have "DS" in the name. (If you have an earlier version of Live on your system, you may also have the first generation drum synths installed, which have "DrumSynth" in the name.)

Just drop one of these devices into a MIDI track or into a pad of a Drum Rack, and you're ready to go. The drum synths don't respond to pitch, so you can trigger them with any note. To preview the sound, click on the drum icon at the top. Most of the drum synths have familiar names like kick and snare (see Figure 13.10). The only exceptions are FM (a simple FM synthesizer for creating electronic sound effects) and Clang (a TR-808 style cowbell).

There are too many of them to discuss all of the parameters in detail, but since they are all customized to produce one particular kind of sound, it's hard to go wrong. Twist some knobs and experiment.

**FIGURE 13.10**
The drum synth Kick.
*Source:* Ableton

You may find that because these devices all produce a particular sort of synthetic sound, they aren't suited to all your needs. They can still be quite useful, however. For example, you may want to use a sampled kick and snare to form the backbone of your song but use synthetic hats and claps. It also works well to layer synthetic and sampled drums. Just drop a Max for Live drum synth into a pad that already contains a sampled drum while holding down Alt (Cmd) to create a layered pad containing both the sample and the drum synth.

# Modulators

Max for Live includes several devices that are totally unlike any of Live's built-in devices. These devices (Envelope, Envelope Follower, LFO, Shaper) are strictly in the business of controlling the parameters of other devices. The other devices could be effects or instruments, or even Live's Mixer. By getting clever with these modulation devices, you can essentially turn Live into one big modular synthesizer.

Instead of comprehensively covering every modulator, I'll be diving deep on a couple of devices and covering all of the core concepts that you need in order to figure out how they all work. What all of the modulators have in common is a Map button that is used to set the target of the modulation (see Figure 13.11a).

**FIGURE 13.11A**
The LFO modulating the Tune parameter of the drum synth Clap.

To get started with a modulator, click on the Map switch, and it will start blinking. Now, move the control you want to modulate. This can be a device or mixer parameter in the same track or on another track. As soon as you map a control, you'll see it become grayed out—it can't be adjusted manually while the modulator has control. At the far right, you'll find the Multimap button. Clicking this displays additional mapping controls. Use these to have the modulation device modulate multiple parameters simultaneously (see Figure 13.11b). To remove a modulation target, click the X next to the Map button.

**FIGURE 13.11B**
The Multimap screen makes it possible to modulate up to eight parameters at once.

## MODULATING PLUG-INS

If you want to modulate a plug-in device parameter, you'll have to first make sure that the parameter is visible to Live, as explained in the "Remote Controlling Plug-In Devices" section of Chapter 11, "Remote Control."

The Target Minimum and Maximum controls make it possible to adjust the overall range of the modulation. The default values of 0% and 100% allow modulation across the full range of the control, from its minimum value to its maximum. These values are fine for many situations and can usually be left alone until you have a handle on the main controls of the modulator.

# LFO

This device is a great example of how Max for Live can change your world. Want to do rhythmic modulation of a reverb's decay time or randomly change the waveform in Operator? Piece of cake.

As soon as you map LFO to a control, you'll see that control start to bounce back and forth to show the LFO's modulation. Adjusting the LFO itself is similar to adjusting the LFO on Live's built-in devices, but the parameters have different names and there are a few additional options.

Depth changes the amount of modulation, while Rate adjusts the speed. Next to Rate are switches to allow modulation in hertz or tempo-synchronized divisions of the beat. Offset determines the LFO's center point. To get a clearer understanding of this, set Depth to 0% so that no modulation occurs. Then move Offset to adjust the mapped parameter to whatever sounds like a good starting point. As you increase the Depth, you'll hear the LFO modulate the value farther away from this point.

Above Rate, there's a menu for selecting the shape of the LFO. Jitter is used to introduce some randomness into the LFO shape, while Smooth rounds off the edges. Small amounts of jitter can be very effective for introducing some subtle irregularities, while higher values are downright chaotic. Smooth doesn't have a big effect if you've selected Sine in the Shape menu, but when combined with harder-edged shapes like rectangle, it can produce some interesting results.

## Shaper

Shaper is like LFO on steroids. While LFO makes you pick a standard wave-shape, Shaper lets you draw your own. Waveshapes are drawn in an editor that occupies the majority of Shaper's interface. Click to create breakpoints or Shift-click to delete them. Hold down Alt (Option) while dragging to bend lines.

The editor has a beat grid, so it's easy to create modulations with rhythmic impact. The Rate parameter specifies how much time is shown in the editor. For example, a Rate of 1/4 means the shape drawn in the grid will play out over a quarter note. Adjust Grid to change how many grid lines are shown in the editor. If you set Rate to 4 bars and Grid to 16, you'll be editing on a quarter note grid to create a pattern that's four bars long. If you prefer to work without the grid, turn off the Snap switch.

## Envelope Follower

Envelope Follower is a Max Audio Effect, which like LFO does not actually process the audio directly. Instead, it measures the gain of the incoming signal and generates a modulation curve, which can be mapped to a device parameter. For example, if you place Envelope Follower in a snare drum track, it will measure the volume of the snare drum. Envelope Follower will then measure the snare drum's volume and modulate the mapped parameter in response.

To change the range of the modulation, adjust the Target Minimum and Maximum values. If you set Max *below* Min, negative modulation will be generated. This means that the mapped parameter will get turned *down* as the volume of the source increases.

For example, if you place the Envelope Follower in a snare drum track, but map it to the volume of a synthesizer part, you could cause the synth part to swell after every snare drum hit by leaving Max and Min at their default values and adjusting Rise and Delay to taste. Or you could make the synth part duck on every snare drum hit (just like you would with sidechain compression) by setting the Max value *below* Min.

## Envelope

Envelope is a Max MIDI Effect that generates freely assignable ADSR modulation in response to note input. It works just like the built-in envelope on an instrument, but you can assign it to anything you like. This opens up not just the possibility of adding additional ADSR envelopes to instruments, but also to have effect devices controlled by an envelope.

The envelope is triggered as soon as MIDI note input is received, after which it modulates the mapped parameter through a range of values, according to the ADSR settings and the Min and Max boxes. The Time parameter sets the envelope's overall speed. It acts as a multiplier to the values shown under the Attack, Decay, and Release knobs.

# Sequencers

The next two devices are very different, but since they're both based on a similar step-sequencing concept, I've decided to call them *sequencers*. The first is a MIDI sequencer in a more conventional sense—it generates a series of notes at varying pitches. The second is in the business of chopping up an incoming audio and sending it out transformed in a variety of ways.

## Mono Sequencer

The Mono Sequencer offers a different approach to MIDI sequencing. Instead of using MIDI clips to sequence devices, the Mono Sequencer allows you to use an approach based on the step sequencers from the early days of analog. While this might seem like a limited way to program parts at first, what you may find is that its limited tool set and approach send you off into unexpected areas and get you making parts you might not have otherwise come up with.

The Mono Sequencer (see Figure 13.12) is organized around a main window that displays the steps of the sequencer (16 by default). At the bottom of the window is the step-enable area, which is used to determine whether or not a note will be sent at that step. Above is an area for editing five parameters of each step: pitch, velocity, octave, duration, and repeat. Repeat determines

Click here to select which
lane you want to edit.

Use this menu to choose
the playback behavior
of the current lane.

Set this to Transpose to
enable repitching of the
sequence via MIDI.

Click here to turn steps on or off.

**Figure 13.12** Try creating MIDI sequences using Mono Sequencer instead of MIDI clips. Then create MIDI clips to transpose the sequences as they play!
*Source:* Ableton

how many rapid-fire repeats of the note occur in the step. Even at the lowest value, the repeats are *really* fast and generate buzzing, machine-gun type effects.

One of the very cool and unusual things about this sort of step sequencing is that you can decide to play the sequence forward, backward, or even randomly. Each parameter can have its own behavior, so you could have the octave sequence play in random order, while the pitch plays backward and forward. It's true that 16 steps may not sound like much, but techniques like this allow you to generate quite a lot of variety from a small amount of programming.

Also of particular interest is the way that Mono Sequencer handles MIDI input. By default, it is set to Transpose, which re-pitches the entire sequence based on note input. This makes the mono sequencer into a very powerful tool, a sort of arpeggiator on steroids. You can experiment to create cool patterns and then grab your MIDI keyboard and turn these patterns into bass lines or leads. In the Transpose and Gate setting, the sequencer will only run as long as a note is held down, as opposed to standard Transpose mode, which keeps the steps running all the time.

Also be aware of the Pattern knob at the upper-left corner. Turn this, and you'll discover that this device can hold up to 12 totally unique sequences. The Pattern knob is an enormously powerful performance control. Not only do you have transposable, randomizable sequences, but you can also switch between them with the turn of a knob. My one piece of advice when you start playing with this device is to make sure that your loved ones can reach you, as you may disappear for several weeks.

## Buffer Shuffler 2.0

The Buffer Shuffler is an experimental, glitchy beast that may not make a lot of sense at first. If you find that to be the case, first get your head around Mono Sequencer, and you'll have an easier time with it. Instead of generating a sequence of MIDI notes, this device takes incoming audio, divides it into slices, and then transforms each slice using a step-sequencing paradigm.

The centerpiece of Buffer Shuffler is a grid that displays a user-adjustable number of steps (see Figure 13.13). These steps represent how many slices the incoming audio will be divided into. The individual steps can then be modified in a variety of ways. The default view is used to rearrange the slices. (This view is labeled Left, which refers to the left channel of the stereo signal. By default, the left and right channels are linked, but you can unlink them if you want to rearrange the two channels independently.)

Move the blocks up or down to determine which slice gets played on which step. The default diagonal pattern plays the slices in order; move them up or down to trigger earlier or later slices on a given step. Below each step is an arrow or an X, which determines the direction of a particular slice and whether or not it is muted. Click to cycle between forward, backward, and mute.

**FIGURE 13.13** Buffer Shuffler: gateway to glitched-out mayhem.
*Source:* Ableton

Along the left of the grid are the other parameters that can be sequenced. These are basic parameters, such as Amp (volume), and special effects, such as Shift and Stutter. Click on one to reveal a sequencer for this parameter. Along the bottom of each view, you'll see a Min and Max value for specifying the range across which the parameter can be sequenced.

For example, when Gate is selected, you can move a block upward to allow more of the slice to play, while moving it to the bottom mutes it completely. With Shift selected, you can move a block upward to increase the amount of frequency shift that is applied, or move it to the bottom to bypass the effect on that step. Get a feel for how these parameters work, and the others will be easy to figure out.

Below the grid is a button marked Dice, which is used to transform the sequence for the currently displayed parameter. Select Random in the adjacent menu and click Dice to generate a random pattern, or Permute to apply limited randomization to an existing pattern. You'll also find options to shift the pattern in a variety of other ways (left, right, invert, and so on). Click Auto to automatically Dice the parameters every time the sequence cycles around.

# Convolution Reverb

For some, this device alone may be worth the upgrade to Max for Live. Convolution is a technology that allows the ambience of a space to be re-created from an audio sample called an *impulse response* (or IR). Not limited to real spaces, impulse responses can be created from hardware effects units or synthesized to generate wild, new Reverb and Delay effects.

Convolution Reverb is the basic version of this effect, while Convolution Reverb Pro offers more comprehensive tweaking at the cost of greater CPU usage (see Figure 13.14). To get started with Convolution Reverb, load an impulse response by navigating the two menus below the display. The top menu contains categories such as Halls and Real Places, while the bottom one lists the available IRs.

**FIGURE 13.14** A much more powerful alternative to Live's built-in Reverb device.
*Source:* Ableton

Loading an IR is not the same as loading a preset. When you load a preset into Reverb (Live's built-in reverb device), you're just setting the parameters to a saved configuration. When you load an IR, you're loading a particular reverb with certain immutable characteristics. You can customize it up to a certain point, but no further. It's more like loading a sample into a sampler.

The Mode menu makes it possible to go one step further. Select Split, and you'll be able to load two different impulses simultaneously—one for the early reflections and one for the reverb tail. Click Early to load the reflection and Late to load the tail. The right side of the Pro version can be unfolded to expose several different editors for further tweaking. Damping lets you change the characteristics of the reverb by adjusting which frequencies are absorbed or reflected by the space, while Modulation can be used to apply subtle pitch effects or full-on chorus. Shape gives you control over the level of the early reflections, and it allows you to tweak the length of the impulse response with fades.

All of these options make for some very interesting sound design possibilities, but be aware that convolution uses some serious processing power, and each of these modules adds more to the burden. Disable any modules you're not using to save CPU power. Consider using it on a Return track and sharing the reverb between multiple tracks. Alternately, use it as an insert and then freeze and flatten the track. Doing so opens up all sorts of fun sound design and editing possibilities. Try it!

## Adding More Devices

A quick Internet search for "Max for Live devices" will reveal numerous sites where additional devices can be downloaded, many of them for free. Max for Live devices are files with an extension of .axmd. Strictly speaking, they can be dragged from anywhere on your hard drive and dropped into a Set. Realistically, however, you'll be much better off if you keep them all located in one place. Making a folder in your User Library is the easiest bet.

When you are moving a Set to a different computer, any Max devices used in the Set must be included with the project. The Collect All and Save command handles this for you. Execute this command before moving the project folder, and you'll be all set.

# Link

Synchronizing computers or hardware music-making devices has always been a problem. It has been possible for a long time, but configuration problems and unreliable behavior have always been the norm. Ableton's Link technology is a breath of fresh air—not only is configuration almost entirely automatic, but devices are also connected using a standard local network and it works over Wi-Fi! That means the router that you use to connect your computers and tablets to the Internet will also work as the hub for a digital jam session.

To get started, you'll need two Link-compatible programs running on devices connected to the same network. For an up-to-date list of programs that support Link, visit https://www.ableton.com/link/apps/.

Unlike traditional MIDI setups or ReWire, Link doesn't need for you to decide which device will be the "master." The first device to have Link enabled will broadcast its tempo to the network. When other devices join the Link session, they will set themselves to this tempo as well. If you change tempo on any device, all of the other devices will follow the tempo change.

Let's look at an example using Live and Novation Groovebox, an iOS application running on an iPad. Both devices are connected to the same Wi-Fi network. First, turn on Link in both applications, as shown in Figures 13.15a and 13.15b.

**FIGURE 13.15A**
The Link switch. If you don't see it, you'll have to visit the Link/MIDI tab of the Preferences screen. After Link is turned on in Groovebox, this switch will read "Link 1" to indicate one other Link application has been detected.
*Source:* Ableton

**FIGURE 13.15B**
Turn on the Link switch in the application you want to sync to, and you're all set. It's almost too easy. Notice the "Connected to 1 app" message, indicating that Groovebox has detected Live.
*Source:* Ableton

In Live, the Arrangement Position box now displays a "progress bar" that moves from left to right once per bar (see Figure 13.16). This is letting you know that a global tempo has been established for both devices. Starting playback in either Live or Groovebox will be delayed until the progress bar reaches its left-most position. In other words, it's a lot like launching a clip with a launch quantization of 1 Bar. The clip doesn't begin playback immediately—it waits until the start of the next bar.

**FIGURE 13.16**
Once Link is enabled, the Arrangement Position box gives you visual feedback about the current tempo.
*Source:* Ableton

Link applications can also be configured to share Start/Stop messages so that they begin and end playback together. This feature may not be supported by all Link applications yet, so if you don't see this option, a little research may be necessary. To enable Start Stop Sync in Live, right-click on the Link switch and select Start Stop Sync from the context menu.

## LINK TO MIDI

Don't worry! Your MIDI gear is not excluded from Link jam sessions. Download "Link to MIDI" for iOS, and you're all set. This app joins a Link session and then generates the MIDI clock that you can send to your MIDI hardware.

# Parting Thoughts

As you can imagine, there are many more tricks and tips still waiting for you to discover. There are as many different ways of working with Live as there are different kinds of music. The more time you spend experimenting, the more you will discover what works for you. And that's really all that matters. There's no "right" way to work with Live, just different methods, some of which you will find more efficient and inspirational.

Also, check out Ableton's user forum, which will teach you that no matter what you've learned, someone else is doing things totally differently. Sometimes you'll pick up tricks that will greatly enhance your workflow, and sometimes you'll just be reminded that finding your own way is the most important thing of all. Either way, you're invited to share your ideas and interact with other Live users. It's a great community to be a part of.

Please visit me at hobo-tech.com for my latest Live tips and musical releases. Feel free to me drop a note and let me know about the music you've made with Live. Thanks for reading!

# Index

473

## V